THE BANKERS

THE
BANKERS

Martin Mayer

W. H. Allen · London
A Howard & Wyndham Company
1976

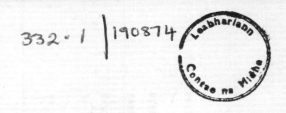
FOR those who taught me,
so many years ago they can no longer be blamed;
especially Hans Staehle, Joseph Schumpeter
and Wassily Leontief
And for Jack Hirshleifer,
who will find on every page
something about which we can argue,
as we have for thirty years

CONTENTS

CONTENTS

It is necessarily part of the business of a banker to maintain appearances and to profess a conventional respectability which is more than human. Lifelong practices of this kind make them the most romantic and the least realistic of men. It is so much their stock-in-trade that their position should not be questioned, that they do not even question it themselves until it is too late. Like the honest citizens they are, they feel a proper indignation at the perils of the wicked world in which they live—when the perils mature; but they do not foresee them. A Bankers' Conspiracy! The idea is absurd! I only wish there were one! So, if they are saved, it will be, I expect, in their own despite.

—John Maynard Keynes

Preface to the British Edition

This book was the most surprising big bestseller in the United States in 1975—surprising to its publisher, to most commentators in the trade, and to me. Without for a moment neglecting the importance of its selection by the Book-of-the-Month Club or the penetrating atmosphere of concern about the economy that dominated the first half of the year, I should like to believe that the success of *The Bankers* draws at least in part from the increasing maturity and sophistication of the consumers of non-fiction books. Though neither publishers nor critics have entirely caught up with the change in readers' attitudes, a writer can now assume, I think, that people are willing to work for their understanding of large and important subjects, and that he can indeed face up manfully to the job of tracing out the labyrinth of small institutions, small decisions, small events that in real life determine the direction of major developments. Politicians still get elected by the use of slogans, but writers do not need them.

Because the book rests on a philosophy of concern for detail, there is no way to transfer its cultural referents: it must be a book about *American* banking. But American banking has been making an impact on British banking for a century and a half. Brown, Shipley is of American foundation, sharing a common ancestor with New York's Brown Brothers, Harriman; Morgan was long as important in London as he was in New York. Hanging on the wall in the anteroom of the Money Market and Bank Regulation Office at the Bank of England is a framed text entitled "Advice to Banks From 1863", taken from a letter to national banks written by Hugh McCulloch, first Comptroller of the Currency, in the Administration of Abraham Lincoln. On request, officers of the Bank will supply a printed copy:

"Let no loans be made that are not secured beyond a reasonable contingency. Give facilities only to legitimate and prudent transactions. Make your discounts on as short time as the business of your customers will permit, and insist upon the payment of all paper at maturity, no matter whether you need the money or not . . . Every dollar that a bank loans above its capital and surplus it owes for, and its managers are therefore under the strongest obligations to its creditors, as well as to its stockholders, to keep its discounts constantly under control . . . The capital of a bank should be a reality, not a fiction; and it should be owned by those who have money to lend, and not by borrowers . . . 'Splendid financiering' is not legitimate banking, and 'splendid financiers' in banking are generally either humbugs or rascals."

During the last fifteen years, the American influence has extended far beyond homilies and advice: the American banks, for better or worse, have been setting examples. Just as it is necessary for students of American government to get a grip on the development of British political institutions during the seventeenth and eighteenth centuries if they hope to understand their own history, it is now necessary for British economists and financial analysts to master the more significant intricacies of American banking before they can claim true comprehension of the organization and operation of their own financial system.

Most of the larger differences between British and American banking derive from other differences between the two societies:

Britain is compact, and thus a small number of large banks with a large number of branches can blanket the country. The United States spans a continent, and is divided into four dozen separate political jurisdictions, each of which has at various times in history spawned banks. The laws prohibit all but a handful of banks to conduct banking business in any state other than the one where their main officers are housed. Our very largest banks—Bank of America in California and First National City in New York—are in fact larger than even the four British giants, but we have more than fifty others with assets greater than £1,000 million. Thus the system is to a large extent decentralized; prices tend to be set and information exchanged in public or quasi-public markets rather than in conversations.

Though egalitarian philosophies command much wider and more passionate assent in modern Britain than in the United States, the control of actual day-to-day operations in Britain is much more hierarchical. The Bank of England can manage the money system of the country by passing appropriate, rather informal suggestions to the executive cadre of four clearing banks and a dozen or so discount houses. Contrary opinion is of course permitted, and tolerance for eccentricity is prized—but the American notion that the way a man makes money is through acting on his contrary opinions is an ungentlemanly thought in a British context. Thus a handful of men and women at the Bank of England can do the work that requires a large bureaucracy and endless refinements of system in America.

Though commercial law is largely a British creation—and the great name in the field is still Lord Mansfield, two hundred years later—it is probably fair to say that money has never loomed quite so large in British legal and political thinking as it has in America. (Property counts for more.) From the days of Alexander Hamilton and the problem of what to do with the debts of the revolutionary government (long since passed into the hands of speculators), questions of the currency and its soundness were central to American politics. Bryan's "cross of gold" speech that won him a Presidential nomination was not a metaphor for oppressions by the big rich; it was a direct attack on the dominant role of metallic gold in the national currency. Because banks create money, their activities have always been subject to close governmental scrutiny in the United States, and their instruments have been given a quasi-official status which has always (except for the Bank of England banknotes) been resisted in the United Kingdom.

We have deposit insurance, which in effect puts the credit of the United States government behind both current accounts (we call them "demand deposit accounts") and savings accounts in private banks: juridically, the FDIC is only a quasi-governmental body, and its resources for backing the deposits are as an ordinary matter the fund gathered from its members; but as an extraordinary matter the fund has an automatic call on the Treasury. American law protects the sanctity of cheques to a remarkable degree. Writing a cheque when you don't have an account in the bank is a criminal offence, and there are a number of states where it is the third or fourth largest category of crimes for which women have been imprisoned. In Britain, a cheque on a non-existent account is a civil offence, and the victim brings suit; in America, the police enforce the banking law. Thus, quite apart from questions of snobbery, American banks always felt much safer about soliciting current accounts and issuing cheque books; and people writing cheques are much less concerned about crossing them (which you can't do in the United States) or otherwise protecting the operations of the cheque system.

Finally, there is the nature of the interpenetration of business and government. In Britain, the tradition has been to seek control of end results, and let the participants determine the means by themselves—a great invitation to collusion and the protection of incompetence. Where the business done is foreign in its end results, the tendency is strongly toward *laissez faire*, making London immensely hospitable to international operations. In the United States, the tradition has been to seek control of ways and means, allowing the end result to emerge from patterns of competition, which government seeks to compel through the activities of regulatory agencies enforcing anti-trust laws. This did not produce in banking the go-getting atmosphere that it produces elsewhere, because a bank really is a money machine, and something even worse than routine incompetence—crookedness or gullibility—is required to go bust in a bank. But it meant that when go-getters did appear in this business, at the First National City Bank of New

York in the years after World War II, they could work vast changes in the operations of the banking system in a handful of busy years.

Those changes I have called a "revolution", and it came to England, too; indeed, the *lider massimo* of the revolution, Walter Wriston of First National City, established his position partly by his expansion and manoeuvring of the bank's international division. London was the largest of the First National City offshore operations, with a solid base of sterling-denominated business, and Wriston extended the principles of his American operations to his English affiliate. "Base rate" for loans—a variant of the American "prime rate"—came to London through First National City, ultimately shaking the British banks loose from their old and rather brainless dependence on an officially announced Bank Rate; so did the principles of "liability management". (And so did the "money shop", the bank-operated small loan office for working-class customers, sitting on the High Street not far from the British branch bank that catered to middle-class customers.) It is at worst a small exaggeration to say that First National City rolled down the hill the first stone that ultimately became the avalanche of Competition and Credit Control, the new policy of the Treasury and the Bank of England that in 1971 brought the banking revolution, fife and drum, full panoply and all, to London.

And it may be only a slightly greater exaggeration to say that the British banks began their own American banking operations in the latter 1960s and 1970s mostly to see how the thing was done. Certainly, American banks in England have remained resolutely American; while except for a little swank at Barclays (which has secured state charters under its own name in both California and New York) the British invaders have been more Yankee than the Yanks. Lloyds Bank has a controlling interest in one of the largest California banks; Midland is part of the consortium called European-American that took over the failed giant Franklin National Bank of New York in fall 1974. Going into the credit card business, Barclays simply purchased the complete BankAmericard system; and its competitors, in founding Access, went to Omaha, Nebraska to find the software their machinery would need. The

City of London is the centre of world banking, and barring utter folly in Whitehall (not, of course, an impossibility) will remain so. But its technology and its objectives grow increasingly American.

To the extent that this book has a thesis, its argument is that the costs of the banking revolution now dangerously exceed its benefits; that in an economy where most of the money supply is manufactured by banks—and the improvements in banking technology that can increase the velocity of money at low cost may multiply the effective size of the money supply while no one is looking—the observer cannot completely exonerate banking practices from blame for the disasters of contemporary inflation. The parallels between the Heath–Barber policies of the early 1970s and the Kennedy Administration policies of the early 1960s are very close (both were seeking "to get the country moving again"); and so are the removals of restrictions on the operations of banks that occurred under those governments. How you get the genie back into the bottle after you have let him out is a question to which nobody on either side of the Atlantic has yet found any very good answers. But those seeking resolution in Britain will need an understanding of the role of banking in modern America. It is on these terms that this detailed, circumstantial, not always solemn report on American banks is offered to a British audience.

Some material that struck me on rereading as entirely parochial to America has been eliminated from the following pages; and I have added some dozens of pages to point up similarities or significant differences between British and American practice—and to introduce a few British personae into my cast of characters. In some sections, I have substituted British for American procedure, where the point to be made is the same; in others, I have supplemented a description of American practice by a discussion of British techniques to accomplish the same purposes. I have also added an epilogue to bring the story into the third quarter of 1975.

It has been a hell of a job; I hope the reader enjoys the book, and finds its information useful.

New York
August 19, 1975

PART
I

—

BANKERS
AND
MONEY

1/The Revolution

Just remember this: if bankers were as smart as you are, you would starve to death.

—HENRY HARFIELD, Esq., of the New York Bar, addressing a meeting of lawyers (1974)

*   *   *

A spectre is haunting American business and government in the 1970s: the spectre of banking. During the course of the last decade, Congressional committees have published studies purporting to prove that through a combination of lending powers, investments by their trust departments and interlocking directorates the banks have acquired preponderant and effective control of American industry. Savings and loan associations and organizations of home builders have denounced the banking system for draining away to other uses the money needed to finance the nationally proclaimed goal of decent housing for every American. Ever-growing lists of professions and industries have sued or lobbied to make the cops keep the banks off their turf: mutual fund

3

managers, stockbrokers, management consultant firms, real estate brokers, computer systems suppliers, leasing companies, lawyers, travel agents, insurance agents and underwriters, courier services— all have come complaining that the banks are marshalling their unique resources of prestige, muscle and money to take over other people's livelihood. And the president of the Federal Reserve Bank of New York has suggested—in public—that the banks no longer understand their own business very well and have run wild in ways that harm the economy.

This agitation and criticism seeks to counter a real revolution, one of the most striking changes in America in the last generation. In American history, banks were most frequently passive instruments, "intermediaries" that carried to differing sections of the economy financial pressures generated elsewhere. J. P. Morgan, basically a banker, was the giant of Wall Street; individually, as lenders and collectors of loans, bankers were important, even dominant, members of their communities. But collectively they were highly predictable, responding along paths of least resistance to developments at the South African gold fields, on the farms of the Great Plains, in the shops of the master mechanics who made the country great—or in Washington. Milton Friedman and Anna P. Schwartz could write a monetary history of the United States from 1867 to 1960 without paying much attention to any bank or banker, resting the entire analysis on events external to banking. The "monetarist" prescriptions for government policy that grew from their work assumed that banking was neutral in the development of the national economy, that if government pushed certain buttons, banks would necessarily respond in a predetermined way.

But even as Friedman and Schwartz were writing, in the early 1960s, a handful of big-city American banks—aided and abetted by a Comptroller of the Currency who was curious about what would happen if the government relaxed some restrictions on what banks could do—were beginning to act as prime movers in the economy. Congressman Wright Patman, chairman of the then Banking and Currency Committee of the House of Representatives, once said that the most powerful group of men in the country are the Open Market Committee of the Federal Reserve System, which in theory and in law controls the American money supply. ("It's a sham and a shame and a disgrace, the way the Fed has secretly operated this country".) But Alan Holmes, a slight, bespectacled, scholarly economist who is the "manager" of open market activities for the Fed, said sorrowfully in 1973 that "these days the banks are always about two years ahead of us".

In the mid-1970s, banks consciously acting in their own self-interest (like everyone else) strongly influence the money supply and hence the price level in the country, and by their lending activities increasingly determine the ratio between consumption and investment. The institutional structures they have built in the last ten years set a floor under interest rates much higher than such a floor has ever been before, thus profoundly affecting the spirit of enterprise, the opportunities available to the young, and the directions of economic activity. The banks have created a national credit market almost as important as the broadcasting networks in homogenizing the regions of a big country—and now an international credit network that threatens the ability of governments anywhere to control in any meaningful way the development of their national economies.

Like all revolutions, the one in banking can be admired or loathed, depending on one's other attitudes. What it should not be is ignored—yet not one American in a thousand has any idea a revolution has happened. (Nor is this incomprehension restricted to the man on the street: Harry Keefe, the second largest dealer in bank shares on Wall Street, says that "of the fourteen thousand chief executives of banks, maybe forty really know what's going on".) The roots of the revolution lie in technical and structural changes only some of which are visibly significant when first disclosed. But it is hard to see how we are to get sensible public policy applied to what has become the key industry of the society unless some reasonable chunk of the public (and the Congress, and the executive branch) understand the implications of the how and why of banking, and the reasons for revolution. And because this is a revolution made by men, not by circumstance, we had better know something about the people, too.

2

As the traveller nears almost any American city, the first building he is likely to see on the skyline is the headquarters of the local bank, partly because it's good publicity for a bank to be identified with a city's salient monument (few banks occupy all the space in their skyscrapers), partly because the bank very likely is the largest of local enterprises. Almost one hundred banks or bank holding companies held more than $1,000 million in total assets in 1974, and their headquarters offices were scattered around fifty cities. Both people and businesses need a bank near home—if they don't need one now they feel they may need one someday—and with only a handful of exceptions banks are forbidden to branch across state lines. And to the extent that the money is being loaned locally, common sense argues that local people should make the decisions about who is to borrow it.

Banking is for most people the quintessential capitalist activity, and the standard caricature of a capitalist in journals of the naïve left (or naïve right, for that matter) shows a pot-bellied man in a top hat carrying a bag of money. In fact, banking is a necessary activity in any economy in which the division of labour has proceeded to the point where most of the community works for a money income. By definition, money is a scarce good (if money were not scarce, people would not work for it), and if it is to be allocated rationally there must be an institution that deals primarily with its uses. To make its Gosplans work at all, the Soviet government found it needed a Gosbank. (Expressing concern about the availability of equipment for the 1974 harvest, "the party's Central Committee and the Government, in their joint decree, authorized the state bank to grant immediate short-term credits to state and collective farms to finance the purchase of spare parts, repair of agricultural machinery", etc.) Among the sources of the tragedy of India is the inability of any government on the subcontinent, colonial or independent, to convince the Indian landlord that he ought to put his money to use through a bank instead of burying it in a hole; among the sources of the tragedy of South America is the flight abroad of money that ought by rights to be in banks—or direct investments—at home.

Physically as economically, then, the bank sits atop the city. The building is likely to be new: banking has been prosperous (in 1973 the banks earned about 6 percent of all profits in American enterprise), and nobody has a greater stake than the banks in the continuing vitality of the cities. When urban renewal programmes provided subsidies for those who would build in the centre city, the banks were the first (sometimes the only) institution on the bandwagon: in Detroit, especially, the fact that there still is a downtown can be credited mostly to the banks. Architecturally, moreover, these are usually something more than minimum efforts. In Cincinnati, Minneapolis, Chicago, Phoenix, San Francisco, Boston, Tampa, Jacksonville, Atlanta, and many other cities the new bank building is the not unworthy centrepiece of a serious effort to make the centre city something other than what it was. Chase Manhattan gave Wall Street its first large open space that was not a graveyard. First National Bank of Chicago pioneered the construction of the glass façade that curves inward from its base (creating some spectacularly open lower floors and odd-shaped corner conference rooms; designers then filled them with appropriate space-age plastic free-form furniture). In Charlotte, North Carolina, the North Carolina National Bank hired young Nancy Collins away from her own art gallery and gave her a budget of $24,000 a year to buy art for the bank and its branches.

One element in the planning, however, has been sadly counterproductive. Banks have long fed their employees—organizers who have tried to unionize banks speak bitterly about the gratitude for the free hot lunch that kept appearing as a reason not to join a union—and the new buildings include elaborate, often handsome cafeterias (sans serif type on shaped signboards to say here salads, there desserts). Whatever gain downtown receives from the new buildings is diminished by the elimination of those who work there

7

from the street life of the city, the patronage of restaurants and stores. But it is a hot lunch, in many banks for nothing.

Inside the new buildings, the banks operate in big spaces, with a minimum of walls. Not so long ago, the public and the operating areas of the banking floor itself were separated by high partitions, and the tellers' windows were barred; and behind the tellers, invisible to the public but part of the work-force community, the bookkeepers laboured over the ledgers, posting people's accounts. Theoreticians of banking always worried a little about this propinquity, because of the obvious dangers in a situation where the person handling the cash and the person keeping the books could become friends, and there were sighs of relief breathed in supervisors' offices when the decision was taken to make banking floors bright and airy, with tellers' stations out in the open behind low counters and bookkeepers exiled to elsewhere. Security presumably was to be achieved by the very openness of the floor, and by the big plate-glass windows through which passersby could idly note anything unusual that might be going on within the bank.

Then bank robbery, which had formerly been a relatively skilled trade, became an occupation for amateurs who often behave more or less nuttily, and now some banks are considering the installation of bullet-proof glass partitions to protect tellers' stations. In some of the less secure neighbourhoods of Manhattan, there are branch banks that have eliminated personal contact entirely: the customer and the teller see each other on television screens, and the paper passes through a slot in the wall. But it is impossible to imagine a central office that worked that way. Bank robbery, while memorably terrifying to the individuals who experience it, is not a significant source of losses to the banking system: discovered and admitted embezzlement (which is by no means all the embezzlement) costs the banks four to six times as much. And everything is covered by a "blanket bond" insurance policy.

The bookkeepers who once stood behind the tellers are upstairs now in enormous bullpens on floors every bit as free from walls as the banking floor itself. They are not resentful of the bullpen: in banking it is the lot of man and woman both. At most big commercial banks, nobody below the level of a senior vice-president is likely to have a private office. Trust officers who handle tens of millions of dollars of other people's money sit side by side at adjacent desks in one big room.

Traditionally, lending officers worked on the banking floor in an area separated from the public by a railing and a step up—indeed, a man authorized to commit the bank to a loan is still a "platform officer". Transactions between a bank and its customers are secret unless somebody has a reason to talk about them (a troubled company may get quite a lot of value from an announcement that a big bank has given it a line of credit; and a bank may get some value, especially in the international field, out of an announcement that it has been the chosen instrument in "arranging financing" for a multinational corporate empire or a foreign government). But banking holds itself out as a public business, and in theory anybody who needs a loan can make contact with a banker who could give it to him. Now the banking floor is consecrated to the general public, and the lending officers on the platform deal with consumer loans. For corporate lending, the business is now upstairs—but the men in charge still sit in one big room.

Sometimes the effect is breathtaking. A senior banker may not have a private office, but he has a lot of space. On the fortieth floor of the Bank of America building overlooking Nob Hill, each officer has a twenty-foot bay to himself. He faces away from the view; the visitor seated beside his desk is surrounded not by walls but by the magnificence of the San Francisco harbour, the bridges, the hills, and the bay. The carpeting is thick, the ceiling is sound-proofed, and the bells are dulled in the telephones on the secretaries' desks far away. One does not speak loudly in this ambiance; but if the visitor is someone who would rather not sit in the open, the officer can commandeer a conference room beside the elevator shafts in the central core of the building. Those few executives of the bank who do have a private office keep their doors open: A. P. Giannini, who founded the bank and made it the biggest in the world, never had an office of his own and would have been appalled at the idea of a banker working behind a closed door. His own greatest moment as a banker, indeed, was staged in the open air, when he set up a table on the street in front of his ruined building before the dust from the great earthquake had settled, and began writing reconstruction loans for his compatriots and neighbours.

The open-space system is probably in decline, not because business has grown more secretive over the years but because the desk in the open leaves no place for couches, and on the executive level Americans now like to hold their meetings on couches. One does not place a coffee cup on another man's desk; a couch comes with a coffee table, on which coffee may be served. A corner arrangement of couches, which is the most common, allows for the sharing of a table and an ashtray, an intimacy undistracted by whatever is on the desk. There is a pleasant flavour of democracy not obtainable when one man is behind a desk in a padded swivel chair and the other is beside it or before it in something necessarily more stiff and less comfortable.

The idea of everybody in one big room goes back to the days before the telephone, when the easiest way to consult a partner was to wander over to his desk, and the only way to convey a change in business atmosphere as rapidly as might be needed was to have everyone, in effect, in the same atmosphere. There was no division of staff and line functions: the man who made the loan was making the bank's loan policy as he did so. The bank sat there: some people came in and made deposits, others came in and asked to borrow money. Now there are policymakers, determining how and on what terms the bank will buy money, how and on what terms the bank will lend it. They do not meet the public much, they do business on the telephone and in meetings, and they work in offices —though still, at most banks, in offices with open doors.

3

Bank executives have not been recruited from the community at large. At this writing, according to information from the American Jewish Committee, none of the nation's fifty largest banks outside New York has on its senior executive level a woman, a Negro, an

Oriental, or a Jew. (There are a few Jews in big New York banks, perhaps half a dozen in the eight giants taken together. Until 1973, there was a Jewish executive vice-president at the Valley National Bank of Arizona, Lester Goldberg, but having fought through and won an insistence that the bank had to raise its interest rate on savings to the highest level permitted by the government even though Bank of America in adjacent California was not doing so, he became the victim of the directors' annoyance when earnings declined.) When John Bunting of First Pennsylvania Bank & Trust was given an award by B'nai B'rith in Philadelphia for having entered into a partnership with an Israeli bank, AJC's Executive Suite programme noted in a memo for internal circulation that there was not so much as an assistant vice-president of that bank who was Jewish. In fall 1973 only 2 of 285 officers of the First National Bank of Boston were Jewish, although, according to a statement by Ephron Catlin of the bank's personnel department to a committee that came calling on the subject, "two-thirds of its customers were Jewish".

Ethnic banks have a long and interesting history—the nation's largest, Bank of America, began as the Bank of Italy in San Francisco—but only a handful of medium-sized Jewish banks in the largest cities still flourish. Black banks have been started in a number of places, but except in Atlanta and North Carolina, where established black insurance companies provide a financial anchor, they have done very poorly. In New York, The Movement has secured a charter for a First Women's Bank, which would have all female officers (and would be located in the 57th Street and Park Avenue space recently vacated by Henri Soule's great restaurant Le Pavillon); and late in 1975, after a long struggle for capital, the bank opened its doors.

There are examples of bank presidents who started at the bottom. Thomas Wilcox, now head of Crocker National in California, went to work for First National City in New York as an office boy; his talent was recognized, and the bank paid the bills to send him to Princeton. Walter Bimson, who created Valley National in Arizona, was a poor boy from Colorado working as a YMCA Secretary at a navy demobilization centre in Chicago right after World War I. Mr. Harris of Harris Trust came to give Bible lectures to the sailors, was much taken with Bimson, and invited him to come work at the bank. Later Bimson learned; he liked to say that all he was interested in was power and position —once he had those, the rest would come.

From the beginning, banking has been a trade for the people up top; when the Bank of Massachusetts was chartered in 1784, its president received among other privileges the right to a seat on the dais at Harvard commencements. "There's nobody you'd rather be liked by than the banking group," says John Bunting of First Pennsylvania, a bantam-sized bank chairman who presents himself as young (under fifty), feisty, and unpopular with his peers. "They're all smooth, they're mostly well-born, and they're certainly all rich." William Reidy, research director of the Office and Professional Employees Union AFL-CIO, which has managed to organize about a thousand of the nation's 850,000-odd workers in banks (there are also about 175,000 "supervisory workers" and officers not eligible for unionization), says disgustedly that "fellows who are glorified clerks like to refer to themselves as bankers; it carries prestige". (In Britain, the National Union of Bank Employees has successfully organized a fair fraction of banking staffs, but in the clearing banks must compete against in-house unions that bargain for workers at their bank alone, tapping the loyalties that have defeated OPEU in America.) Morris Schapiro, the largest bankstock dealer in America, puts the compendium in a phrase: "A banker is a man who lives on the side of a hill."

In the upper echelons, bankers live exceedingly well. They too get a free hot lunch, upstairs in clublike surroundings, with many small rooms in which a man can be a gracious host for a small party of customers—or for a visiting reporter. Morgan Guaranty unquestionably does the best, with two restaurant floors atop Broad Street to do it in. Lunch offers not only excellent steak or salmon, and a salad for the weight-watcher, but also a pastrami sandwich for jaded palates. In Paris, in Morgan's share of the Place Vendôme, two wines are served at lunch for a properly recommended visitor, and one of them is a first-growth claret of a fine vintage. And always at Morgan—people who have worked there are loyal to the place all their lives—one's companions are gracious, patient, informed, a pleasure to be with.

Though Walter Wriston of First National City has demonstrated that a man who radiates nervous energy can flash to the top in American banking, the Morgan manner is for most bankers the desired if not always attainable model. Walter Bagehot in an article in *The Economist* in the 1860s wrote of a London banker friend who said that if he had chosen the priesthood he would have become a bishop, because he never said anything that offended anyone. Bluntly, what makes the difference between the Morgan banker and many of his imitators is often something so simple as the level of intelligence. Gaylord Freeman, chairman of the First National Bank of Chicago, a grey owl of a man who combines great ease of manner with authentically high wattage, was promoted in 1950 from that bank's general council staff to his first senior job in the corporate lending division, and for some reason was asked to develop a statement of the bank's goals and how to get there. Among the areas he considered was personnel. "Banks," he wrote, "offer an opportunity to an educated, personable, but uncourageous young man, for a pleasant, interesting, dignified life. One of our major jobs is to avoid the employment or advancement of such men. . . ."

Adam Aronson is a large and rambunctious entrepreneur who sold out a substantial photo-supply business and wound up building from scratch a chain of suburban banks around St. Louis. He likes to say that every rich St. Louis family had three sons: "The best became a professional man, the next best went into the family business, and the third went to Yale and came back to the bank." Bruce Carl, who left Monsanto Chemical to help Aronson run Mark Twain Bancshares, has found the insight valuable: "Whenever I find out a man in a bank here went to Yale, I know I have to deal with him *very slowly*." Maxwell Brandwen, a lawyer who runs Amalgamated Bank, with $800 million in assets the largest bank owned by a labour union, says of the generality of his colleagues in the big New York banks that "if they could make money only by relying on their competence, they wouldn't make any money". The First Vice-President of one of the nation's twelve Federal Reserve Banks sums up the matter flatly: "You don't have to be smart to run a bank."

There were reasons for this. "The business of banking," Bagehot wrote in *Lombard Street* a hundred years ago, "ought to be simple: if it is *hard*, it is *wrong*." When he shifts his attention from competitors to customers, Adam Aronson no longer gives such high value to brains alone: "I know an accountant who's a Harvard Phi Bete; and if he sends somebody, you know the guy has larceny in his heart." The soundness of the banking system may be too important for either brilliance or imagination to be the sole consideration in choosing the leadership cadre.

It has long been fashionable to make fun of J. P. Morgan's insistence that he loaned money solely on the basis of a borrower's character. Even *The Bankers' Handbook*, a far from inconoclastic document, suggests in one article that the classic "three C's" by which bankers judge borrowers (CAPITAL, CHARACTER, and CAPACITY) could also be seen as "three R's" (RESOURCES, REPUTATION, and RAPACITY). But the fact is that, like any individual told by a friend that he needs some money to tide him over till Tuesday, a banker confronted by a potential borrower will think first about whether this is the sort of fellow who pays his debts. "An open line without security does not necessarily require a higher interest rate than a secured loan," says Robert Long, who supervised the $1·6 billion portfolio of loans to farmers by San Francisco's Bank of America before becoming Undersecretary of Agriculture in 1973. "It all depends on the borrower, and that's an art, not a science."

More than most people these days, bankers believe in living up to one's obligations. Loyalties are expected and given: it is rare for the chief executive of a large bank ever to have worked on the officer level for a bank other than the one he now heads. In the countryside, small-town bankers can abuse their position to get business for their own insurance and real estate brokerage operations, and in the cities there is more self-dealing and accepting of favours by lending officers than anyone wants to believe; but there is a lot less than one would expect, given the pervasiveness of temptation. "And," says Nathaniel Bowditch of First Pennsylvania, "banks have no divorces". Bankers have been known to get girls for customers, but they are rarely customers of such commercial services themselves: their business conventions are bibulous but uxorious.

The need to make personal judgments and to behave yourself means that there is often a stiff back behind the gracious front. In their business lives, bankers are not heavy on faith, hope, or charity, and the shadow of sternness people feel in a bank cannot be brightened away by advertising campaigns about how friendly the neighbourhood bankers are. Despite what the sociological researchers say, lots of opinion leaders don't want a banker to be all that friendly, anyway. "Bankers as a breed are different from other men," says Gerald T. Dunne, editor of *The Banking Law Journal,* who was a vice-president of the Federal Reserve Bank of St. Louis before he became a law professor. "The function of bankers is to be trusted, not to be liked."

4

"I happened to have dinner with the head of one of the larger banking groups," Kay A. Randall of United Virginia Bankshares told a meeting of bank directors, "who commented that one of his men had been honoured for having fifty years of service. He said, 'We thought we would celebrate this occasion, and we stopped all operations in the bank the other day and had punch and cookies in the lobby. We brought everyone in to tell this man how pleased we were. It was quite an occasion.' My friend got up and honoured him and gave him his watch. The retiree said, 'Thank you.' Therefore, my friend got back up, went to the microphone and said, 'Won't you think back in your career in banking. Think about everything that happened and tell us what is the most important thing, the most important change that you have seen in banking in this half-century of service.' The man paused for a few minutes, finally got up before the microphone, and said, 'Air conditioning.'"

5

Banking has been an industry for a long time, but until the present management of New York's First National City Bank came out of its cocoon in the early 1960s a bank was never, really, a business. Freeman's youthful report to his masters in Chicago in 1950 opened with a flat statement that the goal of "the Bank" must be to "make a profit—and as large a one as possible". This did not go down well, Freeman recalls: "The then-chairman of the bank didn't accept it. Bankers were still coming out of the depression, when the whole goal was to stay alive; and for those who survived, the goal was to build their strength. Building deposits and being bigger than the guy down the street had always been more important than making profits." Even today, banks are rated by the press and even by their industry associations not according to their profits but according to the size of their "footings"—the total money at their disposal.

Quite apart from the fact that "profits" is a dirty word to so many people who are considered experts on the economy, the bankers' stress on size rather than earnings was understandable. Size—the number of dollars in deposits, loans, investments—is really *known*, regularly registered with and verified by government agencies. The profits of a bank, on the other hand, are in part artifacts of the accounting procedures employed. "When I was a newspaper writer—banking editor, so-called," says George Mooney, chairman of New York's Washington Federal Savings and Loan (and once New York State Superintendent of Banking), "I used to twit my friends, tell them, 'A guy running a candy store knows what his costs are, and you don't.' Cost accounting in banks was really a joke."

Not the least of the costing problems is the widespread confusion, even among bankers, about the fundamentals of their own business. Howard Crosse while vice-president in charge of bank supervision at the Federal Reserve Bank of New York in 1961 pointed a scornful finger at the typical bank public relations statement that "'all we have to sell is service'. Actually," Crosse wrote, "what banks have to sell is credit." The basic services a bank performs—processing cheques, preparing and mailing statements, supplying references, introductions, and information—are simply the price the bank pays for the money that enables it to make loans, to "sell credit". When a modern bank thinks about a new service, "operations" experts try to evaluate the size of the deposits the service may generate as an offset to the expense of providing it. Cost accounting under these conditions is not a simple operation: John Reed, the thirty-four-year-old whiz who spends $200 million a year to operate the First National City Bank of New York and knows where every penny goes, reports that "Somebody calls me and says, 'Hey, John, what does it cost you to process a cheque?' And I say, 'Why do you want to know?' Because the purpose of clearing the cheque has a lot to do with the cost."

Until fairly recently, moreover, the practical importance of profits was surprisingly slight at a bank. Bank stocks were closely held by small communities of local investors (fewer than half a dozen bank stocks were listed on an exchange prior to the 1960s), and when shares were sold the price was individually negotiated. Dividends were paid out at a steady rate, regardless of earnings: higher profits built the undistributed surplus faster, lower profits built it slower, and that wasn't too serious.

Competition among banks was significant within each of the great money centres, but elsewhere relations were usually cozy: everybody who was anybody knew everybody else, and you got a given piece of business because you knew one of the right people a little better than your rivals did. Full-scale competition from outside the local market was not only unthinkable but impossible: laws forbade banks to cross state lines, and in some states restricted any individual bank to its own county or city—or even, in fifteen states, to its own specific location. In Chicago, growing banks built bridges high over downtown streets to link two office buildings they were using: the bridge kept the business "under one roof", as the lawyers interpreted the Illinois banking law.

Business was significantly different from city to city. "When I came to this bank in 1951," says C. M. vanVlierden, the Dutch immigrant who built the international division of Bank of America, "there were different interest rates on the East Coast and on the West Coast." (The separation of money markets is not necessarily a bad thing, incidentally, and not exclusively American—as late as the 1960s, the Swiss had separate currency exchanges with different prices in Geneva and Zurich. What kills it is inexpensive instantaneous communication: by keeping a telephone line open, the First National City Bank of New York was able to buy, say, French Francs from the Union Bank of Switzerland in Geneva, simultaneously sell French Francs to the Union Bank of Switzerland in Zurich, and turn a modest profit.)

In ten breathtaking years, all this casual isolationism and inefficiency has been broken. Bank shares are now aggressively traded on national exchanges, and middling-sized banks like Philadelphia's First Pennsylvania and Charlotte's North Carolina National (less than one-sixth the size of giants like Bank of America and First National City) find it worth their while to send teams of executives to Wall Street for meetings with stock market analysts. American banks, with a few minor exceptions, are still forbidden to take deposits outside their home state, but they can and do open lending offices all over the country, and branches all over the world. In 1972, when Chicago's Continental Illinois offered some big borrowers "cap" loans (long-term credits with a fixed-interest ceiling), not only the neighbouring and pugnacious First National Bank of Chicago but also the distant and relatively sedate First National Bank of Boston and Morgan Guaranty Trust felt compelled eventually to match what they considered old-fashioned and foolish terms rather than risk losing customers. "We're vulnerable," says chairman Richard D. Hill of the First National Bank of Boston, "because of the international aspect: we can lose business in London and Paris and Latin America if a corporate treasurer gets mad at us."

New York's First National City already finds more than half its profits overseas, and with the growth of multinational enterprise more and more banks feel a need to be in place to service their customers worldwide. "If a corporate customer has to take part of its business to New York," Paul S. Nadler of Rutgers told the *Wall Street Journal*, "the regional banks are through." In spring 1974 the Comptroller of the Currency reported that ninety-four American banks had a real business, not just a post box and a representative, abroad. The "career path" for tomorrow's bank presidents leads not through the Porcellian Club at Harvard or Skull & Bones at Yale (though having known the right people at the right college will never be a handicap) but through the foreign branches. It is already true that the leaders of the great American banks are familiar with the furnishings and fixtures of the diffused corners of the globe—but what it means to have internationally minded men at the head of banks, nobody knows.

By reputation, banks still buy and sell people; in fact, people now buy and sell banks. In various ways and for various reasons, bank accounting is still dubious ("You have to keep in mind," says Jeffrey Howles, who runs Bank of America's English branches, "the difference between true profit and accounting profit"); but the published profit figures have become increasingly important. Apparent trends in profitability will determine the price of a bank's stock, and the price of the stock has become the name of the game. For banks are fighting to diversify, to acquire control of finance companies and leasing companies and computer service bureaus —and even, when the government will allow it, other banks. Like any conglomerate, an expanding "bank holding company" seeks to acquire new properties not by cash purchase but by an exchange of stock. The higher the market price of the bank's stock, the smaller the number of shares that must be offered to pay for any given acquisition, and the greater the future profits-per-share that the bank can buy.

Expanding industries employ not only more people but brighter people, and banking became so active at the business schools so fast that Peter Drucker, for one, worries about what is to be done with all the good recruits: "Within seven or eight years many of them rose to positions of substantial pay and exalted title such as vice-president and senior vice-president. Before they were thirty large numbers of these 'young comers' reached, in other words, what must be their terminal positions. Yet—in large part because these young men did not have much experience—these jobs, whatever the big title and good salary, are quite limited in scope and authority. By the time they reach forty, these men are going to be bored, cynical, and no longer excited about the job and its challenge." One of the unspoken reasons for the expansion into holding companies and international banking is the need to find suitable employment for all the new talent.

First National City has been aggressive in personnel policies too. "They'll give you a job that demands 105 per cent of your capabilities," says a young Englishman who worked for Citicorp in London. "If you grow into it, they do the same thing again. Both as a training process and for job satisfaction, I don't think you could ask for anything more."

It is possible to take another view of these developments. Van Vechten Shaffer, a ramrod-straight old man who retired some years ago as chairman of the Guaranty Trust Company of Cedar Rapids, Iowa, chuckles about "all these young MBA's from the Harvard Business School who are wizards—just wizards—at making loans." Shaffer pauses, then adds, "Not *quite* so good at collecting them . . ."

Bank stock dealer Harry Keefe has yet another perspective on what was and what will be: "My thesis," he says, "is that banking was the one business in America that was controlled not by its owners but by the people it did business with. Look who's on the boards of directors of the banks—all the big borrowers. These days are gone. Your best friend now is the capital market, which will allow you to leverage. From now on my clients—the stockholders—are going to call the tune."

A book such as this one would not have been possible ten years ago, because until bankers had to raise money in the market they had no interest at all in talking to reporters: "Mr. Brown's philosophy," Gaylord Freeman recalls, speaking of his predecessor, "was,

'Never tell anybody anything'."

No doubt it is a mistake to idealize what used to be. At a private gathering in 1973, Arthur Burns, Chairman of the Board of Governors of the Federal Reserve System, contrasted todays' "mark-up bankers" against a description one of his auditors repeated as that of "the old-time fatherly banker as a man who was concerned with his community, who put service to customers above other considerations, who did not bother about comparing his earnings with some other banker down the street, and who never gave a thought to the price/earnings ratio at which his stock is selling". Thomas Storrs, chairman of North Carolina National Bank, "was reminded of a gentleman who operated the one bank in a small town in the Carolinas several decades ago. He had many of the attributes which Dr. Burns enumerated: he *was* concerned with the growth of his community, for he owned a substantial part of it and managed his holdings through the information which he acquired in his bank. He did *not* worry greatly about bank earnings, for while he owned enough of the shares of the bank to protect his position, he did not look to them for any substantial income. He did *not* concern himself with the price/earnings ratio set by the market; he *was* the market for the stock. Sellers came to him and he placed their shares in the hands of new owners who he considered friendly to himself—the transaction taking place at book value. He did *not* worry a great deal about internal efficiencies since the help did not get paid overtime and he played golf several afternoons a week regardless of the workload. . . ."

What Keefe and his stockholders and bankers like Freeman are demanding is what the stock market in the palmy days of 1968 called "performance". Bagehot wrote that "Adventure is the life of commerce, but caution, I had almost said timidity, is the life of banking". Walter Wriston says that "People around here are tired of hearing me say that Babe Ruth struck out three thousand times and nobody remembers it". Both these men cannot be right; which attitude makes more sense in our economy, in our society, is a subject better discussed at the end than at the beginning of this book. But there can be no question at all that Keefe's perception of the current scene is correct: that's what's happening: that's the revolution.

As noted in the preface, this revolution was imported to England in 1971 under the name Competition and Credit Control, the policy statement that turned topsy-turvy the entire monetary regulatory machinery of the United Kingdom. In the postwar years prior to 1971, the Bank of England had controlled the banking system mostly through limitations on the credits each bank could extend. "The banking system was in a straightjacket," says Geoffrey Bell of the merchant banking house of Schroder Wagg, a dashing young economist who used to work for the Bank of England and now puts most of his time into advising the government of Venezuela on what to do with all that oil money. "To say the least, the quantitative restrictions were debilitating: you protected all the deadheads. The most innovative houses might get the new business, but then they would bump into their ceiling." After 1971, the Bank moved toward the American system of controlling bank liabilities rather than bank assets, enforcing reserve requirements against customer accounts. Banks could now bid for money to lend (against each other, because the total money in the system was presumably limited by the Bank of England); and if they could find customers to pay more than the new money cost the bank, they could profit by expanding both their borrowings and their lendings.

Unfortunately, as the Bank has had to learn the hard way, the control of liabilities is much less precise than the control of assets. From the first quarter of 1970 to the fourth quarter of 1974, total liabilities of British banks rose from £16,400 million pounds to £37,300 million pounds, figures that express but also in part explain the disastrous inflation in the U.K.

"The tragedy of Competition and Credit Control was that it was so long delayed," says R. S. Sayers, historian of the Bank of England and the world's leading authority on central banking theory (he was adviser to a large fraction of the Third World countries in setting up such institutions). "An enormous pent-up force was released. People were so ready to jump in, there was lots of room for the rogues, and for the extreme optimists. People not trained for it were thrown into the water, sink or swim, and many of them sank. Inflation rusts a banking system, because the banks are always able to pay out less in interest than they can charge."

Before Competition and Credit Control, there had been an odd dichotomy in banking in the City. The merchant banks, competing against American banks in the Eurodollar market, managing people's money in the stock market and advising companies on their financial structure, were staffed with university graduates trained in economics or business or both, aggressive, bright, at home with the ways of the world. The discount houses—historical anomalies performing a highly routined intermediary function between the Bank of England and the clearing banks—were proprietors of a narrow expertise but performed their duties mostly on a face-to-face basis that rewarded social class and *savoir faire* more than imagination or ability. The clearing banks themselves— Barclays, National Westminster, Midland and Lloyds, more than three thousand branches each, survivors of a massive merger movement—were closed social systems through which grammar school boys rose from menial starting jobs through branch management to great prominence in the City; rarely was the managing director of a clearing bank or any of his senior assistants a university graduate. Suddenly the work of both the discount houses and the clearing banks required both speed and power, and British banking became something it had never been before: a young man's game. The British revolution may have been even more profound—and more dangerous to the ordinary citizen who likes a quiet life—than its American predecessor.

2/Introducing Money

If this Colony be in any respect happy and flourishing, it is paper money and a right application of it that hath rendered us so. And that we are in a flourishing condition is evident from our trade. . . .

— Report of Governor RICHARD WARD of Rhode Island to the Lord Commissioners of Trade for the Foreign Plantations, January 9, 1740

* * *

Only in so far as paper-money represents gold . . . is it a symbol of value.
— KARL MARX

* * *

Money is a manufactured item. The amount of money available to the economy is determined by the manufacturers. . . . Under the Constitution, it is the right and duty of Congress to creat money. It is left entirely to Congress. Congress has farmed out this power—has let it out to the banking system.

— WRIGHT PATMAN

* * *

The functions of banking as distinct from the procedures are not changing, and are not likely to change. They are two in number. First, in symbiosis (bedfellowship might be a better word) with the government, the banks provide and administer the money supply of the country. Second, they make loans to selected borrowers: in the deliberately indiscreet phrase once used by John Bunting, "We determine who will succeed and who will fail." They operate what Robin Pringle of *The Banker* has called a "judgments system". A great deal of the health of the economy and of the polity hinges on how well these functions are performed.

"Money" is a word variously defined, to say the least, but not entirely undefinable. The "essential feature of a money economy,"

24

writes R. H. Clower, "is the existence of institutional arrangements whereby at least one commodity becomes universally acceptable in exchange for all other commodities." Given the chance, virtually all human societies opt for money made of precious metals, because they are relatively scarce and because when properly refined they will not corrode or otherwise deteriorate. "Although gold and silver are not by nature money," Karl Marx observed, "money is by nature gold and silver." Obviously, the substance employed is much less important than the arrangements made for handling it: "The physical characteristics of *money commodities*," Clower continues, "are no more relevant to the *institution* of money than different forms of courtship are relevant to the *institution* of marriage". Wampum is every bit as good as gold if everyone says it is: money is "universally acceptable . . . by virtue not of individual choice but . . . of social contrivance". This does not get us all the way home by any means; there remains the problem dourly stated by R. S. Sayers, that "the money quality of assets is something imposed by the business habits of people. . . . To label something as 'money,' the supply of which is to behave according to rules laid down by legal authority, is to build on shifting sand. . . . There is no hard and fast line between what is money and what is not money". More than one money commodity may be universally acceptable (as both silver and gold have been at various times in history), and some money commodities may be acceptable only in certain places or for certain purposes (like a tax anticipation note, or a credit card slip, or a plastic chip from a gambling casino).

Among the functions of government was the coinage of money made from precious metals: the U.S. Constitution, in fact, establishes this authority as one of the short list of powers specifically given the Congress. The design stamped on the coin certified the weight (and thus the unit-value) of the piece. A good government maintained the weight and quality of precious metals in its coins, which would thus be acceptable in international trade as well as for domestic uses; a bad government "debased the coinage".

One of the central functions of money is that it serves as a "store of value"—that is, instead of spending his income today, a man can save it in the form of money for future spending. This goes wrong two ways: both the holder and his community are losers. First, as Keynes put it, "[M]oney as a store of wealth . . . is barren; whereas practically every other form of storing wealth yields some interest or profit. Why should anyone outside a lunatic asylum wish to use money as a store of wealth?" To which Keynes gives a disturbing answer: "Because, partly on reasonable and partly on intuitive grounds, our desire to hold money as a store of wealth is a barometer of the degree of our distrust of our own calculations and conventions concerning the future. . . . The possession of actual money lulls our disquietude."

Second, money held as money is withdrawn from current use, which damages the economy. "African savings," Theodore Geiger and Winifred Armstrong wrote gloomily in 1964, "are among the most liquid in the world, since they are often held in the form of small cash hoards. Precisely for this reason, however, they are . . . nonliquid and nonproductive; they remain idle and cannot be mobilized . . . for the use of other entrepreneurs."

The tendency of any coined money to leak off into barren stores of value creates a need for banking. The first function of banking is to substitute pieces of paper for coinage, releasing money for circulation. In the early banks of the Renaissance, as we shall see in the next chapter, this substitution was merely a matter of giving investors an agreed-upon partnership share in the proceeds from the employment of their money, and taking from borrowers a written promise to repay on a certain date the coin that had been placed at their disposal. Neither the document attesting the partnership share nor the promissory note was easily negotiable, however: the "money" was still almost entirely the coinage.

Money as we know it—pieces of paper suitably engraved which will be accepted as payment for goods and services—starts with the incorporation of the Bank of England under the Tunnage Act of 1694. Stock in the bank was bought either with coin or with the "bills of exchequer" which were the seventeenth-century version of government bonds, and all the proceeds were turned over to the state, in return for a new interest-bearing government bond issue. The bank received in return the right to issue banknotes up to the full extent of its capital. These banknotes were exchanged for the promissory notes of customers, and thus the bank earned double interest on its stockholders' money—once on the government bonds, once on the loans. Meanwhile, the banknotes served as money for merchants, manufacturers and farmers, who had no direct dealings with the Bank.

The full development of "credit money" came a quarter of a century later with the spectacular ventures of a Scotsman named John Law, who sold the King of France on his rather academic and abstract theory that pieces of paper would continue to be good as gold however many of them were printed, so long as people believed they could get gold for the paper whenever they wished. And people *would* believe it if the state itself accepted the pieces of paper in payment of taxes. Then, instead of borrowing from the old bankers, who would be limited in what they could lend him by the precious metals at their disposal—and worried about how much they lent him because the experience of banking through the Renaissance had been that banks went bust when sovereigns failed to pay their debts—the King could borrow from Law, who would make the loan by printing paper.

To make this arrangement plausible, Law needed a substantial store of precious metals to start with, and an enterprise that people would regard as a steady producer of inflowing streams of metal. The initial store was gathered through an immense stock issue, sold to the public partly for gold and partly, as in England, for evidences of the outstanding Royal debt. And the enterprise was given two highly profitable monopolies: first, the collection of taxes for the crown (which the king pledged as backing for the paper); second, the exploitation of French colonies initially in America but soon all over the world. Everyone knew how much the bumbling Spanish had got from their American possessions; the Mississippi could scarcely be less valuable. The scheme got into full operation at the end of 1718, and for two glorious years Law pumped up the currency of France. Interest rates fell to $4\frac{1}{2}$

percent, about a third of what they had been before, and the country was immensely prosperous. And then, of course, the "Mississippi Bubble" broke.

But credit money (*credere:* to believe) was an idea that would not down. If A signs a piece of paper pledging himself to pay a certain sum to the person who presents the paper, those who are confident that A will in fact live up to his pledge have no reason not to accept the paper as the functional equivalent of coin.

Money is someone's promise to pay, made money by universal belief that the promise will be kept. A merchant's IOU to his supplier, in return for credit to purchase the inventory on his shelves, is not money because most third parties would not accept it. But if the IOU is written to a bank, and the bank buys it as an asset by creating a current account against which the merchant can write cheques, the IOU does become money, absorbed into the national monetary totals. The social function of the bank, simply stated, is to monetize the liabilities of those who borrow from it.

Obviously, this is an easy way to enlarge the money supply. Such enlargement was necessary if prices were to remain stable at a time of expanding trade—especially "trade" that took more time to accomplish because the buyers were in another country or because the manufacture required the prior construction of factories and infrastructure. And a number of acute observers had noted that economic activity seemed to flourish when money was plentiful and prices were rising.

Exactly why this should be true was (and for many observers still is) much of a mystery. Clearly, if pound notes (and bank accounts and other assets representing pound notes) behaved for an instant of time like living cells and divided so that each made two pounds, the results would be trivial: prices would immediately double and nobody would be better off or worse off than before. "Money of account" that merely "facilitates exchanges," Keynes argued, need never "itself come into the picture as a substantive object. . . . It is a convenience which is devoid of significance or real influence". Yet human observation when Spanish galleons began bringing home the silver from Mexico and Peru, and when John Law inflated the French currency, indicated strongly that a mere increase in money quantities *did* have an effect, and a beneficial one. "We find," David Hume wrote a generation after Law and a generation before Adam Smith, "that in every kingdom into which money begins to flow in greater abundance than formerly, everything takes on a new face; labour and industry gain life; the merchant becomes more enterprising, and even the farmer follows the plough with greater alacrity and attention".

Hume had an explanation: "Some time is required before the money circulates through the whole state. . . . By degrees the price rises, first of one commodity, then of another; till the whole at last reaches a just proportion with the new quantity of specie which is in the kingdom. In my opinion it is only in this interval or intermediate situation, between the acquisition of money and the rise in prices, that the increasing quantity of gold and silver is favourable to industry." In more modern (though not contemporary) terms, an increase in the money supply and the resulting rise in prices benefit the commercial debtor class, which is enterprising and innovative and finds uses for the money, at the expense of a rentier class which reaps without sowing. This leads to the notion, widely accepted in our century, that the way to get out of hard times is to inflate the currency.

This notion, as we are now learning the hard way, is wrong-headed. "Inflation does give a stimulus," Sir John Hicks wrote in 1967, "but the stimulus is greatest when the inflation starts—when it starts from a condition that has been non-inflationary. If the inflation continues, people get adjusted to it. But when people get adjusted to it, when they *expect* rising prices, the mere occurrence of what has been expected is no longer stimulating." More than that, the rentier class finds means of self-defence in the ever-rising interest rates that must be paid to persuade money holders to save and lend their money. We shall take a longer look at some of these problems in the last chapter; for now be it noted merely that Law's bubble was only the first to break.

2

The banking system, then, is first of all the instrumentality through which credit money is created. In the early years of this country, this function was directly expressed: banks issued "banknotes," promises to pay specie (monetized gold or silver) to the bearer on demand, and these banknotes formed a considerable part of the money in circulation.

The fact that this vital governmental power lodged in private hands was always offensive to many political leaders. "Money," Abraham Lincoln said when he was trying to talk Congress into authorizing him to print greenbacks, "is the creature of law, and the creation of the original issue of money should be maintained as an exclusive monopoly of the National Government." This was distinctly *not* the principle upon which his country was founded, however; the Constitution, written by men who knew about the Mississippi Bubble and the similar South Seas Bubble in England (not to mention the heavily depreciated Continental currency of the Revolution), had given Congress the power to coin money from precious metals but not the power to print it. The man who had shepherded Lincoln's original legal tender laws through a reluctant Congress in 1862, having moved on to become Chief Justice, voted to hold the greenbacks unconstitutional when the question came before the Supreme Court in 1870.

The reason for preferring banknotes to government paper was, simply, a general belief that bankers would be more trustworthy than governments. Banknotes, Tom Paine wrote approvingly, were not really money, but "hostages to be exchanged for hard money". Legal tender that could not be converted to coin Paine considered counterfeiting by the state; he wrote that the punishment of a legislator who would "move for such a law ought to be *death*". Nothing but revolution could prevent a government from printing such pieces of paper without limit, destroying the foundations of economic life, whereas the private banker would be restricted in his quantities by his need to redeem the notes on demand. "Mr. Wilson," Walter Bagehot wrote, explaining the monetary principles of his predecessor as editor of *The Economist* (who was also his father-in-law), "considered that bankers might be trusted to keep such a reserve, as they would be ruined, sooner or later, if they did not; and if the notes issued by them were always convertible at the pleasure of the holder, he believed that the currency would never be depreciated".

Actually, American colonial experience with government-issued paper money had been nowhere near so bad as reputation had it: Benjamin Franklin had started promoting official paper money as early as 1729 (to relieve the colonies' desperate shortage of specie), and never saw a reason to change his mind. Bray Hammond cites several studies to support his contention that at least five colonies—Pennsylvania, New York, New Jersey, Delaware, and Maryland—had managed state-issued paper money intelligently and successfully. When banknotes from private, state-chartered banks became the paper medium, however, American experience was by no means entirely cheerful. A $1 note issued by a bank far away from the place where its possessor tried to spend it might well be accepted only at a discount, because the man to whom it was offered could not fully credit it, could not be sure that there was specie to back it. Long before Lincoln, the federal government itself did not take banknotes in payment of customs or excise (the only taxes there were in those dear, dead days when freedom from direct taxation by the national government was part of the American birthright); payments to the Treasury had to be made in specie.

Many private banknotes were in fact fraudulent: in the 1830s especially the country suffered a rash of banks started in places like the upper Michigan peninsula, "out among the wildcats", where people were unlikely to come to redeem a piece of paper they had been unwise enough to accept. The Michigan banking commissioner reported in 1839 on his attempts to inspect the specie reserve in his state's banks: "The singular spectacle was presented of the officers of the state seeking for banks in situations the most inaccessible and remote from trade, and finding, at every step, an increase of labour by the discovery of new and remote organizations. . . . Gold and silver flew about the country with the celerity of magic; its sound was heard in the depths of the forest; yet, like the wind, one knew not whence it came or whither it was going."

Lincoln, who had an expensive war to finance, coupled his call for greenbacks with a call for the national chartering of banks. The national banks would also issue banknotes, limited not by their possession of specie (though the notes would be redeemable) but by the quantity of government bonds they bought. (Again, the Bank of England pattern of interest earned both ways.) State-chartered banks would be invited to take national charters, and a tax on the issuance of banknotes by any but national banks would, Lincoln believed, force them to accept the invitation. But he and his Treasury Secretary Salmon P. Chase were behind the times. By 1865, when the tax on state banknotes came into effect, most of the credit money created by banks was expressed not by banknotes but by chequeing accounts. Instead of issuing banknotes the banks were creating deposits, giving customers the power to write their own money in the form of cheques that the banks would cash "at sight" (on demand).

Businessmen's willingness to accept cheques from their customers came as a great surprise. Nicholas Biddle, while president of the Second Bank of the United States, had written in 1832 that checks could not substitute for notes "because they would represent only individual responsibilities, not those [of] recognized corporations established by law". Through the device of the clearing house, which enabled banks to settle their net accounts with all their fellows once a day rather than making bilateral exchanges all day long, the banking system minimized its need for cash. And the New York Clearing House got even with Lincoln: for clearing purposes among banks, it would not accept the banknotes of the national banks.

Assuming that the writer of the cheque does have the requisite current account at the bank, there is no meaningful difference between a cheque and banknotes totalling the same amount: both are liabilities of the bank, and the man accepting either relies upon the bank to redeem the piece of paper. The man who owns a demand deposit in the bank has the same money he would have if his pants were stuffed with bills. The demand deposit system, however, is credit money raised to a higher power: it requires more belief. If the depositors lose faith in their bank, they will demand cash.

But a bank that accepts deposits does not have the cash in its vault, because it uses money to create more money. In the old days, it would accept a deposit in specie and make a loan by issuing banknotes; and both the owner of the deposit and the holder of the banknote then had a claim on the same specie. In the New York system, the bank would accept a deposit in specie or greenbacks or national banknotes or in cheque drawn on another bank, and lend money by creating a new deposit for the borrower. In both cases, the total of deposits was necessarily considerably larger than the cash on hand. A "run on the bank" by depositors, holders of notes, holders of cheques written by depositors, could drain all the specie or "lawful money" out of the bank, at which point the bank would have to close its doors. Depositors and noteholders and holders of depositors' cheques who had not yet removed their funds would be out of luck. Socially, the bank would lose its central function: it could no longer "monetize" the IOUs of its borrowers.

With a limited amount of specie in the country, a fixed issue of greenbacks, and a limit on banknotes set by the size of the national debt (which was steadily being reduced in the latter nineteenth century), the American monetary system was uniquely ill-qualified to cope with financial "panics" in which people lost faith in bank deposits as money. In 1913, Congress created the Federal Reserve System, which was empowered to issue legal tender money backed by assets other than government bonds; in 1933 and 1935, the Fed's power to issue currency was extended. Though the one-dollar bill was convertible to precious metals until Lyndon Johnson's administration ("payable in silver to the bearer on demand", it said), and the rest of the currency was theoretically tied to the nation's gold stock until Richard Nixon's administration, it has been roughly true for a generation that American cash is simply a piece of paper that must be accepted in payment of debts in any place subject to the authority of the United States Government. For "the pound in your pocket", to use the felicitous phrase Mr. Wilson employed to calm fears roused by his first devaluation, value has been a governmental *ipse dixit* for two generations. In America, deposit insurance has supplied so much belief that nobody considers demand deposits less safe than cash; in Britain, the sheer size of the four giant banks guarantees that the government would never permit a default. Even without deposit insurance, the Bank of England made arrangements to protect the depositors in the fringe banks that went up in smoke in 1973-74.

Oddly enough, American paper money continues to be different from money elsewhere. In other countries, to use the pleasant description of Britain's Radcliffe Committee in 1959, currency is "the part of the National Debt on which no interest is paid"—the notes are obligations of an agency of the national government (the Bank of England was nationalized in 1946), and are printed to pay part of the expenses of government. But all the bills in an American's pocket are Federal Reserve Notes, obligations of one of the twelve regional Federal Reserve Banks, which are publicly controlled but privately "owned" by their member banks. The apparent result of this arrangement is that the United States Government unlike all the others in the world must pay interest on all its debt, a situation that infuriated Thomas A. Edison. "It is absurd", he wrote, "to say that our country can issue thirty million dollars in bonds but not thirty million dollars in currency. Both are promises to pay. But one promise fattens the usurers, and the other helps the people".

In reality, however, the American system gives results similar to those of other systems. The proceeds of the note-issue operation are invested in government bonds, of which the Federal Reserve Bank now own something like $90,000 million. The interest on the bonds makes the Federal Reserve System as a whole the most profitable enterprise in America—the totals reached $5,000 million in net earnings in 1974. But the Banks do not keep the money; they assess a tax on their own note issue, to return about 98 percent of their profits to the Treasury. In America, then, the currency is the part of the National Debt on which the interest is refunded to the government. The practical effect—which is not insignificant in the nexus of government—is to make the System independent of the federal budgetary process: as a profit-making institution, the Fed need never seek a Congressional appropriation. The Chairman of the Federal Reserve Board annually informs the Speaker of the House of the System's results for last year and plans for next year, and that is an end to it.

In Britain, by contrast, the Bank of England functions essentially as an arm of the Treasury; an MP with a question about monetary matters will ask the Chancellor, who could not possibly reply, like an American Treasury Secretary, that the subject is not part of his competence. Expressing the other side of the coin, an officer of the Bank says that "if the government decide to have a wildly inflationary borrowing policy, we have no choice but to finance it". In America, the Fed has a *little* choice.

Except in Scotland (where the notes of the private banks trade at par with the official U.K. currency of the Bank of England), paper money is issued only by agencies of the state, but it is entirely interchangeable for current accounts in the banks. At some times of year (near Christmas and at the big holidays) people want more cash than at others, and there continues to be one non-trivial difference between money in your pocket and money in your chequeing account: only you can use the money in your pocket, while the money you deposit in your chequeing account can be loaned to others. But the easiest of the many tasks of the government's "central bank" is adjusting the reserves of the banking system to meet the annual cycle of seasonal demands for cash without cutting off loans.

Taken together, currency and current accounts are what the Fed calls "the narrowly defined money supply;" what economist Milton Friedman was the first to call M_1. This is the money immediately available for spending. On the average over the year, these days, the proportions within M_1 in the United States run about 23 percent currency, 77 percent demand deposits; in Britain, about 27 percent currency, 73 percent current accounts. Money as a medium of exchange in both countries, then, is mostly cheques drawn on demand deposits—in 1974, banks in the United States processed more than 28,000 million of them, banks in Britain, about 1,500 million.

Now, there are three ways that a demand deposit can be created at a bank: the customer can plunk down cash, or he can bring in a cheque, or the bank can create a deposit for him by making him a loan. The middle one of these three possibilities is ambiguous, because the balance behind the cheque the customer uses to create his new deposit may itself have been derived from a previous deposit of cash, or a previous loan—or (you will remember the experience of standing between two mirrors that face each other and noting the receding infinite series of diminishing images) by a previous cheque with ambiguous antecedents.

Each time a bank creates a deposit by making a loan, it sets in motion a chain of money creation. The borrower writes cheques on his account, the proceeds of those cheques are deposited at other banks, the other banks make loans, the borrowers at the other banks write cheques on *their* accounts, still other banks enter new deposits on the proceeds of those cheques, and so on. A bank cannot safely lend the entire proceeds of a deposit—and cannot legally do so in Britain where the Bank of England enforces a "reserve asset ratio", or in the United States, where all bank supervisory agencies (except the State of Illinois) set "reserve requirements"— so the quantity of new money created diminishes at each stop, as the images diminish in the mirrors. But unless somebody breaks the chain by taking out currency the banks will keep creating deposits, creating new quantities of M_1. If the retained reserves are 20 percent, a \$100 deposit of new money—dug out of South African gold-fields, printed by a government, imported from abroad—can produce a chain of \$80, \$64, \$51·20, \$40·96, etc., to a total of another \$400.

Presumably, the Government has close control over the banks' expansion of the money supply. Like the paper money, the reserves of the banking system are central bank liabilities; and, by various interesting devices we shall examine later, the Government can increase or decrease bank reserves at will. Because the banks live by making loans and investments, they will tend to add new demand deposits to the money supply to the maximum permitted by their reserve position. In the depression this did not work so well, because interest rates were so low the banks were willing to let their reserves sit rather than run any kind of risk at all. These days, banks are loaned to the gunwales and have no excess reserves.

The limits of M_1—money as a medium of exchange—appear to be controlled by the government; but it turns out that the effective quantity of money in the system is recalcitrant to controls. No doubt money is a "commodity" but it is a queer sort of commodity which is not used up when it is consumed: the money I spend shows up good as new in someone else's pocket. Thus "velocity" is always important in determining the relationship between a given "monetary aggregate" and the effective quantity of money. "Tight money" tends to become fast-moving money, working contrary to the purposes of the central bank that makes it tight. Moreover, M_1 leaves out "time deposits" like savings accounts and other "near moneys" that can be put to work as a medium of exchange with little time or trouble.

Information about money quantities is meticulously gathered every day, and everybody tells the truth in dealings with the central bank because it would be insane to do otherwise. Yet the fact remains that even the Bank of England has only a vague notion of what the meaningful "monetary aggregates" in the country are at any given point in time. In the words of Sherman J. Maisel when he was a Federal Reserve Governor in 1969, "the changes in money or credit as reported in the weekly or monthly statistics can differ greatly from the true situation". Certainly in the short run and probably (though this will be denied) in the long run, any central bank is likely to be off by thousands of millions in any prediction its experts make about the effects of its actions on the "money supply", however defined.

Anyway, the Government is by no means the prime mover in

what happens: the textbook model presented above—the banks expanding or contracting their deposits in response to actions by the central bank—is simply inaccurate. "In the real world", Alan Holmes of the Fed's Open Market Committee said ruefully in 1969, "banks extend credit, creating deposits in the process, and look for the reserves later. The question then becomes one of whether and how the Federal Reserve will accommodate the demand for reserves. In the very short run, the Federal Reserve has little or no choice about accommodating the demand. . . ." England, at considerable cost expressed by inefficiency and sloth, avoided this problem before 1971 by directly controlling bank lending: banks restricted in the totals they could lend could not increase the money supply. With the move to Competition and Credit control in 1971, the Treasury and the Bank moved to the American system, and inherited its weaknesses as well as its strengths.

In the absence of direct asset control by the Government, the activities of the banks will influence profoundly, and at times determine, the quantity of money in the economy. What the central bank *can* control, by making money feel "easy" or "tight", is the range of interest rates the banks will charge for loans. It stands to reason that a period of tight money and high interest rates will restrict borrowing and thus the money supply, while a period of easy money and low interest rates will expand borrowing and the money supply. But what actually happens will be the result of decisions made independently and in great numbers by banks and borrowers, acting in part as they always have and in part as never before.

3/Introducing Banking

The whole community derives benefit from the operation of the bank. It facilitates the commerce of the country. It quickens the means of purchasing and paying for country produce and hastens on the exportation of it. The emolument, therefore, being to the community, it is the office and duty of government to give protection to the bank.

—THOMAS PAINE

*   *   *

By means of the banking system the distribution of capital is taken out of the hands of the private capitalists and usurers. But at the same time banking and credit thus become the most effective means of driving capitalist production beyond its own boundaries, and one of the most potent instruments of crises and swindles.

—KARL MARX

*   *   *

Milton Friedman and the Chicago school of economists before and after have taught the world that "money matters", but in its incarnation as a medium of exchange it clearly doesn't matter much.

Considered as a "store of value", however, money becomes a more complicated and interesting phenomenon. The phrase "store of value" is deceptively clear; what it means, in operation, is that money can be used to bridge the passage of time. This is the second social function of the bank: its loans make possible the bridging of time.

Early banks were not creators of money at all. The myth speaks of goldsmiths with whom citizens left gold for safekeeping; and the goldsmiths found that because these depositors did not all need their gold at once it was possible to lend much of it to other citizens who would put it to work and pay for the use of it. But the Medici were not goldsmiths, and their banks did not accept "deposits". They were partnerships of moneyed men, who financed foreign trade, enabling a Florentine merchant, for example, to purchase English woollen goods without paying for them until after they had been delivered (and, presumably, sold) in Florence.

That credit was necessary for trade to flourish was quite apparent to the entrepreneurs of medieval and Renaissance Europe: Iris Origo points out that in the twelfth century the *Arte del Cambio* (money-changing) and the *Arte di Calimala* (silk embroidery) were commonly parts of the same guild. But the merchants had a cultural problem because the prevailing religion forbade the exaction of interest on loans as the sin of usury. While the extension of credit was something accomplished privately between sellers and buyers, the costs and risks implied by an arrangement for delayed payment could simply be loaded on to the selling price of the merchandise with nobody the wiser. But once there were banks as credit intermediaries, and the money-changers guild was separate from the manufacturing guilds, the culture began to get in the way.

An aura of sin hangs about the usury question even today and a little attention is required to get the answer straight. There are two quite different objections to the exaction of interest, one of them theological and the other ethical. In theology, the problem was the certainty of reward over time. The religious man was enjoined to live as though each moment might be his last on earth. Time was God's, and what it would bring only God could say for sure. Thus a contract providing for a sure reward in the future was blasphemous in its foundations and could not stand.

To get around this ban on payment for the risks of time, the early bankers switched the basis of their compensation to the need for someone to take the risks of place. Currency values fluctuated from sovereignty to sovereignty (which in Renaissance Italy meant from town to town), and presumably the borrower in agreeing to pay back his borrowings in another currency was giving the lender a profit on the exchange, not a sinful certain gain from interest.

Raymond de Roover in his book on the Medici Bank quotes a bill from the year 1438, by which a Barcelona merchant borrowed 4,425*s*. of his currency with a promise to pay 300 Florentine florins, in Florence, sixty days later. The exchange rate specified was 14*s*. 9*d*. per florin. But the real exchange rate was 15*s*. 3*d*. per florin, so when the 300 florins were paid in Florence the bank could turn around and get 4,575*s*. to return to the Barcelona branch. Roover assumed two months' travel in each direction, which gives four months' elapsed time between the loan of the money in the Barcelona office and the closing out of the loan in the same office. The 150*s*. profit was 3·4 percent of the borrowings—times three to get an annual rate, because the transaction took a third of a year— and the annual interest rate, to put the matter in modern terms, was thus 10·2 percent, which is less of a bite than an American or British bank would have taken from this fellow in 1974.

But the elimination of the theological objection, which is not now in anyone's head, did not destroy the ethical objection. Unfortunately, the ethical objection is usually seen as a matter of unconscionably high rates. Usury survives as a criminal offence in American state law, but the crime relates entirely to the amount of interest charged. (The permissible maximum rates vary dramatically from state to state; New York at 42 percent per annum on small loans from finance companies is the highest, and a number of midwestern states at 12 percent per annum tie for lowest. Maximum rates on mortgages are set in some states as low as 8 percent, and were even lower until 1973.) The real objection is less a matter of rates than a matter of the purpose of the loan. If B is hungry and borrows from A to buy food and A demands the return of the money with interest, A is a usurer and for his want of charity will assuredly fry in hell. But if B wishes to buy a television set now rather than wait until he has saved enough to pay the price—or if he needs money to buy fixtures for a boutique on which he expects to make a profit—morality argues that he *should* pay for the use of A's money over time. The distinction is felt by most people, though rarely articulated; the small-loan company is regarded as a shady enterprise, while "acceptance corporations" or finance houses that make loans for the hire purchase of automobiles or big-ticket white goods are almost as respectable as—well, as banks.

Early banking developed internationally partly to escape the religious prohibition of interest, but also, of course, because foreign trade needed intermediaries as domestic commerce did not. A seller who was willing enough to extend credit to a local buyer would worry about doing business the same way with people he didn't know located in places he had never seen. (These worries persist, too: virtually all the developed countries have governmental insurance schemes to guarantee export credits.) To make an international banking system work required a bank at each end of the transaction, and in the early years it was considered best for the same family to own both, establishing a son or a nephew or an in-law as at least a partner in the remote enterprise. Banking being predominantly Italian, the early banking houses all over Europe were Italian. The place where the money market grew up in London was called Lombard Street, and even today a secured loan is known in Germany as a "Lombard loan". In France, a "Lombard rate" on a short-term loan means that the interest is calculated on the basis of a 360-day rather than a 365-day year. Thus a borrower for 90 days at 12 percent pays 3 percent rather than 2·96 percent for his loan. This sort of tip for the banker is not unknown in Britain too.

As early as the fourteenth century, the Italian bankers had developed the "four-name paper" we now call a bankers' acceptance. In this document as it is today, the four signatures are those of the importer (who gets the credit he needs to buy the goods), the importer's bank (which for a fee "accepts" the importer's liability as its own, guaranteeing to pay up if he doesn't), the exporter's bank (which provides the actual money in the transaction and holds the "acceptance" as its asset), and the exporter (who gets paid). The advantage for the importer's bank is that it can perform a service and earn a fee without putting up any money; the advantage for the exporter's bank is that it winds up not with a loan that ties up its money but with an investment that can be sold, usually at a small profit, if the bank finds other and more profitable uses for the money. Meanwhile, the importer and exporter can do business with each other without troubling themselves over credit risks or possible movements in the exchange rates.

As concentrations of wealth in a time when money was scarce, the Renaissance banks were always in danger of being taxed out of existence by rulers who had no other easy way to raise cash, and they bought safety by making loans to the state or (what might or might not be the same thing) to the head of state. This bucket goes to the well only so often, and the remarkable thing is not that the Renaissance banks rarely endured as long as a century but that so many of them did in fact provide profitable employment for three and four generations of the families that founded them. For all the hazards—and the damnable insecurity of being part of an inter-national banking *system* in which the failure of somebody else's customer far away might severely erode your solvency even though you did no business yourself with either party—banking on one's own capital must have been a good business.

The bank of issue that creates currency arrived with the founding of the Bank of Sweden in 1674, and was firmly established with the incorporation of the Bank of England in 1694. Even the Bank of England was blown about by the bursting of the South Sea Bubble in 1720, but survived and secured a guarantee that no other bank would be incorporated in England (there were also some private banks, necessarily much smaller). Like all banks—even today—the Bank of England was especially useful to the government in war-time, when it was a captive market for government bonds. Its monopoly survived into the nineteenth century; and though its banknotes were not made legal tender until 1833 (as a quid pro quo for a Parliamentary decision to permit the incorporation of other banks in London), the Bank of England became, especially for the American colonies, the model of how this business should be con-ducted. George Washington owned shares in it.

The theory on which the Bank of England operated was Adam Smith's. The function of a bank for Smith was to supply the work-ing capital of industry and trade—to let the shoemaker buy the leather for his next pair of shoes before the ultimate customer put on and paid for the last pair. Sellers often could not or would not carry the expense or risk of extending credit to purchasers. The bank would perform this service, buying at discount the purchaser's promise to pay, variously a bill of exchange, a promissory note or, simply, "commercial paper". The shoe factory offers enough shoes to stock a shoe store for £500 cash; the shoe store agrees to pay £510 in sixty days (12 percent annual interest); the bank prints £500 in banknotes to buy the promissory note from the factory, and in sixty days collects £510 from the shoe store. Meanwhile, the shoe factory pays its workers and buys leather from the tanner with the £500 in banknotes. This purchasing of "real bills", Smith believed, was the only legitimate function of a bank. Money would flow out of the bank when needed to start a transaction that required time, and would flow back into the bank when the transaction was completed. The money supply would always match the needs of trade: the invisible hand would have leverage.

This sort of bank in its pure state does not take deposits of money: it prints money, to a maximum set by its capital. Because most of that capital is invested in government bonds, it has earning assets even if it does not make loans, and is therefore under no pressure to seek actively for business which does not take the form of "real bills". And because its loans are all short term, it need not worry about running out of money, which is forever flowing back as the bills come due. If the government pays interest on its bonds in specie, the bank will have enough specie on hand to meet any demands for redemption of the banknotes, which should in any event be relatively slight because paper banknotes are a more convenient circulating medium than coin and nobody would have any reason not to accept the paper.

The first American banks were formed very much in imitation of the Bank of England. In 1781, still a colonel on General Washington's staff, Alexander Hamilton proposed the organization of a bank to Robert Morris, the newly appointed Superintendent of Finance for the Continental Congress. He urged that the charter incorporating it should forbid the organization of any other bank on the American territories, public or private, for a period of thirty years. Morris seems to have believed that one bank was all America could take, regardless of legal monopolies, and the bill he urged on the Congress that spring merely chartered an institution called the Bank of North America, without restriction of any possible competitors. In a letter to John Jay while the bill was pending, he described his bank as "an institution that most probably will continue as long as the United States and will become as useful to commerce and agriculture in the days of peace as it must be to the government during the war". There was some doubt that the Continental Congress could legally charter a bank—James Madison, for one, was sure it could not—and a few months after the doors were opened, in early 1782, Morris secured a vote of the Pennsylvania Assembly awarding him a charter identical in terms to the national charter. Today's First Pennsylvania Bank (wrongly, says Bray Hammond, but harmlessly) claims direct descent.

Hamilton started his own bank, the Bank of New York, in 1784, and this one really does survive in direct descent. Also in 1784, the Commonwealth of Massachusetts gave a charter to a Bank of Massachusetts, absorbed in this century by the First National Bank of Boston, which carries the date of 1784 and an American eagle in a design printed on all its stationery and publicity. (On the executive floor of the bank's spanking-new brown-glass building, an interior room has been furnished and decorated in Federal style, with beautifully conditioned real antiques, to convey to visitors the insistence on continuity; and one of the executive dining rooms is done up as an eighteenth-century tavern, though no booze is served.) All these banks were banks of issue, financed by their founders' capital, and lending only very short term through the purchase of promissory notes. The Bank of New York would not buy a note that ran longer than thirty days, the Bank of Massachusetts took nothing longer than sixty days, and in both cases there was an absolute rule against renewing. When the farmers in the Pennsylvania legislature sought to revoke the charter of the Bank of North America (they succeeded, briefly; then a renewal was secured), their argument was that the bank did nothing to benefit country interests because its longest loans were forty-five days, much too short for a farmer who wanted money to improve his property.

In 1791, Hamilton got his national bank, the Bank of the United States, modelled closely on the Bank of England. But there was a significant difference in the limitation placed on the bank's activities. The Bank of England was forbidden to issue banknotes or otherwise incur liabilities beyond the amount of its paid-in capital. In Hamilton's law incorporating the Bank of the United States, the limitation on liabilities was on those "over and above the monies . . . deposited in the bank for safe keeping . . ."

Deposit banking had arrived.

2

Deposit banking is where the goldsmiths come in: there *were* goldsmiths in the history of banking, though they first appeared on this scene several hundred years after the Italian bankers who served international trade. They offered a place of safekeeping for the plate and bullion that had accumulated especially in London in the high prosperity of Jacobean England. And they found that they could make loans by emitting bills of credit that would be accepted as money, based on the precious metals in their vaults.

The theoretician of deposit banking was Smith's contemporary Sir John Steuart. A bank operated on deposits, Steuart pointed out, really needed no capital at all from its owners: capital and deposits were just two different forms of liability. People had to have a place to keep their transaction balances and their savings. They did not wish to buy stock, which could rise or decline in value, or might not have a market at all when its owner wished to sell. A bank that took safekeeping of their money could pledge its return quickly on request, if not necessarily immediately on demand—and could use that money, as it could use capital, to purchase bills of exchange, even by the issuance of banknotes. The only thing that counted was the quality of the loans: so long as the bank was paid back, the depositors' money was safe.

There is no question this can be made to work. In 1975, the

Banque Nationale de Paris, the largest outside the United States, had $340 million in capital to support $38,000 million in footings. (Of course, this is essentially a state-owned bank, and like all European banks it publishes whatever figures it feels like publishing.) In 1972–74, the American banking system expanded entirely on the logic of Steuart's argument, increasing its loans and total deposits by more than one-third, while total ownership capital rose only slightly. Something very close to Steuart's logic, but much more sophisticated, was offered in 1973, in pamphlet form with mathematics, by the First National City Bank of New York as a reply to efforts by the Fed to make banks issue new shares of stock and increase the proportion of capital to deposits in their total of liabilities.

Hindsight and logic argue that Smith's real-bills doctrine should apply to deposit banks more than to joint-stock banks. A bank's capital is permanently there unless squandered: the bank will not have to pay back its stockholders, and if long-term loans look attractive there is no intrinsic reason why the bank should not make them. Deposit banks must be liquid, because the depositors may wish their money back at any time. But Steuart disagreed with Smith on restricting banks to short-term loans. Steuart saw no reason why banks should not be "land banks", issuing their notes in return for the security represented by a pledge of real estate. Such loans, he wrote, "give credit to those who have property and a desire to melt it down".

The great advantage of Steuart's sort of bank was that it allowed everybody to participate. Only the largest cities were likely to have enough merchants with money to launch a bank on a permanent float of capital or support one with a flow of bills, but any number of local or regional commercial centres could show enough accumulation of transaction balances and savings to maintain a decent deposit base, and more than enough land to melt down. A country bank, however, will usually not lend all its resources locally; indeed, this is part of the reason for establishing it. Quite apart from Renaissance casuistry, bank loans do bridge space as well as time: some places, like some people, have excess cash, and other places have a need for it. "In England and Scotland," Bagehot wrote in 1873, "a diffused system of note issue started banks all over the country, in these banks the savings of the country have been lodged, and by these they have been sent to London. No similar system arose elsewhere, and in consequence London is full of money, and all continental cities are empty as compared with it."

The deposits in the early American banks, which Hamilton sought to exempt from statutory limitations, were of a different kind: they were the bank's own money. When the bank bought a bill of exchange or a promissory note, the borrower did not need all of his money at once. The bank clearly had no desire to give out more specie or issue more banknotes than strictly necessary; a borrower who did not need all his money at once would be encouraged to take as much of it as possible in the form of a demand deposit at the bank. He could get the money whenever he needed it, and until he needed it the bank would prefer that he left it where it was. Observation of modern American banking practice suggests that borrowers may have been given to understand that subsequent loans would be more easily and cheerfully made if they kept a "compensating balance". The greater the proportion of its loans that a bank limited in its note issue could persuade borrowers to leave in deposit form, the more loans the bank could make, and the more interest it would earn.

Bray Hammond has given an interesting explanation for the growth of deposit banking in American cities. With the passage of time, legislatures chartered more and more banks around the country, producing the desirable results Bagehot described but also a deluge of dubious banknotes from far away in the hands of city merchants. By Gresham's Law, this bad money—dirty, decrepit, convertible to specie only by those willing to take a long trip to the country—drove out the good money of city banknotes: people preferred to pay their bills in doubtful money, shifting the currency risk to their creditors. Men who did business with each other regularly, however, had no desire to poison commercial relations by passing what might be wildcat money, and they began to pay each other by transferring deposits instead of handing over notes.

"City bank notes could not compete with country bank notes," Hammond comments, "but city bank deposits could."

In New England, note issue was policed by the city banks, which banded together under the leadership of the Suffolk Bank of Boston. Whenever any quantity of a country bank's notes began showing up in the city, Suffolk would approach that bank "with an offer in one hand", Hammond writes, "and a threat in the other". Generally speaking, country banks issued their notes at par: that is, a merchant would sign a promissory note for $100 plus interest and receive in return $100 of banknotes. But the country banknotes circulated in the city at a discount: that is, a bank like Suffolk would give only $99 credit for a $100 banknote from a country bank.

Now, Suffolk offered to let the country banks get the benefit of this discount for themselves if they would leave specie on deposit at Suffolk to the amount of $5,000 plus whatever was necessary to cover the notes actually turned in to the Boston banks. Suffolk would continue to give people who came to the windows $99 for the $100 country banknote, then it would deduct $99 from the country bank's account, returning the bill to the country bank which could reissue it at $100. This would considerably increase the country bank's income—provided it really had enough specie to cover its metropolitan note issue. The threat was, Hammond writes, "that if the country bank refused the offer, the Suffolk would pursue it into the woods and demand redemption of its notes on the spot" —very likely putting it out of business.

The germs of two vital institutions grew in this scheme—reserve requirements and correspondent banking. The idea that a small bank's reserves should be kept in a larger bank became a centrepiece of Lincoln's National Bank Act forty years later, and remains at the heart of the Federal Reserve System today, though the banks that hold the reserve are now nonprofit quasi-governmental institutions. And the idea that banks outside the money centres should leave money on account in the big city banks in return for services still provides the metropolitan centres with a respectable proportion of their deposit base. The other side of the coin is (before New York's Franklin National got into openly admitted trouble in May

1974 one would have said "was") that the collapse of a big-city bank could mean disaster for an ever-widening circle of correspondents in the countryside.

Some deposits, then, came from borrowers who left their money on account; some from transaction balances left in the bank by merchants who did not care to use country banknotes any more than they had to. And deposits could also be bought: a bank could pay interest on them. Fritz Redlich traces the first payment of interest on bank deposits to the Farmers Bank of Maryland in 1804. In the 1810s, banks in Massachusetts began to pay interest on large deposits left for a stretch of time (Suffolk's practice of giving the country banks the benefit of the discount on their notes can also be seen as interest on deposits). In 1825, the Bank of the United States paid interest on specie deposits, however long or short the time they stayed in the bank.

Well before theory (or government) had caught up with practice, American banks were making most of their loans by creating deposits rather than by printing banknotes. The New York Clearing House opened in 1853 to meet the banks' need for a place where they could balance their accounts with each other as businessmen deposited the cheques that transferred money from bank to bank. Boston got its own clearing house in 1856; Philadelphia, in 1858.

In London, an informal clearing house had been operating since the 1770s at a pub called the Dove Court off King William Street, and since 1833 there had been a building devoted to clearing purposes at 10 Lombard Street. But it was not until a year after the New York operations began that the joint-stock banks joined the Clearing House and gave it the universal coverage such an institution requires.

3

Adam Smith's banks were merchant banks: the sort of loans Smith recommended were those that merchants needed. They were obviously not adequate to the other needs of an explodingly expansive economy on the brink of the industrial revolution. Indeed, by

1792 Hamilton's Bank of New York had begun to violate its rules against renewing thirty-day paper or making longer "accommodation" loans, and had given a long-term credit to the newly formed Society for Useful Manufactures in Paterson, N.J. And nearly all of them loaned money to the government that chartered them, usually by purchasing bonds. Not infrequently, renewal of a banking charter was made contingent on the assurance of loans to the state to fulfil some worthwhile public purpose, the completion of a road or the construction of a canal or a school.

As banks were chartered in more and more places, they acquired new purposes. Some banks took charters that forbade them to make loans beyond the borders of the community in which they were located. Some stated a purpose in a name: Farmers Bank, Mechanics Bank, Planters Bank. The farmers of the Plains states were deeply suspicious of all banking (Texas came into the Union with a constitution that absolutely prohibited the organization or operation of a bank), but ultimately they were converted by the utility of crop loans, the chance to fatten that many more cattle or or hogs if money could be borrowed to buy the corn. What Bagehot considered a virtue of the banking system, however—its ability to draw money from the countryside to the city—was hated and feared in rural America, and ultimately produced a widespread prohibition of branch banking and (in 1933) of the payment of interest on demand deposits, which was and despite the prohibition still is the device the metropolitan banks use to draw money from the outback.

Recent years have seen a revival of nineteenth-century country attitudes in opinion centres like Ralph Nader's law conglomerate. The first, mimeographed Nader "report" on the First National City Bank of New York denounced the bank for taking deposits from poor people at its branches in Harlem and lending the money to The Man. (The accusation was false, and was quietly dropped in the printed book—First National City's loans to black neighbourhoods actually exceed its deposits in those neighbourhoods—but most of the loans are consumer-oriented, for purchases made outside, so the fight is a stand-off.) What Nader's people (among others) plump for is black banks to lend black money to black businesses in black neighbourhoods. "That's wonderful," Chairman Walter B. Wriston of First National City says scornfully; "socially desirable. But you've got all the bad risks in one place, which denies the principle of banking, the actuarial base—spreading the risk." There may indeed be excellent sociopolitical reasons for increasing bank loans to poverty neighbourhoods (though it is not necessarily a favour to an honest man to lend him money he will not be able to pay back)—but only a bank with a strong base of top-quality credits can afford to take the losses.

(The promoters of New York's First Women's Bank, while stressing what its organizing agent, Eileen Preiss, calls "the vastly underserved market of women", insist that they can draw a range of business wide enough to keep them out of this cul-de-sac. "We will have a better staff and provide better service," says Ms. Preiss, who is also a vice-chairman of the New York State Democratic Party; "we can provide the function of treating middle-sized customers with the same concern the big banks show only for big customers". Late in 1975, more than two years after the press conference announcing the formation of the bank, the money was found to open the bank: and now we shall see.)

In the later nineteenth century, big-city banks became active in the bond markets, especially in New York, Chicago, and San Francisco; and American banks performed—as European banks still do—most of the functions of stockbrokers. The First National Bank of New York was incorporated by brokers (aided by a twenty-three-year-old clerk from the New York State banking department in Albany named George F. Baker, who some years later would endow the Harvard Business School); with the approval of the national banking authorities, it became the nation's largest underwriter and distributor of government and (for a while) corporate bonds. Large underwritings needed commercial bank support both to finance the distribution and to raise customers around the country. "It has become quite a common practice in recent years for parties about to put through big deals to first obtain control of a bank, whereby their efforts could be facilitated", the

United States Investor wrote in 1899. "Big deals are not possible if banking assistance is withheld."

Early in this century a number of banks, not just in New York, formed "securities affiliates" to play in the stock market, a development greatly stimulated by the federal government's reliance on the banks to sell the Liberty Bonds of World War I. The Wall Street house of Goldman Sachs gained control of the Manufacturers Trust Company; National City Bank organized a securities affiliate that became "the largest agency in the world for the distribution of corporate securities". These securities affiliates could branch out away from the home city of the bank, and their charters gave them virtually unlimited powers. Delaware in 1928 granted Detroit's Union Trust Company a charter empowering a securities affiliate "to do everything except solemnize marriages and hold religious services".

These organizations were without exception a disaster, as the Comptroller of the Currency had warned in 1920 that they would be: he saw them borrowing from their parents and other national banks "in an endless chain . . . for the accommodation of speculative cliques". National City Company got into the habit of buying bonds, especially from Latin American governments, before studying their quality; those that later looked all right on examination were put into the bank's own portfolio, and those that looked sour were pushed onto the public. Others ran real estate syndicates through their securities affiliates, or manipulated the shares of the bank's own stock. But Congress refused to ban this activity until the bubble burst; then, in 1933, the Glass-Steagall Act forbade commercial banks to own common stock or to underwrite and sell stock or corporate bonds to their customers or depositors; and the banks slowly, grumblingly, returned to banking.

In Britain, the clearing banks have not fiddled with the stock market at all (some of their critics would like them to do so, by "taking equity positions" to help British industry raise badly needed capital). The first difference between the clearing bank and the merchant bank is that the latter will probably be active on the stock exchange and the former will not.

Except for their occasional indulgence in such Wall Street aberrations, American bankers normally tried to keep a balanced and diversified portfolio of loans and investments, some of which came due soon or could be cashed fast if the bank needed money, some of which would run for a considerable period of time, earning interest. A good deal of wishful thinking might go into the judgment that some assets were "liquid". Well into the 1930s, banks kept lending extensively into a "call money market" on Wall Street. In theory, repayment of these loans could be demanded overnight, but the economic conditions that might make a bank wish to call such loans would make the borrower unable to pay. (This market was ignorantly imported from London, where it worked because the Bank of England does its business with the discount houses, which are the customers for call loans, rather than with the banks. Thus when the banks called their loans Daddy almost automatically stepped forward with the money. Even today the Fed would have trouble gearing to handle this market; and before 1913 call loans in America were a prescription for sporadic catastrophe.) It was not uncommon for a bank to make a demand loan allegedly secured by real estate, or a ninety-day loan to build a factory— which would then be renewed every ninety days for years. Some of this dream world persists: George Scott of First National City spoke scornfully of a friend who had made a loan to the Brazilian railroads to buy a locomotive, and thought he had lessened his risk on the loan by writing it for only nine months.

It was also true—and is—that somebody has to get the work started on long-term projects. Risks are greater when a bank makes a loan expecting to be "taken out" by an insurance company or a sale of bonds in the market, but the bank can be compensated for such risks. The ever-renewing ninety-day loan, Joseph Schumpeter pointed out in 1911, is "a method of periodically testing the soundness of the enterprise. . . . Moreover, if it is true that long-term enterprises are financed by short-term credit, every entrepreneur and every bank will try for obvious reasons to exchange this basis as soon as possible for a more permanent one."

Nevertheless, the obvious fact was that short-term loans for straightforward rapidly concluded business transactions were much more safe than any other employment of the money. The State Bank of Indiana, a publicly owned institution that never suspended specie payment in any of the financial panics of the years before the Civil War, started with loans for the purchase and improvement of farm land, but quickly shifted to the financing of trade: "The choice of policy," Hammond suggests, "was a pragmatic one, such as may arise from experience impinging on brains."

A legislative committee in Kentucky, demanding adherence to Adam Smith's doctrines without necessarily knowing they were Smith's wrote that "the bill business is limited by the actual operations of commerce, the accommodations business is as limitless as the want of money, the rage of speculation, or the spirit of gambling. . . . The past experience of this country when bank paper obtained upon accommodation loans has been attempted to be invested in real estate and permanent improvements has given bitter proof of the fact that banks, properly understood, are strictly commercial instruments, a part of that machinery by which the annual productions of the labour of men are circulated to the points destined for their consumption." Britain in the 1960s forgot this lesson from its former colonies, with results that are visible in the carnage of the "fringe" banks.

British building societies and American savings banks are clearly in a different position from commercial banks. In a sense, a mutual savings bank has nothing but capital; this was, the form, for the organization of the federal savings and loan associations, which until 1968 gave shares rather than statements of deposit to those who supplied the funds, and paid "dividends" rather than "interest". The savings banks and building societies were not and are not engaged in money creation; they merely invest the money left with them, which thereupon goes out into the business world and appears in the commercial banks as demand deposits or repayments of loans. "The people who work here call us the bank," says George Mooney, who was New York State Banking Superintendent before he became chairman of Washington Federal Savings &

Loan, "but it's not a bank, it's a savings society, a Jewish burial society, a cooperative. The savings banks were started by business-men who were tired of paying for the funerals of their improvident employees. The law specifies our purpose: 'to encourage thrift and facilitate home ownership'. That's not banking."

Building societies and insurance companies can safely make long-term investments because their liabilities are not subject to call. Even today, when every American savings bank and association in fact pays out on demand, the contract the depositor signs when he puts his money in the bank gives the bank the right to delay pay-ment for at least thirty days whenever the bank may find it incon-venient to pay at once. The flow in the business world, then, is that a commercial bank makes a short-term loan to a builder who builds houses, and a savings bank "takes out" the loan by writing the long-term mortgage for the purchaser of the house; the money comes back into the commercial banking system via the con-tractor's repayments after the purchaser has paid *him* with the proceeds of the mortgage loan.

These distinctions were well recognized in the nineteenth cen-tury. Lincoln's national banks were forbidden to write mortgages; mutual savings banks in those states that organized them were usually obliged to hold mortgages as a high fraction of their assets. When the Federal Reserve Act and its amendments permitted the writing of mortgages by commercial banks, such loans were limited to a proportion of the bank's time deposits—savings accounts (though those words could not legally be used)—and were not under any circumstances to be financed by drawing on demand deposits. These provisions recognized the futility of the previous ban, for state-chartered banks in most states had long blended their time and demand deposits and made "accommodation loans" on real estate, and the big-city nationally chartered banks (like the British clearing banks) had learned to use subsidiary corporations or trust affiliates to do what the National Bank Act forbade them to do.

Historically—and we live today in a repetition of this history—banks have got in trouble by forgetting that real estate loans are neither so safe nor so liquid as other loans, and that the values pledged to their repayment can plunge drastically and overnight, so that loans publicly proclaimed as "well secured" are really expressions of faith rather than items of business. What drove three-quarters of the banks in Iowa into at least temporary bankruptcy in the early 1930s, Van Vechten Shaffer of Cedar Rapids remembered, was a preposterously high valuation of farm land pledged as security for loans. Today's valuations of that land are, in constant dollars, several times as high as those of the 1920s. Meanwhile, the same principles have been put to work in urban land, and bank loans to Real Estate Investment Trusts, many of them sponsored by the banking community itself, are counted in the thousands of millions of dollars.

What is new in the current banking scene—the other blade in the scissors of the revolution—is the term loan to business, explicitly recognized as such and not hidden behind the fiction of renewable ninety-day paper. One can put a date on the first term loan by an American bank: 1934. The man who made it was Serge Semenenko, a refugee from the Russian Revolution who had become a vice-president of the First National Bank of Boston, and the loan was to American Metals Company, now American Metals Climax. "It came", Semenenko recalls, "from the development of the Securities and Exchange Commission, which raised problems of legal routine in arranging public financing. The company went over to England and got a commitment of a couple of million dollars, for which they paid a $100,000 fee. I didn't see why that couldn't be done in the United States. We had been accustomed to making demand loans, sometimes for six months—but two years! People's hair stood on end. I said, 'You make ninety-day loans and renew them and renew them and renew them for sixteen years. Why not call a spade a spade?' We got collateral, primarily in some African mines they had. Within six months they had paid back the loan and we had established a wonderful relationship."

Term loans now stretch to as long as ten or even fifteen years, and most of them are made without collateral, secured only by the credit of the large corporations to which they are offered. They are

57

to be repaid not out of specific transactions or even from the profits of the company, but from its "cash flow", the receipts of the business that exceed the actual out-of-pocket production costs (material, labour, sales commissions, etc.) before deductions for depreciation. A company with a poor profits picture may thus be a candidate for a loan—if its poor profits result from heavy allocations to the depreciation of plant and equipment and the purpose of the loan is to modernize the equipment: the cash flow allocated to depreciation will be available to pay interest and amortization on a loan to buy new machinery.

In theory, this approach involves a bank much more intimately with the actual operations of its customers—Semenenko insisted on a veto power over any management changes—and sometimes the practice matches the theory. The other side of this shield is that the reasons for granting or refusing a loan—or charging a higher or lower interest rate on it—have become increasingly subjective. Questions of whether collateral covers risk are easier to answer than questions about projections of cash flow.

With the spread and growth of term lending, steps have been taken to make long loans more like short loans. Among the advantages of short-term paper was that money constantly came back into the bank, which assured the bank of a supply of cash to meet unexpected demands from depositors: in tight periods, the bank could meet obligations simply by not lending out again the money that arrived routinely from the repayment of the loans coming due. This feature is built into the term loan and into the modern self-amortizing mortgage through a schedule of repayments of principal—though "bullet" loans and mortgages with "balloons" at the end, loans that will come to a conclusion with all or much of the principal still owed, are by no means uncommon. Short-term loans also meant that the bank could charge (and the customer could receive) whatever rates were current in the money market; and since 1969, term loans have been written with variable interest rates that are adjusted at regular intervals specified in what has become a very complicated loan agreement.

Most of these innovations have been enthusiastically welcomed at the business schools and among banking theorists, but a larger jury is still out. The contributions made by a Semenenko are clearly enormous: he reorganized to the profit of all concerned, in and out of Boston, the bankrupt paper industry, the decayed Hearst empire, and the rickety movie business. His "special industries" division at the First National Bank of Boston survived his departure in 1967 and is now headed by a tall, amiable banker named John Chequer, who says things like, "Serge taught us that. . . ." Personally, Chequer puts a lot of time into "high technology" industries: "There's a large continuum from IBM down to the hardware store, and within that continuum there is a thin band of companies thought to be unbankable where the situation can be structured so that a bank can safely lend its money." Making something "bankable" that nobody else can see as bankable is the banker's highest contribution to his society—provided his judgment is correct.

For the central principle continues as it was in Adam Smith's —or, indeed, Cosimo de Medici's—time. "The definition of a good loan," says Charles Van Horn, regional administrator and chief examiner of nationally chartered banks in the New York area, "is a loan that's paid back."

4

Like any developing country, early-nineteenth-century America was short on capital; and as it was also blessed with a weak government its citizens were free to indulge themselves in good and bad schemes to make the fortune of those who would back them. Interest rates were therefore higher than they were in Britain or France, and capital was imported to build the railroads and barge canals, fullers' mills and millers' mills, shipbuilding yards and iron foundries. There was foreign capital especially in the banks, because much of the banking of America was done in London, and bankers were happiest on both sides of the Atlantic when correspondents were linked by something a little sturdier than mutual involvement in the business of third parties. By the turn of the next century capital was beginning to flow the other way, and since World War I interest rates have consistently been lower in America than in Europe. This disparity, as much as the phenomenon of the multinational corporation, accounts for the international operations of American banks during the last twenty years—and for much of the pileup of Eurodollars, deposits in American money held outside the United States, which now so grossly complicates the management of both domestic currencies and international trade.

One of the more interesting and long-lived arguments in economic literature swirls about the assertion that there is such a thing as a "natural" rate of interest—a price that must be paid to a whole society to make it forego present consumption and lend to the future. Most sophisticated opinion derides the idea these days (received scholarship says that money is a "commodity" with a price determined by supply and demand), but Sir John Hicks told the Radcliffe Committee in the late 1950s that his studies of money markets in the nineteenth and early twentieth centuries had convinced him that there was such a natural constant, and that it was 3 percent a year for the European countries, perhaps a little higher in Scandinavia. Morgan Guaranty in the early 1970s attempted this exercise independently on big computers, and came out in close agreement with Hicks: the Morgan figure was 3·13 percent for Europe and America. The argument cannot be settled, because many other factors enter into the price of money on any given day, and no amount of multiple regression analysis can eliminate all of them. Perceptions of political risk and possible currency fluctuation are not easily quantifiable, and clearly enter into the differences in interest paid in different countries.

The most obvious factor, right now, is the expectation of inflation. People with money they don't need to spend do not have to lend it, after all—they can buy land or pork bellies in the futures market or gold, or make other investments. If they expect the general price level to rise 5 percent over the next year, they will regard a 5 percent interest rate as the equivalent of no return at all on their money. In a deflationary time like the 1930s, money may be available for loan at a very low price (some short-term U.S. Treasury issues in the 1930s sold to yield $\frac{1}{8}$ of 1 percent a year) while in an inflationary time like ours even government paper may carry an interest rate of 12 percent without in any way contradicting the concept of a "natural" rate of 3 percent.

The influence of inflation on the cost of money underlies Milton Friedman's persuasive theory that government cannot ultimately control the interest rate, despite its command of the money supply. If money is created to meet increased demand for loans at a low price, the excess money in the economy produces inflation, which makes borrowers more eager to borrow (because they will be able to pay back later in less valuable money) and lenders less willing to lend—and thus generates yet another flood of money from central banking authorities dedicated to holding down an interest rate that would otherwise rise. Hyperinflation *á la* Germany in the 1920s being a clearly unacceptable alternative, government will at some point be forced to permit increased interest rates.

On any specific loan, the rates of interest respond also to all sorts of prejudice for and against industries, regions, neighbourhoods, individuals (for reasons that may include race, creed, sex, education, social class, family connection). All this gets subsumed into an overall judgment about the degree of risk involved in the loan. A negative judgment may be expressed by a flat refusal to lend (especially to women, even today), or by an insistence on a higher interest rate (especially to blacks). Sometimes the judgment can be reversed—or at least set aside—by the offer of collateral that clearly secures the loan, or by the signature of an endorser whose credit-worthiness the bank can scarcely question.

Among the considerations that have always influenced the perception of risk is the length of time for which the loan is taken. It stands to reason that long loans are more risky than short loans to the same borrower, and historically the line that graphs "maturities" against interest rate has a "positive slope"—that is, the further away the maturity, the higher the rate. Historically, this apparent extra profit was what tempted the banks to make mortgage loans and "accommodation" loans not secured by evidences of a specific transaction.

When money is tight, however, and interest rates are rising, the customers for short-term money (who will be paying the high rates for only a brief period of time) can outbid the customers for long-term money (who face what may be years of larger interest payments), and the yield slope becomes negative—that is, short-term money costs more than long. This development should be profitable for bankers, because it lures savings from building societies, insurance companies, and the stock market into the credit market, but banks that rely for their liquidity on short-term investments that can be sold (Treasury bills and the like) find that the drop in the price of such "money-market instruments" more than eats up the profits from higher rates or greater lending. Meanwhile, the need to do something for the borrowers who depend on the savings institutions creates a raft of quasi-banking governmental agencies, most of them conjuring up credit for housing. When the money crunch is gone, these agencies remain with us, still working to convert credit to savings, and promoting inflation.

When rates were high in the old days, loans were hard to get: that's why rates were high. In the 1970s banking systems and governments have been experimenting with a world where rates are high but money is still available in any quantities to those who will pay the price. This phenomenon has been made possible by adding a third source of money the banks can loan: direct and open borrowing (with interest to be paid) now supplements the deposit base and the bank's capital whenever loan demand rises. "Bought money" lies at the heart of the banking revolution; and "interest-differential banking" is the jargon phrase that describes our post-revolutionary procedures.

Because they are conscious of how much their money costs them in an age of interest-differential banking, bankers can honestly say that they don't want to see high interest rates any more than anyone else does: "We'll make as much at five percent as we do at ten," says chairman Gabriel Hauge of New York's Manufacturers Hanover, an economist once part of Eisenhower's White House staff; "it all depends on the spread." But the "cost" of the existing paid-in capital has not changed at all, and the services that must be performed to draw demand deposits to the bank do not increase dramatically as interest rates go up. Moreover, at a time when banks secure liquidity by borrowing, rather than by selling their bond and bill investments, they no longer need worry about the drop in the prices of these investments as interest rates rise. High interest rates *do* mean greater profits for banks—assuming their customers don't go broke trying to pay them, an assumption that may hold true only in conditions of continuously accelerating inflation. There is an odour of brimstone about most revolutions; we shall have occasion to analyse the contents of the smoke that rises from this one when the need to make some judgments arises in the last chapter.

Preamble to Chapters 4 & 5

The British system for starting a bank is so wildly different from that in America that this chapter and the next must stand on intrinsic interest, like a sex shop. There is no Banking Act in Britain—a most extraordinary omission from the legal order, because any institution that accepts deposits on current account and lends money by crediting the borrower in a current account (or permitting overdrafts, which amounts to the same thing) performs the essentially governmental function of printing money. To call itself a bank and *advertise* for public deposits, a British company must satisfy the Department of Trade and Industry that it really is a bank; but anyone who can get started in the banking business without advertising and without using the name "bank" may hang out a shingle anywhere in Britain. The only tight control exercised is over foreign exchange, where the Bank of England must approve before the bank can deal in foreign money, and the bank must provide the authorities with highly detailed information about its currency activities.

On the other hand, it should be noted that in Britain a number of companies call themselves "banks" but do not perform true banking functions. If all of the funds in a merchant bank are loaned to it on a term basis instead of being placed on current account, the merchant bank does not create money; it merely acts as an intermediary between a lender and a borrower. An important function is performed here: lenders are made more secure because the bank guarantees the credit, indeed accepts as its own the liability functionally incurred by the borrower; and borrowers who might find it extremely difficult to raise money from the public on their own name may do so fairly easily through the intervention of the merchant bank. The merchant banks are therefore "accepting houses" even when they operate simply as intermediaries rather than through the complicated format of the banker's acceptance, which we shall consider further on in the context of international trade.

In the United States, legislation from New Deal days requires financial houses to be one thing or the other: a Wall Street "investment banker" may not accept deposits; a "commercial bank" may not participate in the underwriting of securities (other than public authority obligations) that will be sold to the public. In Britain, a merchant bank can legally operate in both worlds. A Lazard Brothers, an N. M. Rothschild, a Baring, a Warburg will put together a deal most of which is to be financed by other parties, but take a piece of the action for itself with money left on either current account or loan by depositors. Hill Samuel & Co. has even attempted to establish a chain of branches to garner deposits it would use for such purposes. A number of foreign banks in London (especially the long-established American banks like First National City, Chase, Morgan, Manufacturers Hanover and Bankers Trust) will do an ordinary banking business in sterling, accepting deposits on current account and making loans through establishing accounts for borrowers. And the so-called "fringe banks", actually real-estate investment companies that financed their activities partly by the use or abuse of customer balances, lured accounts into store-front, impressive banking facilities in fashionable neighbourhoods.

But the life stories of the merchant bankers, the Jim Slaters and S. G. Warburgs, are wildly different from the tales that are told below, and resemblances between the London activities of the American banks and the activities they conduct at home should not obscure the fact that many of their London activities would be flatly illegal in the United States. As a law-abiding American, I enforce the separation between banking and the corporate securities markets.

4/How to Start an American Bank

Several states had . . . requirements [that] some state official count and certify the specie paid in as capital before a new bank could be open for business . . . and banking was little the better for them. . . . Senator Thomas Hart Benton . . . wrote in 1858 that some promoters in Kansas, who were organizing a bank with $50,000 capital, met the requirements of the law by borrowing $2,000 in coin, which they put in two valises and brought to the state capital for certification. They kept one valise outside, took the other into the Governor's office, and asked him to count what was in it. When he had done so, they brought in the second valise, asked him to counts its contents, and took out the first. Then when he was through with the second, they brought in the first again, and took out the other. When this had been done twenty-five times, the Governor had counted $50,000 and was ready to give the promoters the certificates they needed. Thus America grew great.

—BRAY HAMMOND

* * *

A man who wants to start a new bank in America needs, first of all, money—but not a great deal of it. There are economies of scale in banking, most of them tracing to the fact that a $500,000 loan costs relatively little more to make than a $50,000 loan, but most operations do not get cheaper as more of them are performed. The large bank always has to pay competitive wages; the small bank often does not. Through service bureaus and the like small banks have access to computers at costs little if at all higher than those of the giant banks that operate their own computers. In 1972, according to the Functional Cost Analysis study of the Federal Reserve System, banks with less than $50 million in deposits earned after taxes an average of ·96 percent on their total assets; banks with deposits of $50 to $200 million earned ·92 percent; and banks with more than $200 million in deposits earned ·86 percent. A bank with $5 million in deposits is probably viable anywhere outside the centre of a big city; a bank with $20 million in deposits is viable anywhere.

Few authorities (none of them licensing authorities) would argue that a bank requires capital greater than one-tenth its total assets. The rule of thumb at the Federal Deposit Insurance Corporation says that capital is adequate if it totals one-twelfth of a bank's assets. "Thus", Bernard Shull and Paul M. Horvitz write in an official publication of the Comptroller's office, "an efficient-sized bank could be organized with total capital of under five hundred thousand. This is much lower than the capital needs in most other industries". The Federal Reserve System requires only $200,000 for a member bank in a big city, and only $50,000 for a member bank in a town with less than 6,000 inhabitants. That's the range of what you need for a McDonald's franchise, and much less than you need for a Holiday Inn. And a good deal of that can be borrowed from another bank without disconcerting the chartering authorities. Low capitalization does limit the size of the loans that can be made; the laws under which nearly all banks are chartered forbid a bank to lend to any one borrower an amount greater than 10 percent of its capital and accumulated surplus.

Next, not unrelated to the money, a man wishing to start a bank will need a board of directors. State laws vary; for a national charter there must be at least five (and not more than twenty-five): and the president of the bank must be one of them. Each director must invest at least a thousand dollars of his own money in the bank; two-thirds of the directors must live either in the state in which the bank operates or within a hundred miles of its office.

The directors are responsible for the conduct of the bank, including the granting of loans, and this is not a joke. A summary of the papers presented at three "Assemblies of Bank Directors" in 1973 presented a collection of horribles: an oldie about J. C. Penney, who put a million dollars of his own money into a Florida bank but was held responsible for considerably more when the bank went bust and it was learned that he had attended only three board meetings in thirty months; a tale of the Parksley National Bank of Virginia which tried to save a failing borrower by making him another loan above its legal limit of loans to a single customer, and the directors who had approved the loan were held liable to the other stockholders for their losses; a recent Illinois case where a director-president had to cough up $99,000 to make up losses on bad loans over the lending limit. The worst such whipping ever administered involved loans to the Kentucky Wagon Works by the National Bank of Kentucky: for "failure to heed warnings by the Comptroller and overconfidence in the cashier", a federal court in 1938 assessed the bank's directors individually a total of about $4 million. This record is now in jeopardy in the multi-million-dollar suits brought by the Federal Deposit Insurance Corporation and the bank's stockholders against the former directors of Arnholt Smith's U.S. National Bank of San Diego, who are accused of approving virtually endless credits to other Smith enterprises although they knew the loans were over the bank's limit and likely to go sour.

"Directors of a national bank," says a pamphlet published by the Comptroller of the Currency, "may become personally liable for losses sustained by the bank due to a statutory breach in which the directors participated or to which they assented, a failure to exercise the requisite degree of care and prudence under the common law or a breach of duty to conduct the affairs of the bank with the utmost loyalty". A bank director who misses a meeting of the board remains liable for the consequences of decisions taken at that meeting. Though banks can buy insurance policies that indemnify directors for most possible losses they might suffer as the result of lawsuits against the board, the safety is never absolute— and even in the litigious New York area, a 1973 survey by the regional office of the Comptroller found that only half the district's 289 national banks (144, to be exact) had purchased such insurance.

Despite the attention and legal work growing out of the Justice Department's insistence that banks are subject to the antitrust laws, banking continues to be the home of the brainless American theory of political economy which demands lots and lots of competition in which nobody ever gets hurt. The thrust of most banking laws is unquestionably to preserve the safety of existing banks: in New York, the legislated "policy of the state" is "to eliminate unsound and destructive competition. . . . and thus to maintain public confidence". The fact that a man is willing to risk his own money on his belief that a community will support a new grocery store gives him an unquestioned right in America to open a new grocery store, but a similar belief about his chances as a banker does not give him a right to open a bank. Neither the federal nor the state government will charter a new bank in a locality unless it is demonstrated that the banks already on the scene, whether they are doing a good job or a bad job, will not be harmed. "What is required", writes Charles F. Haywood, dean of the school of business at the University of Kentucky, "is that within a reasonable period of time the future growth of the banking market will be sufficient for the proposed bank to become a viable enterprise without doing significant competitive damage to any of the existing banks".

The banks already on the scene will fight tooth and nail to prevent the chartering of a rival; and if the market is growing at such a pace that it seems clear a new bank must be chartered, applicants will be lined up at the doors of the chartering authorities. In either case, a man wishing to start a bank would be wise to have friends well-connected in politics. The state banking departments are reputed to be the worse offenders in the awarding of bank charters through political influence, and the Comptroller's office is reputed to be clean, but it is interesting to see how high a proportion of the recently chartered national banks that have got into trouble have a significant political figure among the officers of their boards.

There is nothing new about this sort of thing, of course. The original Bank of America was a New York corporation chartered in 1812 with such blatant corruption of the state legislature (then the only source of charters) that Governor Daniel D. Tompkins prorogued that body in imitation of the Royal Governors of pre-

Revolutionary times in the vain hope of stopping a public disgrace. The historian Fritz Redlich quotes a letter soliciting government deposits written in 1812 by the State Bank of Boston to U.S. Treasury Secretary William Gray: "[this bank] is the property of sixteen hundred freemen of the respectable state of Massachusetts, all of them advocates of the then existing federal administration, associated not solely for the purpose of advancing their pecuniary interests, but for the more noble purpose of cherishing republican men and republican measures against the wiles and machinations of a party which has obtained the direction of the moneyed institutions of the State and used them to check the growth of republicanism and thus indirectly to weaken the constituted authorities of the nation".

This sort of approach was not at all offensive to even the most highly placed public servants. "I am decidedly in favour," Jefferson wrote to his Secretary of the Treasury in 1803, "of making all the banks Republican by sharing deposits among them according to the dispositions they show; if the law now forbids it, we should not let another session of Congress to pass without amending it".

2

The fact that a bank can be chartered by either the federal government or a state—with absolutely no distinction drawn between the two by the public or by the business—is the really peculiar element in American banking. There is, of course, a lot of history here, social and political. "Our banking system," says Walter Wriston of First National City, "was built by the wagon trains going west. Wherever they stopped, somebody hung out a sign reading BANK, somebody else a sign reading SALOON, and somebody else started raising horses. Our banking system grew by accident; and whenever something happens by accident, it becomes a religion".

This is, charitably, a simplification. Bray Hammond has written two brilliant and beautiful books, glories of American historical scholarship, about how dual banking came to be the rule in America; and the subject was worth his time. At the start, there was no question about the power of the states to charter corporations; they were sovereign. But the national government was a union of sovereign states, with no powers other than those delegated to it in the compact of their union, the Constitution, and it took all of Hamilton's persuasiveness to convince Washington, against memoranda from Jefferson and Madison, that he should sign the act chartering a Bank of the United States. This was a private venture, though the government held much of the stock issue and the bank undertook a number of obligations with reference to the management of federal payments and receipts. It was a more or less unified Bank with headquarters in Philadelphia and branches presumably controlled by that headquarters in various commercial centres. The charter ran twenty years, and was allowed to lapse in 1811, partly because of Congressional distaste for the bank's foreign stockholders.

Financial experience in and after the War of 1812 led to strong views that some national institution was really needed, both to handle the government's financial needs and to supply a note issue more uniform across the country than that of the state banks. Hammond points out that the New York bankers were mostly opposed, and that the Second Bank of the United States was established by law largely through the arguments of Westerners and Southerners like John C. Calhoun, then chairman of the House Finance Committee, who personally reported and fought for the bill. The community that had supported Alexander Hamilton in 1791 had mostly fallen by the wayside as promoters of a national bank, because their fortunes were now intimately involved with the success of state banks that would at best lose some freedom of action and at worst lose profitable business to a revived national institution.

Andrew Jackson's fight to block a rechartering of the Second Bank of the United States is the centrepiece of American history in the 1830s. Hammond insists that the Bank was done in not by populist agrarians slavering for easy money, but by a coalition of aggressive metropolitan businessmen whose style was cramped by the conservatism of the bank and farmer representatives who distrusted banks and paper money entirely (as Andrew Jackson undoubtedly did) and wanted no banks at all. The upshot, in any event, was that the Second Bank of the United States was destroyed and the states were on their own. They reacted to their opportunities, as states will, in very different ways.

New York was the leader; indeed, Hammond wrote, Jackson's "proud victory over the Second Bank of the United States served directly the calculated purposes of Wall Street". But the New York banks had done so well—and seemed likely to do so much better once government deposits were moved from the national bank and made available to state banks—that the entire entrepreneurial community of the state wanted its own pieces of the action. In the state legislature at Albany a demand arose for "free banking"—a law that would allow any man, or association of men, to open a bank.

Prior to the passage of that law in 1838, banking in New York had been restricted to corporations; and corporate organization of business, which carried the great privilege of limited liability for investors, was available only through a charter specifically voted by the legislature. Thus the word "association", which still survives (sometimes in the letters "N.A.," standing for "National Association") in the names of banks with national charters that do not wish to call themselves the National Bank of Such-and-Such. An association is not a corporation; the legislature would not have to approve a charter; anybody could open a bank. In some of the states that copied the New York law the requirement was a reserve of specie supposedly available to redeem notes; in others—and this made free banking especially attractive to states that were trying to raise money—it was the purchase of a certain quantity of state bonds, against which the newly formed bank (operating the Bank of England model again) would be empowered to issue banknotes. In Congress a quarter of a century later, Justin Morrill of Vermont (who has passed into history as the author of the bill that established the land-grant universities) denounced free banking as a procedure by which "men without means, skill or character, if able to obtain a temporary loan so as to purchase the first batch of bonds, may establish a bank".

But the fact was that free banking had worked reasonably well in New York (as even Morrill admitted), and while it had been a disaster in a number of midwestern states, especially in Michigan, it had even there supplied money to needy governments. The Lincoln administration, lacking the machinery for direct taxation and fearful of unlimited issues of greenbacks, was fresh out of money: Union soldiers had not been paid for two months. New York's legislation was the model for Lincoln's; it passed the Congress in 1863, rather unexpectedly, as a wartime finance measure. There was no thought of forcibly putting the state banks out of business; nobody believed Congress had that power, and the country had enough troubles without adding bank failures to the litany.

For reasons nobody has ever been able to understand, Treasury Secretary Chase required all his newly chartered national banks to take a number rather than a name—hence all the First Nationals and Second Nationals—but otherwise the only requirement was the purchase of government bonds. After he departed, the names rule was dropped (permitting the formation of a Chase National Bank); and Hugh McCulloch as the first Comptroller of the Currency began a long march through the institutions, hoping to persuade existing state banks to take national charters rather than to start a banking system *de novo*. McCulloch was helped a little by the tax on state banknotes voted in 1865, and by a provision in the law that country-based national banks could keep their reserves in nationally chartered city banks but not in state-chartered city banks, which gave the national banks a considerable leg up in the quest for correspondent banking business. But he was hindered by the prohibition against mortgage lending and trust departments at national banks. Nationally chartered banks predominated from the early 1870s to the early 1890s (though never in New York), then fell back. Today about two-thirds of the nation's banks are state-chartered, and the deposit base is split roughly fifty-fifty. Of the new banks formed—and we are running at a rate of roughly

300 a year—about three-quarters are state-chartered.

But the day of "free banking" has long passed. In the chaste words of David C. Motter of the Comptroller's office in 1966, "Past experience illustrates that unrestricted entry into banking is incompatible with the achievement of banking solvency and liquidity". What survives from the struggles is the chance to convince either of two sets of chartering authorities that this part of the country needs a new bank, and that you are just the fellow to start one.

3

Let us now assume a situation where a man by his own persuasiveness or with a little help from his friends has acquired a charter to start a bank at a specified location. (The charter is good only for the location described in the application.) What does he do next? Not unreasonably in an institution that gets its name from the physical facility employed by the pioneers of Renaissance Italy (*banco*, or bench; *tavola*, or table, was more common, but didn't export), his first task is to build a building or rent and expensively refurbish a store. Banking is the most abstract of businesses with the most intangible of products, but it must have a place where depositors can make their deposits and that place must be reasonably solid to limit an unwanted visitor's prospects of walking away with the merchandise. People think a bank *should* look impressive. A new banker in a hurry, however, can start in a specially built trailer—and he may be in a big hurry if both state and national authorities have given charters for a new bank in the same neighbourhood.

The siting of a bank is almost as important as the siting of a petrol station in determining the volume of business it is likely to do, especially in its early years. The higher the traffic, obviously, the more people are likely to find this a convenient place to keep deposits. The ground floor of a big office building is a natural; and so is a shopping centre, though the industry learned about shopping centres a little late. Convenience alone, of course, is not likely to be enough to overcome the inertia of people who are being asked to undertake the nuisance of moving their bank account from its accustomed location, and there is a big bag of promotional gimmicks to get things started. The most common is the neighbour-hood party, with finger sandwiches, cookies, and sodas for the young 'uns, ribbons to be ceremoniously cut, door prizes. The pet door prize recently has been a "millionaire for a day" drawing, which entitles the winner to one day's interest on a million dollars —but only at 6 percent, which is considerably less than what a real millionaire would get for himself. Charter depositors in checking accounts may get a bundle of services for which others will have to pay (fancily imprinted cheques, overdraft privileges, etc.); char-ter depositors in savings accounts may get premiums of the household-appliance variety (up to a maximum wholesale value of $10, by the rules of the Federal Deposit Insurance Corporation). All this will be announced by mailings to all the addresses around, ads in the paper, and so forth.

Basically, however, a new bank in a neighbourhood gets deposits by offering services the established banks are neglecting. This is often less difficult than one might expect: "Any time you have a one-bank dominated area," says Earl S. Francis, president of Marine National Bank, the newest national charter in St. Peters-burg, "the people who run the bank run it the way they want to run it and not the way the public wants it run. A new bank *always* improves banking. Let's face it—you don't open Saturdays unless you have to. We're open Saturdays, we offer no-service-charge checking, we're aggressive. In 1973, eighty percent of my business came from other banks, not from the growth of Pinellas County".

Earl Nelson started Hawkeye State Bank in Iowa City in January 1966; he was forty-two, and none of the people working for him had ever worked in a bank before, because he didn't want to have to break them of bad habits. "It was hard to find even a place to build a bank," he recalls; "we were blocked from the downtown locations. Our slogan from day one was, 'The bank that cares', implying, I suppose, that the others didn't—at least, they thought so. We got eighty-seven accounts the first day. When the other banks got a cheque payable on us, they would call the man and say, 'What do you want to do business with *him* for ?' That got us a lot of customers. Our advantage was that the banks here had been a little greedy, and a little dictatorial. Of course, we had a tremendous pouring in of money to the University [of Iowa] in those days—they were hiring anyone who could walk".

Adam Aronson had Mark Twain State Bank actually completed and open for business in the Bridgeton area of suburban St. Louis before there was anything but cornfields to be seen from its windows. When the industrial park planned for the area took shape, the bank was there to serve proprietors and employees alike—not to mention the builders. Expanding Mark Twain Northlands Bank, in a Mays Department Store shopping centre, Aronson gave full rein to a taste in kooky modern art—fauve colours, textures and bits of wood, abstract sculptures. One such was a business-getter: a "sound sculpture" by Howard Jones, which hangs on the wall by the entrance, stainless steel pieces moving mysteriously and noises emerging when an electric eye is triggered near the front door. Aronson put it there because he likes it, but women are grateful because their children are more than happy to keep breaking the electric eye and watching the funny shapes and hearing the funny sounds for however much time mother needs on the teller's line. Meanwhile, mother on the line can watch silent movies and travelogues and the like projected on to screens above the tellers' heads for those who must also stand and wait. A side benefit of the Jones sound sculpture, Aronson feels, is that it terrifies potential bank robbers. . . .

What really gets deposit business for a small new bank, however, are the loans it makes. "That's the only way a bank is going to grow," says Charles Agemian, "—by making loans. Not by writing FHA or VA mortgages or buying paper." Agemian was retired in 1969 from a vice-presidency in charge of financing at New York's Chase Manhattan, and moved across the river to become chairman of Garden State National Bank, which then had about $120 million in assets. By the end of 1973, it had more than $500 million in assets. Agemian is a large, one could say very fat, grey-haired, informal, sixty-five-year-old go-getter; everybody at his bank calls everybody else, including Charlie, by his first name. "And the way you make a lot of loans," he adds, "is by being ready to give a fast decision, Yes or No, no farting around".

Unfortunately, there is another way: quite a large loan portfolio can be built very quickly by lending to borrowers established banks won't touch. Every town has its failing manufacturer who wants money secured by his weakest accounts receivable, its automobile dealer who will sell cars to every deadbeat in the county if a bank will take the paper on a "no recourse" basis, its mobile-home dealer who will promise good interest on loans allegedly to carry an inventory that exists only in his excellent imagination, its speculative builder whose brother-in-law has a splendid wooded tract on a hillside which a careless lending officer may not know is four miles from the nearest source of water. Banks that start out this way usually have new presidents within eighteen months or so.

They very rarely go bust, however, because the failure of a new bank is an implicit judgment on the Comptroller or state banking superintendent who chartered it. The possession of the charter, in a situation where the authorities issue many fewer charters than are requested, is itself a major asset for even the most poorly run bank. Unless the loan portfolio is really corrupt and hopeless, all to be written off, the authorities can nearly always find a holding company or a previously denied applicant for a charter who will assume the losses as a kind of extra licence fee, and keep the bank open. When the Federal Deposit Insurance Corporation insisted on closing down rather than "reorganizing" the San Francisco National Bank he had chartered to people some of whom should never have been allowed to be customers (let alone proprietors) of a bank, Comptroller James Saxon refused ever to attend another meeting of the FDIC board, of which the Comptroller is ex officio a member. Out of loyalty to a man greatly admired by those who remained in the Comptroller's office after he had left, Saxon's successors made his personal severance of formal relations with FDIC a policy decision that was not breached until half a dozen years after his departure.

No successful bank can be built without somebody—usually, in a smaller bank, the president—who goes out and sells the bank's money to those and only those he would like to have as his customers and depositors. "One of the vices inherent in our type of work," Gaylord Freeman wrote in his 1950 report on *The Goal of the First National Bank of Chicago*, "is a tendency toward staying in the Bank, yet I dare say it is an equally natural tendency for a salesman to want to stay in his office." Later in the same report, Freeman urged that "Our greatest single asset is our loaning policy. Businessmen get to know about that from friends, customers and competitors—not from our advertising". On his visits around the neighbourhood, the new banker simply by looking should be able to learn something about the business conditions in his catchment area, and he will be able to ask a number of people what Martin Griffin of Morgan Guaranty calls "the banker's question: 'Is there anything I can do for you?'"

"You can't be a specialist running a bank," says Earl Francis of St. Petersburg's Marine National. "You've got to know a lot of things." But most presidents of smaller banks tend to be more comfortable with some loans than with others. When First National City Bank of New York was permitted to acquire holding-company subsidiary banks upstate, it picked up six suburban banks to start; two of them didn't write automobile loans, the largest category after mortgages in most suburban banks, simply because there was nobody in the shop really convinced he could handle the paperwork and the problems. Leonard Weil of Manufacturers in Los Angeles says he has built his bank on the expertise of his officers, especially in the clothing industry—on that, and on "always having money to lend". John Dubinsky of Mark Twain Bancshares says that "on our construction loans I try to get my wife to go with me and look at some property every weekend". (This was said at dinner, with the lady present; she mimicked, "Let's take a drive in the country, dear".) In suburban Jacksonville, Florida, present James Kaleel of Lake Forest National Bank says, "I consider myself an expert on building. Most of my family are plumbers, carpenters, electricians. If one of the girls drops her keys down the commode I go over there myself and take the commode off the floor".

Kaleel is a jug-eared, curly-haired southerner with an accent that would qualify him to play the heavy in a television network show about race relations. Four of the neighbourhoods in his bank's service area have changed colour, and "we keep them. We finance their homes, finance their cars, send their kids to college. Of our 836 student loans, 503 are black. I'm going to get these lawyers and teachers and doctors—they're going to feel obligated to our bank". Alton Adams, Jr., who runs the Durkeeville branch of Jacksonville's First Federal Savings and Loan ("the only black-staffed branch of a white savings and loan", he says) is a customer of Kaleel's bank: "I tease him, I keep asking him when he's going to run".

Kaleel's business has held up well (17,000 chequeing account customers, 14,000 savings account customers, $27 million in deposits in early 1973); he gives credit to his willingness to continue lending at the same figures he used before the neighbourhood began changing. His nearest neighbour bank has suffered because its president "can't make a loan over six hundred dollars without going to somebody for authority. We know because when the man down the street can't make a loan, you hear about it from new customers". Among Kaleel's loans in 1972 was one of $90,000 to the local branch of Leon Sullivan's Job Opportunities Industrial Council, to train construction workers and welders for the shipyard; some of them will be his customers, too.

Some new banks start very ambitiously. First National City after acquiring its suburban subsidiaries upstate branched each of them into the local big city—Buffalo, Rochester, Syracuse, Albany. The average age of the chief executive officers sent up from New York for these banks was thirty-three; the man chosen for Syracuse was twenty-seven. "For anyone who wants to establish a track record for himself as a manager, looking toward a senior position here," says John Heilshorn, who shepherded all the New York State subsidiaries at their birth, "it's an ideal job. He starts from zero, he has to handle the political problem, the competitive problem. He's our chief lending officer. He has an assistant in his twenties who's been doing that sort of lending work here for four or five years, and three guys fresh out of school. We go out to guys with fifty or a hundred million in sales, who never saw a banker in their shop before. Our guys get the Dun and Bradstreet reports, look at them, say 'This fellow ought to be a prospect for X, Y and Z. If it means we bring up a leasing guy from New York or a factoring guy from New York, we do it. We've all been brought up in an environment that says, "Treat your client when you visit him as though you were visiting General Motors".' And we've all visited General Motors. . . . But you have to make every second count when it's only a hundred-thousand-dollar loan".

Citibank has been something of a disappointment to the real estate industry in upstate New York. "They offered us building after building," Heilshorn says. "Great big Citibank could easily buy a ten-million-dollar building. When we told them we wanted to negotiate with a clothing store, rent five thousand feet, they couldn't believe it. But then we hired the best architects there are, to turn that brassiere counter into a teller's counter." The slogan for each of these new operations in an upstate city was, "A new little bank with big connections. . . ."

4

The invasion of the countryside by the big-city bank has been a recurring nightmare of American banking since Andrew Jackson put the Second Bank of the United States out of business and Congress dictated that American banks should be licensed to operate only where a state banking authority was willing to accept them—which meant, normally, within one state. There are exactly twelve exceptions, the most notable being the Bank of California, which operates the length of the Pacific Coast (because it got started before Oregon or Washington was a state; Bank of California, incidentally, is now controlled by the Rothschild's interests in Europe). In 1844, the New York State legislature passed a law requiring a bank to operate only from a single location, and this "unit rule", ultimately abandoned in New York, became the guiding principle of bank legislation throughout the West and Southwest.

Among the unit banking states that retain such laws are financial centres as important as Illinois, Florida and Texas; and Massachusetts, among others, still confines a bank to the boundaries of a single county. Bagehot himself thought highly of the principle: "A banker who lives in the district," he wrote in 1873, "who has always lived there, whose whole mind is a history of the district and its changes, is easily able to lend money safely there. But a manager deputed by a single central establishment does so with difficulty. The worst people will come to him and ask for loans. His ignorance is a mark for all the shrewd and crafty people thereabouts".

Branch banking is an issue that has had its ebbs and flows in the United States. For a long time in the later nineteenth century, Carter Golembe has pointed out, the question was seen as one of "the need by rural communities for banking facilities", and "proposals to extend branch powers . . . were discussed quite dispassionately, even at conventions of The American Bankers Association". In this century the rhetoric has escalated again, and Congressman Patman led off his *Primer on Money* with the ringing statement that "the independent bank, locally owned, is a bulwark of strength in our country. Its disappearance is an abuse, and should be stopped".

Neither the National Bank Act nor Wilson's Federal Reserve Act said anything specific about the branching powers of nationally chartered banks, but administrators of the law read it to say that national banks could not have branches. Then A. P. Giannini, whose Bank of Italy was about to become Bank of America, demonstrated that there was an easy way around the rules. The Fed could stop a bank from opening branches, but it could not stop the owners of a bank from opening allegedly independent new banks; and "chain banking", which offered opportunities for chicanery, was obviously less desirable than branch banking, which at least required one set of all the books to be kept in one place.

Congress was seized with this problem for three years, and in

1927 finally produced the McFadden Act, which took what seemed the common-sense approach of empowering the Comptroller and the Fed to permit a nationally chartered bank to branch pretty much as a state-chartered bank could branch in the state where it did business. The ball was now back in the state legislatures' court, but before the struggle could be seriously resumed there the Depression descended, and questions of how banks were to be expanded stopped being discussed. From the end of December 1929 to the end of June 1933 the number of banks in the United States dropped from 24,026 to 13,949. There was some thought that tying the failing country units to larger city banks might save some of them—the proof offered came from Britain, where the great crash produced no bank failures—but the unit bankers fought for deposit insurance instead, and won.

In the 1950s the branching issue returned in a new and interesting guise with the corporate equivalent of chain banking: the bank holding company. Instead of being a branch office of a centrally administered bank, the local operation would be a separately chartered bank, still responsible to the locality by law and custom and still very possibly (not necessarily) locally managed. For the small-town banker, the holding company promised the best of both worlds: he did not have to sell all, sometimes he did not have to sell most, of his bank, yet he could get all the security of being part of a big business. One after another, the bastions of unit banking fell, and in 1974 only Illinois and West Virginia survived as states that forbade holding companies as well as mere banks to operate out of more than one location.

Today, in most cities, a man wishing to start a new bank in his neighbourhood will try to make an arrangement with a holding company, which can help out with capital, political influence, technical assistance, and the beginnings of a deposit base. In point of fact, all the banks mentioned in this chapter (except Manufacturers in Los Angeles) are parts of a holding-company system, but if nobody said so the visitor would never know. The president of the holding-company subsidiary, reporting as he must to his own local board, will almost certainly be a more independent businessman than the manager of a branch. "On the day they come in here and set my goals and tell me what to do", says Earl Francis of St. Petersburg's Marine National, speaking of United First Florida Banks, "they're going to kiss me good-bye. What's my incentive?" Earl Nelson of Iowa City's Hawkeye State Bank is in fact the head of the holding company that controls it, and also controls seven other banks in little towns scattered about eastern Iowa (one of them is a bank in Amish country that has never taken a loss on a loan). "Nobody in these towns knows me", he says. "We are *locally* run. If anyone comes in while I'm there, I'm a visiting salesman."

One of the advantages of the unit bank in rural country is that it enabled each place to have, in effect, its own money market, and this advantage seems to be maintained in the holding company organization. "We operate," Nelson says, "in nine counties through thirteen facilities. It's remarkable the difference in rates within ten, fifteen miles. It's fantastic the difference in forty, fifty miles. We have one bank lending at eight and a half, nine percent, another that never went over seven percent". Tampa is more attuned to the modern world than adjacent St. Petersburg; when money is tight, rates are higher in Tampa than they are in St. Pete, and when money is easy, rates are lower in Tampa. Subsidiaries of a single holding company follow the different pattern of the different cities. Even First National City has found that it cannot enforce identical interest charges on similar loans in its upstate subsidiaries: each must to some extent compete in what is, truly, an independent market for credit. But in California and in North Carolina, the money market is unitary and statewide, because it is politically impossible within a single bank to have lending officers at some branches operating on one basis while those in other branches are privileged to work on another basis.

The relationship between branching and competition has always been complicated. The short and simple statement is that branching reduces, often substantially, the number of independent banks in a state, but increases the number of banks in each market. Holding companies have the same effect. Both encourage the chartering authorities to permit the opening of more banking offices in a given place: a branch damaged by competition can be and will be bailed out by its parent without too much trouble for the community or the banking authorities—and an independent in town wrecked by competition from a branch can always sell out to another bank looking for branches or a holding company looking for markets. Supporting staff services from the holding companies should help set a floor under the possible incompetence of local bank management, especially if that support includes an audit detailed enough to (in Marshall Corns' fine phrase) "protect weak people from temptation, strong people from opportunity, and innocent people from suspicion".

Two studies by the New York State Banking Department indicate that branches do to a small degree take money out of a community; in proportion to their deposits they make fewer loans to local business and fewer small, unsecured loans than unit banks in the same town. But the differences are very slight: in a year-end 1969 study all but a handful of both the units and the branches got at least 90 percent of their deposits and made at least 80 percent of their loans within fifteen miles of the office. Moreover, the author of the report thought there was at least a chance that the branches sent more money out because their broader range of services and higher interest rates on savings accounts brought money in at a faster rate, "and depositors who place their excess funds in time accounts may not generate much increased loan demand, at least in the short run".

Bringing the methods of the big city to the hinterlands is not inevitably a step toward competition; as British experience illustrates; sometimes it can be very difficult to persuade large, sophisticated businesses to compete against each other. New York, with half a dozen very big retail branched banks throwing television commercials at each other on the nightly news, cannot get no-minimum-balance free chequing out of any of them, thought his service or something very much like it is available at thousands of banks in other cities. "The one thing you can write on the front of your book," Edward L. Palmer, chairman of the executive committee of First National City, says scornfully: *"people don't like*

85

competition. That's the church. You go there, and there's nobody in it." But Citibank's pew is sometimes vacant, too: "Mellon is in red ink from the dropping of service charges in Pittsburgh," Palmer's colleague Heilshorn says coldly; "nobody came out ahead because everybody did it". Well, yes. But. . . .

On balance, it seems probable that the spread of bank holding companies has increased competition among banks for deposits and for consumer and small-business borrowings. The benefits have been greatest for the middling-size business, which can now tap a source of large loans by dealing with its old friends and neighbours. The $20-million unit bank that could lend one customer no more than $200,000 has become part of a holding company that can, through the same personnel, lend $10 million. *Can*—but only if the local unit bank or the headquarters staff is persuasive: nay-saying as well as yea-saying is decentralized in the well-run holding company. Each board of directors is still responsible for the operations of the individual bank, and may turn down a participation in a loan made by a fellow subsidiary. At Mark Twain Bancshares, the presidents of all four subsidiaries must agree on the desirability of a loan before anything that involves more than one of them will be undertaken. Elsewhere an originating bank may go ahead with those that agree on the credit, leaving out those it frightens. "I refused to continue participation once in an Atlantic Banks loan," says Jacksonville's Kaleel. "I took the position that they could stand the loss of eight million, but we couldn't stand the loss of a hundred and eighty-five thousand".

The development of holding companies has made possible the construction of banking organizations in regional centres large enough to serve almost any regional needs without reference to the tastes and opinions of the money centre banks. There are still only four cities housing the headquarters of banks that can boast more than $10,000 million in deposits—San Francisco (with the largest, Bank of America, more than a thousand branches and $50,000 million); New York (with the next four largest, First National City, Chase Manhattan, Manufacturers Hanover, and Morgan Guaranty, plus Chemical and Bankers Trust); Chicago (with Continental

Illinois and First National Bank of Chicago); and Los Angeles (with Western Bancorporation and Security Pacific). But there are now bank holding companies with subsidiaries commanding more than $2,000 million in deposits headquartered in Atlanta, Boston, Cleveland, Detroit, Minneapolis, Charlotte and Winston-Salem, Columbus, Buffalo, Rochester, Philadelphia, Pittsburgh, Dallas, Houston, Phoenix, Portland, Seattle, and Milwaukee. And the proportion of the assets of the American banking system controlled by the hundred largest banks has dropped from about 55 percent in the 1950s to something like 50 percent in 1974.

Though many of the very large regional holding companies rely for some of their funds on purchases far away, all have at least a major dependency on their own state for their deposit base: they have the same self-preserving instinct to lend near home that a small-town banker does. Meanwhile, because they deal with very large sophisticated borrowers and depositors, they function in the national money market, interconnected through millions of miles of leased wires. As the holding-company system permits banks to expand their lending and leasing activities nationwide and the source of funds becomes increasingly the market rather than the depositor, everyone worries about whether the balance between localizing and nationalizing forces can be retained. First-class regional bankers like Thomas Storrs of North Carolina National Bank (an economist, graduate of executive office in the Federal Reserve System), complain that "We find the New York banks are bad competition. As recently as four months ago [this was April 1973], they were down here making seven-, eight-, ten-year loans at between seven and quarter and seven and a half percent. Those were bad loans, and they're under water today. But their regional representatives had a profit plan which said anything over prime should be grabbed. . . ." The wholesale banks with their giant money machines can afford a large number of such mistakes; if the regional banks fight back, they can be badly hurt. It is not entirely impossible that the men who run First National City know this.

In summer 1974 these worries were heightened by the disaster of New York's Franklin National Bank, and the catastrophe of

Cologne's Bank Herstatt. Corporations and institutions that loaned money to banks through the purchase of certificates of deposit became reluctant to risk their money in any but the biggest banks, and to keep themselves in funds, many of the regional banks had to pay higher interest rates on their CD's than the market required from the giant banks in New York, Chicago, and California. Presumably, these differentials eased in 1975, as the authorities in Britain and the United States organized bail-outs for the lenders to the fringe banks in one country, the mismanaged commercial banks in the other. Indeed, the big New York City banks lived through several months when fear of the impact of municipal bankruptcy put them among the borrowers who have to pay just a little more. But the impetus toward concentration of the banking business in a few very large banks must persist as long as fears of financial instability are abroad in the land.

5/A Bank of One's Own

*If you feel sick you go to the doctor; if you're in trouble, you go to the
lawyer; and if there's anything else wrong, you go to the banker.*
— GEORGE SCOTT, First National
City Bank of New York

* * *

"Franklin Square," Arthur Roth said, pretending to relax as
he reminisced, "was a little town of thirty-five hundred
people; no railroad station, no industry. I arrived April 30, 1934.
The bank had four employees, deposits were four hundred and
seventy-eight thousand, and the so-called capital was a hundred
and twenty-five thousand. But the bond depreciation was two
hundred thousand dollars, and there were loan losses not yet taken
of fifty thousand dollars. In short, the bank was broke".

This was Franklin National Bank, in a suburb of Long Island,
which became one of the eighteen largest in the United States. A
very tall, muscular young man (forty years later, he could still power
a golf ball 240 yards in one direction or another), Roth had been

working for eleven years for Manufacturers Trust in Manhattan, and had wound up in the comptroller's department, where he learned about forms ("a bank's forms are its *system*", he says) and about keeping the books. Prior to that he had been a successful lending officer. Franklin National should have shut its doors in 1934, but in those days (up to 1937), a stockholder in an American bank might still be liable to depositors for the face amount of the stock he owned—he could lose double his investment. The directors had a stake in keeping the bank open; somebody knew Roth; and his loyalty to Manufacturers was, to say the least, tenuous. He took the job.

Like many other banks in 1934, Franklin was well beyond saving by management alone, and Roth's first mission was to the Reconstruction Finance Corporation, the government agency started by Hoover and greatly expanded by Roosevelt, which was charged with trying to keep viable businesses in being. The RFC put up $100,000, taking in return $50,000 of face value in Franklin National preferred stock and a note for $50,000 guaranteed by the directors of the bank, who secured it with mortgages on their own homes. The $125,000 of alleged capital was reduced to $50,000, the losses were written off, and Roth had a clean bank, if a very small bank. There were few borrowers. "One week we'd make a hundred dollars", Roth recalls; "the next week we'd lose fifty dollars".

About the only business that was active in Nassau County was home building, which the government had begun to encourage. "My father and brother were builders," Roth says, "and I had some knowledge of building; I had kept their books and figured their deals. In those days, banks were afraid of builders' loans, afraid the house wouldn't sell. We were willing to make the loan to the builder and then write the mortgage for the buyer. I went to Mott Brothers in Garden City because they had a good name, I didn't know they were one of the biggest builders in Nassau County. We agreed to take all their mortgages. I found myself originating more mortgages than I had deposits. The only thing I could do was to sell the mortgages. They were government guaranteed mortgages, under the new FHA Law. I took them into Manufacturers, but they wouldn't buy, they said the law would be declared unconstitutional. I'd read somewhere about life insurance companies in New England that were looking for ways to invest money, so I went on the road. National Life Insurance Company of Montpelier, Vermont, agreed to buy my mortgages.

"That was a good business. We'd get a hundred dollars from the builder, and on the sale of the mortgage the premium would be a hundred and fifty. Then we would service the mortgage, for one-half of one percent. I converted a Burroughs bank posting machine to be a mortgage servicing machine, and I kept going out on the road to sell mortgages. Once National Life bought, all the Vermont banks would buy. Then I began to sell to Dime Savings in Brooklyn, and then to all the bigger banks on Long Island. We were doing business all over Nassau County, but after working with forty branches at Manufacturers, I had said I would never have any branches in any bank I ran. It came to the point where there wasn't any place to park. The banking law in those days said a bank could own property only for banking purposes—a bank couldn't own a parking lot. I went down to the Comptroller in Washington and said, 'I'll write it down to one dollar, I won't carry it as an asset'—and on that basis they approved it, let me build a parking lot. Holly Patterson [the town supervisor of Hempstead and a political power in Nassau] used to accuse me of having done something improper in Washington."

At a time when successful banks were earning about 6 percent on their capital—and selling for less than book value: most banks, Morris Schapiro liked to say, "were worth more dead than alive"— Roth's Franklin National earned 20 percent. Once he lost his bashfulness about branching (which was then permitted in New York State only within the confines of a single county), he could easily acquire existing banks by issuing stock. Sometimes the directors of the bank he was buying would worry about the thin market for Franklin's stock. Roth licked that one by personally guaranteeing that for two weeks after a bank merger, enough time for the sellers to get out if they wanted to get out, he would buy the stock at the market price on the day of the sale. Then he would arrange a personal line of credit at Chase National Bank to make sure he could live up to his guarantee. On one merger, early in the war, he arranged a $1·5 million personal line from Chase to assure his purchase. On another occasion, also with money borrowed from Chase, Franklin simply bought all the assets and assumed all the liabilities of a bank after the Comptroller had refused to approve a merger. It would not be a good idea to try anything of that sort today.

As part of his effort to create a widespread market for Franklin stock, Roth in 1941 published what he believes to be the first detailed annual report ever published by a bank. That same year, he became president of the Long Island Bankers Association, and began promoting Nassau County as a place for industry. "Nassau had been the bedroom of the city of New York for a great many years. The newspapers used to run cartoons of industry as ugly buildings belching black smoke; they were against it. I argued for campus-type industry, went before the mayors of the communities. I'd say, 'You have obligations to provide employment for your people. Why should they leave to go to New York?' And then I'd say, 'And you're having trouble with your school tax. . . .' Very little of Nassau was zoned for industry in those days, but once the ball got started, employers found they had a higher quality of worker, and they had a happier worker, because the jobs were near home".

During the war, Roth could see that loan demand in Nassau would again outrun Franklin's resources; looking around for possible future deposit growth he decided to take on the savings banks. New York State law then forbade a commercial bank to call its time deposits a "savings account". The words "thrift account" or "interest account" could be used, but not "savings account". Roth decided this was nonsense, invented the advertising approach that would later be called "the full-service bank", and went into the community to solicit savings. "The New York State Banking Department", he remembers, "protested to Preston Delano, who was then Comptroller of the Currency, and a federal bank examiner called. He said, 'You're only a little bank—do you really think this is worth your while?' It was 1944. I thought to myself, Dewey is running for President, and if he wins Elliott Bell is slated to be Secretary of the Treasury, and we can take care of it then. I said, 'Tell you what. I'll drop it for a year'.

"Well, Dewey lost, and some months later I got a call—the Attorney General was going to sue. I said, 'I gave orders not to use this for a year'. But the Attorney General said that I hadn't taken down the sign above the teller's cage, reading 'Savings'. They were going to sue to make me take down the sign. I said, 'Sue me'. I went to the psychology department at Hofstra and commissioned a public opinion poll, asked for a survey on the use of the word 'savings', what people meant by that word, what they knew about compound interest, and so forth. We went into court and explained sampling, had all these college kids in the courtroom; it was a great case for public-opinion polling. We went all the way to the Supreme Court, and it cost us one hundred fifty thousand dollars. I wrote to all the banks in New York, asking them to contribute. Chase gave us five thousand dollars; we raised a total of thirty-eight thousand dollars. National City wouldn't give us a penny, but the day we won in the Supreme Court they were on the radio, advertising 'savings accounts'."

Roth's greatest war was to keep the big New York City banks from expanding into the suburbs, which were gathering in so many of the people who had once been depositors at the city banks' branches. He was Horatius at the bridge for a decade, a remarkable accomplishment in the face of assaults not only from the big money of Wall Street but also from the political muscle of the mutual savings banks, which had been equally restricted to a single county (or, for the five boroughs, a single city). Even after the state legislature had voted to permit branching into adjacent counties, Roth's bank was an effective spokesman against permitting the city giants to buy up banks of any size in the suburbs. His strongest argument was that little suburban banks will take care of local borrowers a big bank will ignore. When First National City attempted to buy the National Bank of Westchester, Franklin National sent to the Comptroller of the Currency twenty-one affidavits from lending officers in its employ who had formerly been employed by major New York City banks. "These officers on two occasions", Congressman Emmanuel Celler wrote, "examined a total of fourteen hundred business loans . . . which were granted at Franklin National. . . . They concluded that if these same loans had been applied for at their former New York City bank employers, 66 percent or two thirds of them would have been turned down". By the time the banks were able to move significantly into any of the suburbs, Roth was big enough to invade the city with his own branches, most notably a Louis XV décor banking office opened on the Plaza at the socialite tip of Central Park, under the separate name Banque Continentale.

Whatever else Franklin did wrong in the big city, incidentally, this office seems to have paid its way: the European consortium that bought the Franklin assets in autumn 1974, and scarcely needs to build a reputation for Old World sophistication, has kept Banque Continentale in business.

2

Another: a very different man in a very different place.

Walter Bimson had been a commodities loan officer for Harris Trust in Chicago, an outfit which as a native of Colorado he found something less than wholly congenial. ("It was," his brother Carl recalls, "the sort of place where they wouldn't even let you wear a soft-collar shirt on Saturday, when the bank was closed to the public".) Through Bimson, Harris Trust had become a purchaser of surplus agricultural loans made by the Valley National Bank of Phoenix, which in 1933 had $6.75 million in deposits. (It now has more than $3,500 million.) When Bimson became Valley National's president at the start of that year, he, like Roth in New York, called in the RFC to buy preferred stock, and he insisted not only on a "clean bank" (all the bad loans out of it), but also on a voting trust that gave him control of all the stock on a five-year contract. Then he went off to see A. P. Giannini at the Bank of America to find out how it was done. "Giannini," brother Carl recalls, "was a vegetable man and a dirt farmer, and he worked on the theory that you had to be a savings bank and a bank that loaned to individuals. Giannini made a great impression on Walter".

Brother Carl, who would later be president of Valley National and of the American Bankers Association, drove down from Colorado the next winter. "I came out of a blizzard in Alamogordo, New Mexico, so cold it froze the engine block of my car, I came across a desert without vegetation to a place where there were palm trees. I'd been working for a real estate firm in Denver, and Walter asked me to look over some real estate that had been put in his bank's bad-loan company. It was some furnished apartments near the Mormon Church. The Mormons would spend the winters here, and marry their dead through the Church—they converted their dead, then you could come together as a family group in heaven.

"I told my brother to put the place in shape, repair leaky roofs and walls, redecorate, rent the apartments—and then sell it. He said, 'Fine—but we have nobody to do it. Will you stay?' I thought about all this cold up north. . . . They offered a hundred dollars a month plus a free house, free milk and free ice. So I moved in, hired women to make curtains, bought yard-goods at J. C. Penney, repainted the fronts of the houses, fixed the roofs, got it all surveyed to give each house its own yard plot, and went to a fellow in the Mormon Church, the president of the Temple, told him we'd sell it cheap—and he bought it. Let's get this into perspective: we had two-bedrooms, living room, kitchen, bath, screened sleeping porch, and we rented it for twenty-two-fifty [then £5] a month.

"In September or October of 1934 the National Housing Act passed, and they tossed it to the NRA men, who said, 'We need a banker in this damned thing. All the government is doing is insuring loans, somebody's got to explain it'. I was sent to Washington to an NRA meeting, the government paid my expenses—a Transportation Request and five dollars a day. The programme was a loan of up to twenty-five hundred dollars for household improvements, government insured, pay it off in three years. I went to a meeting of the Arizona Bankers at Grand Canyon, but nobody was interested. Our banks were all glassy-eyed, they were frozen in on their bonds, on their business loans, on their mortgage loans, all things they couldn't liquidate—and bankers aren't promoters, anyway.

"About this time, along came a man who was a special-edition newspaper promoter. He'd go to the county papers, say he would sell the ads, you know, buy by the page and sell by the inch. I talked to him, and suggested a double-page spread; and on each page we would buy a big headline and a column down the middle, for every county weekly in Arizona. All these towns had vacant buildings. We would set up a home show in one of them, get the furniture companies and dealers, carpets, paints, roofing supplies, plumbers, tools, appliances—sell them the idea of setting up booths in the vacant buildings. We'd give the paper stories NRA supplied from all over the country, we'd set up speaking engagements in high school auditoriums and city parks and churches, explain the ABC's to people, show them how to fill out applications. In a place like Douglas, down the southern part of the state, where there were two banks and neither bank would handle it, Valley National offered the local banks a deal whereby it would supply the money and take the risk, the local bank would process, and Valley National would pay twenty-five cents per coupon for the handling. Up north sometimes we made arrangements directly with the businessmen. And of course once people knew they could borrow money, they spent their own.

"Arizona was the only state that passed the goal that had been set by the FHA. At one time our little bank had more loans in this programme—more dollar volume—than any other bank in the United States".

When the FHA mortgages came, Valley National expanded from this modernization programme to become the state's leading mortgage banker, opening branches everywhere, and almost immediately ran out of money. Like Roth, Carl Bimson went to New York and couldn't sell his mortgages, because the New York financial market was sure the Supreme Court would declare the government guarantee unconstitutional. Vermont, Bimson knew not of; he went to California, and found Occidental Life, which bought a million dollars worth of Valley National mortgages at ninety-eight cents on the dollar. The day after Bimson returned with the money, Valley National ran a full-page ad: "We Have A Million Dollars to Loan!"

It was clear to both Bimsons that if Arizona was to grow, money would have to arrive from the East; and once the Supreme Court had okayed the FHA guarantees, the mortgage mechanism was the best. "There's a lot of country between here and New York," Carl Bimson says. "How do you get them out here? We sent people back to New York with pictures, to sell the mutual savings bankers on the potential of the state and the health of its economy. And the hooker was, 'Why don't you come for a winter vacation in Arizona? You can charge it to your bank, you won't have to work too hard, and we'll take you around and show you the properties.' We had a lot of mutual bank officers taking two-week winter vacations here, but even they bought only Phoenix and Tucson. We sold Phoenix and Tucson mortgages at a loss to get money to lend elsewhere in the state.

"We went into small-business loans. The government wanted to encourage them, but the big-city banks couldn't do it. They'd say, 'Where are the accounts receivable?' I worked out a form, really like a personal loan, for up to five, ten thousand dollars. I got on the speakers' circuit, told banks about it all over the country. In 1947, there were only three people in the United States who had worked out cost schedules on the different kinds of loan so you could know where you should set your rates, and I was one of them. I built in on the telco [telephone company] system of how much an installer does. I wound up speaking to the national convention about it. . . .

". . . We started a research department, began to publish the rank orders of the states by percentage growth. All our local newspapers and radio and TV stations used our materials to sell national advertisers. Any business thinking of locating down here was told, 'Go to the research department of Valley National Bank, they'll tell you all you want to know. . .".

The young lady who had been given the responsibility of taking a reporter around the bank—and who had parked him in Carl Bimson's office because she had other things to do—came back and ushered him away, apologizing a little for saddling an eastern visitor with this garrulous retired old man. I told her to think nothing of it. We went on to the office of Paul Jones, vice-president of Valley National, a man in his forties with a leathery tan, wearing a redder shirt than might be fashionable in the East, but essentially cast in the image of a conventional banker—as was appropriate for the man responsible for investments and loans in the largest bank between Texas and California. He was in a thoughtful mood, contemplating the bank the Bimsons had built; it was, he said, a sobering fact that Valley National was responsible for one-half the money supply for the entire state of Arizona. . . .

3

There is a nice story, apparently roughly true, about a Lebanese turned Swiss named Edmond Safra, who now controls New York's two most politicized banks—Republic National and Kings Lafayette (for many years the chosen repository of the funds of the Board of Education, the city's most political agency).

Republic has a popular reputation as a racy operation, because it pioneered the exploitation of a loophole in the FDIC regulations that limit the value of prizes banks can give as a reward to new depositors. (Instead of giving a can opener to the depositor himself, Republic offers a colour television set to a friend of the depositor: this becomes legally a money-broker's fee rather than an illegal inducement to open an account; there are enough people in New York who trust their friends to clutter the streets outside Republic's main office every time the offer is made.) But in fact, despite its heavy lending to its own directors, its publicized investments in silver ingots, and its spectacular profits growth of 75 percent per year compounded from 1968 through 1973, Republic has been conservatively operated. Starting early in 1973, it pulled out of the European lending market and kept excess reserves to lend to other banks, avoiding the expensive scrambling about in the money markets that everybody else was doing in New York in 1974.

In spring 1970, the story runs, one of Safra's sons flew from New York to Switzerland and ventured up a mountain where his father was skiing, isolated from telephones, teletypes and other cares of the world. "Pop!" he is reported to have said, "We've finally made it—we've really been accepted in New York. *Penn Central* wants to borrow money from us!" His father paused to check the bindings on his skis, then shook his head. "If Penn Central wants our money, they must be going broke. I won't touch it".

Banks are part of a banking system, a big machine, and the whole is inescapably bigger than the sum of its parts. Banks handle other people's money, and must convey an image of great solidity; they are the home of the committee system of decision-making, and they run to their lawyers incessantly for advice. (Every really big law firm in the country outside Washington pays for its infrastructure with bank business.) Yet the basic judgments the banker makes are still highly individual judgments, and banking is perhaps the most personal of the big businesses. Most of the American banks that interest anybody are the lengthening shadow of one man—a Roth or a Bimson, a Giannini at Bank of America, a Walter Wriston, a Mills Lane at Citizens & Southern in Atlanta (tooling about town in an antique Chevrolet), a Tom Storrs at North Carolina National Bank, a Gaylord Freeman at First National Bank of Chicago. In the banking end of government, too, the impact of individuals has been astonishingly strong, with or against the grain of the institutions—a Wright Patman, a Carter Glass in the Senate, Benjamin Strong at the Federal Reserve Bank of New York, William McChesney Martin at the Federal Reserve Board in Washington, Comptroller of the Currency James Saxon. These men have influenced people's live much more pervasively than other men whose names are much better known, and have done it in highly individual ways.

Serge Semenenko was a young refugee in Istanbul right after the Revolution, studying at Roberts College, an American school. "The professors there thought I had some appreciation for business," he says mildly, "and should go to America. They arranged for me to go to the Harvard Business School. There I studied with Oliver Mitchell Sprague, who was an adviser to General Motors and to the Bank of England, and he was a great inspiration to me". Semenenko held a summer job at Bankers Trust in New York, but on leaving Harvard in 1926 he signed on with the First National Bank of Boston, at a hundred dollars a month.

He came to glory in the Depression, for he had a unique capacity to see around the corners built by panic into values obscured by chaos. The rewards were considerable: he lives and works now in quarters which amount to about half a floor in New York's Hotel Pierre, furnished as aristocratic apartments in St. Petersburg must have been furnished three-quarters of a century ago, icons on the walls, tapestries, and a family portrait by Diego Rivera (because one of the places where Semenenko saw values obscured by chaos was Mexico: "I hated it. Mexico was a place where I went on vacation, it meant having to answer the telephone, but my Mexican friends asked me, their country had no credit, and it turned out to be a wonderful experience, a warm relationship with Miguel Aleman, large loans and large balances. . . ."). He is a rather soft-spoken little man with startlingly black hair and a bulbous nose that gives his appearance a disarming popular flavour; he wears black suit, white shirt, black tie.

"I had a great deal of leeway", he recalls. "I had forty-one years of association with the bank and the bank never had any losses; what they used to call 'the bank within the bank' was made possible by the fact that every deal worked out, which led to a great deal of confidence on the part of my associates". Semenenko and a staff that ran to scores of assistants lived very closely with his "special industries", and he played a significant policy-making role in the companies to which he loaned money, often serving on their boards. "Hearst", he said, smiling reminiscently. "I worked with Richard Berlin, on financing and disposition. One of the problems Mr. Hearst had was that he never liked to dispose of any paper, whether it was profitable or unprofitable; there was a need to prune dead branches. And financing was very difficult because Mr. Hearst had endorsed $150 million of indebtedness, he gave his endorsements very freely.

"I spent thirteen years reorganizing Minnesota and Ontario Paper in Minneapolis. Man named Backus had built the company, but got spread all over the world. They had properties in Finland, I went with him to Finland and helped him dispose of the properties in Finland. . . . I loaned as much as four thousand million dollars to the movie industry, and never lost any of it. M-G-M, Universal —I put together Decca Records—Warner Brothers, I was a director of Warner Brothers; in 1941 I was asked to step in and do Columbia Pictures, and this one has had its difficult days. I started as their banker, for the past seven years I have been vice-chairman of the company, and now it has new management. . . .

"One of the principles I followed was that Boston money was more valuable than money from somewhere else. I would say, 'We are friends through thick and thin, we won't run away when problems arise and storm clouds come up—unlike some other financial institutions'. I obtained very large balances from borrowers Ten, twenty percent doesn't mean anything. Many of my customers would keep *fifty* percent at the bank. Some kept one hundred per-cent. You may wonder, why would they do that? Why would they borrow money and leave it at the bank? It meant they *could* always borrow, if they needed money; these were very unorthodox situations.

"My term loans led me to 'loan financing', and close association, which was new, with the insurance companies. I would say, 'We will take the first five years of this loan, but that's not enough for this company; you take the last five'. Prudential, Mass Mutual, Hancock, I worked with all of them; I would bring in things they could handle. It was very profitable". These profits, in effect, he split with the bank; his departure followed a decision by First of Boston that his share had grown too large.

A banker need not operate on this national scale to become immensely rich: regions or even individual cities offer plenty of scope for a man who is doing something different from what other banks are doing, and is right. He can start small. Leonard Weil in

Los Angeles set up shop as the Manufacturers Bank on a downtown block surrounded by offices of the four largest banks in California; his was the first new bank in downtown Los Angeles in a generation. In eleven years, he built to $250 million in deposits by aiming his services at the well-to-do customer with small needs that don't much interest the big bank—the dentist, the lawyer, the surgeon, the accountant, the small clothing maker. Adam Aronson looked at the crescent of suburban St. Louis and saw there was no way a home builder could miss, and he won the local real estate developers away from the big banks downtown by helping them warehouse land for future projects. This also made him a source of mortgage business for the local savings and loan associations, which, naturally, keep some of their necessary and sizable balances with the four subsidiaries of Aronson's Mark Twain Bancshares.

Hubert Rutland in St. Petersburg, Florida, was in his fifties and running the family department store when a lawyer friend persuaded him to be a more or less honorary chairman of the board of the newly organized St. Petersburg Bank & Trust. The man the lawyer had hired to run it quickly got the bank in trouble with bad loans to consumers, and examiners told the board to find another quarter of a million fast, to replace the losses, or close the bank. "I decided," Rutland says, "if there was going to be a loss of my money I'd rather lose it myself", and he took over the bank.

Fifteen years later Rutland owned three banks in St. Petersburg with total assets over $200 million, all built from scratch. He works in the smallest of them, which is called Rutland Central, and was built to his own designs. His office is where he wants it, built into a corner of the banking floor with floor-to-ceiling glass on two sides so he can see the people and the people can see him. He is a southern gentleman of an older school, with long silky white hair, and he dresses snappily in bright green slacks and checked green jacket, green shirt, and bow tie; on the walls that are not glass are collections of hunting scenes and hunting photographs, taken on his vast estates in Manatee County (behind Sarasota), of which he is reputed to own almost one-third. Among the sights he enjoys through his glass is the prettiest collection of mini-skirted bank employees this tourist saw in some years of visiting banks. Rutland (who has, one hastens to say, been married to the same wife for most of this century) likes women: the chief operating officers of two of his banks are women, one of them his former secretary, who learned on the job and took three summers of banking courses at Louisiana State. "Women officers do a better job than men", Rutland says. "And they're more loyal. You take a man, you make him a vice-president, you're paying him fifteen thousand dollars a year. Somebody comes along and offers him eighteen thousand, and he's gone. . .".

Essentially, Rutland's insight was that there were plenty of good customers for money in the booming Tampa Bay area; the banker's problem was to get people to give him the money so he could lend it. The week after he took over St. Petersburg Bank & Trust, Rutland opened the doors Saturday mornings, which no other bank in downtown St Pete does to this day; presently he started no-minimum-balance free chequeing (with a three-dollar charge for a bounced cheque); when visited in early 1974 he had just begun offering a new service, selling stamps at tellers' windows: "Your Friendly Rutland Bank", the sign at the door read, "Is Now Your Friendly Postal Station".

The Rutland banks have been going head-and-head against the St. Petersburg affiliates of the expanding Florida holding companies, and growing faster than any of them. Rutland is not a member of the Fed: "Can't see anything in it for me except costs". The First National Bank of Tampa picks up his cheque-clearing work every afternoon, via a helicopter that lands on the roof, and returns completed records to him the next morning.

"You know," Rutland said with an old man's expansiveness, stretching his legs under his desk, "people come in and say, 'Can I see Mr. Rutland?' And the girl says, 'Yes, just wait a minute'. He'll come in, and just shake my hand: he just wanted to meet Mr. Rutland. And that's right. You know, banking is the highest profession in the world—doctors come second—though that isn't the way I felt about it when I was a boy. Then I wanted to be a horse-trader. But that business about played out, and now I figure banking is the next thing to it. The other banks here are a clubby lot, but their club doesn't include me; they've opposed every one of my applications down to the last ditch".

4

Most of the country's obviously personal banking, of course, occurs in the small towns, like Lisbon, Iowa, where the road runs past rather than through—but the traveller is conscious that there is a town nearby, well-tended churches and a few two-storey brick buildings off to the left on the crossroad. The buildings are old, because this part of Iowa has been settled for a long time: since 1874, there has been a bank on the corner where the Lisbon Bank & Trust Company stands. Harry Sizer owns it now, a small, white-haired man in a short-sleeve shirt who works in a tiny private office beside the door, up front of the bank. There are three other banks within seven miles of Sizer's, eight banks within seventeen miles. The holding companies are moving in, but Iowa is still unit banking country. What has really made the difference, apparently, is bank advertising on broadcast media. "Cedar Rapids comes out and tells people they'll pay five and three-quarters percent", Sizer comments. "Then they quit, and they don't tell anybody that; they go back to five percent, and you're locked into two-year contracts at five and three-quarters". In the early 1960s, Sizer's deposits were four-fifths chequeing accounts, one-fifth savings accounts; in the early 1970s, they were three-fifths savings accounts.

Sizer is a product of Cedar Rapids Business College; he'd been offered a one-fourth scholarship at Cornell College ($56.25 a year; this is not Cornell University, but a small college on a hilltop with the most beautiful Victorian memorial chapel in America), but even with the scholarship he couldn't afford it. His first job was as an accountant with a bank in Washington, Iowa, in 1928. That one went under in 1931, and Sizer went to work for the state banking department. "But my wife was a Lisbon girl, daughter of a doctor", Sizer says. "The bank here was a private bank, Stuckslager and Auracher. Stuckslager asked me to come work here in 1941, and then he gave me a chance to buy the bank".

Lisbon Bank & Trust has about $3.5 million in footings, and in fall 1972 Sizer's problem was putting his money to work. "Thirty-five or forty percent of my loans are agricultural loans, but we don't have the cattle feeders around here anymore, and they're the big borrowers. We used to have the little fellows, who can go to market only once a year, not like the man with a thousand head who goes to market every week. We're starting now on the liquidation of soybeans, then corn, and we'll drop one hundred, two hundred thousand of loans". Sizer's bank in the 1960s had kept itself about two-thirds loaned up, but with the immense prosperity of Iowa in the early 1970s he was able to put out in the neighbourhood only about half of his money. The rest went into Treasury bills, municipal bonds, and on loan to city banks, who could make commercial loans and handle "Fed Funds". The bonds are kept at Northern Trust Company in Chicago, "which once had a vice-president who was a son-in-law of one of the Stuckslagers". The bank had three employees, plus Sizer and his son; the books were kept on a computer in Cedar Rapids, which cost Sizer $570 a month, including the price of the courier service which picks up his cheques and deposit slips every night and returns the complete computerized ledger of his bank before the doors open the next morning.

"The small-town banker is part of everything," Sizer says. "He has to be on the school board, his church committee. When they issue municipals, they want you to buy, or at least to find bidders. Our local businesses have been so prosperous they aren't borrowing, but there are things we need. If someone wanted to start a restaurant in this town, you'd go out on a limb a little to provide one. . . . And you have to lend the church some money, which is not the best loan in the world—the examiner looks at it and says he doesn't like it, but he understands what you want to do". Three to five percent of Sizer's loans were past due, but he wasn't worried: "Ninety-nine per cent of 'em are honest; if they want to hold the dry corn till after the first of the year, they'll tell me that's why they want the extension. And if there's a new man, our banks are close-knit—I'll call where he came from, and they'll tell you if he's a good man or a stinker.

"We're in the garden spot of Iowa—Lisbon was up twenty-eight percent in the 1950s, twelve percent more in the 1960s. I don't care about making a lot of money—I don't want to bleed the place. I have an insurance agency, and I don't have to pound the pavements at night to sell insurance. You know—old bankers never die, they just lose interest. I'm lucky: I have a son in with me who can take over the bank. But take a man who has no chick nor child—he's going to go, and he'll have to sell his bank to the holding company for one and a half percent of what it's worth".

The holding company is not the only possible buyer, though: there are still some ambitious young men around who long to own a little monopoly bank in a small town, who like the life of the country banker with its opportunities to be a big frog indeed in that local pond—and to make money, too. Nobody is so well placed as a bank examiner to make the transition from salaried working stiff to country banker, and every year some scores of bank examiners buy into a bank and step across this great divide. One of them in 1971 was Alan J. Mannetter, all of thirty-two years old, an FDIC examiner who found in Walker, Iowa, a bank that could be bought at a price he could raise on loan from Bankers Trust in Des Moines —and that needed him, or somebody like him, in the worst way. The need for Mannetter was not universally felt, however. "Nobody invited me into this town", he said a year later in an office at the back of the little bank, papered to look panelled, his desk surrounded by boxes of paper, letters, reports, and contracts he had to catch up with while doing the day's work and trying to look ahead. "I simply bought a controlling interest in the bank".

Walker is a town of six hundred people, shabby and dirty— sloppy lunch counter, grocery store with jumbled boxes in the window, muddy sidewalks, warehouses with slats out of the walls: all the signs of a town where the bank is dead. "There are three people who own half of this town", says Mannetter, looking younger than his age—compact, shiny round face, green shark-skin suit, pea-green shirt. "They don't want anybody making changes. I was the fourth manager of this bank last year, and you know what that's like. It's hard to hold the customers you have, they've had to tell the same story four times. My predecessor had cut off the cattle loans, and I went the other way, followed the prices up from thirty-one cents to thirty-eight or thirty-nine cents. [A year later they would be at seventy-six cents, and then they started down again.] Some of these farmers had too much machinery, they were too heavily in debt; I told them to hold off on the machinery, put the money into cattle and hogs. . . .

"This bank had had absentee ownership, one manager who was an alcoholic, one who took bankruptcy. We live here. I go bowling. I'm a member of the Lions Club. When I first came, I went around to all the merchants—those who had accounts with us and those who didn't. You know small towns: there was a banker here ten years ago people didn't like, they took their business away, and they're hard-headed, they won't come back. And everything goes to the city these days. The county takes the money from real estate taxes out of here in a day or two, and puts it in the city bank. I took my first loss the other day—eight hundred dollars on a car loan. I had another one where the guy took bankruptcy, but I went out to the farm and got his old man to pay it off. Our instalment loans are two hundred thirty-nine thousand dollars, up from one hundred fifty-four thousand a year ago—I've *tried*. I'm going ten years on real estate loans because we need loans so bad. Two of my directors are over seventy. You do the best job you can but you know that some day they're going to get to you. Still, I sell them insurance and I get the commissions on that, and they take their auto loans here, they keep their accounts here. We'll do all right".

(It might be mentioned that he didn't do all right: by summer 1975 Mannetter was gone from Walker.)

5

One-man operation of a big bank is by no means a certain blessing; indeed, it can be a damnation. William H. Bowen of the Commercial National Bank of Little Rock told an Assembly of

Bank Directors about a Georgia bank from which the president had embezzled $4.5 million: "He said his board was not involved or interested. They didn't stay around the bank much. They did not ask for and he did not give them much, if any, information about the bank. And thirdly, he reported, you give me thirty minutes, that's the kind of notice I have when my friendly auditors say they are coming, and I can cover up anything". Bank examiners require that everybody who works for a bank take at least one continuous two-week vacation every year. The theory, writes Ben B. McNew of the University of Mississippi, is "that a defrauder must be present in order to keep his thefts concealed and that a fortnight is sufficient time to uncover most illegal abstractions". The rule applies—most examiners would say that it applies especially—to the chief executive officer of the bank: if he is fiddling, the bank may be in real trouble.

Banks are not allowed to make loans to their own officers except for home mortgages (and those are supposed to be rather modest), but there is no prohibition against loans to corporations in which an officer of the bank is a controlling stockholder. "The largest single cause of bank failures," says Jack T. Conn of Fidelity Bank in Oklahoma City, "is misuse of banking assets by directors and officers". With a little ingenuity, a bank president can conceal almost completely from his directors, examiners, and auditors loans that he is making for his own benefit. A federal grand jury in Los Angeles, for example, has indicted the former president of the small Southland National Bank for a scheme in 1968 by which he and a friend with a chain of proprietary nursing homes planned to take advantage of the "hot issue" status of such properties by selling inflated stock to the public. To get the ball rolling, the grand jury says, the bank president arranged to make loans to doctors who would buy shares in the nursing-home company, using the shares themselves as collateral for the loans. Where there are holding companies with affiliated banks separately audited and examined, the opportunities for such razzle-dazzle are almost unlimited, and the perpetrators won't be apprehended for years.

A remarkable range of possibilities confronts a crooked bank president. He can launder securities by making loans secured by stolen goods, he can arrange kickbacks (preferably through third parties) on the loans his bank makes, he can finance the takeover of a legitimate business by the mob—all without much real risk to himself or (the only thing a bank examiner cares about) loss to his bank. There has been less of this than normal probabilities would have predicted, but now that the federal courts have taken to ruling that the Comptroller cannot deny a bank charter to a man just because he's a convicted swindler (after all, he served his time), we can probably expect more.

During the 1920s, it was standard operating procedure for the senior executives of large banks to mingle their own affairs with those of the banks' securities affiliates in ways that guaranteed them enormous profits, even if the bank and its affiliates suffered losses. Charles E. Mitchell of National City and Albert H. Wiggin of Chase used their banks' funds shamelessly for their own speculations. Such activities would be clearly illegal today. Both Bank of the Commonwealth in Detroit and U.S. National in San Diego may have been subject to criminal misconduct before they fell, but most of the considerable financial collapses of the last decade—Penn Central, Equity Funding, IOS, Atlantic Acceptance, LTV, Francis I. Dupont, Four Seasons Nursing Homes, National Student Marketing—have involved banks and bankers as victims rather than as villains. There is a lot of bad judgment and optimistic incompetence around, and no doubt there is some hanky-panky here and there. And everyone in banking lives with the fear that somewhere in the system a crooked bank president and a computer wizard have got together to concoct a major fraud. But it would come as a great surprise to a number of inherently suspicious observers—including me—if even the grimmest of futures were to reveal any ponderable quantity of corruption of major bankers.

Anyway, an $800,000 million banking system can absorb an immense amount of swindling before any of it even begins to show up in the consolidated statistics. The real problem of the one-man show is not the minuscule chance that the one man is a crook, but the likelihood that what he builds will get too big for him to control, or will fall apart after he leaves.

Semenenko might or might not have been able to pull Curtis Publishing (*The Saturday Evening Post*) out of its slough of despond; but once he was gone there was no chance at all that his successors in the special industries division at First of Boston could perform such magic tricks. Since the Bimsons (there were three of them) and their sidekick Lester Patrick left the scene at Valley National Bank of Arizona, The Arizona Bank has been beating up its giant competitor all over the state. Bank of America was twenty years regaining its vitality after the Gianninis departed, Citizens & Southern began to show reduced earnings within a few months of Mills Lane's stroke. How much the strength of Chase had been that of Winthrop Aldrich became apparent soon after the direction of the bank passed into the hands of his nephew David Rockefeller.

Arthur Roth's Franklin National is an extreme case. There is no need at this distance in time to take sides between Roth and the directors who removed him as chairman and chief executive officer of the bank in 1968. His version of the story is that he was betrayed by his former assistant, Harold Gleason (who took his job), and by an unbusinesslike board on which he had placed political leaders from both parties. The board's story is that Roth had been less than level with them about the extent of the loan losses emerging at the bank. The two explanations are not mutually exclusive.

It seems clear enough now that Roth's decision to expand into New York City in 1964 was a mistake: all the good neighbourhoods were pretty fully banked, and all the best borrowers were pretty assiduously served. (A Wall Street lawyer remembers with malicious amusement that "whenever you had an idea that wasn't really bankable, you took it to Franklin".) The bank did get some prime customers in 1966, when Roth had money (for reasons we shall look at later) and his colleagues did not; but the average quality of the clientele was unquestionably low for a bank that grew to be as big as Franklin. (Roth, not surprisingly, demurs: "Of course, when you open a new branch, people come around who've been turned down elsewhere, and, yes, you take some you shouldn't because the branch needs business. But we had good locations, and so long as I ran the bank, the New York 'metropolitan' division was profit-able".) In any event, real estate was Roth's expertise, and in the 1960s well-meant but unwise government initiatives converted real estate from a legitimate business to a giant tax dodge.

But the directors had nobody to take Roth's place after he was removed as chairman; they wound up entrusting their bank willy-nilly to Larry Tisch of Loew's (who bought the stock in the market with help from Morris Schapiro), and then to Michele Sindona, an international wheeler-dealer from Italy who bought Tisch's hold-ings and whose obvious capability and impressive personality appear to have hidden the temperament of a restless gamber. Neither of these new controlling stockholders knew enough to rescue the bank from men who necessarily, in the absence of direction, kept doing what Roth had taught them to do but with less imagination and worse judgment. Roth spoke out against the impending destruction of the bank he had built while he was still a director, with the result that he was booted off the board in 1970.

As everyone who reads newspapers knows, Franklin blew up noisily in spring 1974, the victim of bad loans too long concealed, overly creative accounting practices, misjudgments in securities trading and investment, over reliance on borrowed short-term money, and speculation or skullduggery in foreign exchange trad-ing. This list may not be complete. At the time its troubles were announced, Franklin was the twentieth largest bank in the United States, and the Federal Reserve System force-fed it with money to prevent its collapse, lending it at the "discount window" sums that in some weeks ran up to $1,700 million. All these loans were secured (loans from the Fed must be secured), but Franklin's "eligible" collateral was quickly used up by its needs and the Fed ultimately had to scrape up some pretty weak paper from Franklin's vaults to back the borrowings. During the height of the agitation, this tourist had occasion to say to a very senior officer of the Fed of New York that it would be fun to watch the Reserve Bank try to dispose of that collateral if Franklin were declared insolvent. "Martin," said the senior officer, "you're not entitled to that much fun."

Though the story is very complicated and many of its details may never be known, the many New York bankers who disliked Arthur Roth as an arrogant parvenu can make a reasonable case for their proposition that the seeds of disaster were sown before he left the bank. (He believes they were always prejudiced against him because they thought he was Jewish, which he isn't.) It is almost certainly a bad idea for a $3,000 million bank to be as much a one-man show as Franklin was under Roth. More interesting, because the answer has policy implications, is the question of whether Nassau County's present deterioration (which is the root cause of Franklin's weaknesses) could have been avoided or at least slowed by keeping Roth's and Franklin's noses to their own grindstone.

When the crunch came, the regulatory agencies were mesmerized by the antitrust division of the Justice Department, too terrified to approve what was initially a viable merger of Franklin into Manufacturers Hanover. The Fed was a natural mark for an experienced operator like Michele Sindona, and on his personal assurance that he would retrieve the situation the discount window was flung open for Franklin. By the time the Fed noticed that its wallet was missing, Manny Hanny was demanding FDIC guarantees of Franklin's loan portfolios before undertaking any salvage work, and FDIC saw no reason why it should rescue the Fed. Finally, after the Fed had undertaken the risks of Franklin's foreign exchange book (which the rising dollar brought over water—indeed, made buoyantly profitable—in 1975), FDIC did come through to make possible Franklin's absorption by European-American, a syndicate that includes Britain's Midland. Despite Franklin's squalid end, three decades of growth in Nassau County remained an important monument to the work begun in Franklin Square. Meanwhile, Arthur Roth is at it again, pretending to be retired, working most days of the week in connection with the new Bank of Suffolk County in Stony Brook, which had $20 million in deposits when he became its chairman in 1970, and was pushing $100 million in 1974.

PART

II

—

WHERE THE MONEY COMES FROM

6/The Cheque System

The nearly 14,000 commercial banks in this country held some 94 million demand deposit accounts in 1972. . . . The number of checking accounts, moreover, is rising faster than the number of households, which in turn is rising faster than the population. . . . With all the steps that have been taken by the banking industry and the Federal Reserve to meet these problems, banks continue to choke on check volume.

—THOMAS O. WAAGE, senior vice-president, Federal Reserve Bank of New York

* * *

The process described below is considerably more complicated than what happens in Britain, though the results are of course the same and much of the machinery now in use in Britain was originally developed to manage the much greater volume and much more varied distribution of items detailed here. I have cut the tale of the processing of my cheque somewhat less than I had thought I would for British publication, partly because most lay readers seem to have enjoyed the narrative and its personae, partly because it seems to me that the detailed description of the actual operation of any complicated piece of social machinery has values for people who seek an understanding of the life of their time. I have pointed out aspects of the cheque system that are different in the United Kingdom, and added some material on the one part of the operation—the Clearing House—where the differences are significantly influential in commercial activity.

In November 1973 I purchased 42.7 gallons of gasoline and 33.6 gallons of fuel oil from Piccozzi's Service Station on Route 114 in Shelter Island, N.Y., and on December 1, promptly, Jake Piccozzi sent me a bill for $27.33. He got my cheque on December 5, and put it together with a number of other cheques for a total deposit of $396.30. Though he has a book-keeper, Mrs. Peggy Payne, who used to work in a bank, Jake runs up his deposits himself on his adding machine, and simply sends the adding-machine tape to the bank with the cheques and a deposit slip for the total amount. His bank is the Shelter Island branch of the Valley Bank of Long Island, and he has been a depositor there since it opened—as a branch of the First National Bank of Greenport—in 1952. That was the first bank on Shelter Island, and Piccozzi, as a founding member of the Shelter Island Lions Club, was one of the men who petitioned the Greenport bank to open the branch. "Before then," he recalls, "I kept a nice speedboat at the dock here, and I would go to Greenport to the bank every day for change. It was some work to get that bank here; at first they didn't care". Donald Deale, assistant vice-president in charge of the Shelter Island branch, is the grandson of the man who owned the dock at which Piccozzi kept his speedboat.

Gene Tybaert, who works for Piccozzi and teaches first aid for the Red Cross and each Memorial Day since World War II has served as first marshal of the American Legion parade, took my cheque to the bank, a neat, neo-colonial one-storey brick building to which was added, a couple of years ago, a rather incongruous drive-in window with a separate portico in the parking lot. The teller on duty in the bank was Mrs. Harriet Case. She looked at each cheque in Piccozzi's deposit and compared it with the adding-machine tape, confirmed the fact of endorsement, and gave Tybaert a duplicate slip to take back to the office. She did not add up any totals herself (and might not have done so on Piccozzi's deposit even if she did so for others: "He never makes a mistake", said Mrs. Case). In a big-city bank, she would not have compared the items and the slip, either: there's not time for that.

The three tellers in the Shelter Island branch (there is no back-office staff) "post" all the deposits, withdrawals, and interest credits in the bank's local savings accounts, but they have no duties other than the work at the window in connection with the chequing accounts. My cheque to Piccozzi's simply sat on the shelf until 3.30, when Pete Pearson, a retired state parks security officer with a lined, cowboy face, came by in a battered Plymouth to pick up the Shelter Island "work". All cheques related to the eastern Long Island branches of Valley Bank are processed initially in East Hampton. There are two basic routes to service the branches, on the north and south forks of Long Island, and the drivers trade runs every week, partly because the drive out to Montauk and back make for a longer day, partly because "Otherwise," Pearson said, "you could get bored". Every once in a while Pearson carries cash from branch to branch, though that is not the game plan— cash is supposed to be delivered by armoured truck. (The Shelter Island branch orders its cash delivered by registered mail from the Federal Reserve Bank of New York; the armoured truck doesn't come on the island.) On December 5, Pearson carried canvas sacks of cancelled cheques; small sacks.

The East Hampton branch is a more pretentious version of the same colonial style. It was closed at 4.15. Pearson unlocked the back door to the bank and a door just inside that opened on to a flight of stairs to a cellar. Downstairs, Mrs. Carol Salisbury and Mrs. Libby Ott were waiting for the work in a spacious room with green walls, a low ceiling, and a vinyl tile floor. They immediately opened Pearson's sacks and took the cheques to a pair of beige National Cash Register machines, about the size of upright pianos, which would "prove" the day's deposits and withdrawals and "inscribe" the cheques and various other slips sent from the branches. When they were finished, the dollars and cents repre- sented by each piece of paper would appear on it in the funny- looking numbers of the "Magnetic Ink Character Recognition" (MICR) code that enables computers to handle the rest of the processing. British cheques are identically encoded by the same sort of machine—though the numbers of course express pounds and new pence rather than dollars and cents.

The MICR code was established by a committee of the Ameri- can Bankers Association in 1956, and today virtually every cheque in a chequebook supplied to a depositor by a bank contains a string of these special machine-readable numbers in the lower left-hand corner. From left to right, the numbers tell the geographic loca- tion of the bank in which the account is maintained (on my cheque, 0210, which stands for New York City), the "name" of the bank itself (0030, which stands for Manufacturers Hanover Trust Com- pany), the branch (009) and the account number (which is my own business) of the depositor to whom the cheque was supplied. The cheque can thus be sorted by machine at a first processing centre for delivery to the appropriate Federal Reserve office, at the Reserve's Cheque Processing Centre for debit to the paying bank, and within the paying bank to be charged against the right account. What Mrs. Salisbury and Mrs. Ott added at their NCR machines was simply the amount for which this cheque was written— 0000002733.

At an inscribing machine, the operator places a small stack of cheques face up on a rack, and bats out on an adding-machine keyboard the amount of money represented by the cheque on top. (Among the intellectual accomplishments of the last generation is the modern adding-machine keyboard, with its single block of number buttons that lie conveniently under the fingers: if operators still had to work on old-fashioned adding machines, with ten buttons in a row for each order of magnitude, the day's work could never get done.) The numbers entered print out on a standard adding-machine tape at the operator's right. She then drops the top check on to a sloping stainless steel tray, at the bottom of which it makes contact with a pair of small rubber rollers that slap it into a stamping machine, still face up. The stamping machine automatically inscribes in MICR numbers right under the signature the dollar value that has just been entered on the adding-machine tape, and simultaneously stamps the back of the cheque with a coloured-in logo that announces (in a form only people can read) the name of the bank that has accepted the cheque and guaranteed all prior endorsements, the branch at which it was accepted, the date, and the place in the day's run of work that this particular slip of paper occupied. My cheque to Piccozzi's Service Station was the 2,067th item processed on Mrs. Salisbury's machine on December 5, 1973. After it was encoded and endorsed, the rubber wheels shot it to the opposite end of the stainless steel shelf, whence it dropped on to a growing stack of cheques in a "pocket" to the operator's left. A new IBM inscribing machine used at some of the big banks sorts cheques into various pockets for various purposes while printing the MICR number for the amount.

It will be noted that apart from the endorsement (which may be ambiguous if the account is in the name of John Smith and there are other depositors named John Smith at the branch), there is nothing on a cheque to indicate *who* deposited it. If anything were wrong with my cheque, however, the information on the rear stamp would help Valley Bank trace the identity of the depositor who was credited with it and should now be told he is out of luck. Locating and debiting the depositor on whom a cheque has been bounced is still a hand operation and a great pain in the neck— and possibly a fundamental constraint on the development of the Electronic Funds Transfer System advertised as the wave of the future. "It's hard enough to reject a cheque", says Barry Sullivan, chief of operations for Chase Manhattan. "How do you reject an electronic blip?"

At Mrs. Salisbury's machine, my cheque lost its individual status as money and become part of a flow of money that—if all went well—would not have to be broken into its contributory streams until the time came to debit the individual accounts. This necessary miracle is accomplished by the magic of double-entry book-keeping, an invention of the Renaissance which is still a mystery to most educated Europeans and Americans, thanks to six centuries of incompetence in our educational community. Mrs. Salisbury processes not only the cheques but also the deposit slips (which are marked with an "01" prefix in MICR, to tell the computer that this is a deposit) and the tellers' slips indicating the receipt of cash. Cheques that have been cashed are recorded twice, as a debit item and a credit item on the adding-machine tape. When all the cheques and slips from a teller's cage have been rung up on the adding machine and encoded with the MICR, the adding-machine tapes should show a zero total: the credits and the debits to the bank should be equal. This "proves" the day's work by this teller. Mrs. Salisbury processed the items that came to her at a rate of fifty or so per minute, the fingers of her left hand dancing on the keys. Then she summed the tape, and the answer came up 00.00.

Working on the bundles Pearson had brought, Mrs. Salisbury made two mistakes, both of which she caught almost immediately after hitting the wrong numbers. She then cancelled out the wrong result on the adding-machine tape and substituted the correct figure—but the damage was done on the cheque, already encoded with an erroneous MICR number, which cannot be erased. Mrs. Salisbury removed each of these cheques from the stack, took a plastic rubber squeeze bottle and dabbed a smear of transparent liquid wax over the wrong number. When these cheques appeared at the cheque sorters for further processing, the computer would reject them as magnetically unreadable for amount, and send them to a separate pocket, to be processed by hand.

As the proof of each teller's work came off the machine, the cheques and slips and the adding-machine tape that expressed them were bundled together with a rubber band and placed in a canvas sack marked RETURN TO THE FEDERAL RESERVE BANK OF (as it happened) PHILADELPHIA. Federal Reserve sacks, like railway boxcars, travel around the system. Mrs. Salisbury and Mrs. Ott had to work fast: they could get started on East Hampton's own paper as early as 3.30, but the material from the north fork and Shelter Island did not arrive until almost 4.30, while the delivery from Montauk would not show until after 5—and everything would have to be ready to go at 5.30. On December 5, this was not an urgent problem—the entire day's work was only about 6,000 items. Mrs. Salisbury even had time to share a cup of coffee with her visitor, and to comment on the Christmas blah playing on the bank's sound system: "Every year it's the same tape. Could you say in your book that the music is *boring?*" In midsummer, however, when the beautiful people are on the beaches, Valley Bank can do 20,000 items of business at the eastern end of Long Island; then Mrs. Salisbury and Mrs. Ott have a third person working with them on a third machine, but it can still be murder to get everything encoded, proved, and sacked before the driver arrives at 5.30.

On this night the driver was a rangy, grey-haired man named Walter Dembeck, an A & P night manager who moonlights in the early evening as a driver for American Purolater, the company that has the courier contract for most Long Island banks and the Federal Reserve Bank of New York. Dembeck drove his own car, a station wagon; American Purolater in late 1973 paid him eight cents a mile (not much) plus five dollars an hour for the sixteen hours a week he spent on the road for them. He was glad to have company on a rainy night, but he rather likes the work—"I never see a boss"—and with a wife and four children he hopes to see through college, he needs the money.

Dembeck's route took him from East Hampton to a bank in Riverhead, where he picked up another pair of gunny sacks stashed in an outside safe he opened with a key, and then to a bank in East Islip, which does the cheque processing for the Riverhead bank. Here he handed over the Riverhead work, and usually left in a deposit box the Valley Bank work to be picked up by the next driver. On this evening, however, the next man—Hank Schaffer, a small and rather weary post office clerk from Commack—was at the Islip bank waiting for him, and he simply handed over the sacks. It was now seven o'clock.

Schaffer put the sacks in the back seat of his family four-door sedan and scooted off to the new, much advertised, and (given the nature of the beast) rather elegant Green Acres shopping centre in Valley Stream. Valley Bank's operations centre is in the basement area of this complex, a remarkably slummy underground driveway (apparently never cleaned, and full of water on a rainy night). Normally Schaffer simply leaves the sacks in a steel box outside the door, but tonight he had a companion in his car, so he rang the bell and handed in the sacks at 7.55.

The arrival of the work from eastern branches started a maelstrom of activity by the two young men and four women on duty in the operations section, which consists of a bullpen with about fifteen desks and a glassed-in area containing the score of green and gun-metal units that work together in the Burroughs bank computer system. The heart of that system, of course, is the mass of spaghetti wiring and transistors hidden inside the big standing steel boxes, revealing nothing to the observer beyond the flickering of a panel of little yellow lights on the face of one of them. But there are fantastic things to see out on the periphery, where a cheque sorter-cum-reader and a high-speed print-out typewriter bang out visible evidence of a job being done.

This is truly spectacular machinery. The unit that physically handles the cheques is about the length of an intermediate-sized automobile. In the Burroughs version, the stack of cheques, deposit slips, and book-keeping tickets is placed on a shelf with the cheques on their side, a hydraulically operated moving-bookend pressing them against a rubber wheel that will pull each from the horizontal stack into a narrow slot between two steel plates. In the slot the cheque or slip is picked up by a transmission belt that carries it around a U-turn, past a magnetic head that reads the MICR numbers along the bottom. Zipping along at about fifteen miles an hour, the cheque rides over a series of thirteen little gates covering other curving slots. Responding to a signal from the MICR reader, one of these gates opens and shuts with invisible speed; the cheque slips into the slot, curves down and around to land in one of thirteen pockets. This machine reads and sorts cheques and slips at a rate of about a thousand a minute. Among its incredible accomplishments is the fact that these fragile pieces of paper, whipped along so fast and changing direction so violently (a cheque that has been roaring along the length of the machine winds up in the pocket facing at right angles to its previous motion), emerge without so much as a crease.

The resting place of the cheque is determined, of course, by the programme that has been inserted in the machine. For the batch of work arriving from East Hampton, six of the pockets were employed: (1) for deposit slips and cash items ("internal documents"); (2) for cheques "on us" (i.e. drawn against accounts in, some branch of Valley Bank); (3) for cheques on other Long Island banks; (4) for cheques on New York City Clearing House banks; (5) for cheques on banks outside New York and Long Island (which would go to Valley's big-city "correspondent bank", the Bank of New York, to be credited to Valley's account there and collected with that bank's other work back to the issuers); and (6) alas!, for cheques the machine could not read.

While the cheques and slips were finding homes in pockets, the high-speed print-out unit and a magnetic tape-recording unit at the other end of the room were registering all the information read off the items in mid-flight. The printer uses the standard large-size striped green-and-white IBM paper, one long sheet folded into a stack, perforated for easy separation of individual pages, with holes along the sides for sprockets that help the platen on the printer pull paper rapidly through the machine, single-spaced or double-spaced. The paper comes to rest for intervals of about a twentieth of a second, and in each interval the electronically controlled printer bangs on a row of five sets of numbers: each line prints the location and "name" of the bank, and the amount of money called for, on each of five cheques that have just gone past the reader.

At the end of the batch, the print-out supplies totals for the machine-readable items in each bundle, and compares the "debit" totals (deposit slips and cash paid out) against the "credit" totals (the cheques or cash received). Unless something has gone seriously wrong, discrepancies between total credits and total debits in each batch must be acccounted for by the items in the pocket to which the machine has sent the pieces of paper it cannot read. Cheques in that category are not ignored on the print-out: they appear as asterisks and blank spaces in the order in which they were processed. But that doesn't solve the problem of "balancing the bank", and the rest of the work must be done by hand.

On this evening, this work was being done at a dead run. Michael Jablon, a fair, slight young man helping at the machine, tore the sheets from the printer, bundled the contents of each pocket of cheques with a rubber band, wrapped the print-out sheets around all of them, and ran his package out of the glassed-in computer room to a large, strenuous, almost miraculously efficient blonde girl, Dolores Johnson, who sat at an antique cash-register-like machine against one wall of the bullpen. This was a noisy black beast, rows of ten keys running down its fat face for each order of magnitude, totals added mechanically (though the impulse for the mechanical motion was electrical). Beside it were a number of pockets—little drawers with black lids—matching in function the pockets on the Burroughs machine. Miss Johnson matched each cheque in her stack with the appropriate hole in the computer print-out, registered the totals on an adding-machine tape, and slotted the cheque itself in a pocket. The machine meanwhile generated a set of MICR encoded slips which would run through the Burroughs unit to keep the computer *au courant* with Miss Johnson's hand-made adjustments.

Each batch of the machine-readable cheques, sorted by destination, now went back to the Burroughs processor, which printed out a list and a total for the bundles of cheques to be sent to each address; and Jablon stacked the bundles, each accompanied by its print-out sheet, in brown stiff-cardboard boxes about one foot wide, half a foot high and three feet long—long enough to hold about twenty-five hundred cheques. These boxes are specially made to the order of the Federal Reserve Bank, which supplies them without charge to its member banks: the work at the Fed processing centres is eased if the cheques arrive in this packaging rather than in lumpy sacks. (In London, cheques move around in rather similar translucent plastic boxes supplied by the Clearing House.) The boxes wound up on a desk near the middle of the bullpen, manned by Ann Kiernan, a slight, quick woman with greying hair and fast fingers. Working on a conventional adding machine, she listed the totals on the bundles, then added in the cheques from Dolores's machine ("Ann, do you want the non-machineable?"). Miss Johnson, the supervisor of the work, finally authorized the "cash letter", the total on Mrs. Kiernan's tapes that expressed the claim on the world's other banks which Valley Bank was entitled to make as a result of the deposit of all these cheques.

Three sets of cash letters were prepared, for claims on Long Island banks, on banks in New York, and on banks reached via Valley's correspondent. The first set of boxes—about three-quarters of the total, because most banking business still involves cheques on nearby banks—would go to the new Federal Reserve Regional Cheque Processing Centre (RCPC) just off the Long Island Expressway in Jericho; the second set would go to Wall Street, to the main office of the New York Federal Reserve Bank, in a gigantically expanded block-square Florentine palace. The two cash letters that went to the Fed in New York, including my $27.33, ran just over $3 million.

By getting the boxes to the Fed tonight rather than tomorrow, Valley Bank will gain a day's use of $3 million. Law and regulation require every member bank to have in cash in its vaults or on deposit at the Fed a certain proportion of its total deposits. Each "cash letter" to the Fed is credited directly to the reserve account. Banks that have insufficient reserves of their own can and do borrow (by convention, "buy") what are called "Fed Funds" from banks that don't at this moment need all the reserves they have. The money in tonight's cash letter can be loaned out to another bank tomorrow (or can save the bank the necessity of borrowing, which amounts to the same thing). With Fed Funds at 10 percent, where they were through most of 1973, a one-day difference in obtaining a $3 million credit means about $822 to the bank— something more than the total daily salary of the night staff that works at processing cheques in this room. "The secret of this business," says George Skoglund, who ran the California branches of Bank of America, "is to collect that cheque as quickly as possible".

On December 3, Valley's cash letters had not been ready when the driver came to take them away, the bank had lost a day at the Fed, and management had discussed the matter with its employees. On December 5, therefore, though the problems earlier in the week had been caused by machine failures, everyone was running—but not uncheerfully. Once the cash letter was finished, the boxes stacked by the door ready to go, the pace could be relaxed. At 8.40—three-quarters of an hour after the work had arrived from eastern Long Island—the four women and Michael and their visitor sat around a table in a back room, drinking coffee from plastic cups and nibbling at a supermarket Danish pastry ring one of the women had contributed to the evening. This is a congenial crew of people. "There's a camaraderie", says Robert Stabile, who heads the night staff at the Data Processing Centre in New York's Manufacturers Hanover; "there are just a few reasons why people work at night. People who work during the day are normal; people who work at night are not-so-normal".

(Indeed so: I am myself a person who works at night.) The women talked about police protection around Green Acres, which was judged inadequate; and about the Danish, which was given high marks.

(In Britain, much of this work would be unnecessary. Because there are effectively only four clearing banks against which cheques presented at an out-of-London branch are likely to be drawn, the basic sorting can be performed by the teller at the window in the branch, who simply places each cheque that comes over her counter into one of four pigeonholes before her. Every so often a messenger comes by and empties the pigeonholes, taking the cheques to an MICR inscriber in the branch itself, and amounts are encoded on the cheques continuously, as a clerk has time. Because the cheques are pre-sorted by issuing bank before they come to the inscriber, the clerk merely takes them in batches and slots them, now encoded, into new pigeonholes by the machine. At the close of day, a rubber band is placed around the contents of each pigeonhole, all the cheques that came in that day are dropped into a grey mailbag supplied by the Post Office, and a messenger carries the bag to the neighbourhood postal branch, for delivery the next morning to head office in London. The only nightwork is done by the postmen, as part of their normal mail delivery services.

(On arrival in London, the cheques go through machines much like those at Valley Bank, except that there is no need to process for destination. A separate cash letter—essentially, as in America, an adding machine tape—is prepared for delivery to each of the other clearing banks at the Clearing House that morning. What the computer does is prepare an "audit list", debiting the bank's own books for the cash paid out and crediting them for the cheques deposited; and a "master list", crediting the customers' accounts for their deposits. The results of this internal bookkeeping on this day's mail delivery are sent out on computer tape to the clearing bank's computer centre, which is in the countryside because rental space is too expensive to be used for such purposes in London.)

2

Before accompanying my cheque on its journey to New York, let us pause for a moment to consider what will now happen to Jake Piccozzi's deposit. All the checks in his $396,30 entry had been machine-readable: his deposit had proved. All his credits had therefore been entered on the magnetic tape that jerked about behind glass, duplicating in its way what was coming out of the fast printer. Later that night, after the girls had balanced the bank, the computer would "merge" the tape of today's transactions into the existing computerized "ledger" of the bank. And the fast printer would then produce for each Valley Bank branch a complete statement of how each account in that branch stood as of the morning of the new day. Donald Deale, arriving for work, would find the envelope in his branch's outside deposit box, left there by Pete Pearson.

In theory, by Valley Bank rules, Piccozzi's deposit would not constitute "good funds"—money he could draw out—for ten whole days. In fact, the necessities of double-entry bookkeeping make Valley Bank credit the deposit of his account immediately. The cash letter that goes out becomes part of Valley's statement of assets, under the heading of "Cash and Due from Banks", and to balance that asset Valley must show a liability under the heading "deposits". The print-out Deale receives supplies for each Shelter Island customer four separate credit figures—Account Balance, 1-Day Uncollected, Total Uncollected, and Available Funds. For a customer Deale does not know, all cheques to be honoured would have to be covered by Available Funds (plus, probably, the "1-Day Uncollected", which is the sum of the cheques deposited nine days ago: if anything were wrong with those, it would almost certainly have showed up by now). But the fact of the matter is that Jake Piccozzi will be able to draw against today's deposit by tomorrow. The North Fork Bank and Trust Company also has a branch on Shelter Island, and if Deale does not give immediate credit to Piccozzi his rival will. For all cheques drawn on New York and Long Island banks (and almost all Piccozzi's cheques fit into these categories), Valley Bank will have credit on the books of the Fed the day after the night the cheques were processed. The chances that Piccozzi's customer's banks will bounce any of these cheques are exceedingly remote—and if it happens, after all, Piccozzi has a solid business and will be able to take the loss himself: the bank has nothing at risk.

In those cases where the bank does collect on the cheques a customer has deposited and then denies him credit for ten days, the bank has a "float", probably best defined (by Russell Fenwick of Bank of America) as "two credit balances represented by the same funds". There is an enormous amount of float in the American banking system, generated in various ways. A situation not unlike that of the customer whose use of a deposit is blocked for ten days is created every time someone writes a cheque to pay a bill and puts it in the mail. He deducts the amount of that cheque from his working balance in his chequebook, but his bank does not see it until it has passed through the hands of the person whose bill is being paid, that person's bank, and the clearing mechanism. During that time, the customer's bank continues to have the unrestricted use of customer money to which the customer no longer has a claim.

This is a bank's float "on a customer". For some banks, it is a known and significant item. State governments, for example, typically make deposits to cover their cheques on the day the cheques are written, and the bank can predict from experience how fast that money will run out; during the time while the cheques are being distributed, the bank invests the money in short-term money-market instruments. Big banks undertake the computerized labour of preparing and mailing dividend cheques for corporations, and charge little or nothing for it, because some recipients are slow to cash them, leaving the bank the use of the money the corporation deposited to cover the payment of the cheques. This situation exists in Britain, too; it is the reason why banks bid against each other for the privilege of handling the accounts of local authorities and government departments.

An unscrupulous bank can do better than that by denying its

customers access to funds for an unconscionably long time after the money is collected from other banks. A lawsuit brought in summer 1974 by a Catholic priest with a penchant for the stock market revealed that at least one (unnamed) Chicago bank will not give its depositors credit for a cheque drawn on a New York bank (and collected within two days) until fourteen days after the deposit; as a result, the priest's cheque to a brokerage house was bounced. In Europe, deliberate expansion of the float is a way of life: French banks routinely debit an account as of the date two days *before* a cheque drawn on that account is actually presented, and date each deposit to the account two days after the money is in hand. When the transfer is international, the delay is even more scandalous. Thibaut de Saint Phalle of the Centre d'Etudes Industrielles of Geneva reports that the average delay in crediting a payment from Italy to Belgium (or vice versa) is "between fifteen and eighteen days". These are the same banks that lease wires between their computers to credit transactions to themselves on an overnight basis—or even on the same day.

In Britain, faith in the Post Office and the ethos of fair play have routinized the situation, leaving no discretion to banks or branch managers. A cheque deposited in a branch of a clearing bank drawn on another clearing bank is "good funds" three days later. Within the City itself, as we shall see, credit is all but immediate.

The most common yet most romantic float in America is the customer's float "on a bank", of which the most obvious example is the cheque cashed by a bank other than the one on which it is written. The customer has immediate use of funds the bank will not recover for at least a day. If my cheque to Piccozzi's had been written on a bank in Pocatello, Idaho, Valley's correspondent bank would not have received credit from the Fed for its delivery of that cheque to the processing centre until two days after the date of delivery. Meanwhile, via float, Piccozzi's would have had the use of the money, because Valley does not hold his account to its ten-day rule.

In the old days, before cheque clearing became as rapid as it is now, "cheque-kiting" schemes exploited the float for the benefit of swindlers, who could write a cheque for far more than was in an account, deposit that cheque at another bank, use the credit gained at the other bank for other purposes, and keep the transaction going by making a deposit sufficient to cover the first cheque at the bank on which it had been drawn, just before it was presented. The new deposit, of course, could be made by means of a cheque drawn on still a third bank, where the swindler's account did not have sufficient funds. . . . Fast footwork was always needed for this sort of fraud, and eventually cheque-kiting schemes were exposed, but in the days when it really took a week to ten days to clear a cheque considerable sums could be generated. Even now it isn't entirely impossible: a Florida real estate developer in 1972 ran a $5 million kite between Hubert Rutland's St. Petersburg Bank & Trust and the First National Bank of St. Petersburg. In early 1976, a federal indictment charged the largest American title insurance company with running a nationwide kite in hundreds of millions of dollars throughout the 1960s.

It should be noted that if I kept my bank account in Pocatello, Idaho, I could generate float for my own benefit, because I could expect that it would take several days for my payment to Piccozzi to be effectively debited against my account. United Air Lines pays its California employees with cheques drawn on Chicago banks to benefit by this sort of customer float "on a bank". Note also that *somebody* necessarily gets this float. If I really am from Pocatello, Idaho, my account is naturally there and I am not kiting cheques on my float, the bank in Pocatello has a float on me because they still have the use of the money I have deducted from my chequebook balance when I wrote the cheque—and after the expiration of the Fed's two days the Valley Bank and its correspondent may have a float on Pocatello.

Bank float on other banks is the largest and most important category of float. Even today, though the big banks are beginning to wise up to what is happening to them, "country banks" like Valley are major beneficiaries of float from their "reserve city" correspondents. (Nearly half the cheques cleared come through correspondent arrangements.) Traditionally, the big bank gives its little correspondent instant credit on such clearings, though it will not receive credit itself for one to three days. The balances on the big bank's books may be very large: when the Fed opened a cheque processing centre in Miami, the First National Bank of Miami showed a $100 million drop in deposits. But the float makes many such deposits an accounting artifact, not real money.

Richard Thornton of First Pennsylvania, which is getting out of the correspondent business, recalls that when he began looking into this situation he found that "some of these million-dollar accounts were a dead loss. We are letting them use uncollected funds, we were borrowing to carry their deposits on our reserves, and meanwhile letting them sell us Fed Funds because they seemed to have excess reserves. We were paying twice for the money, and it was our own money. . . ." According to Gabriel Hauge, chairman of Manufacturers Hanover, which has the largest correspondent banking business in the country, with more than $2,000 million of deposits from other banks, "Calculating the profitability of correspondent bank relationships is a nightmare; it defies rational analysis". How can anyone put a price on the value of local information that can be got from a properly nurtured correspondent bank?

When a Fed processing centre credits a bank for a delivery before it actually debits the bank on which the cheque was drawn, there is a float "on the Fed". Bad weather, which delays the movement of cheques from one part of the country to another, necessarily increases, sometimes dramatically, the size of the float in the system. (In Britain, the postal strike of 1971 was a trauma for the Bank of England.) And whenever a Fed processing centre gets overloaded, which can happen, the Fed gives the banks which delivered the cheques the credit on their cash letter before it processes the paper, generating still more float. On the morning of December 5, the New York Fed had failed to process two million cheques that arrived before (*just* before) its 5.00 a.m. deadline. Credit had been given on these cash letters, which meant that for one day, via float, the banking system would have some hundreds of millions of reserves that the monetary authorities had not expected the system to generate.

The size of the Fed float is known: despite all the new RCPC's and the growing telecommunications network for wire transfer of funds, it still averages well over $2,000 million a day—not far off 6 percent of the total reserves in the banking system. Figures on the other kinds of float are more or less guesses. A study for the American Bankers Association by Carter Golembe Associates estimated that "the volume of transit float in the system as of December 1969 was approximately $120,000 million". The total of demand deposits in the system at that time was (counting inter-bank deposits) about $260,000 million. The size of the money supply turns out to be a significant degree a function of the efficiency of the clearing mechanism.

3

Lou Barbera, a small, careful postman with a moustache, showed up in his Mustang to pick up the Valley Bank cash letters and cheques at a few minutes before nine. He was driving for American Purolator mostly because he wanted a social security cheque he could later add to his postal service pension. He counted the boxes and sacks he was to take, and compared the number with the invoice, which turned out to call for one box more than was there. . . . The documents were changed, the cheques were piled into the back seat of the Mustang, and we were off through the rain to Jericho, where most of the boxes and sacks were unloaded into a receiving window at the shiny new Fed facility, still relatively quiet at ten at night. Barbera said that by 10.30 or so there would be a line of drivers waiting to deposit their loads.

Next, out on to the island a few miles more to Syosset, and Barbera pulled into a truck garage where he was rather impatiently awaited, and his remaining boxes were tossed into a canvas bin together with a great deal of work from other Long Island banks. The bin was loaded on to an enclosed van painted white with a red and blue longitudinal stripe, making it look like an off-beat post office truck. This was an American Purolator vehicle, and its driver, Karl Metzler, a fiftyish former auto mechanic and gas station owner who had signed on to this job only one day earlier, was an eight-hour-a-night employee. He would take this van on two trips from Syosset to the financial district, and then drive whatever other missions might be required (on his first night's work he had carried medicines to hospitals on South Shore Long Island after the bank work was done). Metzler, my cheque, and I pulled into the loading area at 33 Liberty Street in Manhattan at about 11.30.

Getting into the Federal Reserve fortress through the main entrance on Liberty Street in broad daylight can be something of a chore: the place crawls with cops with guns. (The world's gold supply is downstairs in the Fed's vaults, the bars in each room appropriately labelled as the property of the nation that owns them. Among the reputed precautions against possible robbery of these vaults is a steel dam that channels an underground stream that used to run through the rock at the level of the vaults. In an emergency, legend says, that dam can be breached by the turn of a key upstairs and everyone on that level will be drowned. "This is a myth," a Fed spokesman comments, "but we do not discourage its propagation.") At night through the loading dock, however, procedure is casual: nobody could possibly want all these cancelled cheques, and nobody could possibly get into the vault at night without atomic weaponry. I rode a freight elevator to the fifth floor receiving area without so much as a request for identification. Here Metzler delivered his sacks of boxes of Long Island cheques from all the banks Purolator services, took a receipt, and departed.

On the fifth floor at the Fed, the shipments are time-stamped, their contents in numbers of boxes and other parcels are compared with the invoices, and the sacks are dumped into canvas bins on wheels. This is heavy work, and the staff is entirely male, and muscled. On the fourth floor, where an entire block square is devoted to the processing of three to four million cheques a day, the staff is overwhelmingly female, and mostly black. Deliveries are unloaded from the canvas bins (by men) on to a table, where the sacks and the boxes are opened and the cash letters examined to make sure all claims are superficially in order. The official number of the bank submitting this work is circled in red grease pencil on the cash letter to make sure the operators who will start processing it do not forget to enter that vital piece of data, and then the bundles and boxes are taken over to a dozen girls at IBM 1203 proof machines, who begin the preparation of the work.

Either on the cash letter or on adding-machine tapes within the boxes or sacks, the sending bank has supplied its own count of the total value of the cheques in each rubber-banded bundle of three hundred to five hundred items. The girls at the 1203 machine take each bundle, and type out on the 1203 keyboard the subtotal figure supplied with it, producing a machine-readable slip to be inserted under the rubber band with the cheques. Now reasonably small batches of work can be proved separately on the machines that will later sort and decode the cheques. These slips are inscribed with an MICR number 4,000 and are called "4000 slips".

The Valley Bank cash letters, which arrived at the 1203 machines at about 12.45 in the morning, consisted of about twenty bundles. When all had been supplied with 4000 slips, the machine added up the totals of the slips, and the operators compared those totals with the amount called for by the cash letter. This should come out right almost all the time, but sometimes a bank includes in its cash letters some bundles it neglected to send to the Fed, which produces a discrepancy. The morning of December 6, Tinker National Bank, another Long Island bank, had neglected to send in two bundles totalling about $69,000, claimed on its cash letter. If there are any discrepancies, the entire shipment by this bank is put aside on a "difference table", where somebody senior will look at it later. Otherwise the operator prepares a "5000 slip" which states the full amount of the cash letter and goes in with the cheques. She signs it, so if anything is wrong the supervisor will know of whom to inquire.

From the IBM 1203 the box with my cheque in it went to the "block-out unit", a group of a dozen women working at large flat tables. The Valley Bank boxes were divided between two of them, and my cheque was in lot 97, which went to Kathleen Lane, a quick but placid veteran with white hair and rimless glasses. ("Don't judge the average time for this job by her", said William Sledge, the young black supervisor of this section; "she's my best".) Her first job was to take the rubber bands off the bundles and remove any extraneous papers (from many banks, the boxes arrive at the Fed with dividers, cardboard "bundle tracers", still separating the rubber-banded bundles; and it is by no means unusual to find in a box bond coupons, deposit slips or cash slips; in the outgoing work at Manufacturers Hanover a $100 bill once showed up among the non-machineables, rejected by the sorter because it had no MICR bank number, and the girl at the inscriber which had processed it explained that she had never seen a $100 bill before). Then Mrs. Lane rifled through the several hundred cheques in each bundle, her experienced eye out for a bank MICR code that was not New York work, or a misplaced MICR inscribing of the amount on the cheque. As she finished each bundle, she stacked the cheques in a box in the order in which she had received them, facing the front of the box.

A man came by, took the open box, and loaded it on to an odd wheeled vehicle known at the Fed as a "casket", at Manufacturers Hanover as a "Queen Mary". This is a metal construction about four feet high, with two sloping shelves above and two flat shelves below. Each shelf is long enough to hold six boxes side by side. The boxes serve as open drawers; when the cheques have been removed from the boxes on the upper shelves, they are replaced by the boxes on the lower shelves. Each casket thus holds roughly sixty thousand cheques, which is about an hour's work on a machine.

The casket with my cheque among its sixty thousand was wheeled to a glass-enclosed section that occupies the entire end of the fourth floor and holds nine IBM sorter-readers like the single Burroughs machine at Valley Bank. Here the cheques were removed from their boxes in batches of three hundred or so, and placed in one of four sections of a "jogger", a wooden frame the size of a large book, attached to an electric motor that keeps it constantly vibrating at a high speed. The action of the jogger lines up the bottoms of all the cheques to assure a clean feed into the metal slot of the IBM sorter.

Cheques raced through the machine, and fell into one of thirteen pockets. Here there was a pocket for Treasury cheques (by far the heaviest category in the first week of the month, when social security cheques are clearing), a pocket for travellers cheques (bet you never thought of that), a pocket for "country work" (non-New York City banks) to be passed on to the day force, two pockets for non-machineables of different kinds, a pocket for the 4,000 slips that must balance the totals, six pockets for individual New York Clearing House banks, and one for the other six Clearing House banks, whose incoming cheques will have to be sorted down in a second "pass" through the machine. Each cheque as it runs through is stamped with the endorsement of the Federal Reserve Bank of New York: the Fed has now accepted the cash letter from the sending bank, and will credit that bank's account for this amount; the debit of the bank on which the cheque is drawn is hereafter owed to the Fed itself.

Here, as in Valley Stream, the cheques pulsing through the sorter are also being read, and their contents noted. The Fed, however, has no need to make a record on computer tape. The sorter is hooked up only to a printing machine that prints out on a wide adding-machine tape a string of numbers identifying the bank on which each item is drawn and the amount of each cheque—plus a separate narrow adding-machine tape of amounts only for the contents of each of the six Clearing House bank pockets. As the pockets fill up, a man tending the machine pulls out the cheques and transfers them to another casket, where there is a box to match each pocket. When this box is full, the machine is stopped, the adding-machine tape that applies to that pocket is totalled, torn off, and placed in the box with the cheques; and the box is closed up, and labelled with the name of the bank to which it is to be delivered and the total value of the cheques enclosed. Meanwhile, the wide adding-machine tape has been proving the total of processed cheques against the numbers on the 4,000 slips; and that tape, together with the non-machineable items, goes off to a group of seventy-four—seventy-four!—women seated at desks in a "reconciliation section", whose adding machines must prove the cash letter from the bank that sent the cheques.

During this process, my cheque disappeared into a box that was marked 30, which stands for Manufacturers Hanover Trust; and the box in turn disappeared into a large canvas bin on wheels marked 30. And as each bin for each Clearing House bank filled up, it was wheeled to a freight elevator and taken down to a loading dock for delivery to a truck that would take it to the modest whitestone wedge-shaped Clearing House built in 1962 a few blocks north of the Battery on Broad Street.

4

The operation of a money system based on cheques requires a clearing house, and even today, when mergers and acquisitions have reduced the number of New York City clearing banks to twelve (the Clearing House Association had fifty-two members when it was formed in 1853), considerable expense is saved by having everybody deliver to and receive from a central point, rather than making separate deliveries and pickups from every other bank in the city. Moreover, because a clearing house traditionally undertakes responsibility for its members, such an institution gives every bank an added stake in the sound operation of every other bank. Even after the Federal Reserve System was created (but before its directors could begin to learn what they were doing), the New York Clearing House was able to save the country from a financial panic by issuing "clearing house certificates" its member banks agreed to accept in lieu of cash when the outbreak of World War I disrupted the normal circulation of money. On the other hand, the refusal of the New York Clearing House to come to the aid of the Bank of United States in 1931—because, in the opinion of James Broderick, then the state superintendent of banking, it was owned by Jews—sharpened the onslaught of the Great Depression on Wall Street.

WHERE THE MONEY COMES FROM

Many of these functions have now been taken over by the Fed, which operates a kind of national clearing house and since 1972 handles an increasing proportion of the regional and local clearing work. But all the cheques and money transfers involving the major New York City banks—which means, as we shall see later, virtually all international banking—still clear through the New York Clearing House. The Federal Reserve Bank of New York is an associate member, paying about the same dues ($50,000 a year) as everybody else, but none of the assessments for work performed. All the cheques drawn on New York sent with cash letters by country banks like Valley are taken by the Fed to the Clearing House to be part of the daily settlement.

Cheques are brought to the rotunda at the centre of the building for three scheduled exchanges, at seven, nine and ten in the morning. In addition, each bank has a stainless steel hole in the wall of a room in the rear to which deliveries can be made at any time of the day or night either by prearrangement among the banks (First National City, Chase, Manufacturers and Chemical make a scheduled exchange of cheques on each other at 3.00 a.m.) or by the arrival of "pouch loose" sacks full of cheques from distant banks brought there by messenger trucks that meet incoming airplanes. There is another formal exchange at 11.00 p.m., this one for "return items" which for one reason or another (usually NSF—insufficient funds in the account) a bank has refused to accept. But settlement, the balancing of accounts among the banks, occurs only once a day, at ten in the morning, when each bank sends to the exchange floor the last bins full of boxes of cheques, each box to be delivered to another member of the Clearing House and accompanied by a ticket proclaiming the amount of a cash letter totalling this collection of paper and all previous exchanges. All but one of the clearing banks presents each day tickets totalling in the hundreds of millions of dollars, and three or four of them will normally bring more than a 1,000 million dollars of cheques on to the floor. Obviously, so vast an exchange has to run on schedule, and the Clearing House imposes a penalty on any bank that sends its work in late, to wit:

Settling or Delivery Clerk failing to attend punctually, with
statements and tickets complete, at the morning exchanges . . .
$5.00

The room itself is nothing enormous—perhaps fifty feet square,
three stories high. The exchange floor is slightly depressed, and
surrounded by a wall of pulpit-like desks, each with two seats
behind it, each the property of a clearing bank. Everything is very
plain: unadorned white granite walls, marble floor, birch pulpits,
almost Scandinavian in feeling. (Upstairs there is a certain amount
of Victoriana, portraits, original board table and chairs and desks
from the old Clearing House half a mile uptown; and downstairs
there is a gigantic Burroughs computer installation.) Two doors
lead from a modest entrance foyer guarded by one uniformed man
and an old plaque, gold letters etched in marble:

VISITORS NOT ADMITTED

UNLESS INTRODUCED BY

PARTIES KNOWN TO

THE MANAGER

In the days before the Fed kept everybody's reserves, banks would
settle their accounts for real in the clearing house exchange room,
weighing out gold to balance the paper, and it was thought unwise
to encourage the participation of the public.

Even now there is no visitors' gallery, and there is in truth not
much to see. The messengers begin appearing about ten o'clock
(despite the rules, a grace period of five minutes is officially given
and a grace period of ten minutes can usually be taken without any
questions asked: the banks like to keep open until the last instant
the possibility that the morning mail contains a million-dollar
cheque on some other clearing bank, passed on to a New York
correspondent for quick credit). They are mostly routine New
York City messengers, old men and boys of fairly impoverished
appearance, but the First National City Bank messengers wear
snappy Citibank uniforms. The normal conveyance is a canvas or
fibreboard bin held by a metal frame on wheels, but Morgan

Guaranty delivers its cheques on others, and picks up others' cheques on it, in an elegant outsize steamer trunk with green panels and studded black steel borders; Chemical Bank delivers and picks up in shiny all-steel cases. The Fed sends over a separate bin for each bank, which keeps the vehicle, returning it later in the day with its own work for Fed processing: the Fed delivers to the Clearing House, but receives only in its own building.

While the messengers exchange their boxes, the delivery clerk of every bank gives to the settlement clerk of every other bank a statement of the total claims on the other bank represented by all the cheques delivered in the previous twenty-four hours. The settlement clerk has come equipped with a statement of the total claims being presented to the other banks by his bank. He now enters on his settlement sheet the claims against him, adds the total his bank must pay, and subtracts one figure from the other, producing a net debit or credit at the Clearing House. This final figure will be the addition to (or subtraction from) the reserves of his bank as the result of this day's exchanges with the other New York City banks. The figure can be quite large. On December 6, Chase Manhattan owed the Clearing House—i.e., the other New York banks all together—$1,300 million, more than half its entire reserves at the Fed, as the result of this day's exchanges. The key fact is that until the exchanges are completed the dimensions and direction of the figure are unknown—no bank can be sure in advance that it will show a credit or a debit at the Clearing House on this day. As soon as he gets his totals added up (which he does by hand: the morning a little electronic calculator appears at the Clearing House will be the morning the American school system can shut up shop), the settlement clerk calls his home office and tells top management the number that will determine whether the bank has funds to lend or a need to borrow in the interbank market today.

On a podium at the front of the room, Executive Vice-President James Kelly stands beside a table at which young Barbara Gomez keeps a printed "proof sheet", unchanged (except for the names of the banks in the left-hand column) in more than a hundred years. There are four columns beside the name column:

DEBIT BALANCES DUE CLEARING HOUSE
DEBIT AMOUNTS RECEIVED
CREDIT AMOUNTS BROUGHT
CREDIT BALANCES DUE MEMBERS

Each bank brings to this table its settlement sheet, with numbers for amounts received and amounts brought, and either a sum due the Clearing House to put in the first column or a sum due the bank from the Clearing House to put in the end column. The question of an individual bank's balance with any other individual bank is of no importance at all: each of these cheques is now in effect an item on or from the Clearing House itself. Miss Gomez, whom Kelly believes to be the quickest and most accurate adder in the city, had already totalled the amounts received and brought, and they balanced at about $8,645 million, including my cheque for $27.33 to Jake Piccozzi, now a credit to the Federal Reserve Bank of New York and a debit to Manufacturers Hanover Trust Company. To make sure all the clerks had done all their adding and subtracting, she ran down the columns for debit and credit balances. The technique is to write down only the sum for each order of magnitude (cents, dimes, ones, tens, hundreds, etc.): if those are all equal, then the total must be equal, too, and the size of the total makes no never mind to the Clearing House. Kelly duplicated Miss Gomez's work on a sheet of scrap paper while the clerks waited patiently behind their pulpit desks—the messengers with their trucks and bins had already departed. Then he nodded, she nodded, and she read the numbers into a microphone for each bank. Kelly lightly hit a block of wood with a gavel: "We have a proof", he said, and the clerks began leaving.

Signed by Kelly, and copied on an upstairs Xerox, the Clearing House proof sheet will now go to the Fed, which will debit or credit the reserves of each bank according to the totals displayed. There is no great hurry about this, because the books at the New York Fed stay open until 4.30 in the afternoon, and nothing counts but the number on the books at the end of the day. The Fed must also credit to the clearing house banks all the U.S. Treasury cheques they deposit today, and all the cheques on out-of-town banks they deposited yesterday or the day before (depending on how far out-of-town the banks are), and must debit whatever withdrawals ("calls" on the banks) the Treasury has decided to make from its special "Tax and Loan" accounts on this day. There will also be an addition to or subtraction from each of the big bank's reserves at the Fed according to the output of the computerized international clearing operation in the Clearing House basement, and this figure may overwhelm all the others. Chase owed $1,300 million to the Clearing House on domestic exchanges, but was owed $1,200 million by other members on its international exchanges.

If the Fed itself is buying Treasury bills, it will be crediting the purchase price to the banks that sell them (or that handle the accounts of government bond dealers who are selling them); if the Fed is selling Treasury bills, it will be debiting the banks' reserve accounts. And all day long the banks will be instructing the Fed to transfer money from or to these reserve deposits as they lend and borrow "Fed Funds" to and from each other, or clean up their respective "participations" in loans to big corporations, formally made through one "lead bank" on behalf of a syndicate of banks. Though there are occasional surprises in the afternoon, each bank usually knows by noon how large its reserves at the Fed will be at the close of business that day. We shall examine the meaning and importance of this number—it is *the* number for every modern American bank—in a later chapter.

In the meantime, my cheque has gone back to Ur-papa, a burnt-out case; it has served its purpose as part of the nation's monetary system, and has become part of the daily operations problem at the Manufacturers Hanover Trust Company.

In Britain, my cheque would have got to its home bank through a more informal process at the Clearing House, which has separate procedures for big business cheques and ordinary cheques written by ordinary people. The Clearing House has eight members—the big four, Williams & Glyn's and Coutts, which though now a subsidiary of National Westminster retains a clearing function, plus Co-operative Bank, Ltd. and Central Trustee Savings Bank, which joined in late 1975, after this description was written. But ninety-odd percent of the deliveries that a big bank must make to other banks still go to one of three addresses. For this ordinary business, the banks exchange at the Clearing House, downstairs in the garage at about 11 in the morning (after the morning's mail has made its "prime pass" through the machines), yesterday's ordinary cheques and the collection of adding machine tapes, representing what each bank claims from each of the others.

What the Clearing House does that is important is the "Town Clearing", which occurs almost immediately after the close of business. Now banks and branches in the square mile of the City exchange *that same day's* cheques with a value of more than £5,000 per cheque, for credit before the books close at the Bank of England. "Paid in by three o'clock, settled same day" is the slogan. The item traffic is about 20,000 cheques a day, the money volume sometimes reaches £7,000 million pounds. The customs of the other great London markets—the Stock Exchange, Lloyd's, the commodities markets—all rest upon the ability of the Clearing House to make their deals into cash transactions.

The ground floor of the London Clearing House off Lombard Street is now occupied by a Post Office, and since 1967 the Town Clearing has been accomplished on what was once a balcony, now closed off and made into a mezzanine, roughly sixty feet by twenty-five feet. Low ceiling, green pillars rising through the floor, arched windows obviously too grandiose for the space, acoustical ceiling with bright fluorescent bulbs buried in it, rows of long formica-top, steel-clad tables at which rows of girls sit with adding machines, facing pigeon-holed shelves at the back of the table. Starting shortly after three o'clock, messengers begin arriving on the escalator leading up to this floor. Those with cheques received by Barclays (which used this balcony as its Town Clearing cheque-sorting centre before the clearing operation moved upstairs, and has refused to give over its space) go directly to the three tables occupied by perhaps two dozen Barclay clerks, who pile up their employer's claims on the other banks and add the totals, which are then delivered with the cheques to other tables on the floor. The other clearing banks do their

Town bundling and adding in the basement, and their messengers on arrival at the clearing, deliver small packets of cheques to the clerks of the banks that are called on to pay out. Each cheque is examined briefly to make sure it belongs at this table (each of the clearing banks clears for a number of merchant and fringe banks, not to mention its own subsidiary operations, and there are no MICR-reading computers at the Clearing House to verify the accuracy of the process that routed this cheque to this clearing station).

An inspector of the Clearing House supervises this procedure. On this occasion, in honour of the American visitors, it is the director of the Clearing House, K. L. Tibbatt, a stout earnest man who came out of the accounting department at Lloyds. He sits in a small room with three plain tables and hard chairs separated from the clearing room by a plate glass window. He looks out at the messengers and the girls. At 3.25 he pushes a button that rings a brass bell on one of the tables; a microphone picks up the sound of the bell and carries it to the clearing room and downstairs, to the door that leads to the escalators; and the door is locked. This is apparently a fairly solemn moment. Tibbatt points out the uniformed head messenger standing beside the top of the escalator, who has been at the Clearing House thirty years, and mentions the assistant head messenger downstairs at the foot of the escalator, who came to the Clearing House at age fourteen and is now fifty-five. "Never", he says, "have they been allowed to sound the bell; it's an honour reserved for their last day at the bank." Almost immediately after the bell has sounded, however, the door is opened again and the messengers flock in with more cheques; and it is not until about four o'clock or so that the girls at the tables stop receiving new business.

An inspector from the Bank of England then arrives with a ledger book and sits at one of the tables; and an employee of the Clearing House settles at another table with his own ledger book. Out in the clearing room, the supervisors are meeting two at a time, to verify that each bank claimed from and accepted claims from each other bank to such and such an amount. The slips of paper certifying the bilateral totals are slipped through a slot with a hinged door, into a basket in Tibbatt's room, and the inspectors enter the figures in their books. At about ten minutes past four, all the banks have submitted their agreed-upon memos of credits and debits with all the other banks.

Unlike the American system, in which the clearing house itself takes charge of distributing each bank's net debit or collecting its net credit, the settlement sheets in London remain bilateral. Each bank makes an entry in a CHARGE column or an entry in a PAY column for each other bank. When the two columns are added, each bank shows a figure of either debit or credit to be taken from or entered to its reserve at the Bank of England, which is what the inspector from the Bank will take back to his office. The total of charge balances and the total of pay balances for all the banks together are necessarily equal, and the inspectors and Tibbatt go home.

The girls begin to leave at four. "One of the attractions of these jobs", Tibbatt observed, "is that you can leave when your part of the work is finished." The messengers who brought cheques to be charged to others have been returning to their branches from early on, carrying with them the cheques presented to their employer. A few clerks from each bank remain in the clearing room until 4.45, which is the deadline for protesting—refusing to pay—an item presented at the Town Clearing. At 4.45 the representatives of each bank complete their Daily Settlement sheet, adding the "Town Clearing Unpaids" to one column or the other, adding in what is already known from the "General Clearing" that took place in the garage that morning, the totals from the bank giro "credit clearing" (this is done by manual sorting not unlike the Town Clearing sorting, completed before noon), and the results of that day's electronic rat-race in the Bankers Automated Clearing Service, which handles direct debit items and some others.

For the American visitor, used to a system where banks know where they stand for the day a little after ten in the morning, and protested cheques are not returned with their denial memos until thirty-six hours after the settlement, it all seems at least a little unstable. And there are, it seems, occasions when something that misses the Town Clearing leaves a bank with a need to scramble for funds before the Bank of England gets mad. But because British banking is an almost closed system, with only four large clearing banks handling the bulk of the work, the odds are strong that one bank's embarrassment at being caught short in its reserve account will be matched by another bank's *embarras des richesses*. Then the bank with the excess reserves lends overnight to the bank with the insufficient reserves, and everyone goes home with the cheerful thought that the books are balanced, once again.

7/Operations

The office worker who insists on writing so illegibly or in such an individualistic way that the encoding operator has difficulty in translating the handwriting into machine script, or who leaves chewing gum on a paper or magnetic tape, is likely to find that automated office work is not for him. . . . There is an urgent need to teach industrial artists and others who design firms' letter headings, catalogues, etc. that bank and giro account numbers not easily read in all normal types of artificial light, or read with difficulty by people with astigmatism of the eyes (the majority of the office population in some countries), are likely to be incorrectly copied with a resulting massive waste of computer time.

—FRANCIS P. THOMSON

* * *

The Manufacturers Hanover Trust Company processing centre is in 4 New York Plaza, one of the complex of spanking-new, fairly exotically surfaced office buildings down at the very foot of Manhattan Island. The bins of cheques arrived through a loading dock and rode the elevator to the sixth floor. On arrival, each box was weighed, to give a rough count of the number of items inside: "If it's six pounds", says Frank Feldhusen, Jr., vice-president in charge of cheque processing, "we know that we have eighteen hundred cheques. Later if we find thirteen hundred, we know we've lost some." Then the boxes were lined up on long tables and opened, and the Fed's adding-machine tapes were removed for future comparison against the totals that would come off Manny Hanny's

147

machines. Each box was placed on the "Queen Mary", the steel-frame conveyor truck with sloping shelves, and wheeled off to a glassed-in section running most of the length of the floor, where nine Burroughs reader-sorters two generations newer than Valley's —some with thirty-two pockets as resting places for the cheques— are kept clacking away all day and all night. (Machine rooms are always glassed in because the machines and tapes need controlled temperatures and humidities.)

The cheques delivered from the Clearing House will go through these machines often during the next twenty hours. The first run uses the machine as a reader, though it also accomplishes a coarse sort between cheques drawn on branches number 1–100 and cheques drawn on branches numbered over 100. The purpose of this run is to create a computer tape which will be the fundament of all subsequent processing. While making the tape, the machine also prints out a hard-copy list of the information going on the tape— the branch on which the cheque is drawn, the kind of account (business, personal, or special), the number of the account, and the amount of money. And, once again, the non-machineables fall into a reject pocket.

Manny Hanny processes every day more than a million cheques "on us", and every one of them must not only be debited against the account of the person or business that wrote it but also filed in a folder dedicated to this one of the bank's million and a half metropolitan area accounts. The bank cannot afford to do even a major fraction of 1 percent of the posting and sorting by hand. But even if Manny Hanny's own procedures were foolproof (and they are not), the bank in dealing with its "on us" items is at the mercy of the operators at other banks who inscribed the MICR for the amount down at the foot of the cheque. An inscribing machine elsewhere that has set the numbers a fraction of an inch out of whack—too near the edge or the bottom of the cheque, for example —can make nuisance for everybody. And some banks are careless about the paper they send along. Republic National in Dallas has an especially bad name at the Fed of New York: the girls who make the boxes ready for the machine room put aside everything from Republic National and put it together last, because there is always extraneous paper in the box that has be to separated out. At Manny Hanny, there remains every night a batch of some hundreds of cheques that must be entered on the computer tapes manually, by key-punch operators.

At the end of the first run through the Burroughs machine, the tape is sent up to the computer centre that fills the entire seventh floor, where a test programme reads it, edits out the blips from the non-machineables, and then certifies that what remains is a "good tape". Five such tapes of debits and credits to accounts at Manny Hanny will be run over the course of a day, as batches of work arrive from exchanges at the Clearing House and from the bank's 171 branches all around the city and nearby suburbs. Once the tapes have been edited and accepted on the seventh floor, their magnetized oxides are the real world; the cheques themselves are now no more than a gigantic disposal problem.

First the tapes. Deadline pressure often forces the completion of processing on unbalanced totals. "We proof all night as the tapes come in", says Robert Stabile, who is in charge of the night work in the computer centre three nights a week. "But if you're off a million dollars here or there, that's pocket change. You proceed rather than jeopardize the night's work, and they'll do research later, downstairs." With a million and a half cheques passing through the bank's processing centre all told, the target is no more than two thousand errors a day—one in every seven hundred fifty items. Errors always turn out to involve important customers, or so it seems to top management, which doesn't hear about the others. Manny Hanny employs eighty-eight people in an adjustment department to take care of them—eventually, everything *will* have to be in proof. Feldhusen's Law, induced from sad experience, holds that "the more sophisticated the equipment used, the bigger the adjustment department needed."

A little after two in the morning, the computer department shuts down the receipt of new information, and begins massaging the immense quantity of information it already has. Grand totals of debit and credit are taken first: everything subsequent will have to prove to those. All the input tapes are "merged" into a single overall list of the previous day's reported transactions, and electronically sorted to print out in the order of the account numbers for each of the three kinds of account—business (code "0"), special (code "1") and standard chequeing (code "5"). Another code labels each transaction as a cheque or deposit, or an internally generated debit or credit. The sorting is done by transfer of the information from tapes (which must run sequentially) to magnetic discs (which allow input or output in any order), then back to tape to clear the disc system for further use. Meanwhile, an IBM 32–11 printer runs at a rate of 1,600 lines per minute, much faster than the eye can follow, turning out hard copy of what is on the discs.

Once the transaction tape is available in sequence it is compared with a tape of stop orders that have been entered by customers to prevent the payment of cheques they have written. This "stop suspect" run will alert the branches to take a special look at this particular cheque arriving in the morning's work. The listed cheques must be "suspects" rather than rejects, because the computer knows only that a cheque for the amount of the one that has been stopped has now appeared for debit to the account that demanded the stop: there is nothing on the tape about the identity of the recipient of the cheque, and there may be other cheques on this account for this amount that have not been blocked. (In Britain, the head office processing centre does not look for stop orders: that's for the branch. When the branch sees a cheque that must be stopped, the manager immediately puts a message on the terminal at the branch to reverse the debit to this customer's account—and he calls his opposite number at the branch (of any bank) where this cheque that will not be paid was originally deposited. He will send the cheque back to that office by post without involving either his or the other bank's head office. In America, a dishonoured cheque goes back through the clearing process in reverse, which is time-consuming, costly and unavoidable.)

Now yesterday's news must be put into the history books: the items must be "posted" to the individual accounts. Again with the help of the disc drives, the tape of transactions is "merged" into the general ledger of the bank. The sort is first by branch, then by type of account, finally by the number of the individual account. For each branch, the 32–11 printers produce a complete list of current accounts, the size of the available balance, and the float— the money in collection from deposits, calculated by Manny Hanny on a three-day basis rather than Valley's ten-day basis.

Each tape is good for about eighty thousand pieces of paper— cheques, deposits, or records of securities transactions involving this account; the discs can handle several times as much. In the final posting process, the IBM 32–11s print out about 40 branches in a batch. Attendants then remove the box of printed green-and-white striped IBM paper from behind the machine, where the sheets have fallen in graceful folding motion, feed in (when necessary) a new box of paper at the front, and mark the machine ready to strike again.

Messengers carry the print-out sheets to a windowless mail room, where seven mostly aged servitors in loose grey cotton jackets separate the sheets and direct each set to its predestined future. A great deal of work other than the basic DDA (Demand Deposit Accounting) programme passes through this room, but from four thirty to seven in the morning the basic job is stuffing the 170-odd cubbyholes that represent the different branches of the bank. Each gets a complete statement of its customers' transactions processed the previous night, an update of every customer's account, and special pages pointing out matters that should be specially attended to, right now. All this is slid into a plastic portfolio with a metal clasp, marked with the number of the branch. Some time shortly before eight in the morning the truck drivers come up to the room and take away the portfolios for the branches each of them services.

Throughout the night and early morning, meanwhile, Burroughs machines on the sixth floor have been "decading" cheques. The entire collection of cheques on Manny Hanny accounts is sorted into pockets representing branches—first in batches of ten branches, then each branch within each group of ten. Then within each branch the cheques are sorted by account numbers, in ten thousands, thousands, hundreds, tens—until finally the cheques are in the trays on the "Queen Marys" in the order of the account numbers within each branch. There is a lot of unskilled handwork in this, emptying the pockets, stacking the cheques in metal trays between big red file cards marked "Bundle Divider", taking them out again to run through the machine. Perhaps because it involves forever staying on one's feet, it is man's work: the staff tending the Burroughs machines is exclusively male and young. This is the one area where the British machines must handle a more complicated job than their American prototypes, for they must sort the cheques written by their depositors into three thousand separate bundles, each to be mailed (returning the grey mail sacks) directly to its branch.

Completed, the trays are taken to a sixth-floor mail room, where a staff of eight plucks out the cheques in handfuls of several hundred and ties them into bundles on an old-fashioned machine that works with a foot treadle: tie one end, tie the other end, turn lengthwise and tie that way. Here again each branch has its own cubbyhole, with nylon transparent gauze orange-coloured bags marked with the number of the branch, into which the cheques are placed. For cheques tied and bagged by the night force, the twine is white; for those done by the day force, the twine is red. In theory, this difference permits management to place blame for mistakes; in fact, it probably functions more as a device to convince the people doing the work that somebody is paying attention to whether they do it correctly or not. The staff is entirely male, younger than that in the seventh-floor mailroom, and mostly black, including the supervisors. The truck drivers come here, too, shortly before eight, to take the work away. The drivers do not work for the bank, which has a contract with M. J. Santulli Mail Service for all its deliveries.

In theory, the work from 4 New York Plaza is supposed to arrive by nine o'clock at my bank—branch 9, at 43rd Street and Fifth Avenue, the first of the glass banks, designed by Skidmore, Owings & Merrill, and a prizewinner in the 1950s. But C. R. ("Charley") Craffen, a round, white-haired man who runs the back office at the branch, considers himself lucky if the guard brings the orange guaze bags and the plastic portfolio to the third floor by 9.30. The room is a big carpeted bullpen about half the size of the banking floor below, a dull monochrome beige with undecorated walls. Along most of the length of one of the walls is a line of files with check-size drawers for the "tills" that hold the customers' cheques between the day of their return to the branch and the day when the statements go out.

Under Craffen's fussy eye, the orange bags are dumped on to a table, and two or three of the six file clerks are put to work cutting the twine, and re-sorting the cheques by hand into rubber-banded bundles that match the numbering of the file drawers. As she finishes preparing the cheques for each section of drawers, the clerk takes the cheques to a senior clerk (who may well be a younger woman), on whose desk is the list of "stop suspect" and "referral" items prepared by the computer. She removes from the bundles all cheques that somebody in authority should see, and passes the rest on to a man who sits at a Recordak machine at a table across the room. He takes them one by one and slips them into a steel chute, whence they run into the table-top photo unit which takes a picture of front and back for a permanent microfilm record. Then the machine stamps the item PAID. This is why the "referral" items must be removed first: "So they don't get marked paid", Craffen says, "when we're going to return them".

Finally, about eleven in the morning, the clerks begin placing into the drawers, in the individual "tills", the cheques that have been debited to those accounts. At the back of each till, displayed by the motion of opening it, is the signature card of the proprietor of this account (and of anyone else with a power of attorney to sign cheques on it). The theory is that the clerk placing the cheque in the till will look to see that the signatures match; and to some degree, probably, she does.

When my cheque to Jake Piccozzi went into that till, not quite forty-eight hours after he received it, the transaction with Piccozzi's Service Station was really closed. The sum of $27.33 had been debited to my account, debited to the account of Manufacturers

Hanover at the Clearing House, credited to the account of the Federal Reserve Bank of New York at the Clearing House, credited to the account of the Valley Bank at the Federal Reserve Bank of New York, and credited to the account of Piccozzi's Service Station on the daily computer print delivered to its Shelter Island branch.

For all this work, neither I nor Jake Piccozzi had been charged a penny. How this can be so is something we shall look at presently.

2

First, four observations:

1. The basic work force at 4 New York Plaza signs up for a week of three twelve-hour shifts, eight to eight, day or night. The two extra days off, says Vincent Ballschmieder, Stabile's senior assistant on the night shift, "are the honeydew days. It's 'Honey, do this' and 'Honey, do that.' You get a lot done around the house". Break-time conversation among the supervisors of the computer operation seemed to be exclusively about do-it-yourself home repairs and improvements. On the floor, the transition from shift to shift is impersonal; one man leaves off tending a machine, and some minutes later another one arrives to take it over. In the office areas on the computer floor, the outgoing supervisors wait for the incoming ones (who usually arrive about 7.45 in the morning), and will often join them for a cup of coffee to discuss what is left over from the previous night's work, or has been accomplished ahead of time from the forthcoming day's work. The cup of coffee is taken in the bank's cafeteria in the basement, a cavernous space with four short serving lines, where the food is cheap and should be. The cafeteria, like the upstairs machines, works twenty-four hours a day. At 3.30 in the morning, a group of key-punch operators (integrated) were celebrating the birthday of one of their number; they had brought in several barrels of Kentucky Fried Chicken.

2. The immense collection of IBM system-370 machines on the seventh floor are continuously monitored through a read-out

device that forms a separate cubbyhole on the floor. Two IBM "customer engineers" sit at a desk before it, watching messages from the world of electronics on the cathode-ray terminal and in the collection of signal lamps that can tell an engineer exactly what is happening where. One of the two engineers was leaning back in his chair, feet on the table, reading. The book was Alvin Toffler's *Future Shock*.

3. One of the earlier pieces of print-out generated in the Manny Hanny computer centre every night is the complete list of the previous day's international transactions, which run something more than $10,000 million a day in each direction, most of it money transferred between, say, Amsterdam and Sydney, with Manufacturers Hanover as the bookkeeper. In unconscious tribute to the Genoese and Florentines of six hundred years ago who founded this business, the columns of print-out are headed "nostro" (ours) and "vostro" (yours).

4. In most of the cheque-processing centres there are people who remember—it is only a dozen years back—when all this work was done by hand, on tables filled with racks and pigeonholes. The very first computer for bank use was designed by Stanford Research Institute for Bank of America over the five year period 1951–55. General Electric bought the patents and built the thing for the Bank in 1956, when IBM was not interested—a top executive of IBM told the Bank of America planning group that there would never be a market for more than ten big computers in the whole country. Once IBM did become interested, it pushed aside all its competition (except Burroughs) and by sheer quality of equipment and service acquired a quasi-monopoly of the business. (In Britain, all the clearing banks but the Midland use IBM machines, and Midland, in mid-1975, was in the process of switching from NCR to IBM.) The veterans are still astonished by the tricks IBM has taught machines to do. Bob Stabile in his forties has been watching the machines stay ahead of the job since 1961, and has given up on disbelief. "If a man from IBM came in here with a block of granite," Stabile says, "and he told me that tomorrow that block of granite would be making reports for me, I wouldn't doubt it."

The combination of computers and decimal money have changed aspects of British banking practice out of all recognition. Tibbatt remembers that, when young in the bank, "I learned to cast pound, shilling and pence, all at once. There was an old man, though, who could cast much faster than I. He smoked a pipe, and we were sitting on those high stools. He'd lean over and say, '*There* it is'— and bring his knee up, and you'd be lifted right off your seat. After a while, you'd see his pipe moving forward out of the corner of your eye, and you'd move. He'd miss; and he'd say, 'I'll get you next time, you bugger'—and he would. Once I mentioned this knee problem at home, and my father said, 'Does it happen often?' I sensed the way the wind was blowing—'No,' I said, 'Rarely.' He said, 'That's good, because if it happened often it would be your fault, and I'd give you a thrashing.' Things weren't like they are today."

3

Nothing else a bank can do will add so quickly or so substantially to its profits as a reduction in the cost of "operations". New York's Chemical Bank began to take these things seriously in 1972, after achieving the distinction of three straight years of declining earnings—no other bank in New York had done that. Perry Neff was moved into operations from Chemical's legal department on the grounds that he was smart enough to grasp and rough enough to master the problem, and the bank gave him a completely free hand to hire and fire: "I had to interview and pray a lot". Eventually he recruited Bob Lipp, a blond, freckled Harvard MBA '63 who had had enough energy to pick up a law degree too while working in the commercial end of the bank (and who had organized the successful hatchet job on Saul Steinberg when that chubby young man tried to lever his Leasco organization into control of Chemical in 1968). Lipp was put in effective charge of operations at Chemical in 1973 when Neff became executive vice-president.

"The operations division", Lipp says, speaking of the days

before Neff, "had been considered the ass-end of the bank, and its management reflected it. When you brought in professional management, the benefits were tremendous—big dollars". From April 30, 1971, to August 31, 1973, Neff and Lipp reduced the number of people working in operations at Chemical from 4,800 to 3,900. (These economics have been achieved in England too. G. D. Geniver, assistant clearing manager for Midland Bank, reports that "When we had 600,000 cheques a day we had 300 people sorting them by hand; now there are one and a half million cheques a day, and 106 people do all the work.") At Chemical, costs had risen from $35 million in 1966 to $71 million in 1971; two years later, in the middle of the worst inflation in recent history—and in the face of a 25 percent increase in the volume processed—Lipp had them down to $65 million. Even so, he was still charging the other divisions of the bank for his division's work on the basis of an arbitrary rule-of-thumb allocation. For cheques sent by the branches to the processing centre. Lipp charges 6¢ each, not because that's what it cost (let alone what it *should* cost), but because it was a figure that avoided political hassles within the bank. Barry Sullivan at Chase Manhattan, which is only slightly further down the pike than Chemical, said toward the end of 1973, "We are hitting the community bank [i.e., the branches] for $27 million this year. Somebody says, 'Are you sure it shouldn't be $23 million, or $31 million?' The answer is, 'No, I'm not; but I am sure it shouldn't be $15 million or $40 million'".

By contrast, John Reed at First National City, which has been working on these problems years longer than any of the other banks, stands ready to tell any of the bank's operating divisions what any service costs: "We'll do a first-class piece of analysis, and when we sign off we'll defend it." Reed says that the cost of processing a cheque is a function of the purpose of the cheque— but once he knows the purpose, he can give an answer like 4.754¢.

Lean and strong as a steel beam but much smarter, Reed came to Citibank straight out of college in 1966 (though he was a slightly aged college graduate, having taken a couple of years in the middle working for Goodyear); he has risen on brains, brass, and toughness, all real. "My responsibility", he says, "is running a cost centre. I have to know what we spend every morning—in fact, I have to predict what *will* happen every morning, because it's much easier to control these things before they happen. You can't run the place that way without a fairly good information service, and we have one". Reed's job before becoming chief of operations had been at the head of the bank's Management Information Service. "An MIS guy is an artist, as contrasted with an amateur photographer. An artist looks at a scene, and there is a theme that hits him: he seeks to convey that impression. Two different artists will see entirely different themes. If you're an amateur photographer you just show what's there—you might as well give a chief executive officer a batch of computer print-out. The job is to decide what the problem is and array your data to reveal it.

"There's a discontinuity when you get to a certain size", Reed says, warming to the subject. "At the executive offices of the Ford Motor Company, you can't find anybody who's built a car. The manager has a higher-level representation of the world. The guys on the line can tell you only if they tightened these bolts well or badly. It's the same in bank processing. The individuals who do the pieces don't understand what the flows are. You've got to have a good higher-level representation".

Bank operations divisions do a great deal more than the processing of cheques and demand deposit accounts. They handle the many transactions of trust departments (an increasingly hard problem as the trust department managers shift their clients from stock market investments which trade on a five-day payment-and-delivery schedule to money-market instruments that trade overnight). They prepare payrolls for big corporations, transfer stock ownership and issue certificates to reflect stock exchange purchases and sales, handle the billing for utility companies, insurance companies, municipal tax departments. "The important thing", Reed says, "is not to have unit costs vary greatly from day to day. You can do two things—inventory your work and release it at a steady rate to a constant labour force, or vary your labour force by the amount of work that comes in. We try to do both. We analyze the tasks, and hold those that are puttable-off for when we have the free labour force; and we staff by three-day weeks, four-day weeks, overtime, temporary help. We are the largest employers of temporary help in New York. We hire ten agencies; every month we drop one and we add one, keep them churning. Each month every supervisor must forecast the work he expects in his department for the next thirty days—*by day*. He revises the projection for the next five days at the start of every week. He is held accountable for his projections".

Chase's Sullivan, almost as young but much less driven, is not impressed. "How accurate can Reed be as a forecaster?" he argued. "I'd say he's got to be lousy". At Manufacturers Hanover, Frank Feldhusen, twenty years older and playing in a different league, feels uncomfortable with the idea of being that tough about hiring people for specific days, and wonders "how efficient it really is to get people only when you need them. How well do they do your job?" But Reed has error rates no worse than those at the other banks (no better, either); and he is not just boasting when he says that "our costs are way under anybody else." It is a little scary to think how much lower his costs must be than those of the operations at Manufacturers Hanover, which are clearly, especially at the branch level, some distance below the state of the art. When the City of New York asked the banks to bid for the job of processing its tax receipts—a very desirable job in Citibank terms, because it is the kind of work that can be inventoried and fed out to the work force at otherwise slack times—Reed set up a task force to estimate not only his bank's costs for doing such a job but also the costs of the other banks that would be bidding: "We wanted to bid not on our costs but on theirs; if you're the most efficient, you don't want to make too low a bid". The analysis must have been more or less right: Citibank won the job, and claims a handsome profit on it.

4

Every year the Federal Reserve System publishes a pamphlet called "Functional Cost Analysis", reporting the average costs for all the operations of the thousand or so banks that volunteer this information to the Fed. A degree of diffidence accompanies this publication: "Bank cost accounting", says the Introduction, "is not an exact science. There are almost as many systems as there are bank cost accountants. Because of differences in concepts, differences in degree of sophistication, and the heavy reliance on human judgment, it has been virtually impossible in the past to compare with confidence one bank's costs with those of another bank and frequently impractical even to compare year-to-year results within an individual bank". It is not an easy problem: Howard Crosse points out that "in the course of any business day, [a junior platform officer] may take loan applications, open new accounts, sell savings bonds or travellers' cheques, interview an equipment salesman, a representative of the bank's correspondent, and a wealthy woman customer who wants to know what stock to buy. Such efforts cannot be accurately allocated to the cost of processing a cheque".

For the purposes of the pamphlet, the Fed has simplified the categories, and otherwise unallocated expenses have been spread around via a computer programme reflecting "experience factors developed from expense data of participating banks". Though one of the three groupings of banks reported separately in the study is a group with deposits over $200 million (the other groups are under $50 million and $50–$200 million), the operations officers of the big money centre banks seem not to know about the existence of this Fed analysis, so it probably does not very accurately communicate what goes on in the nationally known institutions. But it shouldn't be too far off.

According to the FCA, the average cost of processing a "home debit" (my cheque to Piccozzi's was a home debit at Manny Hanny) varies from 7.334¢ at the middle-sized banks to 8.964¢ at the big banks; the average cost of processing a "transit cheque" (my cheque was a transit cheque at Valley Bank) runs from 3.26¢ at the small banks to 4.952¢ at the big ones. (These figures, unlike Lipp's and Reed's, include an allocation of tellers' and executives' salaries, marble polishing, etc.) One must also charge against my cheque some piece of the 15.074¢ it cost the average bank Valley's size to process its average deposit—plus some piece of the $1.81 monthly cost of maintaining the average account at a middle-sized bank like Valley and the $2.27 monthly cost of maintaining the average account at a big one like Manny Hanny. This cost analysis, moreover, includes nothing whatever for the services of the Fed. In sum, the processing of an ordinary transaction like mine with Piccozzi's must cost about 20¢. Times 27 thousand million cheques: $5,400 million. In 1973, that was the price of maintaining and using the chequeing account component in the money supply of the country: something more than $5,000 million a year. This cost has been rising very rapidly: as recently as 1960, it was probably no more than $1,000 million a year, and extrapolation of current trend lines takes it well over $10,000 million by the end of this decade.

As noted, these services are made available to virtually all businesses and to about two-fifths of all personal chequeing account customers at no charge at all. For the three-fifths of American personal accounts that do pay something for chequeing service (a steadily diminishing fraction), the fees charged represent considerably less than half the actual out-of-pocket cost of servicing the accounts. The average "special" chequeing account in the FCA tabulation shows about ten home debits a month and less than two transit cheques; the average personal chequeing account shows about thirteen home debits and five transit cheques; the average commercial account shows just under fifty home debits and about one hundred transit cheques. The average monthly expense by a bank on a special chequeing account ranges from $1.61 at small banks to $3.17 at big ones; on a personal chequeing account from $2.97 at small banks to $3.65 at big ones; and on a commercial chequeing account (where the averages are uninformative because the extremes are so wide apart) from $6.06 at small banks to $11.89 at big ones.

What pays these bills and leaves the banks a profit is the interest income on the use of the money in the accounts. The most striking example is the Federal Reserve System itself. Its cheque processing services are performed without charge, and it runs extensive research, publishing, consulting, and supervisory services, also without charge; but the end result is the biggest profit of any enterprise in the country (nearly all of it turned over to the Treasury). The income derives from earnings on the government bonds bought with the proceeds of the sale of Federal Reserve notes (currency) the banks buy to meet their customers' needs for cash. Similarly, banks everywhere, in socialist as well as in capitalist countries, pay the costs of their cheque processing work with "portfolio income" on the interest-free demand deposits made by their customers.

In 1972, according to the FCA, portfolio income on special chequeing accounts averaged about $1.25 per account per month at all banks; on personal chequeing accounts, there was a range from $3.47 at small banks to $2.99 at big ones; on commercial chequeing accounts, the range of monthly income per account was from $21.87 at small banks to $36.79 at big ones. Only one of the subcells actually showed a loss—the big banks dropped an average of 30¢ per account per month on special chequeing accounts (and that can be considered a cheap loss leader to draw these customers' savings accounts, and their profitable credit card, personal, installment, and mortgage loan business). But it is quite clear that the significant profits derive from the business accounts. Not the least of the troubles of the banking system is that this fact has become increasingly clear to the treasurers of the corporations, too.

5

The fact that banks perform services in return for deposits has long been understood on both sides. Individuals know that in return for maintaining a minimum balance they can have their chequeing accounts serviced without charge—and businesses know that if they want to borrow money from the bank they have to keep a balance there. This idea of the "compensating balance", so brilliantly exploited by Semenenko, is uniquely American and remarkably nutty, because it divorces the services performed from the payments for them in ways that make it almost impossible for either the banks or their customers to know who is paying how much for what. Companies do not know the real interest rate on their loans, and banks cannot match the cost of the services they provide with the income that can be traced to providing them. "There are some customers we give a prime rate to though they're not prime customers," says Al Rice, chief lending officer of the national division of Bank of America. "Because they keep a big balance".

Case M. Sprenkle of the University of Illinois, in a report to the American Bankers Association, estimated that only 3 percent of the bank balances maintained by the nation's five-hundred largest corporations could be explained by their actual need for money to handle their transactions; the other 97 percent was being kept at the bank because that's the way banks do business in America. Sprenkle compared one of the ten largest industrial firms in the United Kingdom "with the four U.S. firms of roughly equivalent size in the same industry" and found that "the average ratio of cash [i.e., bank balances] to sales of the U.S. firms is 63 times the ratio of the U.K. firm".

The average bank lending officer, however, considers the demand deposits in the bank to be "free money". (This is why, to quote a Wall Street lawyer with banking clients, "The guys who work in the operations divisions say that all the other people who work for the bank are salesmen".) James B. Watt of the Bank Marketing Association observes that "banks are the only businesses I've ever seen that are eager to back off on price. They've always yielded to customers on fees, because the big balances are profitable". Looking at the significance of increased interest rates in a bank's operations, Willard Butcher, president of Chase Manhattan, speaks first of "the increased value of the demand deposits".

Sprenkle says that large deposits—$100,000 or over—account for 20 percent of all demand deposits in American banks, but that figure seems drastically low. In the Fed's published FCA booklet, banks under $50 million had an average of 9 accounts of $100,000 or more, and those 9 produced 23 percent of all demand deposits; banks between $50 million and $200 million had an average of 47 accounts that size, producing 38 percent of their total demand deposits; and banks larger than $200 million averaged 305 such accounts, representing 48 percent of their demand deposits. The money-centre banks which are not well represented in the FCA report have even larger proportions of their total deposits in very large accounts. These figures argue that at least two-fifths of the nation's demand deposits—one-quarter of the money supply—is represented by very large corporate deposits.

This is a dangerous game from several points of view. One of the oddities of American business is that companies in trouble tend to have greater apparent cash resources than companies that are running smoothly. A company in trouble must scour around for loans at more and more banks, and at each bank where it secures a loan it must leave a compensating balance which shows up on its books as cash. "During 1970", says James Coquilette of the $250-million Merchants National Bank in Cedar Rapids, "large corporations went heading for the hinterlands, and we had some interesting approaches. Some very big companies even offered to open a deposit relationship. But this is hot money in the truest sense of the word, and we wouldn't do it". John Dubinsky of Mark Twain Bancshares reports that "We have had some dealings with the mammoth corporations, but it's not as profitable, it's not as much fun, and in some ways it's not as safe. Being the fourteenth bank for Monsanto means dealing with a guy who if trouble comes quits and goes to work for the county."

Compensating balance agreements require the borrower to maintain an average rather than a minimum balance at the bank. Thus on any given day—and predictably around tax payment dates—these deposits may disappear, and the bank may be embarrassed by the need to pay out the money. The more sophisticated big banks have added a daily "profitability" run to their computer programmes, to tell them whether any of the big customers is not paying its way; but in the internal politics of the bank it is almost impossible to force a vice-president to speak harshly to the treasurer of a corporation with which he has had a long and mutually rewarding relationship—a relationship that may indeed be the origin of the vice-president's vice-presidency.

6

The closest thing to really "free" money the American banks can use is the chequeing accounts in the names of the customers of their trust departments. This is a delicate subject, because trusteeship is a serious responsibility, and one of the obligations of a trustee is to keep the funds for which he is responsible continuously invested in earning assets. Money left in current accounts becomes an earning asset for the bank, not the trust; and any trustee who deliberately did anything of that sort would be a sitting duck for a lawsuit. Anyway, the people who gravitate to work in a trust department are almost invariably very scrupulous people with a horror of playing games with other people's money (this is why they were so conservative in the investments they made prior to the go-go years, and why they performed so poorly in the stock market when the performance bug bit them in the late 1960s). Nevertheless, the fact is that trust accounts acquire cash in chequeing accounts, and that the routine procedures of the banks (the "natural" way of doing business) often act to make those deposits larger rather than smaller.

How much demand deposits are worth to a bank is a source of constant political infighting among the divisions of nearly all the larger institutions. In part, this is the old argument between the economist who wants business to operate on marginal revenues and marginal costs (what is the benefit from and the expense of making one more sale or transaction?) and the businessman who actually operates on the basis of his average revenues and average costs spread over all his sales or transactions. Dividing the bank up into "profit centres" and "cost centres" can exacerbate the quarrel.

Chase Manhattan in 1971 adopted a system it calls "responsibility budgeting", under which each division was responsible for and credited with all the income attributable to its activities, but only for those costs within its own control. Under this system, the performance of the division as a division could be judged fairly easily, and fighting between the profit makers and the cost controllers could be minimized. But it left too many difficult decisions for top management.

"Let's say Roger Lyon of the community bank [i.e., he runs the branches] thinks up a gimmick that increases his income a million dollars and adds nothing to his costs," president Willard Butcher says without enthusiasm. "It increases Sullivan's costs in operations by three million, but he manages to hold the increase to two point seven. I have two heroes, and I've lost one point seven million. So we've gone back to profitability budgeting. We try to use responsibility budgeting on marginal cost, profitability budgeting on average cost. Responsibility budgeting is how you administer; profitability budgeting is how you manage." That sounds right, and because Butcher worked his way up in the bank through twenty-five years in its different divisions and is both liked and trusted everywhere, it seems to be generally accepted; on the question of how well it works, the jury is still out. It certainly doesn't solve the problem of allocating the costs of what Butcher calls "the marble palaces" in midtown, which are used by both the "community bank" for its depositors and the "national bank" for the lending officers who handle the big corporate clients in the nearby skyscrapers. Both say they don't need all that polished surface; Butcher has to decide who pays for it whether he needs it or not.

At North Carolina National Bank, which is widely regarded as First National City's major rival in understanding what it costs to do business, the criterion is "product profitability", and top management hears separately every month, via computer, from no fewer than 1,100 "management centres" in the bank and its holding company. These reports allocate costs and revenues both actual and imputed for every one of the bank's "products" (mostly different lending activities) with relation to the five-year profit plan this management centre has established for this product. Results arrive on top management's desk three days after the close of the month. None of this helped in 1974, where NCNB's profit estimates had to be cut 40 percent between May and September. "Our deposit growth", chairman Thomas Storrs says philosophically, shielded by a Harvard Ph.D., "is a function of three factors: (1) the growth of the money supply; (2) North Carolina's share; (3) our share of North Carolina. Number three would be very expensive; number one is out of our control. Fortunately, North Carolina is growing faster than the United States."

"Our orientation is to maximize long-term earnings rather than current earnings", says Storrs' operations chief Rufus Land, who hides a mind that may be as sharp as John Reed's behind a drawl and a manner to match his rural name. (Behind the desk, there is a stuffed fish on the wall rather than a Mondrian.) "Of course, we recognize that the market is irrational".

7

In fact, the entire system is irrational, and it cannot last very much longer. Cheque clearing is one of those phenomena of which it used to be said rather calmly that the quantities doubled every ten years. As the population experts have been screaming for the last decade, and the energy shortage revealed in 1973, expectations of doubling every x years have to be wrong, because there comes a last double when the numbers are unmanageable and the system collapses. Quantum jumps in the cleverness and capacity of cheque-sorting machinery and computers have kept the banks ahead of the task, but the best that can be hoped for from such improvements is a delay of ten years or so—one doubling—in the arrival of the day when the paper overwhelms its processors. Anyway, as Gerald Dunne pointed out in 1966, there is something nutty about "this stop-shuffle-go paper merry-go-round in an age of direct long-distance dialing and other communications marvels."

Not the least of the advantages the Europeans will have in the remainder of this century is their reliance on a "giro" system rather than a chequeing system for the payment of bills. The principle goes back to the Banco Giro in Venice in 1619, but the first fully developed modern giro system comes out of the Austro-Hungarian Empire in the late nineteenth century. Like much else in banking, there is an accidental flavour to the giro story. Emperor Franz

Josef had launched that country's Post Office Savings Bank "on the English model", as a service to the saving public and a source of demand for government bonds; and the director of the bank, Dr. George Coch, turned it into a credit transfer system to minimize the demand for gold coins, of which the country had none too many.

In the giro system, the householder sends the return section of his bills and his cheques to his bank rather than to the person or business he is paying. The bank deducts the total of the cheques from the householder's balance, and credits the amount of each bill to the account of the business that sent it. The debit to the paying account precedes the credit to the receiving account: the bank gets all the float. The householder receives a statement from the bank that it has paid on his behalf the following bills, leaving him such-and-such a balance. The businesses get back the receipted bill forms (each of which is printed as a postcard), and a daily notice of the credits entered to their account. Obviously, this system is most conveniently run from a single central office, preferably governmental and preferably associated with the postal service (in Switzerland, the postal giro accounts are part of the debt of the federal government); but in Britain a Bank Giro system competes with the Post Office, and the Swedes do it all in the private sector through a consortium of banks—and the "Automated Clearing House" already in operation in San Francisco, Los Angeles and Atlanta could be used for giro purposes virtually without modification.

As part of a campaign to sell this sort of banking to the British, Francis P. Thomson wrote in 1964, "Transfer services are entirely free, including provision of the post-free pre-addressed envelopes in which [the householder] sends his postal transfer or cheque forms to the post giro clearing office to process, the overprinting of these forms by the giro service with his name, address, and account number, the dispatch to him of a statement showing his credit balance before and after every transaction complete with the debit notification section of the transfer or cheque form he sent to instigate the transaction. Furthermore, nobody is left in any doubt that the transaction has gone through, for the beneficiary also receives, free of charge, a statement showing his balance before and after the transaction, together with a credit notification section of the original transfer form, which is provided with a space of about half a postcard for a personal or formal message, trade order, etc., from the remitter."

Seven years later, Thomson suggested that "all sectors of the public must be persuaded to accept their salaries, wages or pensions by credit transfer, and to negotiate the majority of their transactions by this means; also to place their surplus resources, immediately they are available, in short- or long-term investments; and to restrict their cash demands to the minor requirements of pocket money. The result is likely to be a wealthier and a far happier human society". In early 1974, the U.S. Treasury took its first baby steps in this direction, asking the Federal Reserve Bank of New York to design a system to pay groups of social security recipients by direct credit to their bank accounts rather than by mailing green cardboard cheques.

In Britain for some years, social service payments—more than 90 million of them every year—have been handled through the Post Office Giro, which also handles rent collections for most local authorities.

The customer in a giro system saves the time of addressing lots of envelopes and the postage of mailing lots of letters. The business (insurance company, mortgage bank, public utility, tax collector) saves the cost and time of making deposits and the nuisance of bounced cheques. The banking system, where the largest savings come, needs to sort the cheques only once and register the data on only two ledgers. And, of course, the giro plan invites computerization. Large companies sending bills could inscribe them in MICR for the company's account number, the customer's account number and the amount of the bill. At the bank, the operator inscribing each transfer cheque would simultaneously prove the householder's payments, and thereafter the whole thing could operate untouched by human hands.

Unfortunately, our banks have been blocking even the first consideration of European experience with giro systems, preferring to give credence to a lot of futurology about "the cashless society" and "the chequeless society". The largest venture in what the banks call an Electronic Funds Transfer System was the work of the Special Committee on Paperless Entries (SCOPE) sponsored by the California banks with help from the Federal Reserve Bank of San Francisco. As Russell Fenwick of Bank of America explained to a press conference in summer 1972, the number of cheques in California had reached a total of 180 million a month—more than 2,000 million a year—and was still climbing at an annual rate of 8 percent. SCOPE thought that as many as 30 percent of these cheques could be handled by electronic funds transfer rather than by pieces of paper: paycheques could be automatically deposited in workers' accounts, and recurring payments could be automatically debited for such things as auto loans, mortgages, water bills, power-and-light bills, maybe taxes. Many banks had done automatic debiting for years, involving savings bonds, United Fund pledges, and the like, but only within the same bank; and some eight thousand banks are involved (though they don't advertise it) in the savings and loan associations' TRANSMATIC system which pre-authorizes monthly transfers of funds from chequeing accounts to savings and loan shares. Under the SCOPE system, through the Automated Clearing House, these procedures would become generalized. The Fed would provide the machinery; the software package had been developed "well within" a budget of $150,000, and had already been sold to Atlanta for use there. Everything was ready to roll in October 1972.

And roll SCOPE did, but very, very slowly. A year after the launching of the system, only 3,500 of what were now almost 200 million transactions a month were passing through the SCOPE computers in San Francisco, and Atlanta was little better off. The problems in San Francisco were various. A number of banks were reluctant to push the scheme because they feared that employers would in one way or another push their employees to keep their accounts in the corporation's own lead bank. A number of corporations were reluctant because they benefited by a float between the deposit or cashing of their paycheques by their employees and the debiting of the cheques to their accounts. But the most important reason for the disastrously slow development of SCOPE was the inability of consumers to see why they should give up control of their chequeing accounts, and authorize automatic first-of-the-month deductions for payments they could otherwise make pretty much at their own convenience. "The biggest and maybe only hurdle on SCOPE", said J. J. Curran of the San Francisco Federal Reserve Bank in spring 1973, "is the marketing effort". You bet.

British banks have been more successful in selling such services to their customers, though it is not easy to see why. In recent years, oil companies and department stores have even been able to persuade customers to undertake variable direct debit obligations, by which the customer's account is automatically charged every month for whatever the oil company or the store says he owes. The British Bankers Association has geared up to handle complaints about creditors' miscalculations in this system, but they haven't arrived in volume. (The most common cause of complaint, in fact, has been the *delayed* bill. A store that has a variable direct debit arrangement with a customer neglects to bill him for two or three months, puts through a charge for several months at once, and the customer is not only horrified but plunged into an unexpected overdraft at the bank. Few problems in banking are so easy to avoid or resolve as this one.) In 1974, bank giro handled interbank clearings of almost 130 million items, about 12 percent of all clearings.

The fact of the matter is that the banks understand intellectually about the need to lighten the burden of paper, but the emotional commitment is lacking: so long as the boat stays afloat, they don't want to rock it. Through the inflation of the last half-dozen years, the total volume of demand deposits in the banking system has grown only slowly. As interest rates rise, the banks' customers "economize" on cash—that is, they try to reduce the proportion of their liquid assets left in places where no interest is paid. In Cedar Rapids, far from the money centres, James Coquilette of Merchants National Bank finds that his corporate customers insist that once a balance passes $50,000 all additional receipts for the account should be invested overnight for the benefit of the corporation rather than for the benefit of the bank. Apart from the compensating balances —an artificiality that cannot survive forever—a steadily increasing proportion of the demand deposits in American banks represents the convenience cash of households rather than the working balances of business.

8

And in the end, even the household balances are likely to disappear from interest-free chequeing accounts—or, at best, diminish. Since 1933, American law has forbidden insured banks to pay interest on demand deposits, but a hole has been opened in that dike and increasing quantities of money seem certain to flow through it. Like so much else in banking, this breakthrough was accomplished by one man acting alone.

The creator was Ron Haselton, an athletic, earnest New Englander, youthful manner under greying hair, evidence of energy being controlled even in moments of apparent repose. Haselton worked his way through Boston's Northeastern University at night, got a job with the First National Bank of Boston, moved on to the First National City Bank of New York; and in 1965, at the age of thirty-four, he was appointed president of the Five Cents Savings Bank in Worcester, Massachusetts. (New York has a Dime Savings Bank and a Dollar Savings Bank; Massachusetts has several Five Cents Savings Banks; it's a difference in attitude. Presently Haselton changed the name to Consumer Savings.) During the credit crunch of 1966, Haselton decided his bank really needed more deposits, and the only way to get them was to offer a service nobody else was offering.

In 1961, the Massachusetts state legislature had passed a law permitting banks to dispense with the passbook for savings. If a customer's record of ownership of his savings was nothing more than a monthly or quarterly statement like his statement on his chequeing account, and if his means of withdrawing money at the bank or by mail was simply a piece of paper very much like a cheque, Haselton could see no reason why the man couldn't pay his bills with pieces of paper drawn on his savings account. In 1969, he applied to the Massachusetts State Banking Department for a declaratory judgment that he could make available to his depositors a service he called "the NOW account", the initials standing for "Negotiable Order of Withdrawal".

"It's a natural extension of daily interest accounting", Haselton says. "The barrier had been quarterly crediting of interest, which made the savings deposit inelastic. When you got daily crediting, the time deposit became a demand deposit." When Massachusetts Banking Commissioner Florence Koplow turned him down, he took the case to court, and early in 1972 he won it. The Supreme Judicial Court could see no special distinction between the sale of a money order, which savings banks were clearly empowered to do, and the issuance of a chequebook allowing the depositor in effect to write his own money order.

Consumer Savings, with something just under $200 million in deposits, moved immediately. Right behind it came Boston's Provident Institution for Savings, the largest savings bank in the state. "My boss", says William J. Maytum, in charge of marketing at Provident, "told me two days before I went on vacation in June '72 that he wanted to get this started. When I came back, my staff had it going. I said to my boss, 'We'll need something to put these things in [referring to the "cheques"]'. He said, 'Oh, get some shoe boxes'. Now it goes on the machine and we get a magnetic tape."

The draftsmen of the Federal Deposit Insurance Corporation rules had never considered the possibility that savings banks might offer interest-bearing chequeing accounts, and there was nothing in them to stop what Haselton was doing. FDIC couldn't have stopped Haselton anyway, because he wasn't a member: the Massachusetts savings banks have long had their own deposit insurance corporation, separate from the federal corporation. There were eight federally insured banks in the state, where FDIC could have prohibited NOW accounts—"but", says Elliott G. Carr of the Massachusetts Savings Banks Association, "there had been other times when the FDIC banks had been disadvantaged, and they didn't want to do that again, so they didn't change the rules". Then the New Hampshire banks got into the act, and the commercial bankers went complaining to Congress, demanding an end to this flouting of the law.

The authority of the federal regulatory agencies to limit interest rates must be renewed every so often by Congress, and 1973 was a year when the law was up for renewal. The Massachusetts bankers, many of whom had been in Washington before only as tourists, descended on the appropriate Congressional committees. This reporter happened to be lunching with banking consultant Carter Golembe on the day they came down to appear before the House Committee, a delegation of a dozen men, mostly beefy, with broad A's. They were, of course, lunching in the same place where Golembe would take a visitor, and they stopped by the table to say hello. Their leader told Golembe they were confident of the result in the committee: "We have a clear majority, it's in the bag". Golembe looked sorrowfully at their retreating backs. "They'll never know what hit them", he said. Both Senator Edward Brooke and Senator Thomas McIntyre were on record as saying that the NOW account looked to them like something of benefit to consumers, and Governor George Mitchell, speaking for the Federal Reserve System, had told the House Committee that he thought it was an experiment worth encouraging, to see what would happen. After a battle somewhat bloodier than the public was allowed to see, Congress specifically authorized banks in just these two of the fifty states, commercial banks as well as savings banks, to offer NOW accounts. Early in 1976, permission to offer NOW accounts was extended to all six New England States.

As of December 1973, Consumer Savings had about four thousand NOW accounts with an average balance of about $1,300. Activity in the average account ran four or five "drafts" a month, at a charge of 15¢ per draft, but three-quarters of the account holders were also taking the personalized printed cheque. "We do offer a free package of fifty plain unattractive drafts", says Donald Hall, Haselton's number two. "We say, 'If you're content with this piece of junk. . . .' NOW account people tend to be younger, more intelligent, white-collar types as distinguished from the blue-collar types who traditionally support the mutual savings bank. We got some press on this when it started, in *Time* magazine, the *Wall Street Journal, Consumer Reports,* and we got requests from out-of-state, even out-of-the-country. We were reluctant, feared we might jeopardize our position with the Congress, finally compromised, wrote people we would establish accounts out of state only with a two-thousand-dollar minimum. That gave the account an element of prestige, and we began getting several accounts out of the same apartment building—people were talking to each other."

Hall, like Haselton, is a veteran of commercial bank experience, in his forties, and not Ivy League. In conversation in his office, he pulls out the bottom drawer of his desk, leans back in his swivel chair, and puts his feet on the drawer. "There's a college professor here", he says, "who went to Commerce Bank and Trust and opened a free-chequeing account there, and a NOW account here. When it came time to pay his bills he would write out all his Commerce cheques, add up the total, write one NOW account draft and mail it to Commerce Bank. He gets interest not only on all his deposits but on the float."

For most of 1973, the Massachusetts mutual savings banks played it cool on NOW accounts. They are old established institutions, bigger than the state's commercial banks (and the largest holders of commercial bank stocks). The totals did not rise very fast or very far—in September 1973, when the Fed of Boston had anticipated $1,000 million in NOW accounts, there were only about $100 million. But as the new year began, the savings banks began to play rough. The ads were in the newspapers and in the windows of the banks: "Didn't you always wish your chequeing account paid interest?" It seemed unlikely that banking in Massachusetts would ever be quite the same again, and this sort of thing spreads, maybe slowly, maybe fast. In 1974, the New York State savings banks began to offer as a special service separate "chequeing accounts" with various fancy names. These accounts did not draw interest except to the extent that the depositor was fast enough on his feet to organize same-day transfer from his savings money at the bank to his chequeing money at the bank. Late in 1975, the state Court of Appeals prohibited chequeing accounts at savings banks, and New York returned to square one.

For cash purposes, nothing so elaborate as NOW accounts is necessary. Savings banks as well as commercial banks have installed outdoors "cash machines" that deliver packets of money in response to a code number and a credit card. In Nebraska, of all places, the savings and loan associations have already introduced at some dozens of supermarkets across the state a "Transmatic Money Service" which allows people with money in a savings and loan account to withdraw it at the supermarket cash register. Looking into the future, Governor George Mitchell of the Federal Reserve System sees today's proliferation of branch banks as "a perverse development. The branch as a way to get deposits will not have a life once the credits can be deposited directly. Once a man can cash his cheque at the supermarket, what does he need a branch for?"

With cash in savings accounts immediately accessible at a variety of locations and giro credits centrally stored, the pressure will be irresistible to create automatic transfer systems between savings accounts and giro credits; today's carefully nurtured distinctions between demand deposits and time deposits will disappear. The end of "free money" is a traumatic thought for American bankers. "The banks have to expect", says Governor Mitchell, "that some-day they won't have any money they don't directly pay for."

Similar developments are predictable for Britain, where the laws are silent on the permissible uses of interest-bearing accounts, the Trustee Savings Banks are offering cheque services, and the distinction between current account and deposit account has been quietly eroding even at the clearing banks for some years. When—if—the inflationary tide recedes, British banks will have to wield a sharper pencil than they have ever used before to calculate how wide a spread they need between the cost of their money and the rates they receive when they lend it to pay for the services the holder of a current account expects as a matter of course.

8/Bought Money

When the first version of this monograph appeared in 1959, it was noted that "corporations make relatively little use of time deposits. . . ." Indeed, until that time corporate time deposits were unwanted at many commercial banks. Corporations and others were reluctant to use for liquidity reserves an arrangement under which funds were tied up for a fixed period of time. The introduction of the negotiable CD, however, has changed the entire picture. . . . A large part of the funds which in earlier literature were not improperly referred to as "idle" has shifted into the high-turnover category, being continuously invested and reinvested in the money market until the actual need [arises] to return them into the money supply . . .

—GEORGE GARVY (Federal Reserve Bank of New York) and MARTIN R. BLYN, *The Velocity of Money*

* * *

American commercial banks have always had the power to accept "time deposits", which can be withdrawn only after due notice. Their function was to give the bank funds that could be loaned on a longer term than seemed safe when the source of the money was a demand deposit that could be removed from the bank at any moment. By and large, however, the big-city banks did not want to make long-term loans and had no desire to handle personal savings accounts. "I joined the bank in 1955", says Richard Thornton, who now runs the operations end of Philadelphia's First Pennsylvania Bank. "In those days if a customer wanted to open a savings account we used to take him by the hand and walk him down the street to the mutual savings bank." When Chemical Bank took over the Corn Exchange Bank in New York in 1954, William Renchard, assigned to merge the seventy-nine new branches with Chemical's nineteen, was amazed to find Corn Exchange still paying a derisory $\frac{1}{2}$ of 1 percent on savings. The business of the commercial banks had been short-term lending to finance the needs of trade. If industry needed long-term money, it could go to the bond market or the life-insurance companies. In Britain, the clearing banks left such matters to the kind attentions of the merchant banks.

But the instinct to save is, thank God, very deep-rooted in humanity, deriving from millennia of experience with bad luck. And one industry—housing—requires great quantities of long-term money that can be raised in the bond market only by governments. Early on, as early as the nineteenth century, it became clear that the financial centre banks would not meet savings needs or housing needs. Special institutions were formed, called building societies in England, savings and loan associations or (confusingly) savings banks in America. These institutions solicited time deposits by paying interest on "savings accounts", a term commercial banks in many states were not allowed to use.

Away from the big cities, commercial banks were needed primarily to make agricultural loans, which as late as 1930 accounted for one-quarter of all loans by commercial banks, half the loans by banks outside the big cities. Though most of this lending was also short-term—financing the purchase of seed, to be repaid when the crop was sold—much of it in the state-chartered banks was mortgage debt of some years' duration. (National banks were not permitted to write mortgages at all until 1914, and were not permitted to write mortgages on residential property until 1927. British clearing banks, except through subsidiaries, still resist mortgage lending. To match such loans, the banks solicited savings accounts. This was profitable business. By definition, time deposits were inactive: the bank had few expenses in servicing them. And when the bank loaned the money it got a good return: normal expectation was that the interest rate curve would have a "positive" slope—that is, the longer the term of the loan, the higher the interest rate. Country banks were therefore willing to pay something for time deposits, but as little as possible. They successfully fought the chartering of mutual savings banks in their states, and expected that their total money available for lending would be a mix of demand deposits ("free money") and time deposits ("bought money"). "The proportions have always varied from state to state", said Robert Mayo, president of the Federal Reserve Bank of Chicago. "Michigan went heavily into purchased funds—savings accounts—years and years ago. Today [this was 1972] the Michigan banks as a whole are up to seventy-odd percent of their deposits in time deposits." In Britain, the proportion of clearing bank deposits on which interest must be paid has now passed 75 percent.

Prior to the establishment of the Federal Reserve System in 1913, the National Bank Act insisted that a deposit was a deposit was a deposit, and reserve requirements were applied to nationally chartered banks on their total deposits without regard to any division between demand and time. In the three central reserve cities (New York from the beginning, Chicago and St. Louis after 1887), the required reserve was 25 percent of total deposits. In the forty-seven other reserve cities, the required reserve was still 25 percent, but half of it could be held in the form of deposits at correspondent banks in the central reserve cities; and in the "country" banks, perhaps reflecting a backhanded recognition of the difference between time and demand deposits, the required reserve was only 15 percent, of which three-fifths could be held in the form of deposits at correspondents in either reserve or central reserve cities. The Federal Reserve Act reduced reserve requirements (to 18 percent, 15 percent, and 12 percent respectively for the three categories of bank)—and made a distinction between demand deposits and time deposits, for which the reserve requirement was reduced to 5 percent.

The logic of the change was entirely straightforward. The first purpose of reserves, after all, was to assure payment to depositors who want their money. Because the Federal Reserve Banks were now available as lenders of last resort which could in an emergency supply a bank with funds to pay off a depositor, the overall need for reserves was diminished. And because time deposits by definition were much less likely to be taken out of the bank than demand deposits, the reserves behind them could be very low.

Money, of course, is entirely fungible: a banker needing money to acquire assets could blend his demand deposit funds (of which he could lend or invest 82 percent) and his time deposit funds (of which he could lend or invest 95 percent). In the prosperity of the 1920s, more and more people had savings to place somewhere, and even some big-city banks—especially National City and Bank of United States in New York—went after their share.

Meanwhile, out on the West Coast, A. P. Giannini's Bank of Italy (soon to be Bank of America) was scattering branches through the countryside, and building mighty flows of money from tiny tributary streams. More than half of Giannini's total deposits were savings accounts. Everyone in the East was envious, and thus suspicious. George Mooney recalls that while still a newspaperman in the 1940s he had occasion to interview a retiring executive director of the American Bankers Association, who had been a force in the industry for a generation. "I asked him", Mooney recalls, "in the fifty years he had been in banking, what was the single most significant development. Without bothering to think, he said, 'When A. P. Giannini introduced the principles of pushcart marketing to the banking business'."

Banks did not offer the option of time deposits to their corporate customers, because they did not wish to discourage the maintenance of big balances in chequeing accounts. (When pressed, the big-city banks would, prior to 1933, pay interest on demand deposits over some fairly high minimum balance; the usual beneficiaries were the out-of-town correspondent banks. When Congress prohibited the payment of interest on demand deposits in 1933, its purpose was to prevent big banks or desperate banks from bidding money away from other banks in the deflationary crunch of the Depression.) Most big-city banks continued to be leery of long-term loans, and thus felt little need to buy long-term deposits. In Britain, the clearing banks were in the business of selling money in the call market and depositors supplied all they could use.

When panic struck, it was the time deposits—their savings—that people hurried to take out of the banks; it was the long-term loans secured by real property that were most certain to be defaulted. The more dependent a bank had been on time deposits and long-term loans, the more likely it was not to reopen its doors after the Roosevelt bank holiday. (The British banks survived not because they were centralized or well managed but because they had neither savings accounts nor home mortgages in any quantity.) Marquis James's history of Bank of America denounces what he (and Giannini) considered a conspiracy in San Francisco and Washington to drive that bank to the wall; and Arthur Roth says he once employed a lawyer who had been with the Treasury Department when the fate of Bank of America was being decided, and had heard an officer of the U.S. Government say he was "going to get that damned wop" (who had been, incidentally, one of few bankers who publicly supported Franklin Roosevelt—once). But the fact is that heroic measures were necessary to keep Bank of America alive in 1933; and the land-holding subsidiary that the bank examiners valued by the acquisition price of the land to maintain an appearance of solvency for the bank did not get above water until well after the start of World War II.

At the bottom of the Depression, demand deposits in American commercial banks were down one-third from their peak in 1930, and they recovered by 1936. Time deposits dropped by 42 percent, and despite the introduction of deposit insurance in 1933 did not recover until 1944.

The holocaust of loans, however, was even worse: they dropped by almost 60 percent, from $35,000 million to $15,000 million. The bankers of the 1930s, horribly shaken by what they had lived through—by the change in their status from pillars to plunderers of the community—were confronted with a situation where they had much more money than they could lend. This phenomenon created the generation of American bankers now retiring, the well-connected but often not very bright men who knew somebody who might want to borrow the bank's money: they were the key to survival. Even they could not scare up much demand for short-term credit, however. What industry needed was money to retire its high-coupon bonds; and through the Reconstruction Finance Corporation the federal government was prepared to underwrite term loans by banks for purposes that would once have sent a prospective borrower off to the bond market. Meanwhile, the new Federal Housing Authority was guaranteeing three-year home-improvement loans and beginning its programme of insured self-amortizing mortgages.

With no little fear and trembling, Semenenko dancing ahead like the Pied Piper, the banks began to write term loans of two and even three years. It was that or government bonds, of which the banks in 1937 already held almost $15,000 million (as against less than $5,000 million in 1929). Government bonds paid less than 3 per-cent; guaranteed term loans could be made for at least 50 basis points more (i.e., $\frac{1}{2}$ of 1 percent—a basis point is 1 percent of a percentage point). This was the first banking revolution, the precondition of the others: a switch of substantial proportions of the portfolio to term loans. During the war, with the government insuring "V-loans" to finance expansion of industrial capacity, the revolution became permanent, like Mexico's.

War should make money tight: World War I had driven the yields on corporate bonds to their highest levels since the 1880s. But the U.S. Government in World War II was to command half the Gross National Product (considerably more, incidentally, than Hitler's government got out of the German economy), and most of the revenues to support that demand for war matériel were going to be borrowed. With the gold standard gone and the Federal Reserve System in place, the government could conveniently print government bonds which the banking system would buy through the creation of demand deposits. "You just put the bond on one side of the ledger", William Renchard recalls, "and the deposit on the other". When new reserves were needed to support these increased demand deposits, the Federal Reserve System would simply buy the bonds from the banks, crediting the proceeds to their reserves. So long as the Fed was willing to buy government bonds at their par value, banking was a great business. In effect, the government was lending money to the banks without charge and then paying the banks to borrow it back. At first it was hard to make the bankers believe the government would really do this (in previous wars the Treasury had raised interest rates for later loans, allowing the market price of earlier issues to sink), and the Fed had to intervene actively in 1942 to make the banks confident that things were as good as they looked. Then everyone became very satisfied with the new system, and the well-connected men who were not very bright began to regard themselves as financial wizards.

The United States had entered World War II with a national debt under $50,000 million; it emerged with a national debt over $250,000 million, of which $84,000 million was in the hands of the commercial banks, representing almost 60 percent of their total assets. Another $24,000 million was in the hands of the Federal Reserve System itself. For President Truman and his Treasury Secretaries the central task of the Federal Reserve System was to hold down the interest the government had to pay on this debt. Right after the war, nobody opposed cheap money: government, business, banking, and academia were united in their belief that Depression would return with peace, and high interest rates could only make things worse. Loan demand on the banks rose dramatically as industry retooled for peacetime production, but it could easily be met by selling off government bonds. This was "asset management": when banks needed money to make loans, they sold part of their government bond portfolio.

Something very similar was happening in Britain, though here the banks' easily liquidated assets included money on call with the discount houses as well as Treasury paper. Until 1958, the clearing banks had more money in British Government stocks than they had on loan to all borrowers.

From 1945 to 1950 the cheap money system worked like a watch. Government TT & L accounts at the banks dropped by $20,000 million, private demand deposits rose by $19,000 million. Loans rose by $21,000 million, holdings of U.S. Government securities dropped by $19,000 million. The total of deposits in the banking system rose by 5 percent in five years. Interest rates on government bonds went from an average of 2·37 percent in 1945 to an average of 2·32 percent in 1950; on Moody's AAA corporate bonds, rates held steady at 2·62 percent. Reflecting the vast increase in money supply during the war, the cost-of-living index rose almost a third from 1945 to 1948, but then it levelled off. The country was unbelievably prosperous: by 1950 average per capita income (for a considerably larger population, already swollen by a baby boom) was more than 40 percent greater than that of 1929, in constant prices.

Then came the Korean War, a renewal of government demand for war matériel at a time when the productive resources of the economy were fully employed in meeting civilian needs, a renewal of government deficits, and a renewed need for the Fed to purchase government bonds from the banks to sustain their reserve positions at a time of mounting loan demand. The inflation of 1950–51, as great as that of 1973–74, threatened the integrity of the American economy. The Fed refused to continue purchasing government bonds at par: if the banks needed additional reserves to support their deposits, they would have to sell their bonds at a loss, which would discourage them from increasing their loans. Interest rates would rise, and the government would have to pay more to refund its existing debt and to borrow any new money for the new war. The Bank of England made the same decision: in 1951, Bank Rate was raised above 2 percent for almost the first time since 1932.

In America, the first steps in this direction were taken unilaterally by the Fed, in the face of furious opposition by the White House and the Treasury. After a seven-month battle, from August 1950 to March 1951, a Washington compromise was effected: the White House accepted the principle that the Fed's activities in the government bond market had to be directed toward the maintenance of a stable economy rather than merely toward the maintenence of low interest costs on the government debt; and the Fed accepted a new chairman from within the Treasury Department. But the new chairman was William McChesney Martin, Jr., who wore no man's collar. Handling President Eisenhower and Congressional committees with equal Missouri suavity, Martin established for the

Fed an independence of political direction that was one of the wonders of American government—he was even able to force a policy of economic restraint in an election year, which almost certainly cost Richard Nixon the 1960 election and saddled the incoming Kennedy administration with 7 percent unemployment.

Before the 1930s, the banks had sought to keep themselves liquid by limiting their assets to short-term loans. In the 1940s their portfolios were already loaded with term loans that could not be called and would not run out frequently enough to produce funds if funds were needed; but the banking system was awash with the liquidity of government bond holdings that the Fed would buy at par if anyone felt the need for some additional reserves. In the 1950s, Martin's insistence that priority be given to the integrity of the currency drove the prices of marketable government bonds well below par—down so far, indeed, that if bank examiners had not been instructed to value the bonds at par for purposes of assessing a bank's condition, fair numbers of country and smaller city banks would have been declared bankrupt.

This was scary to old-fashioned people who felt that nobody should be made bankrupt—or should be made to look bankrupt—because he had bought obligations of the U.S. Government. It was also scary to somewhat less old-fashioned people who found that the assets they had counted on to assure the liquidity of their banks were now frozen by the difference between their valuation in the market and their valuation for examination purposes. The game changed: "You've got to make up your mind", says Gaylord Freeman of the First National Bank of Chicago, "that in the last analysis your liquidity depends on the Federal Reserve, and in the next-to-last analysis it depends on your ability to borrow." The stage was set for the second banking revolution, which is still in progress: the switch from demand deposits to time deposits as the central source of funds for the banks, from "asset management" to "liability management" as the central skill of banking, from good connections to good brains as the requirement for bank leadership.

This American Revolution is the one that happened in London too.

2

Consider the condition of the big New York and Chicago banks. The National Bank Acts of the 1860s had structured a situation in which banks all over the country were eager to keep large deposits in New York and Chicago, where they could get interest and services for reserves they would not be allowed to lend or invest, anyway. Corporations anywhere that needed large loans made a trek to one of the two big cities, where large loans were available; and they kept their balances where they got their loans, because that's what you do in banking, always and everywhere.

With the adoption of the Federal Reserve Act, which they had bitterly opposed, the money-centre banks lost their favoured position; as the years passed, the New York and Chicago banks commanded a steadily decreasing proportion of the deposits in the system. The war accelerated the trend, as factories and payrolls sprang up far away in the Southwest and on the West Coast. Within the city itself, meanwhile, wartime prosperity put money in the neighbourhoods, into the branch banks in the small accounts the great wholesale banks had never cultivated.

In the years right after World War II, while the economy at large was still awash in the liquidity of huge government bond holdings, the giant wholesale banks began to run out of money. Their first line of attack in New York was to absorb the retail banks with their growing branches: First National merged with National City, Chemical took over Corn Exchange, Manufacturers and Hanover joined, Chase made an intricate arrangement with the Bank of the Manhattan Company (which had a queer charter as a water supply company dating back to the days of Aaron Burr: legally, to accomplish the merger, it became necessary for Manhattan to acquire Chase).

But the banking system as a whole was losing to "nonbank financial institutions" in the continuing battle for money. Between the end of 1945 and 1960, the assets of life insurance companies tripled; those of savings and loan associations multiplied by nine; those of trusteed pension funds multiplied by fifteen; those of commercial banks rose by three-fifths. And as interest rates rose in the back half of the 1950s, the situation grew worse: the big "wholesale" banks began to lose corporate deposits.

It was one thing for a corporate treasurer to keep a good deal of loose cash in the bank in the 1940s, when the best interest rate that could be got on a short-term Treasury bill was $\frac{3}{8}$ of 1 percent; something else in the 1950s when short-term Treasuries were selling at 3·5 percent. (And something else again in the 1970s, when short-term Treasuries might yield 9 percent.) The perfection of the market for government securities meant that a company which needed money prior to the expiration of the bill could sell it overnight for cash. As a "money market instrument", the government security qualified as "near money"; and "near money" was really all a corporation required for a good proportion of the reserves being accumulated to pay dividends or taxes or to replace equipment.

The banks themselves were major dealers in Treasuries; adding insult to injury, the corporations began asking them to arrange the transfer of their money from demand deposits to interest-bearing money market instruments. (J. P. Morgan & Company taught them how to do it; when fellow bankers complained to Morgan's George Whitney that his young men were slitting everyone's throat to gain a petty competitive advantage, he said, "My customers are not stupid".) By 1959, non-financial corporations were holding nearly $23,000 million of short-term Treasury issues, at least half of it money that in earlier years would have been part of bank deposits—plus some billions more of commercial paper and bankers' acceptances.

Received opinion was that the banks could not improve this picture by anything they might do. "Federal Reserve operations," Stephen H. Axilrod wrote in the *Federal Reserve Bulletin* in 1961, "govern the availability of bank reserves. . . . the liquidity of non-bank financial institutions," on the other hand, "depends mainly on their ability to compete for the idle cash and current savings of the public." Still, Axilrod thought, the Fed could be counted on not to let the banks fall to the level where they could no longer conduct their necessary business, "the financing of inventories or lines of credit related to day-to-day business operations and needs."

It was especially obvious that the banks could not compete with the Treasury bills market for corporate funds. The Banking Act of 1933 had given the Fed the power (and duty) to set maximum interest rates banks could pay on deposits. In the late 1950s, the Fed by its Regulation Q limited the commercial banks to a maximum of 3 percent per annum on time deposits left in the bank six months or more, $2\frac{1}{2}$ percent on deposits left between ninety days and six months, and 1 percent per annum on deposits left in the bank less than ninety days. (Savings associations were allowed to pay more, to encourage people to put their savings where they would be available to finance housing. Nobody was allowed to pay interest on money left on deposit less than thirty days.) Treasury bills were obviously more attractive: they paid more than 3 percent, and did not have to be held thirty days. Then, in the 1960 recession, the rate on Treasury bills dipped sharply; by the end of the year, it was under 2·5 percent. The aggressive new leadership of New York's First National City Bank saw an opportunity to get corporate deposits back into the bank—and to get them back, moreover, under a time deposit rubric which would require less in the line of reserves against deposits.

The device invented for this purpose was the negotiable certificate of deposit—or "CD". It could be issued for any maturity date beyond thirty days the corporation wished, though under the interest rate ceilings in effect in 1961 maturities longer than six months were virtually dictated. The normal denomination at the beginning was $1 million or some multiple thereof; and the interest the bank would pay was between $\frac{1}{4}$ and $\frac{1}{2}$ of 1 percent above the going rate on Treasury bills.

What was important was that the CD could be sold in a secondary market, just like a Treasury bill—indeed, to the same dealers. This was not an accident. First National City had gone to the Treasuries dealers and persuaded them to undertake market-making in negotiable CDs before the first one was issued, and within a few days of the announcement by the bank that it was going to write such IOUs, Discount Corporation of America announced that it was ready to buy and sell them; Salomon Brothers and First Boston Corporation soon followed. "There's a world of difference", says Walter Wriston of First National City, "between a New Year's Resolution and a plan".

Wriston is a lean, graceful, dark-haired, handsome tough guy, rounded cheeks, a sharply pointed nose and a thrust jaw, son of the man whose presidency made Brown a great university, fiercely competitive, sarcastic, and calculatedly indiscreet. The negotiable CD appears to have been his baby (the scorekeepers give a significant assist to staff economist John Exter), and the chairmanship of Citibank (after a not inconsiderable internal struggle) his reward. "The day we announced the CD", he recalls, "one of the biggest banks in the country called and said, 'Don't you remember we had CD's in Shanghai years ago, and it didn't work? This won't fly, Walt'." I said, "Thank you".

What the CD had going for it on the open market was the chance to get around the Fed's ceiling on interest rates on short-term deposits. Issued at 3 percent per annum, a six-month CD could be bought in a secondary market four months after it was issued; it would then, in effect, be a sixty-day time deposit paying three times the maximum interest rate the Fed allowed banks to offer. Assuming a normal positive slope for the graph that charts interest rates against length of loan, a CD nearing maturity would sell to yield less than the interest rate on its face—that is, it would sell for more than its face value. Dealers could thus "ride the yield curve" and make money on their CD trades over and above the interest they earned when they held the paper in their inventory.*

*This one may be a little easier to understand with numbers. Assume a yield curve sloping upward rather rapidly, so that a six-month loan pays 5 percent and a one-year loan pays 6 percent. (Assume also continuous payment of interest by the borrower, to avoid calculation problems of add-on as against discount interest rates.) A one-year CD for $1,000,000 at 6 percent would yield $60,000 in a year for its purchaser; a six-month CD for $1,000,000 at 5 percent would earn $25,000 in half a year. When six months remain on the one-year CD, there is still $30,000 of interest to be paid on it, and it will sell in the market for almost $1,005,000 to earn its purchaser $30,000 less the $5,000 premium, or 5 percent. Note that the dealer buying the CD and holding it six months makes 7 percent on his money—$30,000 of interest earned, plus a

Though there were some early problems relating to endorsement of the certificates from one owner to another (unlike a corporation issuing a bond, a bank could not print a new certificate for a purchaser in the secondary market), the negotiable CD quickly became an indispensable centrepiece of modern large-scale banking. "There's only one guy I know who was in this business before CD's," says Ralph Forbes, who heads the money desk at the First National Bank of Boston, a self-described "dilettante economist" from Harvard who is still under forty but not drastically so. "He's retired". (Forbes, by the way, has since moved from Boston to Washington to become an Assistant Secretary of the Treasury and help manage the national debt.)

By the end of 1962, the money-centre banks had $5,800 million of CDs outstanding; by August 1966, the total had reached $18,000 million, and half of that could be explained by corporate reductions in corporate holdings of Treasury bills. In 1974, the banks—are you ready?—had more than $90,000 million of CDs outstanding. Most big-time bankers believe that future growth in bank resources will come almost entirely from growth in CDs rather than growth in demand deposits—and they welcome it. "You take the cost of the four walls and the roof in a branch in Reading, Pennsylvania," says president James Bodine of First Pennsylvania, "And the cost of the people in that box—and it's a pretty elegant box—plus the costs of transporting all those pieces of paper to the computer centre, running them through, delivering them out via helicopter and truck to convert them into dollars. Then compare that to the costs of one man on one telephone buying you ten, fifteen million of CDs with a single call. . . ."

The CD came to London as an instrument in the Eurodollar market, an easy way for a well-known bank from any country to buy a deposit base in the world's premier trading currency and for holders of dollar assets to employ them without exchange rate

---

$5,000 premium, for half a year's investment of $1,000,000. Note also that if the yield curve turns negative—if short-term loans begin to pay higher rates than long-term loans—the purchaser of a CD who wishes to resell will have to do so at a discount, and the dealers will get clobbered.

risks or exchange control hassles. In 1968, First National City (having made arrangements with White Weld in London similar to those it had pioneered with Discount Corporation in New York) asked H.M. Treasury for permission to issue sterling CDs to beef up its British business. The clearing banks initially had no interest (CDs, the *Midland Bank Review* sniffed as late as November 1969, "have no special advantage for the issuing banks"), but the merchant banks gleefully bought money in the new market, reducing their dependence on short-term loans from other banks. After 1971, as we shall see, the negotiable CD—and the inexperience of the Bank of England in controlling the use of such investments— became a prime source of expansion of the British money supply.

What made the domestic dollar CD a gamble for American banks was the danger that the Fed could close down the business at any time. Regulation Q could be amended to reduce the ceiling on interest rates for time deposits without touching any other part of the business (savings deposits, which can be owned by individuals and partnerships but not by corporations, are separately controlled). Worse, a failure to lift the Reg Q ceilings if Treasury bill rates went up would immediately dry up the CD supply: corporations that could not get as good a rate on a CD as they could on a Treasury would no longer be willing to buy. At the time Wriston moved, the forests were hearing the first halloos of what the Kennedy administration brains trust called "Operation Twist"—an effort to raise the rate on short-term Treasury bills while keeping long-term rates steady, to counteract a drain of short-term dollars ("hot money") to Europe. Wriston and his allies—especially the Chicago banks and the First National Bank of Boston—moved fast because they hoped to make the negotiable CD so important a support of the big banks that the Fed would hesitate to kill it off.

The gamble was won: every year from 1962 to 1966 the Fed raised its ceilings on time deposits to preserve the CD. In 1965, a single ceiling was set for all CDs, regardless of the time to maturity, provided they ran longer than thirty days. Then, in 1966, rather suddenly, the Fed got in trouble on another front. The Reg Q ceiling had risen to $5\frac{1}{2}$ percent for time deposits—but the ceiling on personal savings deposits was still 4 percent at commercial banks, and 4½ percent at mutual savings banks. The law forbade corporations to hold savings deposits, but it did not forbid individuals to hold time certificates. Arthur Roth of Franklin National on Long Island began offering—*and advertising*—certificates in $1,000 denominations, carrying a coupon higher than the legal maximum interest rate on savings accounts.

Roth modestly refuses credit for inventing this paper, which he called "bonds". He says, "Wachovia [then the biggest bank in North Carolina] had started them. I went to a bankers' convention in the South, and the head of Wachovia told me about them. I hadn't known anything about it. I thought, 'For God's sake, we've been asleep here'. In a month or so, we had four hundred and twenty million dollars." Roth's $420 million nearly ruined the savings and loan associations of California, which had drawn a significant share of their "deposits" from the New York area, by mail, on a promise of higher interest rates than were available in New York. Now New Yorkers could get a return just as good (or better) close to home. Not only did they stop sending money to California, they began taking some out.

The savings banks could not fight back. CD or "bond" rates are what a commercial bank pays on the marginal dollar: most of the bank's money still comes from demand deposits, savings accounts, and older CDs sold at lower rates. Most of a commercial bank's loans, moreover, are either short-term or roll-over, with an increase in interest rate possible at regular intervals. Savings banks and associations if they raise the interest payments must raise them simultaneously for all depositors, not just for the new depositor whose money is being solicited by a CD merchant. And their loans are in mortgages which in the United States carry an interest rate fixed for the life of the mortgage—often enough, in 1966, a rate below the 5½ percent Roth was paying on his bonds. Home building in California began to contract; one of the largest savings and loan associations collapsed over the July Fourth weekend in 1966 and had to be rescued by the Federal Home Loan Bank Board. "We do business with households", says a spokesman for the U.S.

Savings and Loan League. "I've come to think that this is the most avaricious economic unit in the United States." (Of course, avarice is not unknown at the S&L's themselves. In 1974, when everyone was publicly worried about the loss of mortgage money from the withdrawal of personal savings from the mutuals and S&L's, there was really a much larger drain caused by the shift of savings association investments from mortgages to higher yielding instruments in the Eurodollar and Fed Funds markets.)

The Fed is a creature of Congress, and there is no subject on which Congress is more sensitive than home building. In summer 1966, the Fed was given power to discriminate further among the different interest-bearing deposits when setting its ceilings, and that September, in a move that drew no public criticism whatever and is still for some reason held beyond criticism by the consumer movement, the Fed restricted high interest certificates of deposit to denominations of $100,000 or more. The fat cats, in other words, can get the market rate of interest for their savings, but ordinary people are supposed to make do with what the government says is good for them. Paul Anderson and Robert Eisenmenger of the Federal Reserve Bank of Boston have estimated that "in 1970 persons who saved at depository institutions were deprived of almost $7,000 million of income" by this amendment to Reg Q; William Dentzer, former New York State Superintendent of Banks, has inquired acidly: "Who decided that homebuyers as a class were more worthy than [the] lower- and middle-class savers . . . we are penalizing?" (In 1973, the Fed did try to reverse this decision, authorizing—though only for maturities of four years or longer—"wild card" CDs of consumer size; but Congress in one week, without hearings, mandated a return to the *status quo*.)

It seems reasonable to believe that this experience left the Fed disenchanted with CDs as a device. When Treasury bill rates rose above the CD ceilings in 1966, the Fed held firm on its existing Reg Q. By November, $3,200 million of CDs had run off, and the banks had been unable to replace them. "We had felt the CD would be a stable source of funds," says Jim Sheridan of North

Carolina National Bank; "it was a traumatic experience for us." The money-centre banks entered into an anguished decline—"The worst period I ever went through", William Renchard says, and his experience includes the hammer-blow of the Penn Central bankruptcy. "I could see an unlimited demand for loans, and no source of funds, none at all, unless we liquidated the entire investment portfolio at a *tremendous* loss." Losses were in fact taken— banks sold bonds into a declining market to meet their commitments and lines of credit to pinched customers. But the money crunch of fall 1966 did produce the mini-recession of early 1967, interest rates fell, and the banks were able to sell their large denomination CDs again at $5\frac{1}{2}$ percent.

Living through the horrors of fall 1966 stimulated the banks to invent a veritable funhouse of tricks that could be used next time to get around Reg Q and any public policy to restrain the growth of bank assets. "Like a Laurel and Hardy movie," says bank consultant Carter Golembe; "you closed one door, they came through another."

3

Balance sheets, like books, freeze the world at a point in time. This makes them instructive but not always very useful, because the world refuses to remain frozen. When one says that banks are required by law to retain a certain reserve against deposits, the meaning cannot be that this ratio is maintained at every minute of every day. Banks do not control the time at which their depositors will withdraw from or add to an account; they cannot even know for sure when a cheque written on an account will be debited, or a cheque they expect to receive will be credited. Surprise audits, which are a reasonable way to find out whether a bank is keeping its books honestly, are not suitable as a means of verifying the maintenance of proper reserves. Some formalized system for freezing the world at stated intervals must be developed to assure that the reserve requirement is effective.

Different procedures have been followed in the United States at different times. Since 1968, the arrangements have been as follows:

1. Banks are required to keep a ledger showing the condition of the bank just prior to the opening every morning. (The bank doesn't know its condition at the moment of closing; that's what those computer people at Valley and Manufacturers Hanover are doing all night long.) Banks report to the Fed every week the day-by-day total of their deposits by type, their "vault cash" and the cheques they are in process of collecting from other banks.

2. The banking system is frozen for accounting purposes every Wednesday, and a reserve against deposits is assessed. The requirement is a percentage of average daily deposits of each type—demand, savings, time (within which there are subtypes—CDs, deposits by foreign branches, etc.). Since 1935, the Federal Reserve Board has had (and has used) the power to alter reserve requirements for the banking system, within relatively wide limits. In 1974, the precise figures on required reserves for demand deposits were 2 percent of the first $2 million, 8 percent of the next $8 million, 12 percent of the next $90 million, $13\frac{1}{2}$ percent of the next $300 million, and $18\frac{1}{2}$ percent of everything over $400 million; and required reserves for time deposits were 3 percent of the first $5 million and 5 percent thereafter, with higher rates on CDs.

3. But the banks are not held to the reserves that would have been required for the deposits in the week just ended: that would imply a degree of control over their condition that they do not in fact have in this age of telecommunications. Instead, the banks are told that *during the reporting period of the week after next*, they will have to maintain daily average reserves equal to the requirement for the average deposits they reported in the week just past. Thus, the reserves required during the week that will end May 15 are dictated by the deposit figures for the week ended May 1.

4. For this accounting, a bank's reserves consist of its own deposits at its friendly neighbourhood Federal Reserve Bank. (The bank also may count toward its required reserves for the "statement week" the cash it had on the premises during the week for which the deposits were calculated.) Every Thursday morning, a bank knows precisely what its average reserves for the forthcoming

week must be. The Fed allows a 2 percent variation from the requirement in any given week; any deficiency within that 2 percent must be made up next week, and any excess reserves up to 2 percent may be claimed against next week's requirement. Excess over 2 percent, however, goes to waste; and a deficiency greater than 2 percent produces a penalty. Repeated deficiencies will be referred to the Comptroller of the Currency or the state banking authority that licensed this particular member bank, and can result in the loss of a bank's charter.

5. The requirement is for an *average* over the week. The Fed adds up the bank's reserves on hand at the close of every day, and on Wednesday divides the total by seven. Yes, by seven—not by five: Saturday and Sunday count. Reserves at the close of business on Friday, then, are worth three times as much as reserves on hand at the close of any other day.

As recently as 1970, that description of Federal Reserve procedure would have been all but incomprehensible to even fairly sophisticated British bankers. The Bank of England in the old days controlled the banks' *advances*—their loans—rather than their deposits. The two are not unrelated, of course (a loan creates a deposit); but operationally the difference is night and day. To the extent that the Bank took account of reserves against deposits, their interests were in assuring a bank's liquidity (its ability to pay back its depositors) rather than in controlling the money supply. The banks were supposed to maintain a cash reserve equal to about 8 percent of current and 7-day accounts, plus 28 percent in highly liquid short-term assets.

With Competition and Credit Control in 1971, the Bank moved a long way to the American system. As of mid-1975, British banks are required to maintain an interest-bearing reserve account at the Bank totalling 3 percent of their total "eligible liabilities" as of the third Wednesday of the most recent month. In addition, they must keep a sum equal to $12\frac{1}{2}$ percent of their "eligible liabilities" in approved short-term "reserve assets" (call money at the discount houses, short Treasury paper, approved short-term local authority and commercial paper). The 3 percent is an absolute floor, never to be breached; the 12½ percent in Britain as in America is an average over a period of time—but Saturday and Sunday don't count.

British banks have never been forbidden to pay interest on short-term deposits (before the First World War, it was common practice in Britain to pay interest on current account), and the Bank has never had the authority to impose ceilings on interest rates. When the clearing banks began to run out of current account money in the late 1950s, the debate about whether they should bid for deposits was conducted in terms of sound business and banking practice, not in terms of legalities. What resolved it was the growth of Eurodollar business, resting on the negotiable CD market and the interbank lending market (an interbank loan in London is the direct equivalent of a Fed Funds transaction in the United States; the American version has to be called a Fed Funds transaction rather than a loan for legal reasons). Alarmed by the proliferation of these devices, the Bank in 1973 imposed direct controls on the banks' expansion of their Interest Bearing Eligible Liabilities (IBELs—in effect, CDs and interbank borrowings). Like the parallel efforts of the Fed, this device worked only fairly well, for reasons we shall be exploring in the next chapter. The central fact is that by the mid-1970s, the actual practice of banking in London, though not always the terms of art or the apparent customs, had grown remarkably close to the actual practice in New York.

Consider now the situation of an American bank that opens the doors Thursday morning with the knowledge that its anticipated account at the Fed over the forthcoming week will not be enough to cover the reserve requirement imposed by the Fed to cover its deposits of two weeks ago. This is in fact the situation of every large bank in the United States every week. What can the bank do to keep out of trouble? Well, you'd be surprised; the Fed itself is forever being surprised. And since the introduction of Competition and Credit Control the Bank of England has had a lot of surprises too.

9/Fancy Bought Money

I maintain that the Money Market is as concrete and real as anything else; that it can be described in plain words; that it is the writer's fault if what he says is not clear.

—WALTER BAGEHOT (1873)

* * *

First, the obvious things a bank can do when it knows it must increase its reserves at the Fed or the Bank of England.

The bank can sell an asset, probably a securities investment—a Treasury bill, a government bond, a municipal bond—and send the proceeds over to the Fed (or, in the British system, to the call market) to beef up its reserves. This is what the banks did in the years right after World War II, when the Fed was pegging the price of government bonds and buying them at par from anyone who offered them. Once the Fed had stopped supporting the market, this option became less attractive, because it often involved taking a loss on a security that could otherwise be valued at par in the inventory: most of the times that a bank needs money, interest rates are up, which means the price of bonds is down. Anyway, since 1969—when another squeeze on CD rates forced the banks to sell $10,300 million of government securities to meet their commitments to borrowers—the American banks' inventory of Treasuries has been cut to the bone. There is a real bone here, too, because there are laws that require banks to hold Treasury issues as security against the deposits of state and municipal governments. In Britain, there is a gentlemen's agreement between the Bank and the big clearing banks, that the latter will not seek to avoid a squeeze by selling long-term government paper, which would complicate the Bank's work as manager of the national debt.

Also in the area of "asset management", a bank can sell a loan from its loan portfolio, and add the proceeds of the sale to its reserves. Unfortunately, the terms of most loans are such that the borrower would have to agree; and that's no way to keep a customer happy. Mortgages are usually saleable, though, without the consent of the mortgagor, and if the price is acceptable an American bank that needs additional reserves at the Fed may sell some of its mortgages for cash. Many mortgages, in fact, are now written to be sold: the sort of thing Roth and Bimson did enterprisingly in the 1930s has become standard procedure. The purchasers now are usually a quasi-government agency like the Federal National Mortgage Association (FNMA—"Fannie Mae") or a private Real Estate Investment Trust (REIT: larger banks often have their own affiliated REIT). There is less government assistance in Britain, where the government have chosen to put their housing money into council rather than private properties.

In theory, a bank can also call a loan—demand the money back —from a borrower whose agreement to borrow contained a call provision. Such loans were standard on Wall Street fifty years ago, and loan agreements with borrowers in the financial market may still contain such clauses. But experience historically has been that when a bank has a need to call a loan its borrowers have no ready money either, and today a bank that expects it may need the money soon will lend day by day, with the option of refusing to renew tomorrow, rather than risk enforcing a call. (The day-today borrowers are most likely to be government bond dealers, whom the Federal Reserve System will under no circumstances allow to get killed, so it's not tragic if the bank backs away for a while. In Britain, the government, via the Bank of England, uses the discount houses to deal and operate in the domestic market, of which the call money market is a part; but calling a loan to a discount house does not help a bank's reserve position because such loans are themselves "reserve assets".) The great source of liquidity in the banking system is the self-amortizing loan, which gets paid back at scheduled intervals rather than at a lump at the end; portfolios of such loans generate new cash every day. But not enough.

If a bank does not wish to sell an asset at the price that asset commands, it can "emit a liability"—borrow money—to meet its obligations at the Fed. The Federal Reserve Act contemplated that member banks would borrow for this purpose from the Fed itself, by "discounting" their top-quality loans (bankers' acceptances, loans endorsed by other bankers) at the nearest Reserve Bank. Each Reserve Bank has a "discount rate", the interest the bank charges on such loans to its members, and an officer who runs the "discount window". This is the way the Federal Reserve System meets what every commentator since Bagehot has considered the first responsibility of a central bank: to be the "lender of last resort" to the banks themselves. (In Britain, the Bank does not lend to anyone but discount houses, but the principle is the same.) The service offered in America these days is a straight secured loan service: the paper behind the loan is taken into custody and returned by the Fed when the loan is paid off, not "discounted" and held to maturity.

The first large-scale use of the discount window came in 1920, when banks that were squeezed in the postwar deflation borrowed some $2,800 million, a sum greater than the total reserve requirements in the system. Bagehot had insisted that in its function as a lender of last resort the central bank must charge a "punitive" rate, higher than anything the banks could get on their loans, to avoid serving as a generator of inflationary monetary expansion. In 1920, the discount rate was 7 percent, higher than the commercial loan rates of the time. ("Certainly," Benjamin Strong of the New York Fed wrote Montagu Norman of the Bank of England, "it is a better banking investment for any bank to pay off a 6 percent or 7 percent loan than it is to loan the money outside at a lower rate.") But this procedure would greatly diminish the usefulness of the discount window to the banks it was especially designed to serve—country banks which couldn't collect their loans because of crop failures, banks in territories affected by floods or tornadoes or strikes, etc. When credit tightened again later in the 1920s, the Governors of the Federal Reserve System intervened to keep the twelve individual Federal Reserve Banks from raising their discount rates, and ultimately the system as a whole adopted a policy of keeping the discount rate low and rationing Fed credit to banks by administrative action rather than by price. Access to the discount window became a privilege, not a right.

Today a bank must explain why it needs this money, and what plans have been laid to pay it back. The Boston Fed, according to Ralph Forbes of the First National Bank of Boston, "is very civilized in its administration of the window. They never say, 'No', They just say, 'What seems to be the problem?'" All borrowings at the window must be collateralized, and to ease the messenger-service problem each Fed maintains what Thomas O. Waage of the New York Fed calls "a tin box"—a vault full of member banks' government securities and promissory notes that are "eligible" to secure borrowings at the window. Other paper may also be acceptable for this purpose, but then the rate charged by the Fed goes up $\frac{1}{2}$ of 1 percent. Normally, big banks borrow only on Wednesday, to make up a reserve deficiency for the statement week, and the loan is simply cancelled, with a debit to the reserve account for the interest, on the succeeding day. But this is an accounting artifact: a Wednesday loan is really a loan of one-seventh that amount for every day of the week, and a bank that goes in every Wednesday is really in debt to the Fed all the time.

Though there is a real window, like a teller's cage at any bank, the discount window at the Fed is in practice a telephone. "I don't think we've written two letters in twelve years", says Richard Moffat, who runs this operation at the Federal Reserve Bank of Chicago. A phone call from the borrowing bank starts the process, and a phone call from the Fed often ends it. The phone calls are not always pleasant. "In 1966," says Thomas Timlen, a lawyer who rather to his own surprise found himself managing the Fed discount window in New York, "I made loans to fifty, fifty-five percent of the banks in this district, and I wound up talking to one in every three or four and saying, 'The accommodation has been used, and we'd like you now to go away.' If the discount officer is doing his job, the screw is being turned in a personal way, not an impersonal way: the fact is that the discount officer is being critical of the bank's management".

Paul Jones of Valley National in Phoenix describes the situation from the other end: "The Fed will say, 'You borrowed last month and again this month—do you expect to borrow again next month?' To which the only answer is, 'Absolutely not!' It's subtle but it's effective".

Chicago requires a daily financial statement from a bank that is "in the window". Moffat recalls a situation where a midwestern bank called "in extremis"—a loan had gone sour that day, and the bank had a big chunk of collateral in the form of convertible bonds it did not yet know how to sell. "I told him," Moffat says, "'All right—I won't embarrass you. But I'll call you every day at noon till you pay it off, to see how you're getting along in selling that paper.'" Because the Chicago banks had stretched themselves very tight with aggressive lending policies in fall 1972, the Chicago Fed was something less than sympathetic to their problems in spring 1973, but they came to the window anyway. The argument within the banks was that the government was abusing them by holding down the interest rates they could charge their customers while doing nothing about the interest rates they had to pay on CDs: if the Fed discount rate was a bargain (and it was), the banks had a right to get a bit of their own back. "I let us get very devious", says Gaylord Freeman of the First National Bank of Chicago, enjoying himself. "We went in every other week. One day I got a call from the Fed, and somebody said to me, 'Gale, I think I see a pattern. . . .'"

2

The advantage of the discount window as a source of funds was the fact that the borrowing could be instantly credited to a bank's reserves, because the entire transaction took place within the Fed. There was another way this same advantage could be gained: by borrowing from other banks, which had accounts at the same Fed and could transfer the money on the books of the Fed without going through a time-consuming clearing mechanism.

As the discount window began to shut in the 1920s, banks began borrowing these Fed Funds from each other, and a Wall Street broker named George Garvin become the expert in matching banks that needed reserves with banks that had some excess money at the Fed and could lend it. In the 1930s, when the problem was disposing of money rather than finding it, the Fed Funds market fell into decay, and by the 1950s there was almost nobody in banking who remembered it had ever existed—"Except," says Martin T. Griffin of Morgan Guaranty, "George Garvin. He had made a million dollars brokering Fed Funds one year in the 1920s, and a man remembers things like that".

Griffin, who runs Morgan's CD desk and shares responsibility for other Morgan ventures in the money market, is a chunky man with a mane of white-grey hair and the musical, slightly lisped speech that is among the attractions of the very highest social class in New York City. He recalls that he first made contact with the Fed Funds phenomenon in 1947, when he got a call from the treasurer of a bank that was practising asset management to replenish light reserves. His bank, the man said, had $30 million of Treasury bills it wanted to sell for cash; could Morgan buy them? The answer was, Yes; and the next question was how soon in the day Morgan would have to know to get the money credited to the seller at the Fed before the close of business. "About twelve thirty", Griffin said. At 12.30, the man called again to inquire if

Morgan could buy $40 million, and Griffin said, "Yes, but, look, it's getting dark". (Even in 1975, Treasury bill transactions for credit the same day were best made before two o'clock.) Then Griffin didn't hear from the man again, and a few days later he called up to find out what had happened. "Oh", the man said, "I took care of it with Garvin Bantel".

This was the first time Griffin had heard that name: The Garvin Bantel Company, members of various stock exchanges, was not a dealer in Treasuries. He checked into the situation and found that Garvin Bantel was a broker serving a number of smaller banks with which the firm had established relations many years before in the now deceased Fed Funds market. Griffin filed all this information in the back of his head, and recalled it one day in the early 1950s when he learned that money being loaned to Morgan by Guaranty Trust (not yet merged with J. P. Morgan & Company) had in fact been borrowed by Guaranty from Citizens Fidelity Bank in Louisville. Griffin checked Morgan's list of correspondents, and found that Morgan, too, had a relationship with Citizens Fidelity, expressed by a $50,000 balance. No Morgan salesman had ever called on the bank. At Griffin's urging, one of them now did, and suggested that since Morgan was winding up with the bank's money anyway the bank might as well eliminate the middleman.

Morgan was the first of the money-centre banks to be squeezed when the Fed turned off the spigot in the early 1950s: it had maintained its loan customers all across the country but had no retail branches to generate deposits to support its loans. On those days when Morgan did not need money from Louisville, the salesman suggested, it would undertake the work of lending it elsewhere— and if there were ever a week when Louisville needed money, Morgan would attempt (really, *would*, but nobody gives guarantees) to reciprocate past favours. The prestige of J. P. Morgan & Company was such that it had some sort of correspondent connection with a very large number of banks in smaller cities around the country, and Morgan salesmen were soon calling on all of them to offer similar services. In effect, Morgan became a broker of Fed Funds around the banking system. "We were shifting reserves from Pittsburgh to Akron to Detroit", Griffin recalls. "We were very careful never to make a profit on it in those days; we did it for the balances. Within a matter of a few months, that Louisville bank went from a balance of fifty thousand dollars with us to a balance in millions".

Under the urgings of Morgan salesmen, the Fed Fund market grew rapidly in the 1950s, and puzzled technicians from the Federal Reserve System came calling to find out what lay behind the rash of interbank transfers Morgan seemed to be masterminding on the books of the Federal Reserve Banks. At first the Fed's reaction was negative, because the transfer of Fed Funds looked like an end run around the rules: Fed Funds borrowed did not constitute a deposit, and thus were not subject to reserve requirements. On reconsideration, however, the Fed decided to encourage the growth of the Fed Funds market. So long as there were excess reserves in the system, it was difficult for Fed policymakers to tighten the money supply without relatively drastic action. If reserves were fully employed, which would be the end result of an active Fed Funds market over time, the Fed could hope for much greater leverage on the lending activities of the banks.

As transfers of reserves around the country became easier through the Fed's own leased wire system, more banks became participants in the market and the average size of the transaction came down. In 1960, about two hundred banks were involved in the Fed Funds market, and the minimum overnight Fed Funds deal was a million dollars. By the early 1970s, "practically all banks with more than a hundred million dollars in deposits" were trading Fed Funds at least occasionally, and the minimum size had been reduced to $100,000. In New England, nine-tenths of all the banks were in the Fed Funds market in 1974: "We have a policy," said Ralph Forbes of the First National Bank of Boston, "of accommodating all correspondents in the First District, on either side. Then we adjust our position in the national market". Out in Walker, Iowa, in 1972, Alan Mannetter was looking forward to the day "when Fed Funds will get back above eight percent, and banking will be a good business again." He got his wish.

WHERE THE MONEY COMES FROM

Before 1963, Fed Funds had been essentially a source of cheap money—purchased reserves and correspondent balances—for Morgan and the other money-centre banks. The overnight rate on these borrowings was believed to be limited by the discount rate at the Fed: presumably nobody would buy Fed Funds if he could more cheaply borrow at the discount window. Moreover, Fed Funds transactions were considered loans, which meant they were subject to the usual restrictions on how much a bank could lend to any single borrower (10 percent of its capital; normally, in other words, 1 percent of its deposits, unless Treasury issues secured the loan). In 1963, James Saxon, Kennedy's unpredictable Comptroller, announced that henceforward nationally chartered banks were to treat Fed Funds transactions as purchases (by the borrower) and sales (by the lender), not as loans, which multiplied the potential size of the market.

And then, in 1966, it became apperent that the Fed's reluctance to open the discount window for purposes of supplying reserves against routine banking operations would keep the money-centre banks active in the Fed Funds market even after the Fed Funds rate had gone considerably higher than the discount rate. In June 1969, banks paid 4·5 percentage points more for Fed Funds than they would have had to pay at the discount window (a 10·5 percent average for the month, against a discount rate of 6 percent)—but, of course, the Fed was being impolite about providing service at the window.

In effect, the Fed Funds market has become the engine by which the money-centre banks pull money out of the country to support loans to big corporate customers. Instead of lending money in their own territories, the country and small city correspondents of the money-centre banks withhold their loans and sell Fed Funds—an entirely safe form of lending—to the giant banks of New York, Chicago, and San Francisco. "They squeezed down on the instalment credit and on the mortgages", said William T. Dwyer, who supervises correspondent relations at the First National Bank of Chicago, describing 1970, "and they sold the money to us at nine percent".

The *daily* average of Fed Funds purchased rose from about $1,500 million in 1960 to more than $9,000 million in 1970—and $25,000 million in 1973. And the proportion of the nation's banks participating in the market rose from something less than 10 percent in 1960 to something more than half in the early 1970s. "It's unpopular now to go to a cocktail party," says Richard Moffat of the Chicago Fed, "and admit that you don't deal in Fed Funds. It's a status symbol even if you have a million-dollar bank." A study by Benjamin H. Beckhart of Columbia University, using 1972 data, estimated that 8 percent of all the income of the nation's small banks derived from the sale of Fed Funds.

The nature of the correspondent banking relationship in the United States now changed entirely: the crucial function of the money-centre bank in its relations with its correspondents became the purchase of their excess reserves at a price at or just under each day's national market price for money. (One New York bank is reputed to pay $\frac{1}{8}$ of 1 percent *more* than the going rate, as insurance that funds will be available from regular suppliers on rough days.) "We know a relatively small bank in Albany, or Columbus, Ohio," says Ralph Leach, chairman of the executive committee at Morgan. "They let us know they're going to have state money—seventy-five or a hundred million. The state will be disbursing it, but the cheques won't clear for two or three days. So we know we have to dispose of that money; it's in the back of our minds from the beginning". In this case, where every overnight loose penny is being employed, the operation of this market assures the tight and economical use of the money supply. In cases where country banks supply steady streams of money to the Fed Funds market, however, the system has accomplished precisely the result that Congress intended to forbid when it prohibited the payment of interest on demand deposits. Only casuistry—and very high-class casuistry, at that— can find a difference between interest on demand deposits and the overnight sale which turns today's deposit of $1,000,000 into tomorrow's deposit of, say, $1,000,250 at the same correspondent bank.*

*$1,000,000 × 9·2% ÷ 365 days = $250.

By 1973, the purchase of Fed Funds from correspondents had become routinized in a way that eliminated the Fed. Instead of arranging the transfer of another bank's reserves to its account, the money-centre bank simply extinguished a correspondent's "excess" balance on its own books, for the one day. It was understood that no correspondent bank's deposit would be allowed to remain idle under any circumstances. If the money-centre bank that held the deposit did not buy the money itself, it was committed to place the funds elsewhere, either with another purchasing bank or in the Treasury bills market. Any such use of the correspondent's deposit would of course involve the transfer of the money to other hands (the other Fed Funds purchaser or a government-bonds dealer), and would thus be a drain on the reserves of the money-centre bank through which the transfer would be made. By extinguishing the deposit for twenty-four hours, the money-centre bank avoided the drain; and this defensive action was the functional equivalent of a purchase. The Fed, in any event, requires this sort of internal transaction to be reported as a purchase of Fed Funds.

The rate on Fed Funds often fluctuates more than a percentage point during the course of a day, and on Wednesday there may be a difference of five points between the rates at which the cheapest and dearest sales are made. (To get some notion of the orders of magnitude of money involved for the big banks, a percentage point overnight on 500,000 dollars is $13,698.63.) All transactions in Fed Funds must be reported to the Fed, including size and rate, and the Fed publishes a range and an average for every day (the figure used to be a kind of guess at the mean price at which Fed Funds moved through the brokers' offices; since mid-1973 it has been a real weighted average, size times price for each transaction summed at the end of the day and divided by total volume). Because banks really are sort of conservative, the rate on Wednesday tends to be below the rates on other days of the week: the money-desk managers have already taken care of their needs for fear of getting stuck at the last minute. Every so often, however, there is a miscalculation.

For the shortened week ended July 3, 1973 (July 4 was a

Wednesday: the July 3 borrowings counted double)—because they had not wished to show larger amounts of Fed Funds purchased or reserves borrowed on their quarterly statements of conditions as of June 30—banks came to a statement date seriously short all over the country. "The Desk", Alan Holmes of the Open Market Committee reported later, "pumped in $3.34 billion of reserves . . . but the cumulative deficiencies of the banks proved too large. . . . Trading took place at rates as high as fifteen percent for the first time". The average trade that day was at 13 percent (for half a billion dollars, $356,000; and at least ten banks bought that much in Fed Funds that day). On one Wednesday in 1973, a large New Jersey bank actually paid a rate of 30 percent to borrow $25 million overnight, and Mabon, Nugent & Company, one of the two largest brokers of funds, registered trades late in the afternoon at 25 percent. This taught a lot of people a lesson: on July 18 the last trades of a Wednesday were made at 2 percent, and two weeks later a market that had opened around 10 percent ended the day at $\frac{1}{2}$ of 1 percent. "Some banks won't sell at all when that happens", says Gary Whitman, who runs Mabon's eleven-man Fed Funds office. "It's embarrassing to them to be picked off, as they call it".

Of the $25,000 million a day in Fed Funds trading in early 1974, about $10,000 million passed through Mabon and Garvin Bantel, which charge a brokerage fee of 50¢ per million dollars, the best bargain on Wall Street. It is a unique market, a lovely illustration of how smoothly two-way auctions can work when the number of participants is big enough. At Garvin Bantel on the morning of a winter Friday, for example, the market opened at $9\frac{1}{2}$–$9\frac{9}{16}$, with the banks that like to buy their position early taking offers at $9\frac{1}{2}$ percent. In general, expectation had been that rates would go down that week, that the Fed would supply money to the market; but a miscalculation by the Fed on Monday had dried up the offers on Wednesday, raised the rates and driven a number of big banks to borrow overnight at the discount window. "By Wednesday there are no more expectations", said Richard Fieldhouse, a rounded, amiable trader with longish grey sideburns who is Garvin Bantel's Fed Funds manager. "You're right or you're wrong. Higher rates won't draw much money on Wednesday". There is a small futures market in Fed Funds, and "Friday Funds" had traded early in the week in the range of 9–9½, but after Wednesday's experience "the aggressive trading banks", as Fieldhouse called them, were unwilling to sell at 9½ percent, and were waiting for the market to develop.

Garvin Bantel's marketplace is a long table by a window in a room full of brokers who do other things. There are four seats on each side of the table and a set of eight telephone turrets in the middle, each with about fifty buttons that can light up to show an incoming call. One of the seats is held by a young lady named Barbara, who keeps a long sheet of paper previously printed with the names of the twenty or so banks that trade most actively (about two hundred and fifty do some business every week at Garvin Bantel). As the traders match buyers and sellers on the telephone, they call out the results and Barbara writes them down, purchases on the left-hand side, sales on the right, size and rate for each.

At eleven o'clock the market is quiet. If the Fed is going to move, putting money into the banking system or taking it out, the Fed's traders will give some indication of their intentions between 11 and 11.30, after the delivery of the Clearing House settlement sheet. Fieldhouse is on the telephone, on a first-name basis with the bank's trader at the other end: "Looks firm . . . one-half, nine-sixteenths, some trading at a half but it's dried up . . . you'll stay at nine-sixteenths." Fieldhouse expects that most of the banks that call him are also calling Mabon, and will be independently in touch with government-bond dealers and some of the big banks, feeling the market. The phone again: "Provident Cincy has two. What do we do, Barbara?" Barbara is looking at the sheet. "Put it in Wells Fargo". Fieldhouse says into the phone, "Glenda, it's Wells Fargo in California". Wells Fargo has an order in for $50 million, and will check every so often to see how things are coming along; there's no need to make a special call to tell them about $2 million. "In a volatile market, of course," Fieldhouse says, "you have to keep bidders informed, find out, does he want to stay at a half, or bid five-eights, or take three-quarters offerings. . . ."

The phone again: "A half, nine, moving toward nine". The big New York City banks and several of the agencies of foreign banks —which can arbitrage Fed Funds in New York against Euro-dollars in London—maintain leased wires to Garvin Bantel; and so does the Federal Reserve Bank of New York, to which Fieldhouse has just communicated the information that the market continues to hang between $9\frac{1}{2}$–$9\frac{9}{16}$, previous trades at a half, but more bids than offers on the sheet. Another call produces a trade at a half: "Anything further to do", Fieldhouse inquires, "or just the five?" But that's all there is, for now.

Some banks expect to be called once, toward the middle of the day, when they have their figures from the Fed revealing the results of the previous night's clearings. "I call him", Fieldhouse said of such a bank, "and he'll say he has thirty-seven million dollars to sell, and he expects us to do it 'at best'. There's no reason for us to buy money cheap to sell it high—we're not dealers, we represent both sides." A few Midwest banks are large factors in this market, though their total deposits are relatively small. Federal Reserve regulations forbid the subsidiaries of bank holding companies to sell Fed Funds to each other, and the holding-company banks are not willing to work through a rival holding company, so they all work through the biggest unit bank in town, which may be a lot smaller than they are. Every so often a big bank that has done its business for the day comes plunging back into the market un-expectedly with a big order. "Say Continental Illinois gets a call from Allis-Chalmers at noon," Fieldhouse explains, "telling them to wire a hundred million to Chase. The Continental trader calls me, with a lot of obscenities, especially if the market goes against him."

There's a call from down the table: "Starting to trade at a half again!" Another trader: "Hit Marine, hit Marine!" (Marine Mid-land Trust has a bid that can now be satisfied.) Fieldhouse is on the phone, calling out to Barbara, and making notes to himself: "Credit twenty-five First City Houston, fifteen C and S, ten First Pennsylvania. . . . Who's offering it, Barbara?" Barbara, writing hard, not quite composed: "Mellon". The switchboard is lighting up: "We're trading at a half, just saw money coming in. . . . Bank of America is quiet. . . . Barbara, Swiss Credit Bank takes five. . . . We're trading at nine and a half. . . . We're selling money, coming in at a half, bids are getting skimpy. . . . All right Providence? All right Memphis? Mellon will sell twenty more. . . . First National Atlanta will stay at nine-sixteenths. . . . Good trading again at a half. . . . Chase will sell some more, Barbara." Barbara says, "I hear you, Richard". Still on the phone: "First Boston takes twenty-five million. . . . You have any more money to go?"

Not every bank will sell to every other bank: the first source of funds that vanished for Franklin National when its troubles became common knowledge was the Fed Funds market, and the great worry about possible consequences of the near-panic of mid-1974 was that the reluctance of some banks to sell Fed Funds to any but their biggest compeers might concentrate the nation's banking business in a handful of New York, Chicago, and California banks. As a general rule, each trader for a selling bank is restricted to a "line" of a certain size for purchasing banks, and when that limit is reached Fieldhouse will be told to find another customer for the money. When this market was new, the modus operandi was that the seller ordered an immediate transfer of his money at the Fed to the buyer's account, and the buyer sent over a cheque for principal and interest that would go through the clearing mechanism that night and emerge as a transfer on the Fed's books the next day. Now, by and large, the purchasing banks prefer to do business only with selling banks that maintain accounts with them, so the transactions can be expressed simply by the addition of the overnight interest to the selling bank's balance on the buying bank's books.

Aside from the occasional Wednesday frenzy, rates are more stable than they used to be, partly because very active markets tend to be more accurate markets and partly because the Fed has made the Funds rate its primary target, moving during the day to ease money when the rate rises to the top of a bracket, tighten money when the rate falls to the bottom of a bracket. In 1974, when the Fed was really squeezing the banks, these brackets rose month by month, until the jump to a 15 percent rate that had caused scandal in 1973 was just a little bulge on top of the graph. The Fed has much more information than is available to the bankers or the brokers, but it doesn't always help. "Sometimes the Fed sits there befuddled", says Ralph Leach, chairman of the executive committee of Morgan Guaranty, who used to sit on the Fed side himself. "The market isn't moving as it should. Usually, they'll let the banking system hang itself."

"Markets", said Fieldhouse, "*happen*". But now he was busy on the phone.

In London, the timing is different; call money drains out of the discount houses all morning and pours back in all afternoon. Thanks to the Town Clearing, transactions of all sorts can be made in the early afternoon for same day settlement. The London interbank market hots up at about 2.30 in the afternoon, which is when the Bank of England's intentions become clear, and the money brokers who move the interbank loans around would never permit a reporter to observe the transactions. But the similarities, I am told, are striking.

3

Most banks, even the large and sophisticated banks, like to keep on an even keel for the week, paying each day's price for the money they need: First National Bank of Boston, for example, disapproves in principle of playing the Fed Funds market for a profit. "It would make things hard for the Fed if the Funds market became a crapshooters game", says Forbes. "It's not a suitable vehicle for speculation. There are too many random flows exogenous to the market that can move it too much." Morgan Guaranty has no such scruples, however, and may plan dramatically different reserve positions for different days of the same week, according to staff analysis of how the funds market is likely to move from day to day.

Knowing that the bank will need to buy an average of $1,000 million a day in Fed Funds during the statement week, for example, Morgan may nevertheless *sell* $300 million on a Friday, which counts triple, planning to buy $1,900 million in the market on Monday, when, according to Morgan's computer, the rate will be lower. "It is the most incredible change in the commercial banking system", says Bob Dall of Salomon Brothers, who has to find more than a billion dollars a day to support that firm's dealer positions. "They used to react, just as I do. Sometime in the day, they would guess where they would be at the end of the day, and move to stay even. Then Ralph Leach said, 'Why not take a view? . . .'"

There are in fact two views, long term and short term. Morgan's control device, Leach says, is "a thing called the Sources and Uses of Funds Committee. In November we put together our model of the bank for the next year, a forecast of loans and deposits, all the figures except interest-sensitive funds. We lay out the year on a chart, week to week, what you expect loans to be, what you expect demand deposits to be—all the rest has to be raised. Then we keep an interest-sensitive funds book, which says that thirty days, sixty days, six months from now, conditions will be such that we can release or will need more funds." This was early 1973. "Let's see", Leach said, opening the pages of a quarto-sized book. "Our residual looks like three billion dollars.

"The question is, what mix? If you think interest rates are going up, you want longer-term maturities; going down, shorter term. The committee predicts what the rates will be thirty days from now, sixty days from now, and ninety days from now. We 'histogram' the rates—assign probabilities. 'Histogram' is a noun, it describes a chart, but the newspeak people use it as a verb. In the words of our decision-analysis people, it's a means of encoding uncertainty, a way of communicating your feelings about the future without verbalizing. I can say I think CD rates will be 'higher', and you can say you agree, but we haven't communicated. What do we mean by 'higher'? So we quantify, say there's a twenty percent chance the rate will be over seven percent, make bar charts. From the bar charts, you can easily derive what you will be willing to pay for six months money. If the market says you can get that six months money at that figure or less, you'll clearly buy it." (It should be noted in passing that there is some scepticism about this sort of thing in Britain. Midland Bank takes a view, and six senior people meet to determine it once a week. "The prediction you make today will be changed tomorrow", says general manager for finance Dennis Gladwell, a pipe-smoking, round-faced, apparently stolid banker, who is one of the six. "Never embarrasses a mathematician to change his view; never embarrasses an economist, either.")

Managing what Leach called "this three-billion-dollar book" is part of the job of "the tenth-floor group", several score of traders who juggle Treasury bills, CDs, Fed Funds, bankers' acceptances and foreign exchange on an open space the length of 15 Broad Street, recently, expensively, and painfully refurbished in walnut, textured fabric wall covering, and marble. ("You've really never heard a noise", chief Fed Funds trader Ronald Simpson says disbelievingly, "until you've heard them grind marble"). The money desk is subject to the general guidelines of the second-floor committee: "Fed Funds may be providing money overnight at five percent when ninety-day CDs are at six and a half", Leach says, "but if the histogram says short-term rates are going up you ought to go for the longer term that looks expensive today". Within these broad guidelines, however, senior vice-president Donald Riefler handles the operation without interference from the second floor. His work, necessarily, centres around the co-ordination of the trading in the different instruments.

Every day at 10.30, after the settlement clerk has called from the Clearing House to report the results of the day's cheque exchanges, a group of nine men and one woman meet in Riefler's office off the trading floor and go over their expectations for that day and all the days remaining up to Wednesday. The first to speak is a brisk and businesslike lady named Christina Stout, who presented the condition of the bank. She had put together the overnight figures from the Fed, the report from the Clearing House, the report from Morgan's computer centre, opinions from the banking floor about what the biggest customers are likely to be doing, and historical information about what this season and this week have brought in years past. This was a Thursday, so she began with a run-through of the previous week:

"Yesterday we were eight hundred and twenty-eight short on the day [i.e., Morgan's actual reserves at the Federal Reserve Bank of New York, without borrowings, were $828 million below the requirements]; for the week we were eight hundred and fifty short, and I had estimated a billion, two hundred and fifty short. [Riefler whistled: that was unusually far off.] The major improvement was in loan demand. Deposits held up, down only twenty-seven million, and I had anticipated they would go down two hundred fifty, which is what always happens in the first week of the new year. Loans are now two hundred million above forecast, deposits four hundred fifty above forecast. Our CD level was two thousand five hundred and ten [i.e., Morgan had $2,510 million of CDs outstanding]; Eurodeposits were forty-four negative [i.e., Morgan's European branches were taking $44 million out of the New York bank, not putting money into it]; term Fed Funds [Fed Funds bought for longer than overnight] were five hundred average, up forty-four; the T and L [Treasury deposits] was one hundred twenty-four million. For the coming week I have loans going down one hundred million, deposits going down two hundred million, our reserves going up fifty million—the end-of-year deposits [i.e., reserves for next week must cover the deposits that had been in the bank the last week of the previous year]. Our CDs will be two thousand five hundred and twenty-five; term Fed Funds five hundred fifty; and I expect to roll them over. I have us nine hundred and twenty-five down for today [i.e., the current reserve account at the Fed, in the absence of new borrowings, is $925 million below requirements]."

Time has moved forward a year between Leach's description and this meeting: the $3,000 million book has become a $4,000 million book. Note that to meet a reserve requirement of $685 million, Morgan would have to buy $925 million of overnight Fed Funds: the bank was working on net borrowed reserves. (So were all the other big New York banks. "When I came here," says Willard Butcher of Chase, "they told me we were thirty percent loaned. [That is, the total loan portfolio was 30 percent of the total deposits on the books.] Now they tell me we're sixty percent loaned. Hell, we're really *four hundred percent* loaned!") Martin Griffin, who does his CD business out in the world of non-financial corporations, now contributed the information that this morning commercial paper rates were down: there would be no pressure on the banks from that side.

Riefler called on Edward Fecht, described by Griffin as "one of the two original Fed watchers". Fecht reviewed the Fed's interventions in the market in the previous week, and said that in the week ahead "the increase in required reserves [for the banking system as a whole] means they will plug in a billion dollars. The system will be losing about two hundred fifty, taking no account of the Treasury deposits at the Fed, which are heavy, What we don't know is whether the Germans [then busily but quietly defending the mark] will sell bills or draw down their special certificates. Assuming they draw down the certificates, I'd estimate two hundred fifty. And then the Fed will have to draw out five hundred the week after."

(Among the major differences between British and American practice is that the Fed is secretive about its data and projections, while the Bank of England daily informs the clearing banks of its expectation of events in that day's money market; sometimes that guess is no better than anybody else's guess.)

Next, the group's operations researcher, a young Russian immigrant named Dushan Boyanovitch, presented the results of feeding various assumptions into a set of mathematical models of the next week's market. "Last week we bought at nine point seven six average for the week [i.e., Morgan's average interest cost for Fed Funds was at an annual rate of 9·76 percent]. Congratulations, Ronnie [this to Ronald Simpson, the chief Fed Funds trader]. This week the model shows today, nine and three-quarters; Friday, nine and eleven-sixteenths; Monday, nine and five-eighths; Tuesday, nine and eleven-sixteenths; Wednesday, nine and eleven-sixteenths, possibly higher. Average, nine point six nine. Our model still shows a decline of about ten basis points a week until a low point on February eighth, then back up to nine point four. Last year this week there was a discount rate increase from four and a half to five, and the Funds rate was five and three-quarters.

I'm looking for the lowest rate on Monday." But the difference in the anticipated rates during the week was not enough to persuade Riefler that the bank's position should change greatly from day to day: "Sounds essentially flat", he said.

Jim Killeen, the statistician who keeps track of Morgan's actual reserve position at the Fed, had now secured real figures. "We settled yesterday forty-eight red. [That is, the bank's total reserves for the week were $48 million below requirement. Over seven days, the average deficiency was less than $7 million, or well within the 2 percent limit on $635 million. The week before, Morgan had settled "black", with a little more than necessary, and the carryover more than took care of the slack.] Our new requirement is a rocking, socking six hundred and eighty."

The next on line was Simpson, a dryly casual, rather small man in his later fifties. "We picked up a hundred and twenty million from the Deutsches Bundesbank today", he said, "and fifty million in term Funds. We're bidding nine and five-eighths for one month, nine and three-eighths for three months, and we bought twenty, thirty million, all we wanted." Riefler broke in: "Who's selling?" Simpson said, "Continental-Illinois. Everybody." A young man came to the doorway and called to Simpson, "Ronnie, do we want to bid a hundred million today?" Simpson said, "Sure". The young man said, "How much?" Simpson said, "I don't know", and left the room to go to his desk and make a phone call.

Riefler watched his departure reflectively. "I know", he said. "Nine and eleven-sixteenths. He doesn't have to go out. What's the decimal equivalent of nine and eleven-sixteenths?" Killeen said, "Nine point six eight seven five". Simpson returned. "What did you bid?" Riefler inquired. "Nine and eleven-sixteenths", Simpson said, and everybody laughed. Boyanovitch's model had said nine and three-quarters; the bid a sixteenth under what the model called for was the natural bid. But the market might be undergoing a momentary weakness: Simpson had to check it out. Anyway, as Riefler said later, "Whenever the Fed expert and the operations researcher agree, we have a lot of confidence, and that's when we get in trouble".

At the end of the meeting, Riefler announced that he was knocking $100 million off Mrs. Stout's estimate of the daily Fed Funds needs of the bank—the same factors that had pushed her to the up side the week before were probably still working. Moreover, he explained later, Morgan would rather come to the last day needing money than (in Simpson's phrase) "trying to get out of our own way". During the week, consistent with the estimates, Simpson would buy whenever the rates went below the committee's projections, and sell when it got above them, hoping to clip a few sixteenths of a percentage point off Morgan's net cost of funds. By and large, Simpson does his own buying, from steady suppliers, but sells through Mabon, Nugent & Company, because Morgan cannot in the nature of things develop steady relationships with purchasers.

Leach expects his tenth-floor group "to be right seventy-five to eighty percent of the time; in fact, they are right ninety percent of the time". Obviously, the money desk is a "cost centre" for Morgan, which must buy and pay for funds every day. Riefler does his own accounting on a "profit centre" basis, however, and keeps track of his average net cost of Fed Funds as against the average price for each day announced by the Fed. The "profits" (really, of course, savings on interest costs) run $2 million or so a year.

In 1969, the Fed tried to limit the use of the Fed Funds market as a speculative medium by informing the money-centre banks that they would be well advised never to run their daily reserves down below 50 percent of the average required for the week. By 1973, however, the Fed had accepted the inevitable, and while the suggested floor was never eliminated Morgan spent a number of days below the 50 percent figure and heard only occasional mild complaints from Liberty Street. "But we do try to maintain fifty percent, and it's certainly not a good idea to let the balance fall below zero", says Riefler. "They *really* aren't pleased if you're running an overdraft over there." (The Bank of England has permitted an overdraft by the clearing banks only once—in 1972, when sterling fled the country the week before the introduction of worldwide floating exchange rates.)

As late as 1966, Roger Lyon of Chase Manhattan wrote that "the ability to effect very short-term borrowings [e.g., Fed Funds] should be looked upon as a temporary expedient . . . or as a safety valve for the liquidity reserve sector, and not as a permanent source of funds". Eight years later, his bank was buying almost $3,000 million a day in the Fed Funds market—and spending at least $300 million a year in interest on Fed Funds purchases. From an outside point of view, all the big banks are in an "overdraft" condition on their reserves. (The one exception is Bank of America, which when rates were dancing on the roof in 1974 could smugly tell its stockholders that during the first half of that year the bank had been a net seller rather than a buyer of Fed Funds.) This is not quite as worrisome as it sounds, because Fed Funds are really just money, and the fact that they are also reserves does not change the nature of the beast. Today's sale of a CD yields tomorrow's Fed Funds, as soon as the cheque clears. (Of course, the money available from the CD must be reduced by the reserves the Fed requires against such certificates of deposit, while every penny of Fed Funds purchases is usable money.) Still, when the nation's hundred largest banks have purchased Fed Funds to a total greater than their required reserves, which was the case in early 1974, one is talking about something quite a bit more than a "temporary expedient". Riefler says, "I can remember half a dozen years ago, when we were buying three or four hundred million dollars a day, we thought it was a lot of money. . . ." Some people still think so.

4

Despite the opportunities offered by and taken in this market, the money-centre banks have never been entirely happy about their growing reliance on Fed Funds—essentially for the same reasons that the Fed itself finally decided to promote their use. Ultimately, the Fed does control the total volume of reserves, through devices we shall consider in Chapter 15. As Edward L. Palmer of First National City in New York puts it, "The Fed says, 'All this depends on our willingness to expand the money supply'.

And then I guess we have to say, 'You're right, Fed'." After the 1966 squeeze, the big banks went out looking for ways to assure a supply of money for their customers which was not so easily subject to control by the Fed; and ways were found.

The first was the banks' own foreign branches. Because foreign money cannot be used directly in the domestic economy, governments do not usually apply reserve requirements to bank deposits denominated in money other than that of the country where the bank is located. Through the 1950s and 1960s, because of the American deficit in balance of payments and the fact of higher interest rates and greater investment returns in Europe, dollars piled up in European banks. Though overseas branches of American banks deal in all currencies, their basic stock in trade is the dollar. If these branches were to compete effectively in the "Eurodollar" market, against European banks which did not have to keep reserves against their dollar deposits, they would have to be excused from the reserve requirement; and they were.

But Eurodollars are really just ordinary dollars, book entries showing the ownership abroad of money from American banks. In 1966, a few of the banks squeezed out of their CDs by Regulation Q looked abroad to their own branches overseas, which could buy dollars on the London interbank market and hold them without reserve requirements. This was expensive money because it was in short supply—the American government had been trying to block the outflow of dollars through administrative controls—but it was money that the banks could get, and in fall 1966 the money-centre banks were willing to pay anything for short-term money. By the end of the year, about $3,300 million in Eurodollar deposits in American branches abroad had been brought home for use by the parent banks. Then the domestic interest rates dropped below the Reg Q ceilings, CDs came back, and the Eurodollar borrowings were allowed to expire.

In 1969, the Fed once again squeezed the banks by holding the maximum rate they could pay on CDs below the rate on Treasury bills—and $12,500 million of CDs ran off in six months. In the intervening years, the total of dollars abroad had probably tripled (no figures on Eurodollar quantities are any good), and the number of American banks with foreign branches had certainly tripled. As their CDs ran out, the money-centre banks put their London offices to work, and by fall 1969 no less than $13,000 million of Eurodollars had been brought home—much of it at interest rates well over 10 percent, still considered unthinkable at home. President Frank Morris and Jane Little of the Federal Reserve Bank of Boston estimate that the float on the clearing time between New York and London was worth more than $3,000 million a day to the money-centre banks in the heyday of Eurodollar borrowings. In October 1969, the Fed, which had held down the Reg Q ceiling because it wanted the banks to slow their lending, finally blocked the Eurodollar channel, applying a reserve requirement to all such borrowings brought home by American banks, over the total that had been on their books at the end of March 1969. The retroactive application of the new regulation gave it an element of overkill, and the banks ran down their European borrowings as fast as they could; by 1971 almost nothing was left.

The Eurodollar transactions had been, in effect, "nondeposit borrowing" by the banks. There were also domestic borrowings that were not, in 1969, subject to reserve requirements. During the credit crunch of 1966, a number of large corporations had begun to issue promissory notes—"commercial paper"—to borrow needed funds from other corporations that were heavy with cash, or from insurance companies, pension funds, endowments, other institutions. Provided the borrowing was for less than 270 days, the Securities and Exchange Commission permitted the sale of this paper without the expensive formalities of registration. Banks themselves were forbidden by law to borrow money this way, but through the 1960s they had been forming holding companies— and holding companies could issue commercial paper. Richard Thomas, president of the First Chicago Corporation, recalls fondly that the very first act of this newly formed corporate entity had been the issuance of $100 million in commercial paper, which was immediately employed to purchase $100 million of loans from the subsidiary First National Bank of Chicago, then hard-pressed for money in the 1969–70 crunch. Several billion dollars were switched from the commercial paper market to bank reserves in this manner, until the Fed somewhat wearily closed the door by applying reserve requirements to commercial paper issues by bank holding companies used to support the money needs of the banks they held.

All right. What about the "repurchase agreement"? In this arrangement, a bank "sells" an asset, a bond or a mortgage, to an insurance company or government or other institution, with an agreement to buy back the same bond or mortgage, at today's sales price plus interest, on a specified date in the future. Surely that isn't a deposit, is it? And eventually the Fed said, Yes, that's a deposit, too, subject to reserve requirements and to Reg Q maxima.

Suppose we sell a loan on the open market, packaging it as what Morgan called a "Marketable Time Draft", what First National City called "a finance bill", and the Fed called an "ineligible acceptance". This instrument would represent a transfer to its purchaser of the promise to pay made by one of the bank's big borrowers. The bank would guarantee that the borrower would really pay (hence the idea of an "acceptance"). Some big corporations were less happy than others about this scattering about of their debts, but some were understanding and agreed to go along. "To say that the sale of an asset is a deposit is just ridiculous", Ralph Leach commented in early 1973. "But that's just what the Fed is going to say." Every banker believes that he could win a lawsuit on this one, but no banker wants to get the Fed that angry at him—or to place the issue before Congress, which is what the Fed would do if the banks went to court and won.

As amended, Section 217.1(f) of Reg Q now reads, "For the purposes of this Part, the term 'deposits' also includes a member bank's liability on any promissory note, acknowledgment of advance, due bill, or similar obligation (written or oral) that is issued or undertaken by a member bank principally as a means of obtaining funds to be used in its banking business." It is very nearly the only sentence in the Regulations of the Federal Reserve System that is written in English, and it has about it a quality of quiet desperation.

One possibility remains: the sale of bonds or subordinated notes representing a claim on the bank. Since every deposit is also a claim on the bank, and depositors' interests must be placed first, the notes are necessarily "subordinated" to the prior repayment of all depositors. "It's the worst investment I can possibly imagine", says old Van Vechten Shaffer in Cedar Rapids. "I can't see why anybody buys them." Until 1964, the very idea of bonded indebtedness of a bank would have provoked guffaws in the world of finance, but then James Saxon, having forced the Fed to accept the proposition that Fed Funds borrowed ("purchased") were not a deposit, okayed the issuance of subordinated debt by national banks. He even went a step further: he permitted banks to incorporate these notes or bonds into their capital base for purposes of setting limits on loans to individual customers. Capital clearly cannot be subject to reserve requirements or Reg Q.

Once Saxon was gone, the Fed began chipping away at the sale of debt by banks. Since 1970, banks have been permitted to sell subordinated debt only after specific approval by the Comptroller (for national banks) or the Board of Governors (for state member banks); the minimum maturity for the paper has been set at seven years; and the note must bear "on its face, in bold-face type, the following: **'This obligation is not a deposit and is not insured by the Federal Deposit Insurance Corporation.'"** It *can* be done. In 1973, Mark Twain Bancshares was selling 7 percent bonds in $500 denominations; money-centre banks sold issues through Wall Street underwriters in $100 million pieces; country banks through the Midwest sold subordinated notes to their correspondents in the big cities. The Fed's reasons for leaving this loophole was a desire to force additional capital into the banking structure, liabilities the banks cannot run down when business turns slow, as an inducement to increased caution.

The British banks have not had to be quite that clever to escape inconvenience from Bank of England policy under Competition and Credit Control. Because some of their earning assets qualify as "reserve assets", they have been able to improve their reserve position simply by shifting items in the asset book. On the simplest level, a bank can put money on call at a discount house which uses that money to buy the bank's CD: the bank has a wash transaction on its cash position, but shows an increase in its reserve assets. The discount house is required to keep half its assets in Treasury paper; if the transaction with the bank creates awkwardness in that department, the discount house can in effect swap the CD for a Treasury bill in the hands of a corporate customer. Some of these flim-flam games have been stopped; but so long as different assets qualify as reserves for banks and for discount houses, arbitrage that evades the purposes of monetary regulation will be hard to prevent—and the ease of transfer between money in the banks and near-money in Treasury bills will, as G. T. Pepper of W. Greenwell & Co. has pointed out, distort the significance of all monetary statistics.

Moreover, if the government insist on deficit financing for the public sector, the Bank will have no choice but to create reserve assets that permit the government to borrow—and some of these assets will ultimately become available to support the expansion of private lending.

In both America and Britain, the results of central bank policy in the first half of the 1970s were, to put it mildly, contrary to what the authorities wanted. The figures the central bankers were watching—the narrowly defined "money supply"—did, as hoped, rise only sluggishly. But meanwhile, the numbers expressing what the Americans call "the bank credit proxy" and the British call M_3—the total of lendable and loaned funds in the banking system —all but exploded. From 1971 to 1973, M_3 doubled in Britain; and in the second quarter of 1974, when everyone in America was screaming about tight money, the "adjusted bank credit proxy" rose at an annual rate of 21 percent. Interest rates went out of sight (Ralph Leach observed sourly that "the Bank of England used to say seven percent would draw money from the moon; they must have smarter people on the moon these days"). But the banks felt very little pain. They did not have to dispose of assets at a loss in order to fund their loans, and their apparent profits kept increasing—assuming that all those new loans at high rates will be repaid.

In December 1973 the Bank of England began scrambling back

WHERE THE MONEY COMES FROM

to at least some direct controls (especially over consumer credit). The Fed in 1974 put pressure on "capital adequacy", and held down hard on the creation of new reserve assets; but until the inventory accumulation bubble burst and recession bailed out the American monetary authorities, there continued to be major reliance on what Friedman and Schwartz once called "moral suasion, urging banks to discriminate between 'essential and nonessential credits'—a formula that successive use from that time to this has rendered neither less appealing to the Reserve System as a means of shifting responsibilities nor more effective as a means of controlling monetary expansion".

This is material for Chapter 15, where we shall look at some of the phenomena described in the preceding pages through the somewhat differently tinted glasses of public policy and governmental powers. First we had better know something about what the banks do with the money they buy.

PART
III

—

WHERE THE
MONEY GOES

10/Lending to Producers

We have entirely lost the idea that any undertaking likely to pay, and seen to be likely, can perish for want of money; yet no idea was more familiar to our ancestors, or is more common now in most countries.
                                        —WALTER BAGEHOT (1873)

* * *

Denied a $2,000 loan at the Merchants and Miners Bank of Tucson in Eugene Manlove Rhodes' novel *Copper Streak Trail*, Peter Wallace Johnson presented for cash a cheque for $86,000 made out to him by "Henry Bergman, sheriff of Pima County, and the richest cowman of the Santa Cruz Valley.

"'This is sheer malice'," the banker said.

"Not a bit of it", Pete said. "You're all wrong. Just common prudence—that's all. You see, I needed a little money. As I was tellin' you, I got right smart of property, but no cash right now; nor any comin' till steer-sellin' time. So I come down to Tuscon on the rustle. Five banks in Tucson; four of 'em, countin' yours, turned me down cold. . . . I hunted up old Hank Bergman and told him my troubles", said Pete suavely. He expressed quite some considerable solicitude. "Why, Petey, this is a shockin' disclosure", he says. "A banker is a man that makes a livin' loanin' other people's money. Lots of marble and brass to a bank, salaries and other expenses. Show me a bank that's quit lendin' money and I'll show you a bank that's due to bust, *muy pronto*. I got quite a wad in the Merchants and Miners", he says, "and you alarm me. I'll give you a cheque for it, and you go there first off tomorrow and see if they'll lend you what you need. You got good security. If they ain't lendin'," he says, "then you just cash my cheque and invest it for me where it will be safe. . . ."

2

Today, as we have seen, a bank's profitability depends to a remarkable degree on the cost of its funds. But despite the growth of fee business and the spreading activities of bank holding companies, the revenues that make profits possible at all are still, as they were in Gene Rhodes' day, the rewards of lending money and owning securities. The more loans and investments a bank makes, the higher its profits are likely to be. The year 1973 clearly illustrates the rule: despite the ceiling imposed on interest rates early in the year by the Cost of Living Council, and despite the steadily mounting cost of funds, most American banks came to the accountants at year end with record-breaking profits, because they had written record-breaking quantities of loans.

Beyond the parochial question of bank profitability, decisions to lend or not to lend are the way a bank influences the economic development of its community. Paul Jones of Valley National in Phoenix asks, "Why has Arizona grown so much faster than New Mexico? Well, there was the Salt River project, the Roosevelt Dam built in 1912. And the climate is a little better. But I think it's mostly the banking system in this state. I come from Dallas, from a state with unit banking, and I've seen agricultural communities strangle because local banks didn't have money. Here we have branches with loan portfolios a hundred and fifty percent the size of their deposits, because that area needs the money".

And, of course, the value of a loan to an individual may be even more striking. At the party staged in New York's Lincoln Centre to celebrate the gift of her papers to the New York Public Library, dancer Martha Graham looked back half a century to speak a special thanks to "Francis Stella, the man who went on the loan for me for a thousand dollars so I could give my first recital. . . ."

What vitality midtown urban renewal has had derives to a large degree from the willingness of the banks to build new headquarters offices downtown at the cost of recruiting the work force from the collapsing centre-city high schools rather than the adequate suburban high schools—and, on the other side of the coin, the decay of the inner ring has been hastened by the decision of bank lending officers to "red-line" the black slum, to mark off that area (often in a real red pencil) as one to which home improvement loans and mortgage and small commercial loans will not be made. The Route 128 complex of electronics manufacturers bottoms on the nearby presence of Harvard and MIT, but it probably would not have developed as it did without the vigorous, sometimes gambling support of the Boston banks. Franchised fast-food establishments sprang up around the country like dragons' teeth in large part because the First National Bank of Chicago was willing to supply the money. ("We are the leading bankers for Kentucky Fried Chicken and McDonald's; we got out of Minnie Pearl before it collapsed".) Though the multinational corporation was undoubtedly the wave of the future, that future arrived much sooner than anyone could have expected because First National City Bank of New York scattered branches around the globe to make an interface between the culture of the arriving corporation and the culture of the place to which it was coming. Some of these arrangements would be fascinating to know in detail—for example, First National City's role as Pandarus in the consummation of the romance between Aristotle Onassis and Standard Oil of New Jersey, back in the early postwar years—but wild horses could not drag the information from any of the five people who possess it.

Less cheerfully, the mania for conglomerates in the late 1960s was nourished by the banks: the funny money certificates printed by the Lings, Geneens, Riklises and Bluhdorns (not to mention the crooks) were made to seem plausible by the great banks that put real money into these deals. At a time when Ling's companies' "coverage of interest charges did not meet conservative standards", security analyst Benjamin Graham has pointed out, "the banks advanced the enterprise nearly four hundred million dollars additional. . . . This was not good business for them. . . ." There were the nursing homes and the computer companies that were going to challenge IBM (Bank of America may have taken a $100 million bath on one of these); there were the idiocies of National Student Marketing which was going to ride the waves of Consciousness III and (who can forget it?) the corrupt accounting practices of Penn Central, all supported, heavily, by banks. Those losing bets on the future were matters of judgment; more disturbing, as signs of systemic weakness, were the raid on the dollar in early 1973 and the fantastic run-up of commodity prices in mid-1973, both irresponsibly funded by the big banks. In fairness, it wasn't something the banks really wanted to do, but these were good customers who wanted to buy the money.

Before the 1960s, American banks had customers and companies had a banker: the great majority of lending and borrowing relationships were stable, long-standing and buttressed, very often, by social relationships. Even now, a businessman opening an account with another businessman will be asked the name of his banker, and a query will be sent; and the best answer to the query is the one that says "a customer for twenty years". (James Coquillette of Merchants National Bank in Cedar Rapids says he has given up on querying his big-city correspondents about potential borrowers because that's usually *all* the answer he gets— "and even that comes on caution stationery: 'true to the best of our knowledge'.") A very successful New York advertising agency miffed at its treatment by one of the giant New York City banks in 1973 (the agency tried to arrange a loan to buy out a principal, and like Pete Johnson was told money was tight) finally decided not to take its business elsewhere simply because of the value it placed on being able to say in account solicitations that there was a long-standing relationship with this bank.

But in a world of long-standing relationships, the bank's loans will be a function of established customers' needs. In the old days, a banker would no more have advertised money to lend than an attorney would have advertised law for sale. "A bank doesn't loan money to farmers because it wants to loan money to farmers", says Van Vechten Shaffer, looking back on fifty years in Cedar Rapids. "It loans money to farmers because farmers come in and demand the money". That attitude went under in the 1960s, when banking became so much more professional in skills and so much less professional in attitudes. Warren Marcus, bank stock analyst for Salomon Brothers, speaks of the modern bankers who "are trying to *engineer* their loan portfolio, to look at the cycles and moderate the swings. They've said, "We're not going to sit here anymore and be like a can in the water".

Now someone has to go out and sell loans. "I *know* health care is going to need a lot of money", says Bruce Carl in the planning section of Mark Twain Bancshares. "I'm targeting some customers. . . ."

During the 1960s, banks trying not to be a can in the water found many new ways to lend money, often involving loan agreements longer than this book. Some banks reached so far for business that they became in effect endorsers of other people's loan applications, selling "letters of credit" to support requests by their customers for loans from other banks. Others became proprietors of equipment that they leased to people to whom they probably would not have been willing to make a loan at all. In banking as in education (but to somewhat greater effect), "innovative" became the adjective most closely synonymous with "good".

Still, almost everyone in banking would agree with George Scott, a recently retired vice-chairman of First National City, who was right in the middle of everything clever, that despite the revolution the essence of lending did not change. Scott, who is salty and self-educated, was one of the last major executives of a major American bank who never went to college and never went through a training

233

programme: "When a guy comes into a bank today he wants to know what's his career path. When I came in 1929, I said I wanted a job. They said, Messenger, one hundred dollars a month. I said, Fine—it's the only offer I've had". On loans: "I've been up and down this business, and there's still no substitute for 'What do you want the loan for? How are you going to pay it back? And what are you going to do to pay me back if your theory doesn't work'?"

3

Lending, as noted, is the use of money to bridge time. While banking so-called started as a way to carry the manufacturer from the sale of his product for export to the arrival of payment from abroad—and to carry the merchant from the acquisition of his inventory to its sale—observation in India and elsewhere argues that the rural money-lender has long been endemic even in subsistence agriculture. "The farmer," Tawney wrote in *Religion and the Rise of Capitalism*, "must borrow money when the season is bad, or merely to finance the interval between sowing and harvest. The craftsman must buy raw materials on credit and get advances before his wares are sold. The young tradesman must scrape together a little capital before he can set up shop. Even the cottager, who buys grain at the local market, must constantly ask the seller to 'give day'."

Much of the image of the banker (and of the Indian money-lender) reveals the fear and hatred felt historically by the productive worker for the moneyed man who profits by the misfortune of others, appropriating to himself the fruits of fields he has never tilled—and ultimately, often enough, the fields themselves. "The lender," Tawney continues, "is often a monopolist—a 'money master', a malster or corn monger, 'a rich priest', who is the solitary capitalist in a community of peasants and artisans. Naturally, he is apt to become their master". The American banking system of the nineteenth century was particularly suited to the creation of such horror stories. Though farm land was originally purchased with what it is now fashionable to call "sweat equity"—the homesteader got freehold title by developing the property—subsequent transfers of ownership involved mortgages. And the American mortgage until the 1930s was a straight loan requiring the periodic payment of interest, with the entire amount of the principal coming due at the end of a period of time, commonly five years. The long deflation of the late nineteenth century meant that the burden of the mortgage was continually increasing (hence William Jennings Bryan and the Cross of Gold)—and God forbid that the mortgage came due on a date when money was tight, when people were hoarding cash for fear of bank failures and the stock market was in collapse.

Worse yet, the farmer's security for his seasonal loans—and for the equipment loans that permitted him to buy barbed wire and reapers—was often his land rather than a prospective crop. Gene Rhodes' dream of glory for Pete Johnson, the discomfiture of the banker who would not make a needed loan, expressed the populism of a large piece of the rural community of the late nineteenth century—and also Rhodes' sense, virtually unique in American fiction of any period, of how the machinery of daily life actually functioned in the United States.

The disorganized beginnings of the Federal Reserve System and the start of World War I, arriving simultaneously, shocked American government into the exploration of new ways of financing agriculture. A large part of the credits to American farmers (especially the cotton farmers of the emerging Southwest) had been European, and were withdrawn in the first panicky reaction to war. In 1916, the Federal Farm Loan Act set up twelve regional Federal Land Banks to write mortgages on farm properties and twelve Federal Intermediate Credit Banks to meet the seasonal borrowing needs of farmers and stockmen. Like all the rest of the nation's financial institutions, these ran out of money in the Great Depression, and the spirit of experimentation of the early New Deal created a third establishment, the Banks for Co-operatives, which loaned through farm co-ops. All three now flourish, all essentially farmer-owned though government-guaranteed through the Farm Credit Act of 1971. Their total resources, raised in the bond market, are very nearly $20,000 million; among the portfolios that hold the bonds is that of the Federal Reserve Banks. In California these co-operative agencies do a fifth of all the lending to farmers, and though they tend to make the bigger loan to the bigger farmers they supply a valuable yardstick by which the farming community can measure the performance of its banks.

Bank of America, though now a huge international operation with most of its money on loan to suitably huge corporations, is still the largest private lender to farmers, with about $1,600 million out at the top of the season. In tight money times, by bank policy, farm lending has first priority. "We don't have a cow bank here", Robert Long said while he was the San Francisco staff officer for this lending area. "Lending officers specialize in lending, not in categories of loan. But, of course, men who stay any length of time in a branch where fifty percent of the portfolio is agricultural will become very knowledgeable. Some of them come out of rural areas, some are self-instructed farmers; and some—it's a great back-ground—come out of the agricultural school at U-Cal, Davis".

Of the state's 55,000 farms "of commercial size", about 13,000 borrow from Bank of America, which means the average loan is a little more than $100,000; but the figure is distorted by a hundred or so very big borrowers who take more than a million dollars in loans (one of them took $26 million each year in the early 1970s). "With the hundred big ones out," Long says, "our average loan is probably fifteen thousand dollars". The bank prefers to lend on an "open line of credit", with the farmer taking down his money as he needs it, and paying for what he uses; then the lending officer, and the separate appraisal officer, can keep up with the man's budget and see whether he's doing as projected. No farmer borrows twice from Bank of America without an experience budget. "In some cases," Long says, "we do a complete budget for him, including his living expenses".

The rates vary, in part according to the perceived risk, which may be the man or the kind of crop: lending officers at the branches are empowered to set the rate on each individual loan themselves, within a bracket established in San Francisco. The loans tend to be profitable to the bank in years when business lending is light, unprofitable in years when business lending is heavy, because the interest rates on farm loans move much less rapidly than interest rates on business loans. The security for the loan—three-quarters of the seasonal loans are secured—is the crop being raised or the livestock itself, and only rarely the land. Though there are lots of two-year and three-year term loans to spread the cost of purchasing machinery, the loans made on the line of credit are classic old-time bank loans, which are supposed to be cleaned up when the crop is sold, putting the farmer "out of the bank" for at least part of the year.

Iowa would seem to be a little ahead of California in some of these areas—perhaps not surprisingly, because agricultural loans account for more than half the business in three-fifths of the state's banks. Tom Smith, president of the First National Bank of Perry, Iowa, and chairman of the American Bankers Association section on agriculture, has been at it all his life. "Brenton Banks", he said, referring to the holding company that owns 85 percent of the stock in his $19 million bank, "employs sixty agricultural college graduates as lending officers; I was one of the first". He is a small, round, balding man wearing square Ben Franklin eyeglasses with a gold nosepiece. His bank, he says, "was one of the first to really insist that our farm borrowers bring us good records. One big farmer said, 'I don't have to go through this to borrow money'. I said, 'That's right—but you have to go through it to borrow money here'. He walked right out. We lost several big customers; it made you want to bawl. But then it turned around, we got a lot of young aggressive farmers, and they kept getting bigger. It's a joy to do business with people who want to succeed".

At Perry, a town of 7,000, the central management tool in 1972 was the computer, run on a programme called Computer-Eaz, which the Brenton Banks buy from a systems company in Manhattan, Kansas. The farmer activates the programme by coding every one of his cheques according to the purpose for which the cheque is written. "We ask him", says C. R. Collins, Smith's first vice-president, "to do cash-flow projections. He says farming is too uncertain, you can't predict yields, you can't predict insect damage

—and that's true, for one year. But over several years you ought to be able to hit an average. We are less concerned about how much clear land he owns or what his net worth is; we're interested in the profit potential of the operation. If that's all right, everything else will be, too".

In a place like Perry, Iowa, of course, a banker still lends to the man, not to the business. "Each customer," Collins says, "has an individual credit file, the complete track record over his whole history at the bank. If it comes down to stretching a little, you can look back and say, 'Here's a performer'—or 'Here's a non-performer'. His consumer credit also is in the file: I expect him to undress completely. It's like a doctor: if he comes to me for a head-ache I don't expect him going to another doctor for a stomach ache. There isn't any problem he has we can't solve, provided we know the whole problem. We have a few instalment loan losses, but our customer loan losses are nil. . . . Oh, once in a while. But we document things, set 'em up properly, try to do it right the first time. And we have the advantage in these little towns that you do know the people you're dealing with".

Elsewhere nature is not quite so benign as it usually is in Iowa, and agricultural lending is somewhat riskier. An officer of the Barnett Banks in Jacksonville said that in lending to the orange groves and truck farms of northern Florida one had to expect that one out of every three years would be catastrophic. At Valley National in Phoenix, Paul Jones commented that "lettuce is an important cash crop to this state, and growing lettuce is like rolling dice in Vegas. It requires supervision by the loan officer. . . ."

4

"I was up at two in the morning today," says David Lambert, an earnest young lending officer in the home-office San Francisco branch of Bank of America, "worrying about a travel agency loan I have to say Yes or No on. The people are good but the business is shaky. They want to go into corporate travel, which means they would bill every thirty days, but they have to pay the airlines every ten days. If I make the loan, I'll keep in touch with their receivables. The place is on my way home, and one night every so often I'll leave here at four and stop off. I find some excuse to call most of my accounts once a week—not snooping, just catching up".

Lambert is about thirty, black hair, brown eyes; he wears a pepper-and-salt checked suit, white shirt, broad tie, wing shoes. "I went to Georgetown and Pittsburgh, graduate school in political science, then two years in the military, where I met guys who were going back to business school. I was in a hole in Vietnam when I had to fill out the applications. Harvard sent me a fourteen-page application, 'What's your favourite activity? Way to spend time? Why do you rate that number-one?' Stanford had a two-page application, so I went to Stanford. I worked one summer at the bank, in the international division, and I decided all these hotshots didn't really know much about banking. They were handling all these hundred-million-dollar items, but not really making any decisions; the glamour of the six zeros can snow a person. I decided I wanted to go into a branch, learn how the cheques are processed, what happens to the money—and really make the loans. The largest unsecured loan I'm allowed to make is now thirty-five thousand dollars, but you bend it, go to sixty thousand, tell somebody about it afterwards.

"In effect, we're the contact men. I talk to people about trusts, computer services, boat design, pollution control. You have to pump people, plead ignorance. We have guidelines—anybody with a balance sheet of more than three hundred thousand dollars ought to be a trust customer. I ask, 'Are we the executor of your will?' If I can see an international possibility—we're trying to encourage exports—I'll tell him I've heard of a possible foreign market for his product. If he has more than twenty-five people on his payroll, we're interested in selling him a computer payroll service. If he's buying a house, we want the real estate loan.

"I find people like somebody to give them ideas. I have a retailer on Maiden Lane who thinks his bread and butter should be the socialite visiting San Francisco, and the locals should be the icing. It doesn't seem to me to make sense, so I'll put my two

239

cents in. That's the fun part of being a banker. I wouldn't want to be a fashion store operator or a real estate broker or a stockbroker".

Most banks stress the value of the consulting services their lending officers can supply. First National City's loudest explosion of rage against the interference of government regulators came when the Federal Reserve Board ordered the bank's holding company to divest itself of Cresap, McCormick & Paget, an established management consulting firm the bank had bought. "They ruled that management consulting was not a proper adjunct to banking", Walter Wriston snorts. "The first management consultant was a banker on the banks of the Euphrates, telling a guy he had to build a wall around his inventory. That's all a banker is, really, is a management consultant".

Young George Campbell, running the North Carolina National Bank operation in London, says that "Our future is where our history has been—in understanding our customers' business well enough to make a loan other banks may not know enough to make". (Unfortunately for NCNB, Campbell, far from his home and history, then proceeded to make some loans that better established international banks had known too much to make.) Back home in Charlotte, F. Walter Lockett of that bank, a young man in a white shirt and navy suit, at a desk almost bare except for a slide rule, will talk learnedly about the North Carolina textile mills that have switched their output to "warp-knit" fabrics, and point out that the companies most committed to the warp knits are the ones that missed the boat on double-knits, "which were big business here. But we don't know if the market is there for warp-knits. There's a lot of turnover in textiles. It's not to say they aren't able—but they're flashy and they're fast movers; it's very challenging for the banker. . . ."

"There aren't enough banks that understand the industry," John Chequer of the First National Bank of Boston says about the movies, "and that's bad for the industry. Back in the sixties, Twentieth-Century Fox was having trouble because its banks were all reading scripts. Without looking at a script, we made a large loan, in effect we bought out the other banks, and a year before it expired we voluntarily reduced the interest on it, because the risk was obviously so slight. We don't want to read a script or tell people what movies to make. If the head of that studio can't tell whether something will make a good movie or not, we shouldn't be lending him money. The day we say we want to see a script before we'll finance the movie our shareholders are in grave trouble".

First of Boston has been in this business one way or another since the movie companies were first coming out of bankruptcy at the end of the Depression. When an antitrust case split the theatre chains off from the studios in the 1940s, Chequer recalls, his then boss, Serge Semenenko, was delighted: First of Boston had been restricted in what it could lend to the industry by the legal limits on its loans to any one company; now, with two companies where one had been before, the bank could double its exposure. "Forty, fifty percent of our business is in the chains", Chequer says. "I think of the theatres as ways to pay taxes on the land, which accretes ten, fifteen percent a year in value, which doesn't show up on the P and L. Even if his balance sheet shows one million dollars in assets and thirty million dollars in debts, we don't get scared. We'll look at his properties, see what isn't reflected in the balance sheet. We like to say we'll make the balance sheet".

"We have mining engineers, chemical engineers, petroleum engineers, on our payroll full-time", says Reuben F. Richards, who heads a staff of almost five hundred lending officers for the First National City Bank of New York—another of the lean and hungry-looking young men the top management of that bank prefers, wearing a conservative suit, a conservative haircut, a white shirt and a striped red-and-blue regimental tie tastefully ornamented with a pattern of the star-shaped symbols of the bank. "The engineer is a staff man for the banker in that area. He may say, 'That process has never worked—what makes you think you can make it work now?' We can take months on one of these loans; sometimes these are *governments* we're dealing with. But a 'make-and-sell' company we don't know very well, we could probably do enough homework to make a decision about him in a week. A company we've done business with we could usually tell him that afternoon".

Once a month in the early 1970s, the First National Bank of Chicago ran an ad in *Broadcasting* magazine, announcing that the two men whose pencil portraits were the visual feature of the page were waiting at their telephones to hear from people in the television business. Actually, First of Chicago, while involved with the ABC network and a few station groups, had not been an all-purpose lender to the industry: the purpose of the ad was to explore, not to exploit, a position. "People call us", says Ben Lenhardt, the younger of the two men in the ad. "They ask us to comment on the entertainment industry. As the result of the ad, we've become experts. . . ."

There is relatively little movement of personnel from customer companies to banks, though people fairly often go the other way. And lending officers at banks tend to be specialized as lending officers, not as experts on an industry—it is not uncommon for a man to be lending one year to metals companies, the next to drug companies, the next to public utilities. King Upton, an older man who supervises all real estate lending for the First National Bank of Boston, says that "customers want to deal with someone who is even-steven with them, who can bring something to the conversation". But a strong knowledge of banking is likely to be what the customer wants: he already knows, or thinks he knows, about his own industry.

Lending officers for big banks as well as small banks, then, are normally what people who use such words call generalists. "I thought I would be a weird duck here", says young Peter Culver, a hefty, earnest, round-faced young man who finished a two-year apprenticeship at Morgan Guaranty and received his lending officer's stripes in late 1973. "I went to Oberlin, got a bachelor's in music; I was interested in organ and choral conducting, and I was working on a masters in music at Union Theological Seminary when I decided I didn't want to be a musician and went across the street to the Columbia Business School. I fell into banking. I've found that's not atypical". North Carolina's Walker Lockett wanted to go to graduate school and couldn't afford it: "I found the New York banks would pay for a year's education at night school, so I took a job with a bank; it worked out nicely".

Because the accident of assignment is so important in determining who becomes a lending officer, the value of a banker's advice is by no means guaranteed on every occasion—though the banker, who is putting somebody else's money at risk on his judgment, has to think it is. Out in suburban St. Louis, Adam Aronson doggedly recruits MBAs from Harvard and Stanford in competition against the giant banks, and does reasonably well at it, but every so often he worries about them. Unlike most bankers, Aronson ran a non-financial business himself, once upon a time. "It amazes me," he says, "the number of bankers who are in no way qualified to tell a businessman where to go or what to do, who will say they are helping him. We constantly scream at our people—*don't* advise people in an area where you're not competent; send them to somebody who is competent".

5

Most business lending, fortunately, is repetitive, to the same customers with the same needs at the same time of year. The men's clothing store borrows in May and June, pays some of it back in July, cleans it up in August; then borrows again in October, peaks in early December, and cleans up by the end of February. The manufacturer of school supplies also borrows in May and June, but does not start repaying until September and October. The bank's files contain a history of each borrower and his business; the lending officer prepares "spread sheets"—outsize pages of graph paper, sometimes scotch-taped together, which show five or ten years of balance sheet items—to prove out the viability of each loan request. These are "commercial loans", usually sixty-day or ninety-day credits. The lending officer can back up his judgment with numbers in reference books that tell him what proportion of inventory is usually carried by bank loans in this industry, and what the profit margins should be; and a credit agency can tell him whether anything strange has been happening with this borrower since the last time he borrowed. The incentive for the customer to pay back the loan on time is the strongest possible—the knowledge that he is going to want to borrow again at the same season next year.

In Britain, such loans tend to be made via an open line of credit, the borrower paying his bills through the use of the overdraft facility, as he needs the money. Even so, an alert lending officer is supposed to note and query when the borrower's use of overdrafts varies much from his or his industry's usual patterns.

Term loans—the loans that buy the butcher his walk-in freezer, or the dentist his fancy chair, or the toy-maker his injection-moulding machine—are necessarily somewhat trickier. The Bank of America guide for lending officers, *Term Loans to Business*, bluntly explains the difference: commercial loans are repaid by "conversion of inventory and receivables to cash", while term loans are repaid from "business profits". By definition a term loan is one that will not be repaid in full for a year or more. Like consumer loans, term loans to business are usually "self-amortizing"—the monthly instalments pay back the loan as well as paying the interest. The lending officer is expected to analyze the applicant's business—and personal life—thoroughly enough to be sure that the profits from the business will indeed be great enough to get all the instalments paid. The borrower's wife signs the loan agreement. Sometimes there is also a "co-maker" whose endorsement obligates him to repay the bank if the borrower fails to do so.

In a well-run bank, no more than $\frac{1}{3}$ of 1 percent of the loans are supposed to go sour. Unlike the venture capitalist, who can cheerfully take his lumps on losers, because the pay-out is big on the winners, the banker has to live and pay his expenses (including his loan losses) on the proceeds of a limited interest charge. Sometimes the loan agreement does give the banker a partial participation in a borrower's early success, through a "net earnings settlement" clause that accelerates the repayment of the loan by a proportion of the borrower's profits. Since the total sum the borrower pays back remains the same, the effect is to give the bank a higher annual interest rate through shortening the length of time the money is out.

On the European continent, banks often take equity positions—occasionally controlling positions—as well as making loans. This would be illegal in the United States, but does pertain in England.

The dramatic rise in interest rates in the late 1960s did create some situations where a suitable premium for a risky borrower would have put the cost of money completely beyond his ability to carry, and a bank that wanted to lend him money anyway could decide to take its premium in the form of an "equity kicker"—a share of profits in addition to the interest payment, as long as the loan runs. (For legal reasons, these arrangements will probably be made through the holding company rather than through the bank itself.) On some really dicey loans, First Pennsylvania has pioneered a technique of adding to interest charges a small percentage of the borrower's gross receipts, which means that the bank can be appropriately rewarded for its courage even when the borrower has no profits. "The trick", chairman John Bunting says rather complacently, "is to get compensated as you should be for the risks". As a normal matter, however, the bank's extra reward for making the term loan is the growth in the borrower's business, and thus the growth in the size loan he will need next time around, when presumably he will return loyally to the bank that helped him when not everyone would.

Term loans are part of the firmament of small business and professional life today, but within the memory of living bankers such lending was something not permitted by theory, custom, or the bank examiners. The term loan agreement a small businessman or professional man will be asked to sign is thus quite a collection of constraints on his activity. The Bank of America form is not unusual. First, the borrower must agree to report his business results to the bank at regular intervals, preferably with a statement certified by his accountant. He must give the bank's lending officer (or auditor) complete access to all his books and records. He must agree not to borrow money from anybody else without the bank's consent, and must procure the agreement of anyone to whom he already owes money to "subordinate" that claim to the bank's claim if it turns out there isn't enough to go around. He must promise not to increase his own take-home pay or drawing account without the consent of the bank, or pay dividends on his stock (if he has stock). He gives the bank veto power on any important hirings or firings. He promises to maintain a given level of working capital in the business, and to pay all his bills promptly. He must provide evidence of insurance on the business and on himself sufficient to repay the bank if anything happens to it or him.

These loans are normally secured by the pledging of all the assets in the business (not just the assets being bought with this money). "Although it generally is of insufficient value to pay off the loan," the Bank of America guide intones, "securing capital equipment provides three valuable functions:

1. LEVERAGE. As long as the applicant remains in business, the equipment and machinery necessary to his business operation are important. . . . Therefore, the fact that it is secured gives greater incentive to the borrower to meet his payments.

2. COLLATERAL CONTROL. Often a security agreement is taken simply to prevent the applicant from obtaining an additional loan from another lending institution. . . .

3. LOSS REDUCTION. When a loan is in default, security can be sold and proceeds applied toward the loan balance. . . ."

In the sample form supplied in its guide for lending officers, Bank of America also got the applicant to pledge that if he sold his home, the proceeds of the sale would have to be applied first to the payment of the term loan to his business.

To say that the borrower "offers as security" the capital equipment of his business does not entirely convey the dimensions of what happens. The bank wants to make sure that if anything goes wrong, no other creditor—no unpaid supplier, for example—can pick up any part of the proceeds of the sale of such equipment. Thus the bank will insist that a "Notice of Intent to Make Bulk Transfer" be filed with the appropriate state agency and advertised in a newspaper of general circulation, informing the world at large that this businessman has placed this chunk of his flesh in hazard to the repayment of a new loan. The bank is thus assured two ways that the equipment is really available for this purpose and that the borrower is at least minimally trustworthy: the state agency will inform the bank if such a notice has already been filed on behalf of someone else covering the same equipment, and any prior creditor reading the notice in the paper can raise hell or forever hold his peace.

Two kinds of relatively small loans to relatively small businesses are especially tricky for banks and lending officers. Automobile dealers carry their inventory with loans; indeed, the normal procedure is for the factory to bill the bank (or commercial credit company) rather than the dealer himself whenever a new car (or mobile home) is sent to the dealer's address. The dealer expects this "floor planning" service at rock-bottom interest rates, because he will subsequently act as a salesman for the bank's auto loan department, pushing his customers in the direction of that bank. Banks hate to lend people the total value of what is being bought with a loan, for obvious reasons (and also for an interesting non-obvious reason: if it becomes necessary to liquidate security, the borrower's other creditors and the trustee in bankruptcy will be very helpful in arranging a sale if something will be left over for them, very unhelpful if the only beneficiary is the bank). But an automobile dealer can normally borrow 100 percent of the invoice for what the factory sends him, and when money is easy and banks are hungry a dealer sometimes can borrow up to 110 percent of the factory price of his vehicles, making the bank advance some of his rent and salary and tax expenses, too. These loans necessarily give the dealer a fine opportunity to keep the use of the bank's money after the car or trailer has been sold to someone who pays cash or arranges his own financing away from the bank. Lending officers are strictly enjoined to pay unannounced visits to automobile dealers at frequent but irregular intervals, to make sure the merchandise the bank is financing is still in stock.

Even trickier is the loan to the building contractor, which is paid out in pieces, as the construction progresses. Normally, the construction loan is paid back neither with the conversion of inventory

to sales nor with the net profits of a business, but with another loan
—the mortgage. Where commercial property is involved, the bank
may not legally make the construction loan without proof that the
builder has already arranged a "take-out"—a final mortgage to be
supplied by an insurance company, a savings bank, or some other
"responsible lender".

"I don't do that business", says Garden State's Charles Agemian.
"Sure he's got a take-out, but I can be sitting with the construction
loan till the building is eighty or ninety percent full, because that's
what triggers the take-out. I don't want to be anybody's partner; I
just want to be his banker". A. G. Weichert of Bank of America's
home branch sighs, "The boilerplate on some of these take-outs is
so complicated and so clever; we don't always have the expertise
we should have". Early in 1974, a syndicate of New York banks
headed by Irving Trust Company had to call a $62-million loan
and acquire actual ownership of a big office building in New York
because the builder's take-out failed to materialize.

On homes, the bank must wait for the sale, when a savings
association will supply most of the take-out. Some commercial
banks write commercial mortgages themselves, nearly all write at
least some home mortgages (if only for the finance officers of big
borrowers), and a few (notably Bank of America) regard construction loans as advantageous in part because they give the bank the
inside track on the mortgage business; but most consider real
estate mortgages a wrong-headed use of the limited funds at their
disposal. They will write the long-term mortgage for the purchaser
only when something has gone wrong with the builder's original
take-out arrangements. "We never make a mortgage loan", says a
suburban midwestern banker, "on purpose". Such loans can then
be sold—sometimes at a slight loss, sometimes at a slight profit—
on what is now a highly developed nationwide "secondary market"
for mortgages.

The normal arrangement with a builder is that the bank "com-
mits" to lend a sum which will cover perhaps 80 percent of the cost
of the building, a third of it at the start of work, a third when the
foundation is completed, and the last third when the basic structure

is topped out (or all but the top floor is completed), leaving only the inside work to do. Like the British borrower using his overdraft privileges, the American builder pays interest only on the money that has actually been placed at his disposal, but from the day the agreement is signed he must pay a "commitment fee", most commonly $\frac{1}{2}$ of 1 percent, on the total amount committed. "The commitment fee is golden", says Hyman Minsky, a professor of economics at the University of Washington at St. Louis, who also runs a weekly seminar for the executives of Mark Twain Bancshares. But John Dubinsky, Mark Twain's vice-president for planning, is not so sure: "I don't like commitments; when you make commitments you find everybody wants his money at the same time. . . ."

Keeping up with the progress of a construction project is even more important than verifying the existence of the automobile dealer's inventory: only a few automobile dealers will sell a car without paying the bank's loan that put the car on the floor, but nearly every builder will try to get the next piece of the construction loan released before the completion of the work that the agreement says will trigger the next advance. Ancient wisdom in banking urges the visitor to the loan department to look at the shoes of the lending officers: if nobody has mud on his shoes, it means nobody is out visiting the construction projects, and the builders are stealing the bank blind.

Any lending associated with land or buildings is made doubly complicated by the fact that nobody can ever say what a large real estate project is "worth". Stocks and bonds are traded in a market, automobiles have an invoice price, but the market for real property is lumpy, with few buyers, few sellers, and rapid price changes. An early 1974 story in the *Wall Street Journal* told of Deil O. Gustafson, proprietor of the Tropicana Hotel in Las Vegas, who went from a teaching job at the University of Minnesota to a high-flying real estate career. "In 1963", Frederick C. Klein reports, Gustafson "learned that Nicolette Village, a development of one hundred sixty townhouse-type apartments in the Minneapolis suburb of Richfield, was available at a bargain price. He went to a bank in search of the financing.

"'They asked me what I was paying for the property. I told them to go out and appraise it and tell me how much they'd put up,' he says. 'They did and said they'd give me one point three million, which I guess was eighty percent of what they thought it was worth. I said fine. The actual purchase price was one point one million. I used the two hundred thousand that was left to start some other things. It wasn't income, so I didn't have to pay taxes on it. When you're young and need funds, that's a great way to get it'."

This is not respectable banking practice, of course; respectable practice would have offered Gustafson 80 percent of whatever he was paying, up to $1.3 million maximum. The mind boggles at the idea that a bank with that kind of money to lend on real estate security did not, in fact, require a look at the sales agreement before putting out the cash. Like Tertullian, one believes because it is absurd: nobody could have made up a story like that. It is also a nice story, because everybody lived happily ever after, which in the situation as described is far from guaranteed.

6

Like Rhodes' story, Klein's points to a truth the observer finds it too easy to forget: that in the relationship of banker and borrower, despite all the fine print in the loan agreement, it is the borrower more often than the lender who has the preferred position. The boxes at the ballparks, the hefty expense accounts at the restaurants, are paid for by banks entertaining borrowers, not borrowers entertaining bankers. "There's a growth company on Route One Twenty-eight", says Tom Fitzgerald of First of Boston. "He outgrows the legal limit of his local bank. He has a choice—he can go to Boston or to New York. New York is crawling around up here. They have a v.-p., he'll take you to theatre and such things. I'm not complaining, that's competition. But it puts a lot of pressure on us."

An American bank lending officer is first of all a salesman; he sells money, at a price. Junior lending officers are expected by their superiors to make calls, much as any industrial salesman makes calls. A man who has a good case for a loan of a profitable size can do business with any one of a number of banks, just as he can buy stationery from any one of a number of printers, and the lending officer's job is to convince him to do business with this bank. Most business lending relationships start not with the businessman coming to the bank but with the lending officer coming to the office. It was this sense that the banker performs services for the borrower, not technique or muscle, that made the American banks such effective competition when they came to England en masse in the 1960s.

Take for example the relationship between Inforex, a Route 128 electronics company, and the First National Bank of Boston, a relationship that ultimately produced a pioneering loan agreement permitting the company to offer its equipment on cancellable leases and thus to compete with IBM in the marketing of computer peripherals. Thomas H. Lee is the v.-p. in charge for the bank— a few years older than Bank of America's Lambert—blond, fair, blue-eyed—and Jewish. ("The only Jew in corporate banking". Not quite, of course, as Lee knows, but close enough; in any event, it is not easy to know what one says next. "Do they", I inquired, "know this at the bank?" "We talk of nothing else. Usually, I bring it up myself". Presumably the feeling is that scientists don't care. Shortly before these pages were first published, Lee moved on to operate his own venture capital business, with help from First of Boston; among his early investments was the Sol Hurok office that manages concert artists and sponsors tours of America by opera and ballet companies.)

"My wife", Lee reports, "had a friend to the house, who said her husband was sales manager for Inforex. I asked what Inforex was, and she told me, and I said, 'I know about that. That's like Viatron'. Viatron was a customer of mine; this was before Viatron went broke. She said, 'Oh, we're *much* better than Viatron'. So a few days later I went around to visit at Inforex, and I left with a cheque for half a million dollars of their money, which we put to work for them immediately in the Treasury bill market. . . ." The lending relationship came later.

In general, the bigger the company is, the more eager a bank will be to have it as a customer. Large loans cost little more to make than smaller loans, apart from the cost of the money itself, and are thus necessarily more profitable (provided the big borrower doesn't demand too many free services, which he will when money is easy). Though situations like Penn Central, Stirling Homex, Yale Express, Equity Funding and Lockheed have shaken everybody's confidence just a little, on the whole bankers like other citizens find it hard to imagine that great big enterprises can really go broke and leave their creditors gasping on the beach. Except for AT&T, which almost never borrows money from banks (it borrows from its customers, by making them pay for each month's service in advance), all the nation's largest companies maintain relations with several, sometimes with scores of large banks; and each of the ten largest banks is involved in lending to at least 150 of the *Fortune* 500. First National City lends to every one of the 100 largest industrial corporations (AT&T is a utility, not an industrial), and to 199 of the top 200. John Schroeder, executive v.-p. in charge of "general banking" at Morgan Guaranty, says that "we lend to all of the top one hundred to whom we choose to lend."

Giant banks lend to giant corporations on a national—indeed, an international—market, a fact now recognized by the regulatory authorities, which have approved applications from some of the big banks for the establishment of scattered loan production offices that can carry the bank's money around the country. First National Bank of Chicago has been the promoter of this idea. "Our industry specialists travel all over the country", says vice-chairman Chauncey Schmidt. "They're in Seattle today and Florida tomorrow and Boston Friday—it's terrible, and very inefficient, too. We hope to open regional offices all over the United States in the next few years." Others are not so certain this makes sense: Morgan's Schroeder says, "I don't see how they can communicate, how they can make decisions, how they can keep out of the hair of the correspondent banks." Reuben Richards of First National City argues that "a man going out to San Francisco can do a better job—and he brings the New York money market to the guy on the coast, which is one of our contributions." Both First of Boston and First Pennsylvania expect to plant loan-production offices around the country, however: First Pennsylvania, in tribute to Chicago's invasion of its market, put down its first distant roots in Chicago itself.

About three-fifths of the lending big banks do to big business is in the form of term loans. Originally, such loans were variants of the builder's loan: a corporation wanted to build a factory, which at some point would be paid for by the sale of a mortgage bond or debentures in the bond market; the bank put up the cost of building the factory, and was paid back—"taken out"—by the proceeds of the bond sale. But this "bridging" function became increasingly complicated as the banks grew more adventurous, and now the bank loan may be calculated to last not merely until the company can conveniently go to market but until the success of the factory has been demonstrated. "Take a Boeing Company", says Roy H. Dickerson, who came out of the domestic lending end of First National City to the direction of its British branches. "Boeing has a seven-year product cycle from the design to the delivery of the airplane. Isn't it appropriate for the bank to lend on their product cycle?"

Such loans may not be self-amortizing; indeed, the borrower may be excused from paying anything at all toward the reduction of the principal until some time after the factory is up and running, and when the term runs out there may be a "balloon" of 50 percent or more still outstanding. In 1972, the Chicago banks and First National City began turning the clock all the way back to the old-fashioned home mortgages, and wrote a number of "bullet loans" under which the borrower paid only interest through the full term of the loan, and seven or eight or even ten years later still owed the full amount. In fairness, it should be said that such loans were written only for top-rated public utilities, which can easily put the interest on a loan in their rate base but get into hassles with consumer advocates when they add on the amortization.

Ideally, all these loans should be so thoroughly collateralized that if the borrower were to go broke, saints preserve us, the bank could get its money back through the sale of the security. In the real world, this doesn't happen anymore; and, really, it never did. In most cases the forces that would make a borrower fall would also destroy the value of his collateral: a cigarette-making machine would not be worth much to the bank that loaned the money to buy it if the cigarette maker were put out of business by a law prohibiting the sale of cigarettes. Given the immense variety of interesting activities now known to go on under the certified blanket of Generally Accepted Accounting Principles, a bank's acceptance of the stock of a subsidiary company as security for a loan to a conglomerate corporation is really an expression of faith in the management. Though secured lenders do tend to come out of bad situations less severely injured than unsecured lenders, a high and increasing proportion of the term loans to big companies are now made on an unsecured basis, relying on the general credit of the business, the fact that it is expected to survive. The question is the extent to which anticipated earnings before depreciation and taxes are *sure* to "cover" some multiple of the interest costs the borrower has assumed. If that number looks right—if, in other words, the "cash flow" is adequate—everything else is assumed to be all right, too. At least quarterly and sometimes more often banks will send lending officers around to big borrowers to chat about this and that, have a drink with friends, and make sure the number still looks right.

How large a loan any one officer can make on his own authority depends on customs that vary a great deal from bank to bank. At First National City, rather surprisingly, one officer alone cannot go above $2,500—but two sets of initials can lend an applicant $5 million. At Bank of America, the theory (not always the practice) long forbade even senior people to go to the bathroom without a vote by a committee; since 1970 the regional vice-presidents have had lending authority reaching in some cases over $10 million. And at the First National Bank of Chicago, every lending officer

is technically empowered to commit the legal limit of the bank—
at this writing, about $60 million. People normally consult with
each other, and especially with their superiors, before putting out
anything like that much money (and when money is tight all loans
must pass an allocation committee), but every so often somebody
takes a plunge. A few years back, a junior officer was making a
visit to the treasurer of a large company the bank had been wooing
unsuccessfully for some years. While he was in the office, the
treasurer got a call from a rival bank, which was for some reason
delaying on a loan agreement. When the treasurer hung up cussing,
the young lending officer asked him how much money that delayed
loan was supposed to be. "Thirty million dollars", said the corporate treasurer. "You got it", said the loan officer, whose age in
years was lower than the loan in millions. Then he went back to
the bank and told his superior what he had done, and his superior
said calmly, "For your sake, I hope he pays it back. . . ."

Some loans are bigger than even a very big bank likes to undertake on its own (some exceed the lending limits of even the biggest
banks). No one bank, for example, could by itself finance the
construction of a fleet of LNG (Liquefied Natural Gas) tankers at
$100 million per boat. Such loans are "syndicated" to groups of
banks, each of which takes a specified percentage as its "participation". Other syndications may occur when an old and good customer whose business a big bank would hate to lose wants a loan
the bank is none too eager to write. Citibank's Rueben Richards
explains: "The division head may say, 'This price is a little bit thin
—but we've been doing business with this company for a jillion
years'. Then we'll offer some of it out". Or there may be other
relationships: "We have a correspondent bank in St. Louis,"
Richards says, "that we know is the leading local bank for this
company. We are their leading capital bank. We'll say, 'Fair's fair',
and we'll share the business".

Even when the loan is syndicated, the "lead bank" receives fees
and other benefits greater than those received by the others, and
the competition is fierce among the giants for special relationships
with special very large customers. Computer work that would cost

a customer quite a lot of money in the outside world may be done by the bank without charge, dividend cheques may be handled as "payable through" drafts (which means no deposit is placed in the bank to support the draft, but the corporation forwards the money to cover the disbursements when notified that the dividend "cheque" has been presented). The range of possibilities is substantial, especially for a borrowing customer that keeps good balances and does not haggle unduly about interest rates. But this ceaseless competition for a small number of very large accounts has driven down profit margins on the largest loans to the point where the giant banks now speak wistfully of the need to find ways to serve companies with only $50–$60 million in sales. "Highly profitable accounts," says First of Chicago's Schmidt, "and very loyal to their bank".

In soliciting business from the corporate giants, the banks are in competition not only against each other, but against non-bank lenders. Ford Motor Company can sell short-term IOUs in the open market in the form of "commercial paper" just as easily as it can borrow from banks; the Securities and Exchange Commission will issue Ford a "no action letter" freeing the company from the need to register the IOUs as securities, on assurance that the money is really needed only for short-term purposes, like carrying inventory. Or, if it wants to borrow for a period longer than nine months (the maximum the SEC allows on commercial paper), Ford can pay the lawyers a little more for the required papers and sell debentures to the public through underwriters, or place them privately with insurance companies or pension funds or charitable endowments.

It should be noted that except for the private placement, all these apparently non-bank borrowings would also involve banks to some degree. Commercial paper dealers and buyers require each seller to maintain at his bank or banks a "line of credit" sufficient to pay off the commercial paper when it comes due. This is usually a commitment to lend, not entirely unlike the commitment made to a builder, except that the builder is expected to use his and the issuer of commercial paper is not—if he comes to the day of reckoning on the paper without the money to pay it off, he "rolls over" his indebtedness: that is, he sells new paper. (The banks should have known Penn Central was at the brink when the lines of credit presumably securing the commercial paper were drawn down and absorbed by the gigantic losses of the railroad. The crisis threatened to spread immediately thereafter because the commercial-paper buyers, confronted with their Penn Central losses, suddenly realized that Chrysler, too, was operating without lines of credit sufficient to cover commercial paper that would have to be rolled over within a few weeks. While the Fed gets and earns the credit for saving the world the weekend Penn Central went under, Morgan Guaranty would like to see some recognition given to Manufacturers Hanover, which on its own motion in a perilous time increased Chrysler's credit line—a gesture worthy of J. P. Morgan himself.) Depending on the strength of the borrower and the bank's other relations with him, the line of credit the bank guarantees to keep available to back up his commercial paper may or may not earn the bank a commitment fee. It is understood that any corporation that has a truly committed line of credit will keep at least 10 percent of the total of that line on deposit as a "compensating balance" until the paper is paid off. "But that," Thomas J. Wageman of First of Chicago told a correspondent banking conference in fall 1972, "is no comfort to those of us who see our lines of credit converted from active loans to insurance policies".

One of the largest categories of bank loans is the loan to people who use the money to lend to others. The man who buys stock "on margin" owes the rest of the purchase price to his stockbroker—but the stockbroker probably owes it to a bank, which has taken custody of the stock as security for the loan. Factors—who operate by purchasing a manufacturer's accounts receivable at a discount, and then collect at full price from the manufacturer's customers themselves—operate almost entirely on bank loans. Many hire purchase car loans are written outside banks: in Britain, by finance houses, some of them now subsidiaries of the clearing banks; in America by finance companies ranging in size from giant CIT and General Motors Acceptance Corporation down to the local lawful

257

shylock—but these lending organizations get much of their money by borrowing from banks.

Department store and mail-order revolving-credit plans are in reality bank loans through a middleman. In practice, there are two middlemen: the department store organizes a wholly owned "captive" finance company; when the customer buys the merchandise "on time", the finance company buys the customer's instalment plan agreement with money loaned it by the bank. The department store has cash and no debts, a nice clean balance sheet; the wholly owned finance company, which makes no public report, has assets in the form of consumer receivables, and debt in the form of bank loans, and profits or losses that the parent department store may or may not wish to show as its own. Setting up this sort of convenient, legal but potentially misleading arrangement is a management consultant service the banks can offer.

7

An old story in Hollywood tells of the agent who watched a star's belligerent walk down the aisle of the Brown Derby, and said, "There goes the sonuvabitch who's getting ninety percent of my money". Watching the finance companies, factors, and leasing companies, the banks envied them the profits they made on what was (from the bank's point of view) the bank's money. Unlike the actor's agent, the bank could go do this work itself; and, presently, it did, opening personal-loan departments, moving in on instalment credit, ultimately (through the holding-company device) purchasing the finance companies it used to envy. Buying up companies can be a very good deal for a bank, which need not put up a penny of its own money. "One bank bought a finance company for six hundred thousand dollars, which I raised for them in the debt market", said bank stock dealer Harry Keefe. "They paid seven percent. [This was 1972.] The company now generates one point one million in revenues. How do you calculate the return on equity, when there is no equity?"

The move into new ways of business lending was led by the First

National Bank of Boston, which emerged from World War II with the knowledge that it could not greatly expand its retail operation (because state law restricted its branching to the boundaries of Suffolk County in Massachusetts), that it could not compete with the much larger New York and Chicago banks for national business of the usual kind, and that its resources—four times as large as those of the next largest bank in New England—were considerably greater than anything it could profitably employ in its own territory. Lloyd Brace, the chairman of the bank, Nebraska-born and Dartmouth-trained, worked this out for himself. He was blessed with the most imaginative lending officer in the country in Serge Semenenko, and he gave Semenenko freedom to play with the bank's money in markets where the other big banks would be afraid to compete.

Throughout the Depression, railroads had been able to buy new rolling stock despite their bankruptcy, through the sale of "equipment trust certificates", which were in effect bonds secured by the pledge of the locomotive or the boxcar itself. From time immemorial, both the American and the European merchant marine had operated on a basis of ship charters, by which the shipping company bought the use of a vessel for a voyage rather than the ship itself. Assuming that some item of capital equipment was usable by and resaleable to others, a bank could make a safe loan even to a very shaky borrower by securing just the items of capital equipment to be purchased by this loan. Unfortunately, most shaky borrowers already have loans outstanding, with "covenants" that prevent them from pledging anything they own or may acquire to any other lender. Semenenko saw that the desired result could be achieved, without violating previous loan agreements, through an arrangement whereby the bank retained title to the machinery, and the borrower instead of repaying a loan in instalments made a regular rental payment. The legal situation would be different, but the underlying realities would be the same. "Semenenko taught us," John Chequer says with persisting admiration, "to look at leasing as just another way to handle a financial problem. You put together a company's needs, and then look at what the most advanced thinking says the Fed will let a bank do".

What brought leasing to the fore as a banking tool was the investment tax credit the Kennedy administration created as part of its push to get the country moving again. Through this loophole in the tax laws, a company investing in plant or equipment could take 7 percent of the cost of that investment as a credit against its tax liabilities in the year the investment was made. In effect, the government contributed 7 percent to the cost of new productive machinery.

If a bank bought the machinery and leased it to the customer, then the 7 percent credit would go to the bank, reducing its tax bill handsomely. The "borrower" would benefit by a good fraction of that reduction in tax, because the bank could make the deal at a lower than usual "interest rate" and still turn a profit. There was some feeling among commentators on this arrangement that it was cheating, but the fact is that the banks were living up to the intent as well as the letter of the law. A tax credit device could not stimulate a company that was losing money or had already accumulated tax credits from prior losses. By purchasing the equipment and taking the associated tax credit, the banks spread the benefits of the legislation more widely around the business community. Meanwhile, a company that might have had some difficulty adding to its debt got the use of new machinery, cheap. The tax credit law was indeed, as later critics liked to say (many of them Kennedy Democrats quite unconsciously criticizing themselves when young), a form of "socialism for the rich".

In addition to the tax credit, the bank in a leasing deal received the tax benefits from the depreciation of the equipment it now owned. And all these benefits could be greatly increased if the lease was "leveraged"—i.e., if the bank put up only part of the purchase money itself, arranging to have others lend the rest. Now the bank could get the benefit of tax credit and depreciation on the full value of the machinery, for only part of the price.

The legality of aspects of this operation remained questionable for a while, but in 1963 Comptroller James Saxon went all the way for the banks. He ruled that national banks could indeed own and lease "personal property", that such leases were not loans and not subject to legal lending limits, and that it was permissible for banks to arrange leases that would not in fact pay out the full cost of the machinery, leaving the bank with the possible profit or loss from its disposal at the end of the lease. (The Federal Reserve Board has since successfully vetoed bank leasing on any but a full pay-out basis.) What constitutes "personal property" remains something of a mystery. "The law of fixtures is the craziest area of the law in all states", says a young lawyer in one of the state banking departments. "In some states, a refrigerator is fixed equipment, in others it's personal property. What the banks lease as personal property can be fascinating to behold: I know something as big as Yankee Stadium and twelve stories high that a bank owns and leases as personal property".

While Semenenko was out using First of Boston's credit to buy sawmills that could be leased to lumber companies, his colleague King Upton was lending to mortgage bankers to allow them to assemble packages of mortgages to sell to insurance companies ("mortgage warehousing" now accounts for $125 million a day in loans by First of Boston), and Felix Pereira in another room of the same building was putting the bank into the factoring business. "Our interest in factoring really started in the 1930s", says Tom Fitzgerald, now First of Boston's vice-president in charge of such operations, an earnest Irishman with close-cropped greying hair, tailored with impeccable conservatism down to but obviously not including Western boots. "We were in the middle of the textile industry, and we were saying to our clients, 'We can't lend you any more money, your business has gone down, you'd better go to a factor'. We woke up and realized we were telling them to use their best assets, their accounts receivable—and the people who were buying those accounts receivable were doing it with money they borrowed from us".

For very proper First of Boston to become a factor was no small step. A factor does not lend money; he buys his client's accounts receivables. Thereafter, his success or failure is a function of his effectiveness at bill collecting, and historically there have been

WHERE THE MONEY GOES

strong-arm elements in this work. The factor buys the paper on a "no-recourse" basis—that is, if his client's customer doesn't pay up, the factor eats it—and presumably the basic element of judgment is the credit-worthiness of the client's customers. In fact, it turns out that the central judgment is the capacity of the client himself, because once a manufacturer begins to go under even his best customers begin refusing payment for merchandise, claiming defects in quality, failure to meet specifications, tardy delivery, or what-have-you. The great enforcer of morality in commerce is the continuing relationship, the belief that one will do business again with this customer, or this supplier, and when a failing company loses this automatic enforcer not even a strong-arm factor is likely to find a substitute. "If something goes wrong in this business," says James Patmore, who handles the accounting end of First of Boston's British factoring affiliate, 'it goes *really* wrong". The important decisions, then, turn out to be bankers' decisions, and First of Boston, virtually alone as a banker in the factoring world until First National City bought Hubschman Factors in 1965, made pots of money.

Factoring turned out to have additional values for First of Boston. "In 1960," Fitzgerald recalls, "when we decided we had to expand our international operation, we didn't have the disposition, the manpower or the funds to go into worldwide competition with First National City or Chase. But we could do factoring. We wanted to use our correspondent relationships abroad, do joint ventures with them, help them get into this market. Today we have a network of twenty-two countries in which we have a partner, joint ownership of a factoring company".

These operations did not always start off satisfactorily: factoring was a new idea in Europe, where manufacturers often looked askance at the idea of having a third party collect the bills they sent their customers. A British joint venture with the merchant banking house of Hill, Samuel dropped almost $1.5 million in 1964 alone. But today the international and the domestic First of Boston factoring operations each generate about $1,000 million of profitable paper over the course of a year; and the British subsidiary (now based in Brighton and shared with Lloyds Bank) is, Fitzgerald says, the most profitable factoring company in the world. "In England now, people flock to it: 'to sort out the mess', they say". Everything goes on computers, and First of Boston does its factoring clients' accounts receivable bookkeeping. Through this specialized international network, the bank can offer clients a safe way to do an export business, taking not only the credit risk but also the currency risk, at a price.

Domestically, First of Boston now has a lot of company in this business. "I did my graduate work at Rutgers", says Walker Lockett of North Carolina National Bank, which bought an outfit called Factors, Inc. in 1971 (and changed the name to NCNB Financial Services: "factor" still has an ugly sound to bankers). "My thesis was a study of bank participation in factoring. I started on it in 1967, and by the time I finished it in 1970 it was outmoded: the banks had bought all the factors".

This too is part of the revolution in banking: the discovery that the power to lend is the power to take over.

11/Interest Rates and Other Problems

An organized money-market has many advantages. But it is not a school of social ethics or of political responsibility.
—R. H. TAWNEY

* * *

The interest rate is the price of money, fixed minute by minute in a multiform market with a wide variety of participants. Market prices, as people keep forgetting, are the prices that clear the market, matching what the least-eager buyer is willing to pay for this item to the costs of the least-efficient surviving producer. If the price were higher, presumably, some buyers would be unwilling to buy; if the price were lower, some producers would be unable to supply. This equilibrated best of all possible worlds, of course, is not the world we have, neither in the money market nor anywhere else.

First, though money (of one country) appears to be fungible and all-the-same, in fact it is a variety of products. Money, like speed, is a function of time. Money that can be borrowed only overnight is different from money that can be borrowed over a period of one year, or ten years. Each duration makes a separate credit market; some of these markets may be thin and narrow at times when others are broad and deep; and the price movements in the different markets are frequently in different directions.

Normally (though not in all inflationary economies), rates are higher for long-term money because the risks are greater. A classic way for a bank to get in trouble is to try to take advantage of this "spread" between long-term and short-term rates, making long-term loans which it expects to finance by repeated short-term borrowings. If short-term interest rates rise, the bank can suffer severe losses on its long-term loans or its investments in long-term securities. Assuming everybody involved was honest (which may be a larger assumption than the facts warrant), this is what happened to Donald Parsons' Commonwealth Group in Detroit, which went under (one bank) or into reorganization (the others) in 1970. Parsons, an under-forty lawyer with a gift for publicity and creative accounting, had put the banks heavily into low-rated long-term municipal bonds. ("Risky?" a *Fortune* article asked two years before the smash. "Much less so than one might imagine, according to some recent academic studies. . . .") Even after allowing for the tax-exempt feature of the interest payments, earnings did not come near covering what the bank had to pay for money in 1969–70; and in a crunch the bonds were unsaleable. And even if they had been saleable, the bank didn't have enough capital to absorb the losses on the sales. Yecch.

Historically, developments of this sort created money panics in the economy. Now the fact of unrestricted paper currency, the ability of the central bank to create unlimited credit for anybody, presumably eliminates this banker's error as a source of disaster for the banking system as a whole. But it is still a worry in the Eurodollar market, to which the Federal Reserve System has no obligation to act as central banker, and in the administration of individual banks. Men who are nourishing a reputation as "sound" bankers will say that they "match maturities"—i.e., that their term loans are financed by term deposits or long-range borrowings of some sort. This assertion is always untrue, but the recognition that virtue is virtue has a value in banking as in other sectors of the society.

Second, the market for money can never be free of government influence, partly because money, as Lincoln and Wright Patman observe, is a creation of government. In the short-term money market, supply is pretty much what the government wishes it to be; making money (the one proper use of that unfortunate idiom) costs the government nothing. ("*Not* nothing", a Fed spokesman says firmly; "one cent per dollar bill".) If the government wants interest rates lower, it can print money; if it wants interest rates higher, it can in one way or another destroy money. A strongly developed sense of this truth dominated American politics for many years, before the Civil War, when the merchant classes (*not* the farmers and workers, as Bray Hammond has proved) pushed for "free banking" and easy credit; and after the Civil War, when a farming community with fixed debts and falling prices demanded greenbacks, free coinage of silver, and the election of William Jennings Bryan. Interestingly, these matters were never significant political issues in Britain, probably because the Bank of England was regarded as beyond the reach of politics and politicians. Even today, popular mythology and the newspapers proclaim the Democrats as the party of easy money and the Republicans as the party of hard money—though Richard Nixon pushed on the Federal Reserve System more persistently and more successfully than any of his predecessors to enlarge the money supply. "An election was approaching", former Fed Governor Sherman Maisel writes of the Nixon administration's pressure in 1971; "from their point of view, the faster money grew, the better was monetary policy." It should be added that Maisel, a Kennedy Democrat, thought Nixon's policy was right whatever his motives.

The government's power to control short-term interest rates does not, however, extend to the market for long-term interest rates. These rates are profoundly influenced by expectations as to the future value of money itself, and many lenders who see inflation ahead will not lend unless the return looks high enough to compensate them not only for the use of the money but also for the probable decline in its value over the term of the loan. If the price level is going to rise 7 percent over the course of the year, after all, a 10 percent interest rate will yield only 3 percent "real" interest for the twelve months. This problem may be made considerably worse by the movement to tie pension funds to the cost-of-living index. At present, the fact of fixed dollar obligations maturing at some distant future date—insurance policies, pensions and annuities—assures a continuing demand for safe long-term-debt instruments in the face of persistent inflation. It is obviously unfair to make the beneficiaries of insurance policies and pension plans carry the worst burdens of inflation, but the elimination of unfairness in this case could cripple capital investment—and thus the standard of living of future generations. Of course, when inflation reaches the heights achieved in Britain in 1975, one cannot avoid "indexing" pension obligations, whatever the cost in current investment.

The fact that interest rates on longer-term loans are at least partly a function of price-level expectations ultimately limits any government's power to control short-term rates, too. An infusion of new money to reduce short-term rates increases the expectations of inflation, and drives up long-term rates still further. The end result of this process is a flight from money into things, a loss of the willingness to hold money that we call hyperinflation. No government not seeking to subvert society (as Allende's was in Chile) will deliberately create a hyperinflation, and this fear of chaos places a ceiling on governmental efforts to hold down short-term interest rates through printing money. At any given point in time, however, the short-term interest rate is at least partly a function of government policy.

Third, rising interest rates affect different borrowers in very different ways. The American home buyer who signs up for a thirty-year mortgage at a fixed rate will be the worst hit by an increase: for him, a rise from 7 percent to 9 percent in the interest rate on a $30,000 loan means a difference of $32.50 in monthly payments, $11,700 over the life of the mortgage. By contrast, the man buying a car with a $3,000 three-year instalment-plan loan will find the monthly payments up only $3.25, the total cost up only $117, after an increase from 11 percent to 13 percent in the interest rate on a new loan. Ten times as much money compounded by ten times as long a loan means a hundred times as much increase in interest cost. Similarly, the department store borrowing $5 million for two months to carry Christmas inventory will be out of pocket only $16,667 by a 2 percent rise in the interest rate, which means that the cost of the merchandise is increased by only $\frac{1}{3}$ of 1 percent, while the municipality or the paper manufacturer selling forty-year bonds to build facilities to reduce water pollution from sewers or paper mills will find that a 2 percent increase in interest rates adds from 12 percent to 22 percent to the total cost of the project. The in-and-out stock market speculator does not care at all about the interest on his margin account, except to the extent that he believes high interest rates put pressure on stock prices. The commodities speculator doesn't even worry about that. Some American economists believe that these problems can be resolved by variable interest rates on mortgages and long-term bonds; but experience in England in the 1970s argues that the social cost of high rates is intolerable, whether future rates are fixed or variable.

Allowed to proceed unhindered, an increase in interest rates directs money away from future-oriented investment toward present-oriented consumption and toward gambling. Historically, this is a price that governments have been willing to pay (while loudly proclaiming their displeasure with the results) in the belief that total economic activity is significantly restrained by the added cost of money at a time when restraint is essential. Several key sectors of the economy are not in fact affected. Despite piteous appearances to the contrary in 1974, increases in the interest rates influence only slightly the long-term planning of a power-and-light company, a monopoly supplying an indispensable service, which can increase its charges to its customers by the amount of its interest costs and must borrow so often that over the years these costs must average out. Distortions of economic activity that the government finds truly unbearable can be corrected by selective measures on the demand side—by the provision of tax credits for housing, municipal construction projects and long-term industrial investment, and by specific controls on the use of credit in the stock market (high margin requirements) and in automobile purchases (high down payments).

Britain's Radcliffe Committee examined this theory at the end of the 1950s, and decided that it worked—*not* (as American opinion believes the Committee said) because higher interest rates did in fact importantly affect the behaviour of most borrowers but because institutional rigidities in the banking system led to reductions in activity by the lenders. "A rise in rates", the Committee wrote, "makes some less willing to lend because capital values have fallen [i.e., the securities they own and might sell to raise money to lend have gone down in the market], and others because their own interest rate structure is sticky." This is exactly what happened in 1966, when the Fed leaned heavily on the banking system in ways that restricted the growth of deposits and made additional lending possible only through selling off securities portfolios at a heavy loss. "They socked sixteen million dollars of losses onto Morgan", says Hyman Minsky of Washington University, "before they bailed out the system". (Morgan says it took the losses deliberately, to clear out low-rate interest inventory and increase current rates of return at the expense of a one-shot shellacking.)

It should be noted that the Fed succeeded. "Judged by its performance in getting GNP on track", wrote Arthur Okun, chairman of the Council of Economic Advisers in the Johnson administration, "the Federal Reserve in 1966 put on *the* virtuoso performance in the history of stabilization policy. It was the greatest tightrope walking and balancing act ever performed by either fiscal or monetary policy. Single-handedly the Fed curbed a boom generated by a vastly stimulative fiscal policy that was paralyzed by politics and distorted by war. And in stopping the boom, it avoided a recession." The politicians, however, found the price too high: "In the view of most Americans", Okun continued, "the collapse of home-building, the disruption of financial markets, and the escalation of interest rates were evils that outweighed the benefits of the non-recessionary halting of inflation."

More important, perhaps, the banks found the price too high. Prior to 1966, term loans had been written with rates of interest fixed for the duration of the loan, like mortgage interest or bond coupons. When interest rates went up, prospective term borrowers had reason to delay in taking their loans, in the hopes of saving something on the cost of money. At Valley National in Arizona, which has retained the pre-1966 ways of doing business. Paul Jones reported in summer 1973 that "some customers who want an increased line, on being told what the marginal credit will cost in term and rate, will say they want to think about it." Meanwhile, bankers, fearing even higher interest rates in the months ahead, had reason to avoid term lending, afraid of increasing the proportion of their loans outstanding which yielded less than some subsequent prime rate—less, indeed, than the prospective cost of new funds bought in the CD or Fed Funds or Eurodollar markets.

After 1966, the fixed-rate term loan became almost extinct at the major money-centre banks. "You can't win on fixed rates", chairman Richard Hill of First of Boston explains. "If the rate goes up you're clobbered. If it goes down, your customer comes around with a lot of economic clout. You're only a commerical banker. If you won't renegotiate, Chase will," By 1973 most of the big term loans to business were being written to provide that the interest rate would be recalculated periodically over the duration of the loan. "We have more ways of calculating a rate than you can imagine", says Reuben Richards of First National City. "Some are every ninety days, some every hundred and twenty days, some monthly, some every time the rates change."

Now it became irrelevant to such a borrower *when* he borrowed: if his loan said 6 percent today, it might well go to 10 percent next year; if it said 10 percent today, he might well be paying only 6 percent next year. Except for the mortgage borrower and the borrower on the bond market, *all* large term borrowers were placed in the position of the power-and-light company that could count on averaging out its costs.

Meanwhile, the shift from asset management to liability management made the banks much less concerned about the price of their securities portfolio. In the municipal bond area, indeed—as we shall see in the next chapter—they found ways to make profits on falling prices. Traditionally, the Fed had always, as the Radcliffe Committee recommended, sought to control the growth of the economy through the manipulation of interest rates. Now increasing interest rates still did their harm—undermining the housing market and the municipal bond market, displacing demand from long-term development to short-term consumption and speculation—but they could no longer do any good. The ground had been cut out from under the fortress of government regulation; but the commanders of the fortress seemed not to notice that they were standing unsupported in midair.

Bewildered by and angry at the banks' desire *and capacity* to frustrate sound public policy. Chairman Arthur Burns in private and in meetings of small groups found moral turpitude in the "Harvard types who concern themselves with maximizing efficiency . . . who worry unduly about the price/earnings ratio of their stock." They were "mark-up bankers", he said scornfully, and lacked the sense of public duty their forefathers had known. But the discomforts Burns suffered in 1973 had little to do with antisocial attitudes among the men he was supposed to be regulating, and a lot to do with commercial attitudes in the business community, which now had no reason to believe that prudence or taking advantage of swings in the business cycle would have the slightest effect on the interest costs they would have to pay.

2

Precisely how interest rates on loans were determined in the old days is now a mystery to which nobody has an answer. Then as now, there was a floor, which was the interest rate on government bonds or Treasury bills of the duration of the loan: no bank would lend money at rates below what could be earned on an investment in government securities. In Britain, the floor was set rather solemnly by announced decisions on "Bank Rate" by the court of the Bank of England. But the ceiling was not so firm, being a function of what the banker and his customer considered a fair rate at this time, an attitude which was itself a function of what they thought (or knew) was in the deals other bankers were making with other customers. Lending activity was carried on in confidence—not to say secrecy—and there were no published rates. In Britain, where quantitative controls limited the advantages a bank could gain by dropping its rates, the clearing banks with government approval ran a money cartel offering a borrower the same rates and terms wherever he turned.

If they could borrow money at all, blacks in America paid more than whites, women paid more than men, Jews paid more than gentiles. George S. Craft of the Trust Company of Georgia wrote in *The Bankers Handbook* in the mid-1960s that borrowers in the cloak-and-suit industry were often known "to make heavy withdrawals of capital from the business. These withdrawals may be for investment in real estate or securities or for transfer of assets to a wife or child. This is one of the reasons why bankers often require personal guarantees in connection with loans to this trade." Under these circumstances, of course, bankers felt entitled to charge higher interest rates, too. None of this is as bad as it once was; but none of it has disappeared, either. Wearing the right school tie (or knowing someone who does who will sign the note) is still worth a point or so on the interest rate; the wrong race, creed, colour, or sex still implies some small penalty, though it is no longer so likely as it once was to mean a complete refusal to lend.

Today some but not all of the veil of secrecy has been pierced. Banks announce a "prime" or "base" rate—the interest rate charged the best customers on loans of ninety days or less. (In Britain, for some reason not entirely comprehensible to a foreigner, or explicable by the natives, "base rate" is about a percentage point below the rate at which loans are actually being made to the best private borrowers, half a point below the rate to the nationalized industries. Banks report to the government weekly or monthly, and to their stockholders and the public quarterly, on the total volume of their loans and the ratio between loans and other kinds of investment. Nearly all the larger banks publish an average rate of interest earned on loans and investments over the most recent reporting period. But it is still almost impossible to find out the specific interest rates that individual business borrowers actually must pay, or the considerations that enter into the decision on any one loan. Morgan Guaranty tells potential foreign entrants to business life in the United States that "American financial practice depends on thorough disclosure. When a company seeks credit, it should be prepared to supply complete financial records, including a considerable amount of information that may not appear in the published financial statements of the corporate parent. A bank receiving such information will treat it in strict confidence." Part of what is kept in confidence is the nature of the loan agreement, including the size and the price of the credit, with any given customer.

In a general way, however, the factors that determine interest rates are known. The first consideration, obviously, is the risk to the bank in making this loan as against the loan to a prime borrower. To the extent that there really is a market for credit, this judgment of risk is made not by the individual bank but by the market: the premium a borrower must pay over and above "prime" or "base" rate measures his ability to get his money elsewhere. Companies large enough to sell their commercial paper on the open market are prime customers by definition: they have leverage on the interest they pay. "When GM calls and says they want to borrow twenty million dollars", Al Rice of Bank of America explains, "they say, 'What's the rate?' And if you say something higher than prime, you get jawboned back to prime." Recently some of the larger banks have been trying to discourage borrowers in periods of tight money by charging higher rates for loans larger than those this particular borrower has historically taken.

A local company with a lot of other banking business at its

disposal may be almost as well situated. A local department store, for example, with a payroll account and a white-goods department that generates credit applications from its customers, will be able to borrow at a low rate (though not at the prime rate) even if sober analysis of its balance sheet would drain the colour from an accountant's cheeks. Insistence on a rate that would compensate the bank for the real risks would drive all the store's business to another bank, and the banker can be sure some other bank will take it. At times when the banks have a lot of extra money around, word will go out to the lending officers to treat little borrowers as though they were big borrowers, because they can in fact get money elsewhere; when money is hard to come by, the little borrower may find himself brushed off.

"Established banking relationships" are the happiest mark of safety: every banker would rather lend to somebody who has already borrowed and paid back his loan than to a new boy on the block. The fundament of the banking business is the customer who comes back repeatedly for money, and a successfully completed loan should move a borrower's costs closer to the prime rate. The costs of opening the file on a first-time borrower—getting to know his business and his bookkeeping—are not likely to be amortized in the return from that first loan: most banks disclaim any desire to make one-shot deals, at any interest rate. When interest rates go through the roof, as they did in 1969 and 1973–74, the established local borrower from the local bank may be able to borrow for less than the prime rate charged the national borrower from the wholesale bank, if only because the banker is embarrassed to be asking that kind of a price for money from somebody he knows. This is one of the social advantages of the American system of decentralized banking, as opposed to the British national banks.

The arrival of term loans added another element to the pricing of money: longer loans command a higher rate of interest (expressed these days as a percentage over prime rather than as a flat rate). And within the category of term loans, repayment schedules affect (or should affect) the rate: a loan that is to be retired in regular instalments should cost less than a loan that runs to its term to be repaid in a lump. Common sense would argue that a secured term loan should carry a lower interest rate than an unsecured one, but in fact the reverse is true in business (as distinguished from personal) lending—unsecured loans are cheaper because they are offered only to the most "creditworthy" borrowers. (And the bank saves the cost and nuisance of keeping and periodically verifying the collateral.)

Some loans, of course, become bankable only if collateral is available to back them up: Semenenko could never have loaned First of Boston's money to the movie industry without the real estate to put behind the loan agreement. The Philadelphia banks that had mortgages on Penn Central property behind their loans to the railroad will probably get out of the bankruptcy with little damage; the New York banks that had made unsecured loans (or loans secured by the watery stock of certain wholly owned subsidiaries) have been punished.

There are rules of thumb about the size of the rate penalty required to compensate for the greater risk of loans backed by differing kinds of security. Most authorities seem to feel that a loan backed by saleable inventory (raw materials or finished products, not semifinished products) should pay at least 2 percent more than the bank would charge a borrower sound enough to get his money without security; a loan backed by accounts receivable should carry an interest rate at least 4 percent over prime. Factoring is *really* expensive: about the minimum charged is 12 percent flat, which means that the bank assumes the risk on collecting the paper, advances the money to the manufacturer, and performs certain bookkeeping services at a price that probably absorbs a third of the gross profits on the business. This is not a loan at all, of course: whether or not his customer pays, the manufacturer owes the bank nothing.

Prior to the late 1960s, interest rates moved infrequently and by small steps, propelled by demand or the lack of it. "In setting an interest rate," Van Vechten Shaffer of Cedar Rapids said, looking backward, "you first have to determine whether you want to make the loan". Banks tried to keep a sizeable liquidity reserve of securities, and when the need to find cash for loans began to erode that reserve they would raise rates to discourage borrowers. If borrowers complained bitterly and moved their business to other banks, the rate increase might be rescinded; if they paid up with only moderate complaining, it would stay.

Reductions in the rate were stickier: price reductions always are. Bankers have the normal businessman's horror of price competition, but the opportunity to differentiate identical products through advertising is not open to a man whose product is money. To some extent, true competition can be carried on in banking by offering services the other banker does not give, and sending salesmen (lending officers) door-to-industrial-door to tout them. Much banking business is not price-sensitive, because the bank has all that information, and there is a history of close confidential relationships; for a businessman to change his banker is a big step. But if a bank retains a higher rate than its fellows for a considerable period of time, some of its customers will feel themselves unfairly treated and will depart. And a rate cut will draw new business fast from brokerage houses and finance companies, which frankly play for the lowest prices they can get.

Before 1971, price leadership was in New York or, occasionally, Chicago or San Francisco. That year, First Pennsylvania broke the published prime by a quarter of a point. "We needed loans", John Bunting recalls. "We felt interest rates were going to go down, and if we went first we could pick up forty, fifty, sixty million in loans. We needed thirty million to make it worthwhile. We were out there alone for two weeks, and we picked up about sixty million in new loans". Bunting also got a lot of publicity, which he likes and some others envied, and a year later a much smaller bank in St. Louis tried the same trick, announcing a prime rate a quarter of a point below what the money-centre banks were charging. President Nixon, running for re-election and pushing for lower interest rates, sent a telegram of congratulations, but the bigger banks didn't follow, and ultimately the St. Louis bank rejoined the parade.

Today, interest rates are controlled to a large extent by the bank's cost of funds: the experts speak of "interest-rate differential" banking. Cost of funds is extremely tricky, because each dollar the bank lends is a changing mix of demand deposits (for which the cost is cheque-clearing and account maintenance), savings accounts, time deposits, and the range of bought money. One speaks of the "blended" or "melded" cost of funds. But demand deposits are not rising: the new loan, the marginal loan, must be financed out in the CD, Fed Funds, and Eurodollar markets, in the richer part of the blend.

In early 1973, in America, government pressure kept the prime rate charged by the banks as much as two points below the open-market rate for CDs and commercial paper. Corporations that normally raised money in the commercial-paper market naturally came to the banks instead, vastly inflating loan demand. Others performed what Henry Kaufman and James McKeon of Salomon Brothers delicately call "large-scale arbitraging of short-term loans against high-yielding CDs"—that is, they ripped off the banking system, borrowing against their lines of credit at, say, 7 percent and using the borrowed cash to buy CDs at some other bank to yield, say, 9 percent. "It was almost impossible to find out how much of this there was, even in our own bank", says Donald C. Platten, who became chairman of New York's Chemical Bank in the middle of this mess. "We ended up with a sheer guess of maybe four, five hundred million dollars for the banking system as a whole".

Anticipating the political problems, First National City Bank of New York even before 1973 attempted to set up a "floating prime" which would be established every week at a rate $\frac{5}{8}$ of a point above what the Fed reported as the previous week's average price for money in the short-term commercial-paper market. This proposal aborted in 1973, but by 1974 it seemed likely to take over as the basic pricing rule for the banking system—at least as long as the commercial-paper rate remained safely over the blended cost of funds. The knowledge that First National City would move of a Friday to set a new rate based on commercial-paper rates gave other banks some competitive advantage. Every large bank trading department knows the commercial-paper rate before the Fed publishes it, and a bank seeking publicity or a few million dollars in new business from price-sensitive overnight borrowers could jump the gun on the Citibank announcement, confident that its asserted leadership would be confirmed in a few days. First of Chicago, vain of its independence and analytical prowess, established its own, slightly different formula, which led to interest charges a few basis points (hundredths of a percent) higher or lower than First National City's. In early 1975, when interest rates were falling rapidly in the market, First National City discovered a new "principle" of banking—that prime rates should not move by more than $\frac{1}{4}$ of a percent per week, which greatly improved its spread and apparent profitability. In early 1976, Citibank adjusted its formulae to create a $1\frac{1}{2}$ percent spread between commercial paper rate and prime—and everyone wondered why the emerging economic recovery failed to produce increased borrowings at the banks. Perhaps there is still no substitute for judgement.

3

However interest rates are determined, the lowest rates always go to the same borrowers: in Britain, the discount houses; in America, the big Treasury bond dealers. For some years, the largest single borrower from banks in the United States has been the firm of Salomon Brothers, which needs well over a billion dollars almost every day to carry its inventories of federal, municipal, and corporate bonds, notes and bills, negotiable CDs, acceptances and other "money-market instruments". Salomon's needs may vary by hundreds of millions of dollars from week to week (even from day to day), depending on what happens in the trading room. Though lending limits may not be a problem (because much of Salomon's borrowing is secured by government issues, and loans so secured are exempt from lending limits in nearly all banking laws), only a handful of very large banks can manage a loan portfolio with that kind of variability. "We have nice banks that come in to us and say, 'We'd like to do business with you'," says

Vincent Murphy, Salomon's lean and elegant partner in charge of money and inventory. "And I say, 'That's nifty'. And they say, 'We'd like to have a two-million-dollar loan with you every day'. Well, that's not worth the trouble for us; even five million is an accommodation".

Most of Salomon's borrowings must be very short-term, because the loans are secured by the inventory, which must be available for trading; but there is some merchandise acquired for sale at a later date which can be pledged for a few weeks. On these borrowings. Salomon is not restricted to dealing with banks. "General Motors may have fifty million dollars it knows it will need in thirty days for steel stampings", Murphy says, "and we can borrow that on a no-risk deal tailor-made for them. The rate will be under what the banks pay on CDs, hopefully, because the loan is safer: should, God forbid, Salomon Brothers go by the boards in thirty days, they have in their possession these Treasury Bills that make them absolutely secure".

These arrangements are really "repos"—repurchase agree-ments—rather than loans: General Motors buys $50 million of Treasury bills from Salomon with Salomon's guarantee to buy them back at an agreed upon somewhat higher price in thirty days. Another big customer on this basis is the City of New York, putting its balances to work. Repos of Treasury bills are also made by the Federal Reserve System itself; this arrangement is, in fact, the standard operating procedure when the Fed's Open Market Committee wants to pump some money into the economy for a day or two. (What puts the money into the economy is the reduc-tion in the government-bond dealers' demands for loans: the banks, free of the need to lend to the dealers, can lend to others, or reduce their bid for Fed Funds.)

The Fed is on the telephone to the government-bond dealers and Fed Funds traders every fifteen minutes or so all morning long, feeling the market. It keeps in touch with the inventories the government-bond dealers are carrying, to know how much collat-eral is available for repurchase agreements and how much money the dealers are likely to need today. If it is going to take action, the Fed at eleven o'clock or so will request offers for repos (usually overnight, sometimes for several days), raising a cry of "The Fed is in!" that can be heard all over Wall Street.

The Fed buys and sells governments with twenty-four dealers, ten of them banks, and they all get the same message from this contact. Nobody knows how much the Fed intends to buy on re-purchase agreements on this day, or the rate the dealer will have to pay for the money. Each dealer puts in an offer, and the Fed goes through the list, buying first from those who have offered the highest interest rate, on down the line until it has met its needs for the day. "Sometimes the offers are ridiculous", says Alan Holmes, manager of the Open Market Committee; ridiculous offers are almost always rejected. The rates the Fed accepts on repos from the government-bond dealers are always considerably lower than the rate the banks would charge—but how much lower depends on the results of the auction. If the Fed is buying only a small amount, a dealer who offered too low an interest rate will be out in the cold and will have to borrow more expensively from the banks.

Because the Fed and the banks need active government- and municipal-bond markets, Salomon and its peers never have to worry that they will not be able to borrow money: some way will be found to accommodate them on the whole range of their inven-tory, governments, municipals, and corporates. The rate at which they can borrow, however, is a different story. In April 1974, when rates were soaring, the banks that make these big loans—four or five in New York, ten or so out of town—might call Salomon in the morning and say that a certain minimum loan ($20 million, say) would be available to the house on corporate securities at prime rate, but anything over that minimum would have to pay a penalty of a quarter of a point over prime. In 1975, when rates were coming down and loan demand was light, it was not un-common for a big bank to call a government-bond dealer and quietly offer money at a discount from the advertised prime.

On loans from the banks, the collateral is often corporate or municipal rather than Treasury securities, and rates are to some extent a function of the collateral. Corporate and municipal bonds are always available to be pledged, because sales of such merchandise are for delivery five days after the date of sale, and during those five days after it has sold its inventory Salomon can use this paper to secure loans. Governments may not be available, because the Fed has made repos or because the inventory must be on the shelf for expected customers. Treasury bills and government bonds sold this morning are usually sold for "cash" and must be delivered this afternoon. "We can borrow," Murphy says, "only on securities beyond what I need for trading; I have to be comfortable in isolating that merchandise". The other side of the coin is that Salomon does not know until all the trading for same day delivery has been finished—usually around noon, but sometimes later— exactly how much must be borrowed.

Government-bond collateral is all kept at the Fed, and there is no need to move pieces of paper: the Fed simply makes a book entry in the computer, transferring the ownership of such-and-such a Treasury issue. (As of the end of December 1973, $176,600 million in marketable governments—out of a grand total of $270,200 million outstanding—was represented by book entries at the Federal Reserve Bank of New York rather than by certificates.) Corporate bonds, however, must be trundled around Wall Street from one bank vault to another to secure Salomon's overnight loans. "With some of our very good banks out-of-town," Murphy says, "I can keep the paper in my vault. I give them a complete description of the securities, the issue, maturity, quantity, even the number; and periodically, on a surprise basis, they send an auditor who wants to see these securities in my vault".

The man who borrows the money for Salomon is Bob Dall, a compact, easygoing, red-headed trader in early middle age, who works in shirtsleeves (like everyone else, but his are bright red striped) at one end of The Room. This is a huge collection of trading desks assembled in a space almost the length of a city block, two stories high, pillarless, built to Salomon's specifications on an upper floor in a new skyscraper at the foot of Manhattan. High on the wall at each end, the ticker—orange symbols moving on a black background—informs everyone of what is happening a quarter of a mile away on the floor of the New York Stock Exchange, where Salomon deals in large institutional block transactions. On the long wall, which all the desks face, is a monster Telex board, white numbers whirling on a black background to tell him who runs what the prices are here and now on Eurodollars and Fed Funds, all significantly traded Treasury issues and agency issues, the most important municipals and corporates, commercial paper and bank CDs of differing maturities. Actually, nobody pays that much attention to the numbers on the Telex board when there is a trade to be made: they are merely the background for the monetary picture, which Salomon wants people to keep in mind. When a specific bid or offer is to be made, hit, or taken, a trader who needs information about a price yells to anyone in The Room who may have such information. "The only time I quote a price off the board," says one Salomon trader, "is when it's a bank on the phone and he wants to buy some flower bonds". [Flower bonds are old, long-term Treasury issues that carry a low-interest coupon and sell for considerably less than par, but will be accepted at par by the Internal Revenue Service in payment of estate taxes.] Then I know there's a big hurry, somebody's client just died, and I make a deal at the price on the board".

Billy (officially William) Salomon, a slim grey-haired man, formal in tailoring yet casual in manner, loves to show off The Room, but every so often his ace gets trumped. Asked if he had ever seen anything like it, Peter Lee of London's Union Discount Co. replied, "Yes—a Tunisian camel market".

Though only the trades in government securities will require any change in Dall's plans for today—underwritings, decisions to undertake blocks at the stock exchange, trades in corporates and municipals can be financed later because they will not involve paying or being paid for some days—Dall must keep up with everything that is going on in The Room, to analyze his longer-term position and to feel ahead in the market. He also must know a great deal else, from foreign exchange rates and interest rates abroad to the spending and lending habits of great American

corporations, tax dates, dividend dates, Stock Exchange procedures, Fed procedures, much highly technical exotica. On the
phone: "Herbie, he doesn't have the money, he's playing a U.S.-
Canadian game. Some day we'll sit down over drinks and I'll
explain the whole drill. Between Thursday and Monday he has
money, between Monday and Thursday he doesn't; and you don't
want that". The operating philosophy, however, is deliberately
simple: "My mandate is to finance inexpensively, but you have to
think of it as a continuum; there's never any point in taking a
man's last nickel. Wise guys don't last long in this business, and
I want to be here until I retire".

Dall loves The Room and everything about it. "I was a commercial banker for seven years, in the corporate finance handshaking
business; I came here to be in the market". His three assistants—
Dominic and Manny and Bill, everything is first name—he recruited himself from the back office: "I thank God for the very
simplistic business decision this firm made: let's pay the people in
the back office, to keep them." There are black traders and female
traders, not many of either, but enough to lend some small credence to Wall Street's claim that the bias of the customer is worse
than the bias inside. Nobody in The Room works on commission,
or on payment according to the profits that could be credited
directly to his efforts; instead, Salomon takes a sizeable fraction of
its total trading profits and distributes them around The Room in
prearranged shares. "I'm always amazed," Dall says, "that with
a hundred and eighty-five people in this room there's so remarkably little discord that becomes public. Everybody has an invisible
line that he understands. Mostly, I suppose, it's the pooled compensation".

There are also some perks, among them the use of the splendid
dining rooms on the upper level of the two-storey suite, an excellent
cuisine (second only to Morgan's among those sampled) in Georgian surroundings with antique silver service, and superb views
over the harbour, East River, and the spread of Brooklyn out to the
ocean. These lunches are free, but most of the time the traders stay
at their desks with sandwiches delivered from outside delis (also

free). "Must be very quiet in the CD market today", Dall said censoriously, looking a few desks down. "I see they've gone out to lunch".

By the sound of it, The Room is a zoo, with great roaring noises floating in the two-storey space whenever any of the many markets traded within its confines becomes active and the participants yell information back and forth to each other. "Very quiet today", Dall said again as the decibel level ebbed. "I hate that. You get spoiled by the excitement. I call my mother in the middle of a busy day. She's now seventy, went back to work at fifty-four, in a trading room, and worked eleven years at it. She caught the fever. When it gets real noisy here, I'll call her up and just hold out the phone so she can hear The Room".

The functions Salomon performs—and Dall helps it perform—are, of course, those undertaken in Britain by the discount house. This remarkable institution, unknown anywhere else in the world, served British banking as its lungs for well over a century. Because its orientation is heavily toward asset management (from the bank's point of view), the discount house is widely regarded as an anachronism by expert commentators; but in revising the means of monetary policy with Competition and Credit Control in 1971, the Bank and the Treasury decided to keep the discount house on the centre court.

There are twelve discount houses, all in London, all joint-stock companies, publicly held. As the name implies, their basic work is to discount—to purchase at a price less than its face value—the liabilities emitted by others: by government (nearly all short-term British Treasury bills are sold initially to a discount house); by local authorities; by manufacturers, exporters and importers (acceptances and bills of exchange); and by banks (negotiable CDs). The discount houses pay for these assets with money they borrow from others, mostly on very short term. Call money supplied to the discount houses is the first line of liquidity reserve for the banks, which means *all* the banks, the clearing banks, the merchant banks, and in their sterling operations, the foreign banks. But anyone who has money in some quantities that would otherwise lie idle tonight (a corporation getting ready for a tax date, for example) can find a home for it in a discount house.

Call money with a discount house qualifies as a reserve asset for every kind of bank, which means that the discount house can normally buy funds a little more cheaply than anybody else. And if something goes wrong, the discount house is the only sort of institution that has automatic access to the Money Market and Bank Regulation Office (formerly Discount Office) at the Bank of England, which is an almost exact equivalent of the discount window at the Federal Reserve Bank, described some pages ago. Needing money to carry its inventory of assets, the discount house can borrow what it needs at the Minimum Lending Rate posted by the bank. In return, the discount houses every Friday tender for all the Treasury bills that the Bank will be selling all through the next week, and pledge themselves to keep at least half their assets in the form of Treasury obligations.

Unlike Salomon, a London discount house buys up to half its short-term paper to hold to maturity, rather than for trading purposes. Peter Lee of Union Discount estimates that in an average year three-quarters of the profit of his house will come on the "carry", the interest-rate differential between the cost of call money and the yield on short-term investments held to maturity. (In a squeeze, however, call money rates can quickly rise above the yield on the paper the discount house has in inventory, and the house can suffer significant losses; this happened at Union Discount in 1974.) A discount house funds itself on a maximum ratio of thirty-to-one—that is, its capital is only a little more than 3 percent of its borrowings. At the end of 1974, Union Discount, which is the largest, was running at an apparent ratio of fifty-to-one—£622 million in "loans secured on assets of the Company" against £12 million in published capital and reserves. However, discount houses are permitted to hold undisclosed reserves and in Union's case these must be submitted to remain with its thirty-to-one ceiling. The daily turnover may be as much as £250 million.

Because the call money market is so much the most convenient place for a bank to put anything left over, by keeping in touch with conditions at the discount houses, the Bank of England knows whether money is easy or tight today, whether the Bank should buy Treasuries (pumping money into the discount houses and diminishing their need for call money) or sell them (removing some money from the market, which can be uncomfortable for them: "Sometimes you find yourself flooded with money", says Union's Lee, "and that takes really more judgment, because the Bank of England then have a habit of selling you bills at unattractive rates"). The Bank also like the role the discount houses play in policing the quality of judgment at the merchant banks, which discount some thousands of millions of pounds of acceptances in this market. "By vetting a lot of paper", says Simon Brearley, a broad-shouldered, tall, casual young man who is a deputy in the regulation office, "the discount houses perform a great *prudential* function". Lee agrees: Union Discount will not take into a trading inventory or act as broker for any bill it hasn't physically seen. "We trade bits of paper that represent trade. I want to look at the bits of paper and see who the people are."

All borrowings by or from a discount house are against collateral, which is hand-delivered and examined before the cheques are issued; this makes the discount houses major contributors to the pedestrian traffic of the City. (Union, planning new facilities for itself, had a time-and-motion study done of its operations, and found that on an average day its messengers clocked three to four hundred trips out of the building.) One part of the discount traffic makes the discount houses a ponderable element in London's tourist trade, for the bill brokers from the discount houses go calling on their customers in person every morning, wearing striped trousers and a top hat. (The representatives of what used to be called the discount office at the Bank of England also wear top hats when they go out to call on their contacts in the houses.) "When I started in this market twenty years ago," says Lee (he was then newly up from Cambridge with a degree in medieval German), "that's all we did—you put up your top hat at a quarter to ten, walked half the market, returned at eleven to make an oral report and then did the other half. Now we have a two-hundred-and-ten line board up in the trading room, and men on telephones, but we still honestly do believe that the city is a village, and you get much more out of a fellow when you see him face-to-face than if it 's merely a voice at the other end of the phone."

The work Bob Dall does rather privately in a corner of The Room at Salomon is done in a white light of in-house publicity—literally on television—at Union Discount. A camera is focused on the firm's money book, and the picture is carried by closed circuit into all the significant offices and trading rooms. A hand moves across the page, noting all changes in the firm's position—call money repaid today to lenders on the left-hand side of the ledger, new call money borrowed from lenders on the right-hand side. Because one list necessarily grows longer than the other, every fifteen minutes or so the man keeping the book draws a line under the payments and borrowings completed as of that monemt, and casts a running account; and everybody in the house knows whether money is coming in easily or going out beyond normal expectations. This sort of thing is useful information for a trader deciding how badly his house wants a bill someone has just offered. It's a very efficient way—one-up on America—to get the information around; yet it's also suitably traditional, the clerk keeping the company position in a fine, round hand.

4

Loans to American government-bond dealers and stockbrokers are always cheaper than loans to industrial borrowers even if the rate looks higher, for one peculiar reason: the "compensating" or "supporting" balance. Salomon gets to use every dollar Bob Dall borrows; but the average corporate borrower will be required to keep in demand deposits at the bank a sum that over the duration of the loan must average 20 percent of the money supposedly advanced by the bank. From the point of view of the corporate borrower, then, $1 million at 8 percent is really $800,000 at 10 percent: his interest charges are $80,000, and that buys the use of only $800,000. The absence of this peculiar American custom in Britain may be the reason why First National City, in introducing "base rate" to British banking, set it below the actual price for money; otherwise British rates would look higher than American rates even when they really were not.

This system is admittedly nonsensical. "In interviewing both bank and corporate personnel", Case M. Sprenkle wrote in a report for the American Bankers Association, "not one single individual could provide a rational explanation for requiring or preferring such balances except that it was traditional to do so". When money was relatively easy in 1972, several of the more aggressive banks equipped their lending officers with wheels and cards that would show borrowers the precise effect of compensating balances on their real interest rate, and the lending officers would then offer customers loans at differing rates, depending on the compensating balance agreements. The "bullet loans" to public utilities were all made without compensating balances, because says First of Chicago's Chauncey Schmidt, "the state regulatory commissions don't give rate increases for balances. So we charged them a hundred and twenty-five percent of prime."

The excuse for compensating balances has always been the proposition that a borrower should do his banking business where he borrows; and a banking business usually requires a balance. But as the banks expand their lending nationwide this excuse goes lame: there is no earthly reason why a borrower in New Orleans with no business north of Memphis should keep a balance in an account in Chicago. Once the remote bank offers loans without a balance, the local bank must compete. "All-in-the-rate pricing is coming fast", says Willard Butcher, president of Chase Manhattan.

In fact, the compensating balance is something less than an ideal arrangement for the bank, because the requirement is averaged out over the length of the loan—"and," Butcher says, "the value of a balance in March '73 and in November '73 were very different things". But in 1973 the drive toward more rational pricing was drastically slowed: at most of the money-centre banks, compensating balances account for a good fraction of the demand deposits (at Morgan Guaranty, such balances must add up to two-thirds of the total demand deposits), and with money-market rates higher than the prime rate the banks certainly did not wish to risk any part of the deposit base. Moreover, at a time when the government was restricting published interest rates, flexibility in compensating balances was vital to maintain revenues.

"It looks better for us", retired chairman William Renchard of Chemical says. "Instead of charging a guy eleven percent you charge him nine percent and get tougher on the balance requirements. I've often kidded people. They ask me how much I'll charge for a loan, and I say, 'If you leave a hundred percent in the bank, I'll lend to you for one percent'."

Warren Marcus, partner in charge of Salomon Brothers' activities in bank stocks, got curious about what was happening to compensating balance requirements under the pressure of government-restricted rates, and began asking around. "They all said, ten and ten—ten percent on the commitment, and another ten percent and the actual loan. That was exactly what they'd been saying a year before, when money was much less tight. I said, 'How can that be?' They said, 'Well, we weren't getting it then, and we are now'."

The flexible compensating balance would also seem to have some value to a bank that wanted to charge one prime customer more or less than another prime customer without making any noise about it. This proposition was offered to Don Riefler and Martin Griffin of Morgan Guaranty over lunch, and there was a brief, pregnant pause. "Well," Riefler said finally, "compensating balances *do* vary. But it makes such a problem of equity within the bank—lending officers saying, 'Why does *his* customer get this and mine doesn't?' It's better just to move the rate."

Academic commentators and even some government regulators tend to treat the compensating balance as nothing more than a hidden interest cost. "If [the customer] needs ten thousand dollars, for example," Howard D. Crosse wrote while chief examiner for the Federal Reserve Bank of New York, "he will simply arrange to borrow twelve thousand five hundred, leaving twenty-five hundred on deposit". But this is probably not true, because corporations may not wish to assume larger loan obligations (which must appear on the balance sheets published in annual reports), or may not be able to secure higher loans. If they need all the money and the bank demands a balance, they may turn to funds brokers, helping to support what some Congressmen, especially rural Congressmen, consider the worst abuses in the American banking atmosphere.

The funds broker, briefly, is a man who supplies a bank with deposits from third parties. The business grew up to serve savings and loan associations before their dividends were subject to federal limitation. Given a choice between the services of a broker and the costs of advertising campaigns (with bank-by-mail services), a number of savings associations in fast-growing parts of the country chose to build their deposit base by paying commissions to brokers. The association got the deposit, which it would promptly lend to local home builders; the depositor got an insured savings account at a somewhat higher interest rate than was being paid in his locality, and the broker got a fee. No problems.

Regulation Q and the parallel requirements of the Federal Deposit Insurance Corporation prevented commercial banks from paying a broker's fee on top of the legal maximum interest on the deposit itself—but nothing prohibited a bank's *customer* from sweetening the pot for a depositor. A borrower of $100,000 at 8 percent, required to keep $20,000 in the bank as a compensating balance, could arrange with the bank to have others supply the balance. Assume the maximum legal interest rate on a savings account to be 5 percent. The bank's customer contracts with a broker to pay 8 percent on money the broker places in the bank in *demand* deposits. The broker offers his sources bank accounts that will yield them 6 percent, the interest to be paid by the broker. The depositor thus gets 1 percent extra interest on what is still an insured deposit. The borrower whose compensating balance is being supplied borrows this last $20,000 at 8 percent, which is really less than the cost of the rest of his loan (because he is paying $8,000 for only $80,000 of the bank's money). The broker gets a

2 percent fee. No serious problem: good business.

If this sort of thing can be done for the compensating balance part of a loan, it can also be done for the entire loan. A borrower in an area where the banks are short of money (which may include a black slum) works out a deal with a local bank whereby the bank will lend him funds supplied to the bank by depositors arriving through the services of a broker with whom the borrower has established a contact. The funds brokers point out that such an arrangement is really not wildly different from the purchasing of money to lend by the big banks in the CD, Fed Funds, and Eurodollar markets: the existence of funds brokerage allows little banks to compete against the giants for deposits, and to grow even though they are excluded by their small size from the ranges where the big banks roam. The borrower gets his money, the little bank grows (and gets a profit on the loan), the broker gets a fee.

Now suppose the borrower does not pay back his loan. The broker keeps his fee. The depositor still has an insured account, and gets his money back. The bank goes bust.

In testimony to the House Banking and Currency Committee in April 1971, Chairman Frank Wille of the FDIC reported that "in eight of the twenty bank failures occurring from January 1, 1969 to date, the misuse of brokered deposits was a major contributing factor to the closing of the banks. In all of these cases, the receipt of brokered deposits facilitated improper loans to officers, directors or owners of the closed banks (or to their affiliated interests) or to borrowers outside the banks' normal lending areas". The names ring like bells: Peoples State Savings Bank of Auburn, Michigan; Farmers Bank of Petersburgh, Kentucky; Prairie City State Bank in Iowa; First National Bank of Coalville, Utah; Morrice State Bank of Morrice, Michigan. All gone; total liability to the FDIC, maybe $10 million. Who got the money? Who do you think?

The thing works like a watch. A criminal syndicate finds a troubled bank, and offers to place in the bank brokered deposits a little larger than the sum the syndicate will be borrowing. When the loan comes due, the syndicate walks away. The securities pledged behind the loan turn out to be fake, and that is an end to it. During the interim, the syndicate may also be able to use this bank as a laundry for "bearer bonds"—bonds not registered to anyone's name, the property of whoever possesses them—stolen in the rabbit warren of the back offices of a Wall Street brokerage house. A robber might be a little shy about selling such merchandise himself, and it's nice to have a friendly bank that will accept the bonds as security for a loan and then sell them to some other bank when the loan goes into default. Sworn testimony before a Senate committee says that in 1970 Bebe Rebozo's bank on Key Biscayne was used just this way, wittingly or unwittingly, by a known con man.

Banks of some size have been subverted with brokered deposits, but the public never learns about it because the bank absorbs the losses and stays in business. The FDIC has supported legislation to prohibit the brokering of deposits, but the business survives, probably accounting for half a billion dollars in deposits around the country (most of them, of course, entirely legitimate). The government's only current means of control is a list of Mafia figures and corporations known to be controlled by organized crime, supplied by the FBI to bank examiners visiting certain banks. Whenever the examiners find these names on a bank's loan ledger, they are supposed to play Twenty Questions with the president of the bank, and perhaps with the directors who serve on the loan committee. Maybe this procedure will be sufficient; maybe not.

Here the British system of a few large banks, plus well-known discount houses and finance houses, presumably yields advantages: money brokerage, so-called, is a perfectly regulated business in Britain, a national adjunct to the work of the discount houses, greasing the wheels of the interbank market in both sterling and Eurodollars. Still, one wonders: the fringe banks that went belly up in 1973 and 1974 all relied on money brokerage for at least part of their funding. It may be that this is an inherently irresponsible business, and ought to be discouraged everywhere.

12/Bad Loans, Municipal Bonds, and Still More Problems

"Competition works best when competitors are reasonably clear as to their costs—and bank costs are inescapably tied to a cost that is extraordinarily unclear, uncertain, and difficult to appraise. This cost is the risk of loss on assets, especially if they have to be converted into cash. . . .
> —FREDERIC SOLOMON, Division of Examination, Federal Reserve System

* * *

Few of the loan defaults that make trouble for banks can be blamed on criminal borrowers: most represent bad luck or bad judgment. Received opinion says that banks *should* make some loans that go sour: a bank that never takes a risk cannot be serving an important, innovative sector of the surrounding economy. Moreover, bank lending officers are supposed to be educated by the experience of trying to collect a loan that has not been repaid. "The best thing in the world a bank can do," says chairman Donald Platten of Chemical, "is to set up a hundred thousand dollar reserve for a young loan officer, and chalk up his losses to that reserve as a charge for learning. I haven't been willing to do it."

293

There is also a contrary opinion, worth hearing if only because its source is Albert J. Hettinger, a very old man, parchment skin over brittle bones, wisp of white hair on the fine skull, ramrod straight, brisk, to be found at the Rockfeller Center offices of Lazard Fréres (of which he is a partner) when he is not visiting Japan to investigate financing opportunities there. Hettinger is reputed to have made and kept some tens of millions of dollars over his investment lifetime, though nobody knows for sure. He is a modest man: "I'm a jack of all trades, who tries to be as little superficial as is possible under the circumstances. The first fifteen years I was in this business I rode gloriously up and down ingloriously. My great mistake was that I thought the great names in this industry were much abler than they really were. I didn't think I was as good as they were, maybe I was sixty percent as good. But while I was quite right in my judgment of my ability relative to theirs, my overestimate of theirs meant I was overestimating my own on an absolute scale."

Of all the banks Hettinger visited over his career, one was clearly a favourite: he even found a way to work a mention of it into the epilogue he wrote for the Friedman and Schwartz *Monetary History*. "There was a fellow by the name of Schreiner," Hettinger says, "who came from Alsace-Lorraine to Texas, and settled in what is called the hill country, in a nice little town, name of Kerrville, about a hundred and forty miles from Fort Worth. When he died, he owned a million or so acres of land—not the most expensive land, of course. He had introduced sheep to that country, he had capital, he dominated the mercantile distribution of the area, and of course he owned the bank. His sons revered his memory, and never settled his estate. The bank still exists: it's known as the Bank of the Charles E. Schreiner Estate, one of the three surviving private banks in the United States. When Morgan incorporated in 1940, Louis Schreiner came to New York to commiserate with them on hauling down the flag.

"When I was there, the two sons were one of them ninety, the other almost ninety, and they talked about their father. One of them said that in his younger years he would be working with a problem borrower, and he'd go to his father and say, 'We've just got to call this loan'. And his father would ask for the consolidated accounts—what the man bought at the store, at the feed lot, what he paid for shearing—and then his father would say, 'Get hold of that man and tell him we'll stake him for another year. The only time to call a loan is before you make it. You've got your freedom of action then'".

"That's the proper rule", Hettinger concluded. "Be careful when you make it, then see it through".

The most common cause of default on a loan is death; banks can avoid loss from that cause by requiring credit insurance on the life of the borrower, and under present rules bank holding companies can write such insurance themselves. The next most common cause of default is natural or man-made disaster: fire, flood, and windstorm. Some of this can be taken care of by insurance, some is met by the government under disaster relief programmes, which normally have as a major target (rarely discussed in the press) the shoring up of collapsing banks, needed now more than ever to make loans to local businesses seeking to recover. Then there are the problems of consanguinity and friendship, loans to directors, their families, friends and enterprises, which have not been vetted as carefully as they would have been had the borrower been a stranger.

Loan losses for straight business reasons are infrequent: it is a rare year at the average bank when as much as $\frac{1}{3}$ of 1 percent of the outstanding loan volume must be charged off, and consumer loans are more heavily represented among the losses than in the loan portfolio as a whole. But the fact that something is infrequent does not mean it never happens (quite the contrary), and in some years the loan-loss reserve which every bank should keep can be substantially hit. Even in good years, business loans go sour: the energy crisis blows up the gas station, the girls' dress manufacturer founders in the sea of blue jeans, the restaurant loses its chef.

At some banks the loan that looks sick is turned over quickly to a "work-out department" that specializes in finding ways to reorganize or sell a failing business—or, if worst comes to worst, its surviving assets. "We find that the quicker we get it to loan adjustment," says H. G. Weichert, Jr. of Bank of America, "the more likely a settlement: they're specialists". At other banks, however, the lending officer who made the loan continues to be responsible for relations between this borrower and the bank. Tom Hutson, an impeccably upper-class Englishman who came to First of Boston's British factoring operation from eleven years at the Bank of England, puts the principle with patrician precision: "In this company, if you'll pardon a vulgarism, our rule is that when you make shit you have to clean it up yourself."

Lending officers try to keep up with their loans, reading quarterly statements, telephoning, visiting the borrowers' premises at least once a year, up to half a dozen times a year on larger loans. Speaking of really big loans, Peter Culver of Morgan Guaranty says, "We see a few individuals often—treasurer or v.-p. of finance maybe three, four times a year, assistant treasurer every month or two weeks. On the periphery, there are some people we see once a year, to keep in touch, people who are good sources of information about the politics of the company, the internal trends. Almost every meeting produces a memo for the files. There are also people who are sort of dead in their jobs—you entertain them, take them to lunch, buy a martini, put in a memo, 'General conversation'."

Clearly, unless the loan is enormous, yielding enough to pay for constant travel, careful and frequent checking up on a borrower can be done only if he resides somewhere near the bank. "With a local customer," says president James Coquillette of Merchants National in Cedar Rapids, "you run into his guys all the time. You drive past their plant. You hear the gossip. How are you going to hear gossip about a business that's a thousand miles away? Through a personal relationship of an officer of ours, we had an account with a dairy in New Jersey. Every time our examiner came around he would say, 'How's that dairy in New Jersey coming along?' The truth was, not too well. Finally a group of local banks bailed us out."

Even in the case of a local loan, however, the first word that something has gone wrong may be a call from the borrower requesting more money. After that call, a decision usually must be made fairly quickly whether the bank should go the Schreiner-Hettinger route, advancing the man enough money to keep trying for another year (which may well involve throwing good money after bad), or should look for the nearest available exit.

In the fall of 1973, young Tom Lee of the First National Bank of Boston had to face this question in considering an application for an increased loan from a Route 128 company called Iotron, makers of a fascinating gadget called Digiplot. This is a computerized radar plotter for installation on ships. The radar spots all the other ships within seventeen miles; the computer takes the direction and location and plots the course of up to forty such blips, then projects the course of the vessel on which Digiplot is installed; if the result shows a collision it rings a bell and otherwise calls attention to itself. Before actually changing his heading, the pilot can simulate the results of the new course on the computer, and find out what is and what isn't safe. The Environmental Protection Administration has urged, and may ultimately insist, that all oil tankers carry a device of this sort. Digiplot was developed by aerospace engineers; John C. Herther, who was one of them and is president of Iotron, likes to describe it as "a nickel's worth of SAM-D", referring to the Surface-to-Air-Missile made by Raytheon down the pike. About $3 million—including $1 million ("as good a number as any") for R&D—had been invested in Digiplot by October 1973, most of it by a syndicate of Texans; and First of Boston had loaned the company $250,000.

Forty Digiplots had been sold, at prices ranging from $50,000 to $70,000, depending on custom features. The U.S. Navy had bought four, Texaco had bought three (and was considering an order for seventy-five more), National Bulk Carriers had ordered six, and the Russians had bought and installed two on Soviet merchant ships. The only competition was a Sperry Rand device which Herther (and Lee) considered inferior equipment; moreover, the Iotron sales contract included an unconditional one-year warranty, free service on board anywhere in the world, which Sperry did not offer. Unfortunately, not all the purchasers had paid for their equipment: some Norwegian and British distributors were particularly late, and in most of those cases the buyers with whom Iotron had the contract were marine suppliers rather than the owners of the vessels.

The week before, Iotron had run completely out of money; and Lee being out of town the company had borrowed the payroll for its fifty employees from a local suburban bank on an unsecured thirty-day note. "*He* must be worried", Lee said cheerfully. So Lee went out to Route 128 to talk things over at a morning conference in Herther's very utilitarian office beside the production floor in the new one-story factory. Herther was a broad-shouldered, grey-haired man who worked in shirtsleeves; he walked about the room, around the grey metal conference table where Lee and I were seated.

"The balance sheet is very bad from the bank's point of view", Lee said. "The ratio of equity is ten percent, and it shows a terrible cash squeeze. No working capital at all. What are you going to do to raise more equity?"

"In January," Herther said, "we'll go for another half-million. This is in a way a bridging loan, but the risk is an order of magnitude less."

"Mmm", said Lee.

We all went to look at the production line, the integrated circuits on their plastic boards being bolted to steel frames, the guts of a completed unit standing in a big oven, where it would bake at 140° for two hundred hours—"to get rid of weak components", Herther explained. "It's almost equivalent to a one-year service test." The unit was functioning; Herther turned dials and the radar screen showed blips in motion. "The law requires you to plot all courses," Herther said, "but there are so many ships in the English Channel that if you try to do that, you don't have time to do anything else. And forty percent of all the collisions at sea occur between Dover and the Elbe."

Back in the office, Herther said, "We're moving toward four a month. We can get to six without adding more than a couple of very low-priced people".

"Meanwhile," Lee commented, "we have what we call a short-fall". Herther's cash-flow projection showed a November intake of $133,000, a November outgo of $200,000. "And we'd like to clean up some old bills", Herther said.

"I was so worried awhile ago," Lee explained, rifling through some pages, "that I insisted on getting an inventory guarantee. It's a measure I took to protect the bank, those little old ladies in tennis shoes who put their savings in the bank."

"When we get orders," Herther said conversationally, "that runs down our inventories—they turn into accounts receivable."

The accounts receivable are the crux of the matter. Lee runs a finger down the list. "Our rule of thumb is never to have a loan above the good accounts receivable, and you have some cheesy accounts receivable. And we still don't have a perfected security interest in them; we haven't filed in Oslo. I have to talk to our counsel about that". The finger stopped at a name. "This is not a strong company. It's a distributor, three guys and an office".

Herther said, "A. P. Moeller is paying on that one".

Lee said, "If Moeller were responsible. . . ." and left it hanging.

"You'd lend more?" Herther asked, eagerness showing for the first time.

"Well, maybe. . . . We'd be happier".

Herther said, selling now, "Marine budgets run on annual cycles—and they don't buy one, they outfit the fleet. Texaco wants to put in seventy-five, but that's a hell of an order, it takes board approval."

Lee nodded. He said into the air, "The investors, who are friendly with us, haven't known if they have a big success or a bankruptcy. Since the summer, the EPA has been saying it wants collision protection. The big fleets are talking. It's become clear we're the best in the field. I hate to keep putting pressure on the investors, but. . . ." His finger stopped at another name on the list of accounts receivable.

Herther looked over his shoulder. "Nothing to look at, that's a garage operation, but they're strong."

"Can we get figures?" Lee said almost wistfully.

"Oh, yes—twenty million dollars".

"All right", Lee said, and looked at his watch. His time was up. "The question arises—will the bank go for another hundred and fifty? The answer is No. Is the bank pleased with progress? The answer is Yes. Will the bank go in for more on a matching basis with the investors? The answer is Yes". The meeting broke up with a handshake; and presently First of Boston and the Texas investors had put more money into Iotron.

By spring 1974, the company had turned the corner. For the fiscal year ending April 1, it had a solid profit, more orders than it could handle, and big expansion plans, which the bank would help finance. And Lee, incidentally, had been promoted from assistant v.-p. to vice-president of the First National Bank of Boston.

2

"There are lots of stupid loans being made today", John Bunting of First Pennsylvania said in 1973. "The loans to the Penn Centrals, the Stetson Hats, the Horn and Hardarts—not the more ambitious loans my more ambitious younger lending officers are making. I don't worry that the young men will get the bank in trouble. For every bright ambitious lender there are nine senior people trying to get him fired."

Loans to corporations in the Fortune 1,000, even to household names, have indeed begun to look like a real problem for the banks, and for the grave older men whose career asset is a long-standing relationship with the senior executives of big business. As every generation learns anew, mature companies like mature people can grow feeble; juridically eternal, the corporation too can be mortal. And in dealing with the great corporations, banks are normally careless, not infrequently blind, scornful of any lad who suggests that the emperor may not have any clothes. Noting the rapid increase in "criticized" loans at the banks in his district from 1968 to 1970, David Eastburn, president of the Federal Reserve Bank of Philadelphia, was disturbed that "the poorer record is at the larger banks, where credit analysis would be thought to be the more sophisticated."

In 1965, John Brooks reports in *The Go-Go Years*, an investor in the paper of Atlantic Acceptance, a young but large Canadian finance house, queried the Toronto-Dominion Bank for a credit check on the company. "The response—which in retrospect appears dumbfounding—was favourable". Atlantic was a swindle; but such dumbfounding approvals are becoming routine. With no little help from the accounting profession, big corporations in their relations with big banks have been able to make reputation do service for soundness. The officers of bankrupt Mill Factors liked to say that "what was good enough for major New York banks ought to satisfy anybody."

"It's logic rather than human nature that says you can't rest on the reputation of the company", Tom Clausen, chairman of Bank of America, says with admirable candour. "It takes great courage to be wholesale banker—not the courage to say Yes, but the courage to say No". Clausen finally said No to Jimmy Ling, changing the management of L-T-V, Inc. Ling attempted a second bite at the apple with an outfit called Omega-Alpha, and First Pennsylvania's Bunting said Yes for $15 million, some of which will never return again.

Equity Funding was a Ponzi scheme as blatant as Atlantic Acceptance, made more plausible than most by the use of computerized ledgers rather than pen-and-ink, but still—in hindsight—an unbelievable story. What made the fraud possible was not the computer but the business practices of the insurance industry, by which re-insurers bought policies from the original issuer for cash money, simply on the say-so of the issuer. Though the bookkeeping was complicated, Equity Funding (like Bernard Cornfield's Investors Overseas Services, which fortunately for the banks did not require loans) admittedly traced much of its growth to spectacularly high compensations paid the sales force—compensations so high that the normal earnings of an insurance operation could not pay them. Subsequent analysis of the books, by the trustee in bankruptcy, indicated that the company could never have been profitable. Nevertheless, four of the nation's wholesale bankers, First National City serving as chief lemming (or "lead bank") supplied the company with $50 million.

Among the giant banks that stayed out of Equity Funding was First National Bank of Chicago, and the reason is interesting. "First National City asked us to come in for, I think it was fifteen million," Gaylord Freeman recalls, "and we sent out a young man, thirty-one years old, to look at the company. The young man came back and said, 'I just don't think they're our kind of people'. I said, 'Why not?' 'Well,' he said, 'while I was talking to them I asked about the very small accounting firm that was auditing their books. And the answer I got was, 'Our boss says I'm going to do business with Julie baby as long as I live'.'" On the business evidence provided, shoddy as it was, a less flamboyant scoundrel might have put his hands on First of Chicago's money, too.

The worst of these careless gestures by the banks was, of course, Penn Central, "the largest single bankruptcy in our nation's history", to quote Congressman Harley Staggers' Foreword to the SEC report on the disaster. In a way, the heavy involvement of the banks in Penn Central is encouraging at a time when everyone worries about the advantages inside information gives the Wall Streeter in competition with the normal citizen searching for investment opportunities. Of the debts created by Penn Central between its formation in February 1968 and its bankruptcy in June 1970, non-banks at the end held $167 million ($82 million pushed on their trusting customers by Goldman, Sachs & Company as dealers in the railroad's commercial paper, $35 million well and separately secured and safe in the hands of insurance companies, and $50 million in the hands of individual investors, who could bail out through attached rights to convert into the good stock of Norfolk & Western RR). American banks, the insiders of insiders, had advanced Penn Central no less than $300 million of additional credit, all of it after fifteen months of operations by the newly formed giant had demonstrated that the merger was a disaster.

The big lump was in an agreement signed April Fool's Day 1969, by which a consortium of fifty banks led (again) by First

National City took a $50 million revolving credit long extended to the former Pennsylvania Rail Road and made it a $300 million revolving credit for Penn Central. At that time, the cumulative negative cash flow of the merged railroad was already $315.6 million, and cash was draining out at a rate of more than $25 million a month. Joseph R. Daughen and Peter Binzen, in their fine book *The Wreck of the Penn Central*, write about treasurer David Bevan's worries that "some banker, sooner or later, was going to notice the torrent of cash streaming away from the rail-road. So far, nobody had. But Bevan was being forced to rely more and more on the 'other' earnings of the railroad to induce the bankers to come across with loans. If the 'other' earnings were diluted with Chinese money, the bankers didn't know it in 1969". The fact was that until 1970, in the words of the SEC report, "the banks, through their agent First National City Bank, never seriously doubted the ability of Penn Central to pay off its loans". In late 1969, when the national bank examiner put the Penn Central loan in a "special mention" category in his report on the bank, Citibank executives screamed bloody murder.

Yet many of the earnings that made Penn Central appear profitable as an entity were visibly being manufactured in ways that were "unsafe and unsound", to use banker's lingo, even if they were not illegal (and they were probably illegal). Footnotes to annual reports may be too dense for lay investors to follow, but bank lending officers are not supposed to be lay investors. The market price of the stock which was collateral for the First National City line of credit rested upon reported profits from sales of real estate. The footnotes revealed that the prices at which that real estate had been sold were inflated beyond any realistic estimate of its value. And the entire purchase price had been taken into one year's earnings, though the cash receipts from the sale were only a small down payment, and the remainder was to be dribbling in over forty years from purchasers whose track record was nowhere near strong enough to justify confidence that they would really pay. The banks accepted the flim-flam without question.

Worse: some members of the consortium had reason to know

that Penn Central was playing games with its figures. First National City itself had loaned more than $14 million to a Penn Central subsidiary called Executive Jet Aircraft, and knew that the books of that company were being juggled. Manufacturers Hanover, which was in the consortium credit for $20 million, had participated in perhaps the most blatant single misstatement on Penn Central's books. Manufacturers was banker to the wholly owned subsidiary New York Central Transport Company, which twice in 1969 paid $6 million "dividends" upstream to the parent company though it did not have the profits to justify such dividends and in fact needed the money for its operations. Both times, upon receiving the $6 million "dividend" from Transport, Penn Central *that same day* loaned the money back to Transport, interest-free. Manufacturers Hanover saw on its books these nonsensical switches of money back and forth, which left subsidiary and parent in identical cash positions at the end of the day but enabled Penn Central to claim $12 million of "earnings". And said nothing about it.

"Everybody believed that the government wouldn't let Penn Central go", Manufacturers chairman Gabriel Hauge said several years later. "The bankers had a herd instinct for trouble". But the real cause of the trouble was negligence. "Every little railroad in the country had credit officers coming out of its ears", says William Dwyer of First of Chicago (which not only lost its share of the consortium loan but also dropped $8 million in a separate Eurodollar loan made by its London branch). "Penn Central never even had anybody visit in the back room".

In early 1970, Penn Central came back to First National City for another $50 million on the cuff, and the bank began to get nervous, requesting additional security (none of which, in fact, Penn Central still commanded—which is exactly the sort of thing that cannot happen with a properly administered loan). Rebuffed by Citibank, Bevan proceeded to Chemical Bank, already a participant in the consortium, and Chemical became the lead bank for another $50 million. This was completely unsecured credit, intended as a "bridge loan" to be paid back after Penn Central received the proceeds of a projected $100 million bond offering on the open market. When the underwriters of the bond offering backed away and made what had to be a public announcement, Penn Central found it impossible to roll over its commercial paper. The power-and-light bill had not been paid for months. Now there was no money to meet the payroll.

Scrambling to salvage the situation, which blew up during the weeks American forces were in Cambodia, the Nixon administration tried to arrange a loan from the Navy Department to Penn Central under the provisions of the Defense Production Act of 1950, which authorized the military to keep afloat imperilled companies that were vital to national security. Before the Navy Department could move, however, it needed certification by the Federal Reserve System that there was at least a reasonable chance the loan would be repaid. The Federal Reserve Bank of New York, given this investigatory problem, did not anticipate any great difficulty finding an answer: First National City as the lead bank would have all the necessary records. But Fed examiners looking into the Citibank files found the cupboard very nearly bare of the comforting detail a bank should have on the condition of a borrower. After a little further checking, the Fed gave the Navy Department an answer most easily summarized by the words "No way".

Chemical's folly in making the final unsecured loan has drawn the most heavy fire within the banking community; the description of the bank as "the Comical Bank of New York" dates from this fiasco. William Renchard, who was chairman of the bank at the time, feels that all this is very unfair. "That fifty million dollar loan," he said recently, "was to the top company, not to the railroad. It was to be a ninety-day loan, to be paid out by financing. What really brought the house down was the failure of the investment bankers, who didn't come through with the hundred million. We made the loan only on the understanding that if the pay-out wasn't there it would be secured by Norfolk and Western, Buckeye Pipeline, Great Southwest—good assets. First National City's three hundred million was secured only by stock in the railroad company."

Of course, by the time the agreement to put security behind Chemical's loan came due, Penn Central was in bankruptcy. And the First National City credit was in fact secured by all the other garbage, mostly the fraudulently operated real estate subsidiary. Renchard's statement as a whole can be characterized adequately by the one significant contribution made to the language by the hippy movement: "Oh, wow!"

3

A footnote to Chemical's involvement with Penn Central, and something Renchard says about it, opens a glimpse into what may be a larger and more frightening can of worms. While they were raising the money the railroad was to lose, treasurer David Bevan and several of his colleagues in the Penn Central finance group, together with Charles Hodge of the brokerage house of Glore Forgan and a group of their friends, were playing the stock market as proprietors of a private mutual fund called the Penphil Corporation. The initial investment in Penphil in 1962 was only $30,000; the total investment over nine years was only $389,000. The profits and unrealized gain a year after the railroad went under were $3.5 million. The great bulk of the money used to purchase securities for Penphil—80 percent overall, 95 percent of all purchases prior to 1966—came from Chemical Bank, in loans collateralized by the securities purchased, in flat violation of Regulation U of the Federal Reserve System, which limits the money banks can lend borrowers for the purpose of buying stocks. These loans, moreover, were made at prime rate. Investigators from the SEC found a memo from Renchard to his lending officers setting up the deal: "Frankly, the rate on the proposed loan is too low, but in view of the size of the deal and the fact that it has such good friends connected with it, WSR felt it was preferable not to quibble with Mr. Bevan over the rate. . . ."

Renchard is tired of hearing about Penphil. "The Penphil thing," he says, "has been inflated out of all proportion. The fact that a couple of characters got a little greedy had nothing to do with the bust of the railroad". He had felt some concern about the propriety of the situation: "Several times Dave Bevan sat in my office and I asked him whether he was absolutely sure he wasn't getting into a conflict situation. He told me everything he did was under advice of counsel; it turned out his counsel was his brother". Beyond that, Renchard had what he considered a substantial mark to put on his side of the ledger: "They invited me to be part of the group. I said I couldn't possibly do that, not while I am lending them money."

And that was right, of course: he couldn't. What is interesting, if Renchard's recollection is correct, is the idea that Bevan thought he might.

The banking system has a potential systemic weakness: the power of the lending officer, restricted in form but not in substance by the various committee systems, to approve or deny loans that may be matters of commercial life or death to prospective borrowers. Under these circumstances, it would be surprising if successful applicants did not in gratitude seek at least on occasion to give some token of that gratitude to the man who made it all possible. If tokens of gratitude may be offered after the event, then of course they may also be promised before the event. Uncharitable people might call that a bribe, so we won't talk about it, right? Right.

"When I first rose in this bank", says chairman John Bunting of First Pennsylvania, "a man came to me and said I would get some stock in a company to which we were making a big loan. The loan was going to be important to them. Once I was offered a thousand shares. It's not against the law". In fact, it is against the law: Section 18, No. 215 of the U.S. Code provides that "whoever, being an officer, director, employee, agent or attorney of any bank, the deposits of which are insured by the FDIC . . . stipulates for or receives or consents or agrees to receive any fee, commission, gift, or thing of value . . . for procuring or endeavouring to procure . . . any loan or extension or renewal of loan . . . shall be fined not more than \$5,000 or imprisoned not more than a year, or both". Why does Bunting think otherwise?

Late in 1973, a front-page story in the *New York Times* told of

WHERE THE MONEY GOES

a deposition in a civil suit, charging that former officers of the National Bank of North America, the $2,000 million subsidiary of CIT Financial Corp., had taken bribes to make unsound loans to a subsequently bankrupt ship-chartering firm. And there can be no doubt that such things do happen: it has been observed elsewhere that Christ Himself could not trust all twelve disciples, and there are ten thousand times twelve bankers in the United States who have something to say about loans. Direct bribery cannot happen often, however, if only because so many less unlawful ways of accomplishing the same result are available. Lending officers have wives, and they and their wives have brothers, brothers-in-law, uncles, nephews, cousins, friends, some of whom are insurance brokers or real estate agents or lawyers or accountants. Most borrowers of any substance have business to give such professionals; some would be more than willing to direct some of this business anywhere the loan officer considered helpful.

It is very nearly impossible to get a banker to talk about this problem. "You take care of that," one said in the depths of embarrassment, "when you hire the man". It is probably fair to say that the decision to authorize a man or woman to make loans with the bank's money is never frivolously made: there is an element of almost religious ritual, of investiture, when a young banker "receives his lending authority". Moreover, while every big city has its "political" banks that receive far more than their share of public deposits (and have tie-ins with the writers of real property and casualty insurance who are the major support of local politics in America), the banks in general must be given high marks for avoiding loans to people who shouldn't get loans. The *New York Times*, reporting on a study of loans to criminal elements by the federal government's Small Business Administration regional centre in New Orleans, quoted the director of that city's Crime Commission as saying that gangsters were particularly ardent supplicants for SBA credits because "they're barred from the banks".

Every once in a while, a bank gets stung by a lending officer who is simply a soft touch for his friends and acquaintances, and digs himself even farther in the hole as he seeks to help the helpless. In fall 1972 a federal judge in San Francisco had the unhappy task of sentencing a Bank of America branch manager who had embezzled $591,291 through manipulation of phony accounts, without taking a penny for himself. The baffled judge sentenced him to six months in jail and three years' probation, during which he would have to repay the bank at a rate of $100 a month to offset about ½ of 1 percent of its losses.

American banks are audited frequently by internal auditing teams that are hired directly by the board and report to a committee of the directors rather than to the bank's officers; and like all corporations, banks are also audited by firms of Certified Public Accountants who are hired, in theory, by the stockholders rather than by management. Such auditors, who arrive unannounced for periodic inspections, have access to all the files, and are specifically charged with measuring the soundness of loans. Any tendencies they may have to be kind to management are counteracted by the fact that they are periodically second-guessed by an only slightly less thorough inspection by government bank examiners. Neither the examiners nor the auditors are in fact looking for evidence that improper influences have been exerted to secure loans; their responsibility runs strictly to the soundness of the credit, the evidence that demonstrates the borrower can pay back his borrowings. James E. Smith, Comptroller of the Currency and thus ultimately responsible for the examining of all national banks, suggests that improper influence on a lending officer "would probably surface on some loan that showed quite inadequate documentation, an insufficient credit rating to justify the credit."

"Well", says Richard Byrne, a young supervising national bank examiner in the New York area, not wishing to be critical of his boss, "one certainly hopes so".

The chairman of a savings and loan association says that he recently had to fire a lending officer because all the mortgages written on property in an area near the bank went to the customers of just one of a number of local brokers. Such patterns would probably exist on the record of any lending officer who was abusing his position, and while they might not be visible to auditors or examiners looking for other things, they would show up bright and clear in the acid bath of a complaint from a broker or insurance agent or title company that found itself losing business to the loan officer's friend. It has been suggested that a fair proportion of the not infrequent cases when a high-level lending officer departs unexpectedly, or a bank is reorganized with a new chief executive officer, represent the discovery that someone with lending authority has found a way to profit by its exercise. When the *Times* story about the National Bank of North America was mentioned to Comptroller Smith, he very quickly said, "None of the people named in that story are still connected with that bank".

The number of prosecutions for this sort of criminal behaviour, however, seems to be almost invisibly small. No doubt many loan officers who are dismissed under this cloud are men who have seen the error of their ways, for whom an injunction to go and sin no more is defensible charity. (In the securities business, this is called a "consent decree".) But much of the force of any law derives from the belief of those subject to it that if they break it they will suffer a public punishment. Unless the banks are willing to bring charges in cases of this sort, public suspicion that "it's who you know" that determines your treatment at the bank will never be eliminated. Wonders might be achieved with just one prosecution of a bank president as an accessory after the fact in a bribery case where the president failed to report the crime to the authorities. Somewhere, surely, there must be a politically ambitious U.S. Attorney who could rise to this challenge.

4

A bad loan becomes a loss when the bank admits that it is one; indeed, the threat that if the bank denies him money it will have to accept a loss on an existing loan is one of the strongest arguments available to a borrower in trouble when he comes around to seek an extension—even an increase—in his line of credit. Here the auditors and the examiners do play a crucial role, forcing a bank to "charge off" loans which appear uncollectable to the cold eye of an outsider. What evidence there is argues that the examiners are, as they should be, more careful than the bank: more than two-thirds of all actual loan losses occur in loans previously "classified" by an examiner; but most classified loans—four-fifths to nine-tenths, depending on the general economic climate—do not in the end produce a loss to the bank.

There are arguments of varying degrees of bitterness about how loans should be "written up" and whether or not the bank must make "provision" for them—i.e., set aside a loss reserve. One of the reasons American banks change from national to state charters, or vice versa, is that the local examiner is regarded as unacceptably tough. Most commentators on this escape valve feel that its use proves the illegitimacy of dual regulation—that it is proof of what Allan Sproul called "competition in laxity". But there can be two views of the rights and wrongs here. Howard D. Crosse while a chief examiner for the Fed, which keeps an eye on its state-chartered member banks but has no disciplinary powers, "examined several national banks in process of conversion to state member banks as the direct result of what they considered supervisory 'persecution'. Findings bore out the banks' contention that the classification of assets was unwarrantably severe". Bankers claim that they suffer from the bureaucratic arrogance of examiners, and tell horror stories about young twerps who insist on criticizing $50,000 loans to businesses that keep $200,000 on current account in the bank. No doubt some of the stories are true; and so are the stories examiners tell of easing up on criticism of a loan for fear of costing a lending officer his job.

Once the bank has been forced to admit the presence of a bad loan in its portfolio, the accountants, unfortunately, take over. Common sense and Morris Schapiro argue that money lost in a bad loan is a cost of doing business as a bank, and should simply be added to the expense side of the ledger before expenses are deducted from income to yield the residue of profit. This was, in fact, standard operating procedure at the best banks until the mid-1960s, when the banks became terribly conscious of their "bottom line" and the valuation the stock market put on it. In the days of ninety-day commercial credits, they argued, immediate expensing of loan losses was indeed correct; but now that half the loan portfolio was in term loans, it was somehow unfair to deduct all of a loan that went sour in the year you decided (or were forced to admit) it was hopeless.

Because loan losses really are expenses, and because they fluctuate drastically from year to year, the Internal Revenue Service since 1954 has allowed banks to deduct from their taxable earnings an allocation to a "loan-loss reserve". In any given year, the allocation might be larger or smaller than actual loan losses. Manipulation of this figure was an easy way to reduce taxes or improve reported earnings (depending on management's immediate needs); if the bank wished to retain the appearance of a high loan-loss reserve without reducing this year's reported profits, it could always replenish the reserve from undistributed profits accumulated in past years. In theory, this way of handling the problem is perfectly legitimate, because a loan that went sour this year was made last year and can correctly be charged against last year's profits; in practice, of course, the possibilities of deception are considerable, because previous years' profits figures do not have to be (and in fact are not) restated to show subsequent deduction of loan losses from undistributed profits. What worried IRS, however, was tax avoidance through deducting an unreasonably large amount from current earnings (the star performer at squirrelling away profits in this manner was the old Meadowbrook National Bank in New York, which at one point had a loss reserve totalling 7 percent of its loans). Finally the revenuers produced a formula establishing a ceiling for loan-loss reserves as a percentage of loans outstanding. The ceiling was originally 2·4 percent: contributions to the reserve that brought it up to that figure would be deductible for tax purposes; contributions to the reserve that took it higher than that would not be deductible.

In 1969, IRS offered the banks a new way to handle this problem, by allocating to the loan-loss reserve not this year's actual losses but a sum amounting to one-fifth of the total losses over the previous five years—i.e., a "rolling average" of the most recent five years' loss experience. Now even without trying a bank could insulate its reported profits from its loan-loss experience: from 1969 to 1970 First National City showed an increase in profits from $2.57 a share to $2.89 a share, because only a fifth of the Penn Central losses had to be expensed in that year. If Citibank had deducted from profits all the loan losses actually charged off in both 1969 and 1970, its per-share earnings (calculated by Morris Schapiro) would have declined from $2.47 to $2.45. First National Holding Corp. of Atlanta claimed a jump in profits from $4.93 per share to $6.42, which Schapiro's post-loss calculation showed as an actual decline from $3.92 to $2.84; Bankers Trust of New York, a rise from $4.86 to $5.79 that should have been a decline from $4.75 to $4.72.

Loan-loss experience in 1968 was one of the best the banks have seen since banking stopped being stick-in-the-mud. The economy was booming, and inflation (the great cosmetic) was painting all the lilies. Penn Central stock sold for more than $60 a share, only two of Morris Schapiro's sixty-one largest banks showed loan losses of as much as ·2 of 1 percent, and four of them actually showed negative loss figures—that is, the recoveries the work-out department was able to squeeze from loans previously written off were greater than the new losses that had to be taken. Until 1973, then, the rolling five-year average, because it included this splendid 1968, was always below the actual loss experience of the year — *way* below, in some years. Meanwhile, the banks were doubling their total loans. As a proportion of loans outstanding, the loan-loss reserves dropped from more than 2 percent to little better than 1·3 percent. At the same time, bank capital (from the depositors' point of view, also a loan-loss reserve) was dropping from about 12 percent of loans to perhaps 7 percent of loans.

The villain of this piece may well be IRS, trying to wring the last taxable dollar out of the banks. In 1973, some ambitious agents even took a crack at disallowing the 50 percent write-off the members of the Penn Central consortium had taken on the defaulted revolving credit; 25 percent, IRS said, would cover the true losses. This is arrant nonsense: the bankruptcy court, in fact, has been quickly and surely expropriating all the Penn Central creditors, who are most unlikely to get back as much as 50 percent of what they loaned. But it is hard to avoid the feeling that some banks have not fought as hard as they should have fought, because they like the idea of being forced to declare higher profits, which allow the holding company to print more widely acceptable Chinese money for the purpose of acquiring other people's businesses.

Browsing the bank's most recent figures in fall 1973, a visitor noted that First Pennsylvania showed an increase over the year before of about 30 percent in total loans—without any increase at all in loan-loss reserve. Chairman John Bunting was asked solicitously whether his loan-loss reserve had been too high the year before, and he winced. "We're almost identical in ratios with First National City Bank", he said.

In early 1973, First National City published a booklet entitled *Bank Capital Adequacy*, written by its vice-president in charge of corporate planning, much admired as a new statement of theory for what had been a rather ossified area of official analysis. Among the items of information supplied to buttress the theory were the results of a study of "adverse loan experience over a ten-year period from 1962–72. . . . In no year did after-tax loan charge-offs exceed 13·1 percent of after-tax earnings. . . . Average charge-offs as a percentage of loan-loss reserves was 3·5 percent, with a peak experience of 7 percent. After-tax loan losses averaged less than 0·5 percent of total capital accounts and in the worst year—the Penn Central bankruptcy—charge-offs aggregated 1·3 percent of total capital accounts. . . . Prudent expectations would hold that expected future losses would average 6 percent of annual earnings, 3·5 percent of reserves, 0·5 percent of capital accounts". The 1973 results then showed Citibank's actual after-tax loan losses at 14 percent of earnings, 13 percent of reserves, and 2 percent of capital accounts. And 1974 was worse. And 1975 was *much* worse. Prudence seems to mean different things to different people.

Fortunately, the heavy loan losses of 1973 did not blight the annual report. Thanks to the miracles of modern accounting, the severe loan losses of 1973 could be shown on the balance sheet as a reduction of loan-loss reserve (or as a replenishment of the reserve from undivided profits), and not as a debit against earnings. Citicorp had enjoyed a solid profits increase even after charging off the loans—but not quite so solid as the 26 percent claimed.

"Banks owe the holders of their securities a realistic account of how they are doing", Morris Schapiro wrote in 1972. ". . . To the extent that the Loan Reserve is replenished by annual transfers from undivided profits, it may be held that reported income, in effect, includes additions from capital. . . . Loan losses should be counted in full to make disclosure fair and meaningful to the investing public. Managements are not absolved of their responsibility to stockholders just because the regulatory authorities give banks the option of averaging their loan losses with those of prior years. . . . *Bank Stock Quarterly* respectfully suggests to bankers and accountants that 'full and fair disclosure' has priority over 'generally accepted accounting principles'." In Britain, "provision against advances" is in fact deducted immediately from profits at the top of the P & L statement, and the five-year moving average is adjusted to maintain loss reserve percentages against the loan portfolio.

In 1973, according to Robert Morris Associates (the guild of credit officers), net losses on business loans at the 473 largest banks in America ran about $26 for every $10,000 outstanding, up from $21 the year before; by 1975, they were approaching $40 per $10,000 outstanding. Among the 25 giant wholesale banks in Morris Schapiro's index (which did better than the national average), First National City had the fourth worst record. Its brilliance and imagination have for some years met higher standards than its level of care: Lockheed, Penn Central, Equity Funding, Mill Factors, Yale Express—the bank's recent history is a litany not only of good ideas but of bad loans. (In the Yale Express situation, the financial v.-p. who got the company in trouble had come recommended by Citibank: "Money was no problem", president Gerald W. Eskow told *Fortune*'s Richard J. Whalen. "I had my fat friend with the moustache and the little black bag who'd go to the bank and get a million".) A $600,000 loan from Citibank provided the capital with which Donald Parsons first acquired control of the Birmingham–Bloomfield bank in Michigan that later went resoundingly bust. Coming into 1974, Citibank had $600-odd million out on loan to no fewer than seventy of the nation's two hundred Real Estate Investment Trusts, the American equivalent of the fringe banks, all of which seemed likely to be more or less troubled in years to come.

But the mid-1970s look like a bad period for loan losses for all the wholesale banks. Bank of America has already announced that it was adding $30 million to its loan-loss reserve to cover its exposure on a $130 million loan to Memorex, but has not in fact charged off any of the Memorex loan—and not many people in the electronics industry think that $30 million will take care of the difference between what Bank of America has advanced Memorex and what it will get back. All the big banks have money in loans to REITs, to cattle ranches, to fast-buck franchise operations, to conglomerates that used the loan to buy up their own stock, to all the tax dodges that have passed for enterprise in the last crazy ten years. Fraudulent borrowers are turning up with increasing ferquency: following the SEC's exposure of a nutty fake scheme to import cheap wine from Europe, for example, United Virginia Bankshares (headed by a former chairman of the FDIC) had to write off in spring 1974 no less than $3.8 million in loans secured by fictitious inventories of rotgut wine. Plus there are all the letters of credit carelessly written (the U.S. National Bank of San Diego problem is only the part of the iceberg that shows)—and all the loans abroad, to Italy and (alas!) to England, and to the Third World, where there is neither capitalism nor socialism, but the bankruptcy laws are elastic.

Giving banks the option of insulating their reported earnings from current losses has encouraged them to make more risky loans. And there arrives, of course, a day of reckoning, when the costs of inflation seem too great to be borne, and businesses will for the first time in a generation be made to pay for their mistakes. Unless history has lost its power to predict, the greatly expanded loan portfolios of 1973–74 will show increased proportions of defaults before the books are closed. In the last quarter of 1974 and the first half of 1975, the American banks began to face up to the facts; they stopped hiding behind the skirts of Internal Revenue Service rules, and began doubling and tripling their additions to loan loss reserves. That may or may not cover the losses that will soon have to be taken.

5

Loans are not the only source of bank profits and losses from the use of funds. Banks also make investments in securities. Since 1933 American banks have not been allowed to buy corporate stock, and they rarely do buy corporate bonds; but they can buy notes and bonds issued by federal, state, or local governments. In the 1970s, investments have run to about one-third of the total earning assets of the banks. In turn, about a third of those securities investments are more or less involuntary: all U.S. Treasury deposits, and most deposits of state and local governments, must be matched by holdings of government securities of some sort. The other two-thirds of the investment portfolio divide up between securities held briefly to provide liquidity—to assure that if depositors come around for cash or send the money to other banks the bank will have assets easily saleable for cash—and securities held on a longer term to provide profits.

These days, the profit-makers are the state and municipal bonds. They sell to yield the banks only about 70 percent as much as Treasury issues—but the earnings from them are tax-free. In most years in the 1960s, commercial banks bought more than one-half of all the new state and municipal bonds issued in America; and at the end of 1973, they held about 45 percent of such indebtedness. They were careless about what they bought: "Why", Senator Edward Brooke asked Walter Wreston, "didn't you try to protect not only your bank, but . . . New York as well?"

Since 1973, because investment tax credit provisions and leasing deals have offered alternative sources of tax-free income, the banks have reduced their holdings of municipal paper. Though the New York City situation is unique, involving major elements of fraud, the impact of these reductions has been damaging to municipal finance all across the country.

For a bank, the vital difference between a loan and an investment is the fact that there is (probably) a market for an investment and (probably) not for a loan. This cuts two ways. Because there is no market, a loan can be carried at full value unless an auditor or an examiner gives it another value. Thus a bank cannot appear to be losing money on a safe loan—but it can appear to be losing money on a safe security if the market price goes down. In 1938, when the reconstruction of confidence in the banking system was still a prime national goal, the regulatory agencies and the American Bankers Association got together to see if something could not be done to avoid the misleading appearance that a bank's solvency was endangered when the market price of a safe government security dipped below par. The agreement reached gave the banks the right to carry on their books at face value (i.e., a $1,000 bond would always be worth $1,000 on the books even if its market price dropped to $950) all Treasury and other U.S. government bonds. State bonds rated at "investment grade" by Moody's or Standard & Poor's can be carried at 90 percent of face value; municipal bonds at 80 percent. Among the uses of this privilege is the concealment of losses in the trading accounts: securities that have declined in price are simply moved to the bank's portfolio account, where they can be carried at cost (perhaps not legally, but who's to know?). In 1974 there was more of this than anyone admits.

Still, banks often do have occasion to sell bonds from this portfolio, regardless of the present market price. And here we must permit to rear its head—briefly—the great dragon of tax consequences, which breathes so dense a smoke screen around American corporate reality. Before 1969, banks could deduct from their income for tax purposes their net *losses* on sales of securities; but they were charged only 50 percent of their usual tax rate on net *profits* from "capital gains". Thus banks would manoeuvre their investment portfolios in such a way that one year would be an all-loss year, reducing income for tax purposes; another year would be an all-gain year, taking advantage of the capital gains tax break. A bank that took a $100,000 loss in one year and a $100,000 profit the next would show a net gain of $25,000—the loss the first year would be partially offset by a $50,000 tax credit, while the profit the second year would be diminished by only $25,000 in taxes. Only the full-year totals counted for tax purposes. A bank that was foolish enough to balance its profits and losses in both years would show no gain at all.

Now, money made or lost through the purchase and sale of securities is no different from money made or lost in other ways. But because banks had to decide at the very beginning of each year whether they were going to take profits or losses on their investment portfolio in the twelve months ahead, reporting these results as increases or reductions in earnings would put the banks' reported profiability on a meaningless yo-yo. Thus it became traditional for American banks to report their earnings exclusive of gains or losses on securities transactions, which were then reported separately. When banks speak of their earnings, they speak of "operating earnings", before taking into account the results of their securities transactions.

The Tax Reform Act of 1969 took away from the banks most of their privilege of claiming capital gains from the sale of long-term investments, which eliminated the rationale for separate reporting. But the tradition was retained—partly, no doubt, to avoid any temptation an unscrupulous management might feel to inflate the apparent earnings of the bank by selling only those securities on which the bank had a profit. Unfortunately, in a period of rising interest rates it is still possible for a bank to manipulate its securities holdings in a way that overstates true earnings. Edward M. Roob, then in the bond department of First of Chicago (now at the Treasury Department) illustrated the tactic in a lecture to officers of that bank's correspondents in the fall of 1972.

Roob assumed a tax-exempt municipal bond with ten years still to go, carrying a $3\frac{1}{4}$ percent coupon. The bank had purchased a million dollars of these bonds at par some time before, and showed "taxable equivalent" earnings of 6½ percent on its investment. But interest rates were up, and the price of the bond on the open market had dropped ten points.

All set? Hold on to your hat.

The bank now sells these bonds for $900,000, taking a loss of $100,000—of which $50,000 comes back from the government in reduced tax liabilities. So the bank has $950,000, which it invests in a similar bond issue with ten years to run, buying a face value of $1,055,000. Now, 3¼ percent of $1,055,000 is $34,287.50, which is 3⅗ percent of the $950,000 the bank put into it. Instead of showing a 6½ percent taxable equivalent yield on a million dollars, the earnings account now shows a 7⅕ percent yield on $950,000. True, the "bottom line" *after* profits or losses on securities transactions shows a loss on the sale of the original bonds—but some investors look only to operating earnings *before* profits or losses on securities transactions. Clever.

Cleverer, still: ultimately, the loss on the sale is more than made up by the gain in the value of the bonds bought at discount. Held to maturity, the bonds just bought for $950,000 will pay off at face value of $1,055,000; so the original $100,000 loss ($50,000 after taxes) comes back as a $105,000 gain ($52,500 after taxes). Customary accounting procedure now takes this guaranteed accrual of value in our bonds as an *earnings* item, ten slices of $10,500 each ($5,250 post tax). Now the taxable equivalent yield on our bond portfolio is up to 8⅓ percent, every year. We never show the recovery of our old loss on securities transactions, but even the bank stock analysts have forgotten that by now, and they are impressed with the way our operating earnings keep going up. . . .

Even more remarkable things are done at some banks (*not* at First of Chicago) by keeping two sets of books, one for the Internal Revenue Service and one for the stockholders. I R S gets to learn about the actual income and expenses, and a bank heavily involved in municipal bonds and leasing may show a loss in this accounting, because real money received in interest failed to cover the bank's costs. But for reporting to stockholders, the bank shows its receipts on municipals on a "taxable equivalent" basis, which lifts income enough to produce an apparent profit. Now, the loss for tax purposes the bank has taken in its report to IRS has a value for stockholders in the future, because it means that much of future earnings will be tax-free. So we capitalize the value of our tax loss, and show it as an asset. . . . Detroit's Bank of the Commonwealth was the master of this juggle when Donald Parsons ran it; $11,444,000 of such assets were on the books when the FDIC sent in a resuscitation team. In 1972 the new management had to swallow $23.6 million of losses in the sale of the municipal bonds portfolio. As this would be more than enough to make future profits of the bank tax-exempt for the five years that tax-loss credits are allowed to live, the new management also made an "Extraordinary write-off of future income tax benefits" of $9,344,000.

Willard Butcher of Chase Manhattan notes that the separation of operating earnings from securities gains and losses gives him an incentive to buy long-term bonds when rates are high, and then prevents him from selling the bonds at a profit should rates come down, "because my income account can't stand the loss of the high interest. What's focused on in the news reports is always the earnings before securities gains and losses, as though those were the rub of the green. I want to see bank accounting changed to make management accountable for below-the-line as well as above-the-line—the results on securities are not an accident."

What Butcher complains about is the seamy side of the revolution in banking: the pressure placed on the chief executive officers of the banks to deliver whatever figures the stock market wants. So long as management is judged by the short-term profits it reports, the likelihood that these profits will somehow be over-reported is about as strong as the likelihood that water will run downhill. In fall 1974, Butcher's bank was in the headlines because the value of its securities portfolio had been overstated by at least $40-odd million. Under present accounting procedures, to quote bank-stock analysts David C. Cates and Frank L. Harwell, who run a service called Bancompare, "the cleanest certificate in the country covers figures which, by themselves, are patently inadequate and may be misleading".

"Most influential teacher I ever had", said Albert J. Hettinger, "was the fellow who taught me accounting. I'll never forget him. He used to say, 'Accounting is a way to tell the truth'." It would be a pity if that idea died off with Hettinger's generation.

13/Lending to Consumers

Indian County was built on credit and lived on credit. In the Spanish stucco palaces overlooking the lake in Shoreview, and in the toy-strewn, crabgrass-ridden ranch houses of Lakeside, everybody had his little books of perforated coupons payable to the Indian National Bank, or to the Thrifty Finance Corporation. Since nobody ever bought anything with money, nothing could be too expensive. . . . The newcomers to Indian County, looking with endless amazement over the property that they considered their own, filled out the coupon books every month, for the house, the car, the television set, the new encyclopedia, and the piano that nobody ever played. They could own anything when it cost only pennies a day.
—from *The Loner*, a novel by OTTO
FRIEDRICH

* * *

1

In fall 1973, in a nursing home, overfull of years and pretty much forgotten (I had not dreamed he was still alive), died an American lawyer-turned-banker who probably had more influence on the way people live today than anyone else who survived into this decade—Arthur J. Morris, who in 1910 organized the Fidelity Loan and Trust Company of Norfolk, Virginia, the first "Morris Plan bank". Before Morris, ordinary people who needed money could borrow from their family or friends, from shylocks, or from eleemosynary institutions established to give compassionate loans; people who merely wanted money, to buy something they otherwise "couldn't afford", were not likely to be able to borrow at all unless they were rich. Within ten years of Morris's initiative, he had Morris Plan banks in thirty-seven states, and the consumer society, which nourishes itself at the fount of buy-now-pay-later, was lustily crying an announcement of its birth.

Morris Plan was a simple idea. The borrower took a one-year loan to pay back in monthly (sometimes weekly) instalments. He needed two co-signers who would agree to pay if he could not. He had to satisfy the manager of the "bank" that he was going to keep his job and stay in the neighbourhood. And he paid what the Morris Plan called "6 percent interest". Assume he borrowed $100, to pay back in monthly instalments of $8.33(4) over a year. His interest was deducted in advance from his receipts, so he got $94. Over the course of the year, the average amount of the Plan's money that he actually had to use was $51.84; the true interest rate—$6 as a percentage of that—was 11·6 percent.* But to some extent that's

* The Federal Reserve System having copped out on explaining where these percentages come from—if you want to know the Annual Percentage Rate on a transaction you can send $1 for a printed set of tables, but you can't buy instructions to do it yourself—a little arithmetic is hereby offered as a public service.

Annual Percentage Rate (APR) is the interest the borrower pays divided by the average amount of money actually in his hands during the year. If you borrow $120 and pay it back in $10 monthly instalments, you think you have an average of $60 during the year, but in fact you do a little better than that because there is a whole month when you have the full $120 and no time at all when you have less than $10. If you add up $120 + $110 + $100 + 90, etc., your total will be $780. Divide that by 12 months, and your actual average for the year is $65. Divide the $65 by $120, and you get 54·167 percent. On any loan made for one year to be repaid in equal monthly instalments, the average sum in the borrower's hands over the course of the year will be 54·167 percent of the total borrowed.

That's without considering interest. Let us now take the case of a $120 loan with a $7.20 "finance charge". The repayment rate is $10.60 a month. But because the amount in your hands for the first month is much larger than the average amount that will be in your hands over the course of the year, a larger-than-average share of the first monthly payment must be assigned to the finance charge. We come to what the bankers call "the rule of 78". Recall that the "sum of the digits" in a level monthly repayment of a $120 loan was $780. Because you had the use of the full $120 during the first month, $\frac{12}{78}$ of the sophistry—from the point of view of the man borrowing the money, he had the immediate use of $94, at a cost of $6, which didn't seem like, and wasn't, such a lot. And still isn't.

Morris did not, of course, invent the personal loan. Personal loans to royalty had been the licensing fee for Renaissance bankers, and Rothschild once made Benjamin Disraeli an unsecured personal loan large enough to buy the Suez Canal, on the word of the Prime Minister of England. For lesser personages, security was always required. The poor had their pawn shops—still do, mostly in Latin countries—and the rich had access to banks, provided they could pledge land or securities worth more than the money they wished to borrow. Most single-payment personal loans in American banks—and the total runs about $12,000 million—are fully secured by collateral worth more than the loan, in the form of stocks and bonds and savings account passbooks or certificates. (Loans secured by time-deposit certificates, which cannot be cashed without a penalty, make sense; loans secured by day-of-deposit-to-day-of-withdrawal passbook accounts do not. But lots of the world makes no sense, and the passbook-secured instalment loan may well be worth the little it costs for the householder who needs the monthly bell of the coupon to make him salivate savings.)

---

total finance charge should be applied to the first payment. That gives us $1.11, so instead of repaying $10 on the principal of your loan the first month you actually repaid $10.60–$1.11, or $9.49. Over your first six payments of $63.60, $5.17 must be credited to interest, and your actual repayment of principal is $58.43 rather than $60. You make up the short-fall on the final six payments, when $61.57 of your $63 will be credited to principal; but the effect is that you have about $1.10 more of the lender's money, on the average over the year. Add $1.10 to the product of the calculations in the previous paragraph, and the average actually in your hands becomes $66.10. Divide the $7.20 finance charge by $66.10, and the Annual Percentage Rate of Interest comes out to 10·9 percent.

That's the rate for an "add-on" loan—you get $120 and pay back $127.20. The Morris Plan example is a "discount" loan—the $6 interest is discounted from the $100 loan before you see it, so you have only $94 to start. Apply our percentage: $94 × 54·167 percent gives $50.92 average before considering how the interest payments divide up on the rule of 78. In this case, you wind up in fact with an average of 92¢ more of the lender's money. Total: $51.84. Divide $6 by $51.84, and the interest rate is 11·6 percent.

Interest rates on fully collateralized personal loans are just about the lowest in the bank, frequently at commercial prime or even (in the case of passbook loans, where the bank charges 1 percent more than it pays) below commercial prime. These loans, after all, are safer than any business loan, and in the case of the passbook loan there isn't even any cost to convert the collateral if the borrower fails to repay. Thus the purposes for which people borrow against collateral include the full range of human activity—medical, educational, sacramental and celebratory experience. Insurance premiums and tax bills are also common uses of such loans. The Federal Reserve System, however, responsible for regulating the use of bank credit in the stock market, can think of only one thing.

"The 'purpose of a credit'," says the Fed's Regulation U, "is determined by substance rather than form. (1) Credit which is for the purpose, whether immediate, incidental, or ultimate, of purchasing or carrying a margin stock is 'purpose credit', despite any temporary application of funds otherwise. . . ." Everyone who borrows on stock collateral must fill out a "Statement of Purpose", and swear to it under penalties of perjury; and an authorized officer of the bank must accept the statement "in good faith". Those words are defined on the form as follows: "Good faith requires that such officer (1) must be alert to the circumstances surrounding the credit, and (2) if he has any information which would cause a prudent man not to accept the statement without inquiry, has investigated and is satisfied that the statement is truthful". Every "Reg U statement" that arrives in the mail is supposed to be investigated. When the bank examiners check out the collateral behind the loans, they do verify that every loan secured by a marketable stock comes equipped with a Reg U form in the borrower's folder. They also verify that at today's market prices these securities actually add up to more than 70 percent of the loan they secure, as Reg U requires. They do not, however, attempt to follow the money from the loan through the customers' pocket to determine whether or not the Statement of Purpose has been obeyed.

Morris Plan gave people with a good local reputation and two friends similarly situated a chance to borrow like people with collateral—at about twice the interest rate. Its success drew imitators, finance companies and "small loan" companies that cut a level or two below the social stratum of the Morris Plan customers. But their rates were often insupportable—30 percent, even 40 percent or more a year, concealed by the small weekly amounts and by misleading rate tables. Both the Morris Plan institutions and the finance companies got their money from sources other than depositors and thus were not legally "banks": a bank is quintessentially a thing that accepts deposits. Anyway, theirs was not at the start a business banks wanted to be in: in America as in England, the banks were more than satisfied to act as intermediaries, charging the finance companies higher-than-prime interest rates because they were in a risky, maybe questionable, business.

To fight what looked to them like bloodsucking by the usurers of Wall Street, a number of the politically more advanced labour unions took out bank charters themselves. "We felt," says Maxwell Brandwen, now chairman of Amalgamated Bank, "that a person of modest means with a job was entitled to a character loan on the basis of his job". Amalgamated, still owned by the Amalgamated Clothing Workers Union, is one of the few survivors of these ventures by the socialist unions of the 1920s (the banks owned by the United Mine Workers and the Teamsters Union have clearly had purposes other than socially productive lending). It is, however, quite a survivor, sprawling over a collection of storefronts on Union Square, with a branch in the garment district: $800 million in footings. Brandwen, a forceful, fleshy, elderly New Yorker from the vintage generation of immigrants' children that still dominates the professional life of the city, was one of the original incorporators of the bank, which does not mean he was a clothing worker. He was a young Harvard Law School graduate recommended by Felix Frankfurter to Sidney Hillman, then president of the union; and he runs what is in many respects the most conservative bank in New York: as a labour union bank, and Jewish to boot, it could not expect even minimal help from other banks if it ever got into trouble. Amalgamated makes no term loans and writes no mortgages longer than five years. In 1974, the Amalgamated Bank was a significant supplier of Fed Funds to the banking system, with money in nine figures for sale every day.

The tradition of service to what Brandwen always calls "the person of modest means" has persisted. Amalgamated has the only free chequeing account—no minimum balance—offered by a domestically owned New York bank (nearby New York University suggests that its students bank at Amalgamated for that reason); and since the early 1960s the bank has offered savers a way around the interest-rate ceilings through a USave account, which is not a deposit at all but a participation in a purchase of Treasury notes. The bank takes a fee of $\frac{1}{2}$ of 1 percent, and passes the rest through to the saver; the result has usually been at least 1 percent a year better than the legal maximum on savings accounts or short certificates.

Virtually all Amalgamated loans are to individuals, co-operatives or nonprofit institutions. Commercial loans are not entirely prohibited—especially if the applicant is somebody who wants to start a candy store in one of the lower-middle-income co-operative apartment projects the union has sponsored. But the bank avoids loans to the clothing industry, for fear of being in a position where a borrower could blackmail the bank by threatening the elimination of jobs or a flight from the city to the South if it didn't come across with more money. Most mortgage loans are housing-related, and there are lots of customers for personal and auto loans at the lowest interest rates in New York. (The low-cost loan service is advertised once in a while; the free chequeing service is never advertised: Brandwen did it not to get deposits but because he thought he should, and he worries about its soundness as a way to run a bank.) The utilitarian banking floor, broken into sections by plastic partitions and by the walls of the former storefronts, is crowded with the races and ages of man, and calls forcibly to one's attention how middle-class and middle-aged the scene is at the city's other banks.

The other New York labour banks failed. Brandwen feels, because they were not run as banks. "A labour bank as a bank has to meet the same criteria of operations as any other bank", he says. "It must operate efficiently, competently, and profitably. Its tellers must be as competent as those at First National City Bank. A loan is no better here than there". Still, from its very earliest days— when Brandwen arranged a loan programme with the Patrolmen's Benevolent Association to get the cops out of the hands of the money-lenders—Brandwen has been open to suggestions of things a real bank could soundly do (like lending money for the purchase of co-operative apartments) that would serve communities not served by the more narrowly profit-oriented.

Whatever the reasons for the failure of other labour banks, the reason that new ones have not started is clear: credit unions for instalment loans and savings associations (or savings banks) for housing loans have taken over much of the mission Sidney Hillman had hoped to accomplish with a union bank. As clearly as 1928, National City Bank of New York was in the personal loan business in competition with Morris Plan and Household Finance; and the Bank of America personal loan division can trace its history back to 1929. In the Depression—contrary to all expectation—Americans paid their debts to finance companies at the cost of considerable personal hardship. During the war, the Valley National Bank of Arizona gave automatic credit to any graduate of a service training programme in the state—a loan of $300, no questions asked, to pay for a trip home on leave. "There were zillions of these loans made", says Bill Best, the bank's p.r. director, "and the loss rate was infinitesimal".

When the banks emerged from World War II heavy with cash and government securities, consumer lending, even to persons of modest means, seemed increasingly attractive as a source of profits. From 1950 to 1960, instalment credit directly extended by banks nearly tripled, from $5,800 million to $16,700 million; and in the next decade it nearly tripled again, rising to $45,400 million in 1970. In 1975, the banks had more than $70,000 million outstanding in consumer loans. Loans for consumer purposes were about 9 percent of total bank loans in 1945; in 1975, they were approaching 25 percent.

The easiest—and thus the most profitable—way to make a personal loan is through giving a depositor overdraft privileges in the English style. One of the great differences between Britain and America was that the individual customer of an American bank regards his bank as a place to put money, while the individual customer of a British bank looked upon his bank as a place to get money. As a result, British banks were very choosy about whom they would accept as a "depositor", while American banks will give chequebooks to anybody who walks in with cash and can sign a signature card. Thus the British overdraft system was always considered incompatible with American banking procedure, an impossible import. But First National Bank of Boston took a shot at it in 1955, setting up a "cheque credit" plan by which any depositor who paid off one loan from the bank became immediately and automatically entitled to write a cheque for as much as $3,000 that was not in the account.

James Smith, now Comptroller of the Currency, remembers that he was working at the American Bankers Association at the time and asked First of Boston whether maybe there wasn't some middle ground between the traditional American banker's suspicion of the unsecured personal loan and this flat adoption of British practice. First of Boston told him not to worry, and was right—the first approval of the borrower remained good, and defaults ran less than $\frac{1}{4}$ of 1 percent of the overdrafts. (Meanwhile, Britain has gone some distance the other way, soliciting current accounts without overdraft privileges from all sorts of very ordinary people, and making personal loans by individual contract rather than by overdraft privilege. According to the British Bankers Association, only about one quarter of the personal accounts in the clearing banks now command overdraft privileges.) More recently, the Boston bank has been a little less enthusiastic about cheque-credit, largely because public-relations considerations have frozen the interest rate at 1 percent per month on the outstanding balance. Instead, the bank is promoting its Master Charge cash advance, which yields 1·5 percent per month.

In mid-1973, First of Boston had about $50 million outstanding in personal loans, $20 million of it through Master Charge—and that $20 million was one-half of all the Master Charge cash advances made by all the members of the New England Bank Card Association. Next to the $100 million needed to build a single LNG tanker, personal lending is a small business for a big bank, but First of Boston regards it as important to the community status of the bank and has devoted some resources of cleverness to the problems. Chairman Richard Hill's favourite stunt was a heavily advertised offer to excuse people from payments in the month of December, when presumably they need all the money they can scrounge to buy Christmas presents. "Our customers," Hill says happily, "thought this was the greatest thing since sliced bread".

For all the good experience of some banks, however, most are still not really comfortable with unsecured personal loans. Banks now do more than 60 percent of all automobile financing, but only about a third of all personal instalment loans. It is probably fair to say that most banks are interested in making such loans only to borrowers who are also depositors (the approved device is now "no-bounce chequeing"). Even then, the instalment lending officer will be expected to probe the purpose of the loan and the temperament of the borrower. The Bank of America *Handbook of Instalment Lending* summarizes what the officer should look for:

On personal characteristics: "The best credit risks are usually over 30 years of age [never trust anybody under 30?]. . . . Married applicants are usually better credit risks than single persons, because marriage usually indicates a person's willingness to assume responsibility. . . . One full year with the present employer is the minimum employment requirement. . . . Stability of residence usually denotes the applicant is established in the community. . . . Judge the applicant by past credit records, particularly those of the past two or three years. . . . Ask, 'Could I meet the payments if I made his salary and had his monthly expenses?' . . . If monthly income is suddenly interrupted is there secondary source of repayment? . . . Co-makers

. . . should never be used as a crutch. . . . The value of co-makers lies in the persuasive influence they can exert on the borrower to make payments. . . ."

On purpose: "In the case of loans for some services, such as doctor bills and vacations, you must judge whether the benefits are valuable enough to stimulate payment after the service has been rendered. Loans for recurring debts, such as doctor bills, vacations, insurance premiums and taxes, should be, in most cases, repaid in full before the same bill is due again next year. Exercise caution when considering debt consolidation loans. . . ."

Student loans are not mentioned in the handbook; Bank of America writes them, says Kenneth Larkin, head of the personal loan division, as a "socio-political necessity". They are government guaranteed, but only after the bank has tried to collect the money itself, which is expensive and unpleasant and, Larkin feels, made necessary in large part by the government's own slovenly collection practice when the guarantee is claimed: "If you don't put the fear of God into these kids it's like a cancer—the kid doesn't pay and brags about it. Now the government is beginning to get tough, because fellows like myself were leaning on the Office of Education, saying, 'By God, get some fellows out into the field or we'll stop making the loans.'"

An applicant for a personal loan necessarily sacrifices privacy for money. In America, moreover, the invasion of privacy is direct: personal loans are rarely made unless the borrower comes in and fills out the forms in person. In Britain, a high fraction of the personal loan business is done by mail, saving the finance houses the cost of shopfront rentals. In America, a lending bank will call an employer to check statements on length of employment, nature of job, and salary. Many employers will not give salary information; the bank's investigator will then tell the employer what the applicant put down on the form, and ask if that's about right: employers who won't volunteer information will often react, and it helps to keep applicants honest if they know the boss will be told what they claimed. The primary source of information, however, is usually a centralized credit bureau, to which all lenders make reports. The operation of these credit bureaus, now nationwide, computerized, and interconnected, has been a source of concern to civil libertarians, who have a point, though not necessarily the point they think they have.

The problem is that the credit bureau exists to search out negative information about people. "Consumer credit," writes Joseph A. Turner of the Kanawha Valley Bank in Charlestown, West Virginia, "is an actuarial science. It is based on the fact that the large majority of citizens are honest and stable, that they keep their jobs, support their families, and pay their debts. The job of the loan officer is not one of selecting the good risks but of eliminating the poor ones." Turner compares the personal loan to life insurance: "If an applicant can pass a physical examination and show evidence of good moral character, it is assumed that he will live out his normal expectancy and be a good risk for life insurance." Similarly, anybody about whom the bank knows nothing bad is likely to be approved for a personal loan; and like the life insurance doctor the lending officer works by adding up a "point" score on what is wrong, minimizing the exercise of judgment.

What the banks want from the credit bureaus, then, is the reason to disapprove a loan. Part of the back-checking that will be done if a loan goes sour will be a look at what the credit bureau said about this fellow. Until 1971 a credit bureau could get in trouble not when it was unduly pessimistic about a possible borrower but when it was unwisely optimistic. Thus the people who work for credit bureaus were told to dig up dirt. Testimony before a Senate committee has claimed that they were told to dig up dirt even where there was no dirt, to maintain a stable percentage of negative references. Since 1971, federal law has required that the contents of credit files be available to their subjects, and that credit bureaus be required to communicate to their customers the replies by the subjects to any negative comments. But in the absence of malice, the victim of an inaccurate report in a credit file cannot win a libel suit: credit bureau investigators like other people have the First Amendment right to make mistakes. And the fact that the law requires a credit bureau to tell the subject of a file what it says about him does not mean that the bureau always does so: at the least, there are tens of thousands of people in the country who cannot borrow money and cannot find out why.

Still, it is the maintenance of credit files that enables banks to lend—at rates much lower than those charged by non-bank lenders —to ever-increasing numbers of people. To argue against information services, as some civil liberties groups do, is really to argue that fewer people should have the chance to borrow from banks: banks, like people, are reluctant to lend their money to total strangers. And the major victims, of course, would be people who look doubtful to the loan officer but clear the objective hurdles well enough to qualify as borrowers. Though no writer really likes to say so, probably the best approach to the privacy problem lies in the restoration of menace to the libel laws, making it dangerous for credit investigators (or other reporters) to damage their neighbours frivolously.

The major beneficiary of the independent credit-reporting service is the solid citizen who happens to be black. Before the 1960s, it was all but impossible for a black to get an unsecured personal loan at a bank, partly for reasons of bigotry and partly for reasons of realistic observation: all other things being equal (an important qualification), a black borrower is somewhat more likely to be feckless than a white borrower. Political pressure and the possibility of establishing a track record through a credit bureau have since combined to ease access to banking services for black borrowers, though there can be no doubt that prejudice survives.

In recent years, the fashionable remedy for this prejudice has been the development of black banks that would get their deposits from and lend to the black community. Like so much else that has been fashionable in the last decade, this was a thoroughly stupid idea. The black businessman, even more than the white businessman, wants to do his banking at a bank that can be helpful to him in establishing his credit with suppliers. The better established the black business, the more prominent the bank with which it can develop a relationship. Thus the new black bank cannot hope to draw any significant business from the best part of its presumed market, which will be depositing and borrowing elsewhere. But it can get all the risky business it will take.

Outside of North Carolina and Georgia, where solidly based black insurance companies that did business exclusively with the black community were available to provide some foundation for a black bank, there are no successful black banks. In Detroit, Denver and Kansas City the leading black bank went under; in Boston, the black bank could be saved only by a charitable act by the FDIC, which bought a bond issue from the bank to keep it solvent; in New York, Freedom National has repeatedly been kept in business only by the willingness of the bank examiners to ignore seriously unsound practice. Jackie Robinson wrote in his auto-biography: "I had a growing suspicion that the Comptroller's office was patting us on the back when they should be hitting us over the head with a club. I told [the bank examiner] that I thought we were not being judged by the same standards that would have been applied if ours were a white bank. I said that they were doing us no favour if they were telling us everything was all right when things were not right. The response from him was amazing. He never admitted it, of course, but it became apparent that my sus-picions had validity. We were being handled with kid gloves because certain officials did not want to get themselves accused or suspected of persecuting a black institution."

"Personal lending to poor people", says H. Matthew Snorton, a black vice-president of North Carolina National Bank in Char-lotte, "is marginal business that the black bank struggling for survival simply can't do." So NCNB, partly but not entirely for public relations purposes, decided to do the job itself. Snorton, an athletic, large young man with long sideburns, was then working for a housing developer after having acquired experience with American Motors and General Motors Acceptance Corporation: he had seen something of banks. NCNB recruited him in October 1972 to lead what the bank called its "low-income lending pro-gramme". Snorton was amused at the sense of bold innovation that he found at the bank when he reported for duty: "When I was growing up in a ghetto in Detroit, we used to go to the finance company and borrow three, four hundred dollars. I was surprised to hear all this hoopla about low-income lending—the finance companies have been doing it all along."

Over the first nineteen months, NCNB loaned $1.2 million to low-income North Carolinians, most of it in auto loans, "loans to improve oneself, to go to school, to improve the house, or to consolidate debts. Consolidation is the most common," Snorton says, not entirely happily. "You have to do a character determination, decide whether he's in trouble because he has a bad character or whether he was a victim of the retailers.

"You need outside help in this business. You can't take a guy off the street; you want a referral, from the welfare department, the housing authority, some self-help agency. Then you put the agency on the hook a little, too. It takes a different kind of loan officer, more patient, more understanding. He needs flexibility. If the guy loses his job, the loan officer has to find a way to delay the loan; he has to be experienced, and know the ins and outs of banking. So our loan officers are mostly older people. We'll lend money to buy a car for a man to get back and forth to work, give himself more mobility, to get a better job. We try to get a savings pattern established in people, even if it's only a dollar a week.

"What you can't understand until you see it is the increase in their pride—in the fact that they fulfil their obligations. It means they matter to somebody." Out of the $1.2 million in the first nineteen months, NCNB had to take only three losses, totalling not quite $3,000. The interest rate—about 15·5 percent APR—was less than that on the revolving charge plans of the best stores and the bank credit-card plans. "We don't want to make any money on these loans—though you can't get the people who live in a housing project in High Point to believe that. On the other hand, we don't want to lose money, either."

2

By far the biggest business banks do with consumers is automobile financing, and though this sort of loan is predominant everywhere in the country the ways of handling it are very different from region to region. In the East and the Midwest, the banks stress the fact that they are lending to a borrower: "For us," says Richard Hill of First of Boston, "the car is only the excuse to make the loan". In the West and the South, the banks take very seriously the fact that the loan is secured by the automobile, which can be repossessed under writ of replevin (though not arbitrarily: a bank that repossesses without cause can be sued for punitive damages). In the British hire purchase system, of course, title to the vehicle does not pass until the buyer makes the last payment on the loan.

Eastern banks by and large write "no-recourse" auto loans, which means that the dealer takes no responsibility for the credit-worthiness of his customers; western banks normally want "recourse", the chance to make the auto dealer take back the car and disgorge the money to the bank if the customer defaults. Procedurally, the eastern bank usually makes the loan itself; the western bank checks out the customer quietly, but lets the dealer make the loan agreement and then buys the paper from him. Until recently, Bank of America would make a car loan without a dealer's recourse agreement only when the customer had a "preferred" Bank-Americard, which is issued to cardholders who have run up at least $750 of bills and never been delinquent on a payment. Still, Kenneth Larkin does not like to see the lending officer using the dealer's guarantee as a crutch for failure to investigate the buyer. "The way to get in trouble," he reports, "is to do business with the guy who says, 'My name is on the back of it.' When the time comes that you want a hundred and fifty thousand dollars back from him, he says, 'Why did you buy all this lousy paper?' "

Bank of America runs an "advanced sales training workshop" for lending officers who handle automobile business, and one part of the manual presents the terminology of the trade. Among the things to watch out for, the manual includes

337

- the *flake* and the *mooch:* bad credit risks
- the *cancer:* a car that burns oil and smokes
- the *paper down:* when the dealer fakes a down payment
- the *mickey:* a loan the customer gets from a credit union or finance company to make the down payment on the car. The finance company that gives a mickey is a *mouse house.*

"When a loan officer finds somebody is mouse-housing a car loan," Larkin says, "we won't make the loan. But it's hard to find out."

Instalment lending is expensive for banks, but most of the time the higher rates more than make up for the higher costs. Taking the medium-sized banks in the Fed's Functional Cost Analysis, the average cost to make a consumer loan in 1972 was $28.93; the average cost to collect a payment was $2.16. Loan-loss experience on the five-year average ran about ⅓ of 1 percent. In 1974, loan-loss experience was pushing ½ of 1 percent and rising, and competent opinion held that the big-city banks would some day pay for their careless habits in extending credit to people whose best friends would never have loaned them money. Aaron Greene, a New York private detective whose business includes tracing debtors for banks, is appalled by the number of times he is approached by several banks all of which have made bad loans to the same clever deadbeat: "You'd think they'd talk to each other; but they don't".

In 1972, according to the Functional Cost Analysis, the average bank's break-even size was $1,431 for a one-year loan at $6 per $100 add-on interest (11 percent Annual Percentage Rate, which was about the average); for a twenty-four-month loan, $1,031; for a thirty-six-month loan, $901. These figures are somewhat misleading, however, because they reflect average rather than marginal costs. In an already established department, with loan officers on salary and with some spare time on their hands, additional loans may well be profitable even if they are only half the size of the average normally required to make the bank come out ahead. At these middling-sized banks, the average number of consumer instalment loans outstanding was 6,916 in 1972, and the average loan ran $1,387, with an average length just under a year and a half.

Especially when they operate by purchasing dealer paper, banks can get in trouble in instalment lending: writing of the $1,300 million Union Planters Bank in Memphis—which "went out and took a load of auto dealers' paper including, seemingly, a lot from younger folk"—Alan Abelson of *Barron's* commented early in 1974 that the resulting repossessions had put the bank "among Memphis' top ten used-car dealers". Bank examiners say these troubles can be serious enough to influence their rating of a bank, but unless the dealer is cheating, the losses are limited by the resale value of the car—at $1,000 each, for example, the two hundred cars in the Union Planters lot represent losses of only $200,000, which is barely visible in a $1,300 million bank.

In general, banks do not engage in price competition for instalment loan business—until the Truth in Lending Act of 1968, in fact, it could be extremely difficult to find out what the true interest rate was on a consumer loan. Now American law, implemented by the Federal Reserve Board in Regulation Z, does require a simple statement of Annual Percentage Rate, which can be compared from lender to lender. Nevertheless, perusal of a year's worth of sample bank ads distributed to its members by the Bank Marketing Association—perhaps a thousand in all—did not show one that emphasized pricing or, indeed, gave a rate figure. A *Columbia Journalism Review* article quotes a Chemical Bank spokesman as saying that his bank "had a policy not to announce either rate increases or decreases on consumer loans."

Competition is often on a green-stamp basis—borrowing more than $2,500 for a car or a home-improvement loan gives the borrower from the advertised bank a free portable black-and-white television set, or free license plates, or a tool kit. Wells Fargo in San Francisco and First National City in New York have pioneered reverse green stamps—as part of a package of services sold for $4 a month, the bank will graciously give a discount (unspecified) on the $2,500-and-over loans for which its rivals give the merchandise premiums. Getting people to pay for the right to buy the bank's most profitable service is truly exquisite marketing.

Fortunately, there is one source of auto finance credit that does in effect advertise—the credit union, which keeps its membership in touch with rates—and consumer lending by the banks is increasingly policed by the spectacular growth of credit unions (from $10,000 million in instalment loans outstanding at the end of 1968 to almost $20,000 million at the end of 1973). "A preferred rate", says the Bank of America *pro forma* proposal to dealers, "is available to help you retain customers who are now financing directly through credit unions . . .". And as time goes on more and more automobile buyers are conscious of the fact that the auto dealer has squirrelled away in his desk several different loan agreements, with different terms and different rates.

Most authorities believe that instalment borrowing is not greatly affected by changes in interest rates. F. Thomas Juster in a study for the National Bureau of Economic Research divided bank borrowers into two classes—rationed and unrationed: "Rationed households were those that did not have the option, given the market rates they faced, of borrowing for preferred maturities or of borrowing preferred amounts, and they were generally constrained from borrowing except when simultaneously acquiring an asset. That is, rationed customers could borrow to buy a car because the car was collateral, but they could not in general borrow for consumption. Unrationed customers were those who could generally borrow preferred amounts at going rates. . . . Rationed customers were in general quite unresponsive to changes in interest rates: they were already constrained to borrow lower amounts than they preferred at existing rates, and changes in market rates were therefore irrelevant."

John Bunting of First Pennsylvania said in 1973, "We've been looking at the interest sensitivity of consumer loans, and we've found it to be zero. It's the judgment of our lenders that you do much better if you change the terms and the down payments." But the fact that consumer rates are sticky on the downside turns out not to be so harsh a penalty as one might expect, because the political sensitivity of these rates makes them sticky on the upside, too. In 1973, when commercial loan rates soared to 10 percent for the prime customer (actually 12·5 percent, if the borrower was really forced to keep 20 percent of his loan in the bank as a compensating balance), instalment loans held pretty steady at $6 add-on per $100, or 11 percent, up perhaps half a point from the year before. Most banks did not promote them, but some did: First of Boston, with its belief that the bank does best by persuading people to borrow and stay borrowed, even stretched its automobile loan maturities to forty-eight months, thereby doing its own special bit to feed roaring inflation in Massachusetts. In 1974, consumer rates did rise, though proportionately less than business rates. They also came down more slowly in 1975.

Because credit rationing is accomplished by down payments and terms, consumer credit is an ideal subject for government regulation: by insisting on high down payments and short maturities, the Federal Reserve System can reduce loan demand in this area without disrupting the money market or any part of the economy other than the consumer durables section. Regulation W in the Korean war days did just that, to great effect, and in England the alteration of such requirements to meet changing conditions is part of the normal weaponry of the Bank of England. One of the tragedies of 1973 was the inability of the Fed to use this relatively painless tool of monetary control to brake an inflation fuelled to a considerable degree by unprecedented demand for automobiles and a concomitant jump in consumer credit. We shall take a look at what the Fed could have done in 1973 when we consider the labyrinthine ways of American government regulation.

3

From prehistoric times, merchants have offered their best customers credit as part of the inducement to buy—but only their best customers. "What said Master Dombledon about the satin for my short cloak and my slops?" Falstaff asked his page.

"He said, sir, you should procure him better assurance than Bardolph. . . ."

"Let him be damned like the glutton! . . . A whoreson Achitophel! A rascally yea-forsooth knave! . . . I looked a' should have sent me two and twenty yards of satin, as I am a true knight, and he sends me security. . . ."

For the rich, there were charge accounts, and dunning tradesmen at the door. The poor paid cash; Falstaff's problem was that he was poor. ("I can get no remedy against this consumption of the purse: borrowing only lingers and lingers it out, but the disease is incurable.") In the 1920s, department stores and oil companies began issuing credit cards ("courtesy cards") to identify preferred customers when they made credit transactions, and soon after the war the airlines began issuing Air Travel Cards to businessmen who would secure their credit with a deposit of $425 (but one deposit could be used for all the officers of the business). One such businessman found he could make money by letting others use his Air Travel Card and charging them interest on what was in effect a loan, and after noodling over this situation for a while he and some friends founded what they called the Diners Club. It was obscure enough that different authorities give different dates for its organization—1949 and 1950.

Diners Club would issue cards at a fee to qualified middle-class consumers, and would arrange with restaurants and hotels to give cardholders credit for rooms and meals. The Club would promptly pay the restaurant or hotel, taking a commission (originally from 5 percent to $7\frac{1}{2}$ percent) for its services. The benefit to the restaurant or hotel was additional business from tourists, and an undoubted loosening of the purse strings when the patron could sign rather than hand over cash for purchases. To understand the credit card business, it is probably best to regard the card issuer as both a lender and a factor. When he issues the card to the cardholder he is in effect writing a letter of credit; when he pays the merchant for the sales note he is buying accounts receivable.

The first bank to get into this business was Arthur Roth's Franklin National, in Franklin Square, Long Island, in 1951. Though customers could be billed for interest charges on overdue accounts, the hope at Franklin was to make the service pay through the merchant discounts, because the merchants would be the main beneficiaries: the "Franklin Charge Plan" would enable local Long Island stores (which were Roth's customers) to compete more effectively against the invading branches of the New York department stores (which were not). Roth's service neither flourished nor died; it limped along, making a little money every year. Roth also had a more ambitious restaurant credit service in partnership with *Gourmet* and *Esquire* magazines; these did not make money because too many customers did not pay. The problem was a classic chicken-and-egg dilemma: the service was not worth the time, trouble, or discount to the merchant unless there were a number of customers, and the customers had no interest unless there were a lot of merchants.

In 1958 American Express went into competition with Diners Club for the T&E (Travel and Entertainment) card business; and two giant banks—Bank of America in California and Chase Manhattan in New York—put out their own credit cards. Both banks thought they could make their plans attractive to the department stores, and both were wrong; but Bank of America, with a whole state to play in and with more capable management, signed many more merchants and many more cardholders than Chase could find. In what turned out to be the clarion call of an unexpected future, Bank of America slogged along, turned the corner, and, according to Larkin, "recovered our start-up costs in four or five years"; Chase fell further and further into the red and in 1962 went out of the credit card business with losses that have never been published but must have been millions of dollars. (Chase is today a franchised issuer of BankAmericard.)

These experiences were discouraging to other banks, and between 1960 and 1965 only ten banks introduced credit card plans. In 1965, First National City bought into the business big, acquiring the large but foundering Carte Blanche operation from Hilton Hotels, but the Justice Department promptly broke up the deal with an antitrust suit. The breakthrough came in 1966, when all the big Chicago banks moved at once. The Illinois unit-banking rule had restricted them to only one office, which vastly diminished their possible consumer loan business through conventional means; the credit card was an opportunity to build a regional market from a single office. The BankAmericard experience, and statements by Citibank during the Carte Blanche fight, had indicated that credit cards could easily become "revolving credit" systems of the kind pioneered in the mail-order field by J. C. Penney, yielding the bank interest on consumer loan accounts as well as a factor's discount from the merchants.

In the chicken-*v.*-egg dispute, the Chicago banks went for chicken—the greatest number of accounts to be opened in the shortest possible time. To solicit applications for cards was likely to be a slow and unprofitable business. Earlier that year, Marine Midland of western New York State—which had been in the credit card business since 1958, with an existing list of merchants —had sent out a batch of 33,357 promotional mailings, complete with postage-free return envelope, to a culled list of prospective customers who had used the bank's personal loan services or had been referred by local stores. Only 221 applications came back, a return rate of 0·7 percent. Then Marine Midland sent out a number of cards to people who had *not* applied, and within a short period 19 percent of them were actually used.

The Chicago banks' lawyers were willing to let them work together to establish a clearing house to permit every bank's cards to be used at stores signed up by any one of them, and in the course of the planning for the clearing house it became obvious that everybody would be opting for mass mailings of unsolicited cards to get the henhouse in action. Common sense suggested that the banks work together to establish credit verification procedures for the names to which cards would be sent, and to allocate lists of names to one bank or another. But the antitrust laws were not written with common sense in mind, and the banks' lawyers forbade such collusion. Competing for business in this new area of enterprise, then, the banks all sent cards not only to their depositors and their correspondents' depositors, but also to the mailing lists of the department stores and to people whose names appeared on lists available from mail-order services.

"The Chicago banks got greedy", says Eric Younger, marketing director for Interbank Card Association (Master Charge), which later took over the Chicagoans' Midwest Bank Card group. "Babies were getting cards when they were born; cards were being sent to dead people. Dogs got cards. People would follow the postman to the house to steal the cards from the box—you could tell they were cards because they practically printed it on the envelopes."

In the January–June period in 1967, losses from all causes in Chicago's credit-card plans ran $7.2 million, which was 5·73 percent of the total outstanding at the end of September 1967. "It was the fraud experience that was unexpected," wrote a System Task Group of the Federal Reserve System in 1968. "The dumping of millions of credit cards in a market was too much of a temptation. Security procedures were not carefully developed. Cards were placed in a postal system already heavily burdened with Christmas mail and staffed by large numbers of temporary workers. Criminal groups systematically picked up cards in multifamily housing units and apartment houses. In isolated cases, participating merchants co-operated with improper cardholders to bill large quantities of merchandise until the card appeared on the 'hot card list' and then turned in the card and split the 'hot card' reward with the improper holder."

Meanwhile, also in 1966, Bank of America had taken Bank-Americard national, franchising banks all over the country, with experiences not unlike Chicago's. Larkin, in fact, regards Washington, D.C. as marginally worse than Chicago in the level of corruption. "There are", he says mildly, "some interesting people working for the post office these days. The way we do it now is that a postal inspector and a crew come up here and seal registered mail bags, so at least we can trace it to the local postmaster."

Still, the ball kept rolling. Frightened of the growing Bank-Americard penetration of the credit card market, four large California banks joined together in 1967 to form what they called Mastercharge, and made mass mailings. The Fed Task Group claimed that the Californians had learned from the Chicago experience and had "avoided excessive losses", but something must have gone wrong at Wells Fargo, which admitted losses of $7 million on its credit card plan from July 1967 through December 1970. The worst loss from a single theft was that of Riggs National Bank in Washington, where the mob quickly ran up $2 million of bad paper through the use of a thousand stolen cards.

The Interbank system that would eventually absorb California's Mastercharge (and buy the name) was formed mostly at the initiative of Karl Hinke of Marine Midland, who put together a consortium of his own bank, Citizens & Southern in Atlanta, Bank of Virginia in Richmond, First Wisconsin in Milwaukee, Valley National in Phoenix, Seattle First and First Louisville. All these banks had their own regional shopping cards, and all saw a value in establishing a national identity that would allow customers to use their card anywhere in the country and would compete effectively against the franchised BankAmericard. The situation jelled in 1970 when Bank of America relinquished control of its extended operation to a co-operative National BankAmericard, Inc., owned jointly by the licensed users of the card; and Interbank established a single design for Master Charge cards all over the country. In 1970, also, Congress prohibited mass mailings of unsolicited credit cards, limited customers' liability to $50 on the unauthorized use of properly issued cards that had been stolen, and just to be safe wrote into law the obvious fact that a customer could not be held liable at all for the use of a card he had never received. (These "clean cards" were of course the thieves' favourite, because the thief could sign the card himself and not have to worry about forging someone's signature, which takes skill.) From the end of 1970 to the end of 1971, the total number of cardholder accounts dropped from 47·6 million to 29·3 million—but the total number of *active* accounts rose from 15·3 million to 16·8 million. By 1974, the decline in total accounts had turned around, and the number of active accounts was probably over 20 million.

The central rule of the American credit card system is that each bank is responsible for its own. A merchant may sign with both Master Charge and BankAmericard (an effort in Virginia to establish exclusive relationships was blocked by the Justice Depart-

ment); but he signs with only one bank in each system. The arrangements that bank makes with him are strictly between the two of
them. The airlines and some fashionable restaurants and stores that
a bank desperately wants to be able to offer to cardholders are
getting an almost free ride: the bank buys their paper at a discount
of only 1½ percent from face value. Local haberdasheries that wish
to be able to offer a credit service, on the other hand, may wind up
paying 5 percent or even 6 percent, if any bank will sign them on
at all. Issuing an imprinter to a merchant is a much riskier act than
issuing a card to a customer: "The merchant", says Robert Dodge,
who runs the security operation for Interbank, "has the sales notes
and a way of converting them. The average loss on a stolen card is
maybe two hundred or two hundred and twenty-five dollars; seven
or eight thousand would be pretty high on one card. But a travel
agency . . . there was one in Florida that took the T and E cards for
almost three quarters of a million dollars. It's essential for a bank
to have good people signing up merchants. They used to hire
college kids and pay them five dollars a store, and the kids would
walk in and out, not care what kind of store it was."

As of 1974, more than 1·4 million "merchants" were signed up
with one or both of the bank credit card systems. The rule of
thumb seems to be that any transaction that yields a discount better
than 75¢—a $22 transaction at the 3½ percent average discount
charged by the bank—will make money for the bank; and the
banks are still out scouring the land for merchants. In 1973 the
concentration was on hospitals, clinics, doctors, and dentists, all
of whom have collection problems and most of whom are glad to
pay a bank for taking care of accounts receivable. The most successful ad ever run by Master Charge—maybe the most successful
magazine ad of 1973—was one in *Dental Economics* showing a
handsome young man with a slightly crooked smile sitting in a
wing chair with a small pile of envelopes in his lap, and holding up
a piece of paper to be taken by his pretty wife, who leans affec-
tionately over the back of the chair, her hair brushing his cheek.
"It's only the dentist's bill", the young man is saying. "He can
wait." The ad drew responses from more than 40 percent of the

347

circulation of the magazine.

Imprinted, signed by the cardholder, made out for the amount of the bill, the "sales note" from the merchant comes into the bank that signed him up, as good as a certified cheque. The bank gives immediate credit to the merchant's account for the face amount of the note less the agreed-upon discount. In general, banks request that the slips be deposited the next business day, and require that they arrive within three days, to help speed up the process of catching illicit use of a card. When the card used is the bank's own, it keeps the entire discount; when the card-issuer was another bank, the merchant's bank (which is promptly reimbursed for its advance to the merchant through the local clearing house or the Federal Reserve clearing system) keeps 15¢ plus 1 percent of the face amount of the slip, and the rest of the discount goes to the bank that issued the card—provided, of course, that it collects from the cardholder.

The cardholding community of 30 million or so is ranged on an income continuum; about 10 percent of those with incomes below $3,000 a year hold a bank credit card, and just under 50 percent of all those with incomes over $15,000 a year. For most credit purposes, banks prefer richer to poorer, but in the credit card business the ideal customer falls somewhere in the $6,000 to $15,000 range. Over that range, he is too likely to treat his credit card as a charge account, paying each month's outstandings right on time, which means the bank gets no interest. About one-third of all cardholders take what the banks consider a free ride; about two-thirds are using their cards as entry to revolving credit schemes, which in most states run 1·5 percent a month on the outstanding balance up to $1,000, 1 percent thereafter. The proportion that stays in hock to the card system has been rising: "As people have the card longer," Younger explains, "they find themselves in a situation where for reasons of convenience or emergency they use it for a big-ticket item; and then they let the thirty days pass. . . ."

New cardholders are now solicited almost exclusively from the bank's own solid depositors, or from the active charge-account customers of stores that decide to give up their own credit service and go along with the bank. In New York and in the Washington suburbs, several banks no longer mail renewal cards to the holders; instead, they send a notice that the new card is ready and ask the cardholder to come to the bank to pick it up. For a while, banks were offering to laminate onto each card a photograph of its legitimate owner, but this tactic is dying out. "It's a problem getting people in for a new picture every year," says Interbank's Younger. "The women don't like the pictures of themselves, and during the year the men cut off their beards. Besides, the merchant doesn't look at it. Chemical Bank had cards made with pictures of Napoleon, Mussolini, Stalin—and nobody ever questioned the guys who used them."

Interbank distributes to all merchants once a week a thick booklet of numbers of dishonoured Master Charge cards, which the cashier is supposed to consult before accepting the card as payment. The real line of defence now, however, is a computerized on-line authorization service run by Interbank out of St. Louis. Each merchant has a ceiling figure—most commonly $50—above which he must get specific authorization before he can honour a card. He gets that authorization by calling a telephone clerk at his bank. The clerk pushes the credit card number on a keyboard, the message goes to the switchboard in St. Louis, and then automatically to the computer at the bank that is responsible for the card, which equally automatically says yes or no. The elapsed time for the merchant is 15 seconds after he gives the number to the clerk. The bank that issued the card is billed 15¢ for each query processed by this system that produces an authorization, 30¢ for each one that produces a refusal to authorize. Recently, a number of merchants who do a volume of credit-card business have been issued terminals that are permanently on line to the computer; the card is inserted in the terminals which almost immediately flashes a Yes or No. "For several years we were really trying to put our fingers in the holes in the dyke," says security chief Robert Dodge. "Now we've got the holes plugged up and we're moving on to education. . . ."

Whether the credit card operation has been profitable to the banks is an open question. The 1972 Functional Cost Analysis shows small losses for the average bank with less than 200 million in deposits—but the costs in the analysis include a five-year loan-loss average much inflated by the mass mailings now forbidden. Bank of America and Interbank both say that the great majority of the plans are now profitable—"making money", Bank of America's Larkin said in early 1973, "even after the cost of money and of administration. The switchover took place just in the past year—it was rather dramatic, but not unexpected." At First of Boston the picture seems less bright. "In our market," says William D. Coakley, head of the bank's consumer operations, "the hotels and motels and restaurants pay only two percent, two and a half percent. There's continual downward pressure on the discounts. I don't think we'll ever get all our money back on this—the payback will spread over a hundred years." But Edward S. Amazeen, Jr., whom Coakley identifies as "our Master Charge mastermind", is optimistic about "making small loans on the credit card chassis", and reducing processing costs to build profits.

The nice thing about Master Charge cash loans, from the bank's point of view, is that 1·5 percent monthly interest runs from the first day, while on Master Charge purchases there are no interest charges until thirty days after the bill has been sent—which may mean fifty-nine days after the money was advanced to the merchant. "Typically," writes Robert Johnston of the Federal Reserve Bank of San Francisco, "banks average only thirteen percent on card outstandings instead of eighteen percent, because of the effect of the grace period as well as the tendency for balances to be paid off to avoid charges."

Almost ten thousand banks are involved now in credit cards, most of them as intermediaries for other banks that take the risks, and the usual reasons for involvement have little to do with immediate profit-and-loss. Credit cards are seen as the key to a future "cashless" and "chequeless" society, where payments will be debited and credited electronically via a card-processing machine; and nobody wants to be left out of that. A few such machines are already in use in some department stores, on line with the bank computers to give automatic credit to the store and debit to the cardholders' credit card account (or even his chequing account, if the bank can get away with it). Similar devices are in public use as "cash machines", enabling a bank customer to draw a packet of currency from a vault upon punching appropriate numbers and inserting the credit card that goes with them. These machines are made by Docutel in Dallas and sold to banks at prices that range from $15,000 for a cash dispenser to $33,000 for a more clever machine that accepts deposits and makes loans. In many cities, they are an example of marketing gone haywire—they process fewer than a hundred transactions a month, and they don't pay their costs of maintenance except in those instances where a bank has been able to get customers to pay a fee for the right to use them (New York's Chase charges 25¢ per transaction, and Chemical gets a fee of $3 per year). Elsewhere, the machines do better: First of Chicago, for example, finds its machines much used and less expensive than a teller station.

Part of the technology of the cash machine and the on-line credit card is a magnetic strip on the back of the card, which provides the computer system with a statement of the credit available through this card: debiting the cardholder's account, the processing machine also alters the magnetic pattern on the strip. This device was standardized and approved by an American Bankers Association committee, but First National City Bank of New York thought it dangerously insecure, and staged a demonstration.

"We offered", John Reed of Citibank says reminiscently, "a five-thousand-dollar prize at Cal Tech to the student who would come up with the best way to break the magnetic encoding. The contest proved what we knew—that it can be done without great technical sophistication or elaborate equipment—fifty cents' worth will do nicely. The idea of the contest was not revealed to anyone at 399 Park Avenue [the bank's headquarters] until it was done, at which point the argument of whether we should or should not have a contest was academic. I understand students at Berkeley have been using this device on Bay Area Rapid Transit cards, imprinting them with eleven dollars or eighteen dollars, I've forgotten which."

First National City then developed its own system, which is patented and secret, but apparently involves microscopic Hollerith holes (what is punched in an IBM card is a big Hollerith hole; Hollerith was a Dutch mathematician of the nineteenth century). The holes are in an interior section of the plastic card, readable via an optical system in a terminal. At present this card is used mostly as an identification device for Citibank depositors wishing to cash a cheque in a branch not their own, but obviously the bank did not spend research money estimated at more than $10 million for the purpose of producing a cheque-cashing card. First National City is an Interbank member offering Master Charge to its depositors. It would not be too much to say that everybody at Interbank is curious about what Citibank plans to do next.

4

British experience with credit cards has tracked the American example rather closely. Barclays bought the full BankAmericard package and marketed it under the bank's own name, starting in 1966. Its rivals were surprised and a little upset about the success story, and eventually banded together (NatWest, Lloyds, Midland, Williams & Glyn's and the Royal Bank of Scotland) to form Access, which was launched in 1972. They drew their lists of prospective cardholders from their own current accounts, but the bank managers were instructed (via an educational film prepared by J. Walter Thompson) to go after certain depositors especially. "Those with a propensity to borrow money," explains Geoffrey Burdett, chief manager of Access for NatWest, a born marketing man, bright-eyed and eager to communicate, who by some freak had made his entire career, starting as a "walks boy", in the bank. "Do they have standing orders to pay finance companies or television rentals? We want the likely users, the right age groups, not just the most credit-worthy."

The British consortium went for maximum initial impact, sending millions of selected customers a card in a huge mass mailing, although one bank used a variation—a prior "negative letter" (you're going to get a card unless you do something to stop us). A price was paid. "If there is no return address on an envelope in this country and it's not deliverable," Burdett explains, "the Post Office will open it and look at who sent it and return it. Either you decide you want to trust the Post Office or you put on a return address—a postbox—and an experienced crook quickly finds out that if it's postbox so and so . . . In early 1974 we had a team of professionals following the postman about bedsitterland, Earl's Court, Chelsea, where the post is left on a table." Losses to fraud after the second full year ran at under ½ of 1 percent of the total turnover.

Unlike the Master Charge system whereby the bank that signs up the merchant gets the discount on his tickets, Access signs up all merchants in the name of the consortium; the discount, like the interest on the customer's delayed payments, goes to the bank that signed up the cardholder. Merchant discounts run from 4 percent down; the average in mid-1975 was 2·65 percent. The largest single category of use is for petrol at garages, which is not profitable for the banks: the average garage ticket runs only about £5. Access has been luckier than the American banks in signing up department stores; it has Harrod's and Selfridge's (but not Marks & Spencer or the John Lewis Partnership). At the department stores, the average ticket is pushing £15, which is profitable, even at a reduced discount.

"The only real horror stories *we've* had," Burdett says, "have been government inspired." In December 1973, the Treasury lowered the boom on consumer credit, with special attention to credit cards. People who had been told that they could pay off their credit card indebtedness at a rate of 5 percent a month had to be told that under the new rules they would have to pay back at a rate of 15 percent a month. Though it wasn't in the least the banks' fault—if anything, they felt worse about it than their customers—the man who found his budget out of order, because he had to pay three times as much as he had expected on his credit card bill, was understandably furious at his bank.

PART

IV

—

WHAT
GOVERNMENTS DO

14/Regulators and Supervisors: Policing the Banks

Chase's administration of the Treasury . . . fostered what is probably the greatest mass of redundant, otiose and conflicting legislation and the most complex structure of self-neutralizing regulatory power enjoyed by any prominent country anywhere. . . . The immediate result . . . was mischievous complication of the federal effort. Its lasting result is the stultifying bureaucratic complex of matchless redundancy with which the country is still blest.

—BRAY HAMMOND

* * *

[Bank regulation in England in accomplished by calling people in and talking to them. The Bank of England trust the board of directors to inform them immediately if the auditors uncover anything troublesome in the audits; and everybody trusts the auditors. There are no inspections, and no systematic examinations of what banks are doing. "I could open a thousand new branches," said a general manager of one of the clearing banks, "and I'm not sure the Bank of England would even know about it." Nevertheless, the court of the Bank and the government expect the people who work in the regulation office to know everything that is going on (without deliberately seeking to find out about it); and when the fringe banks blew in late 1973 James Keogh, who had been head of the Discount Office and was immensely respected and liked throughout the money market, was taken up to the mountain and sacrified to the angry gods. A young man who used to work in the treasurer's office of an American branch in London tells a pleasant story of leaving the office at 7.30 after one of the rougher days in the money market in early 1973, and finding Keogh on the street, heading for tube or train. Keogh stopped and said, "Did you get that position right?" "Yes, sir." "Good," said Keogh; "I'm glad; I'm glad." The young man remembers with pleasure: "You had the feeling he *personally* cared."

[None of this is any reflection on Rodney Galpin, who now sits at what was Keogh's desk, and was hugely, personally kind to this tourist in spring 1975—he put on his top hat and walked me around the City, like Rothschild taking the fellow to the stock exchange in the famous story, and it worked the same way.

[What is in the following pages is offered as the description of an alternative system; it has no parallel in Britain.]

357

Shortly before 8.30 in the morning of February 22, 1974, the guard at the Union Center National Bank in Union, New Jersey—occupying the bottom floor of a square three-story building in a row of storefronts on the main street of an old suburban town—came to the front door to find eight men, mostly young and in nondescript raincoats, looking through the glass in a faintly hostile manner, carrying what looked like samples case and demanding entrance. Their leader, a tall man with light brown hair and a stooping posture, flashed a card that identified him as Richard Byrne, senior national bank examiner for the Comptroller of the Currency. The guard opened the door, and the men (and one woman) trouped in, each in turn showing identification.

As employees arrived, they were asked to identify all the repositories of the bank's records, and Byrne sealed each of them closed by means of a small rectangular yellow paper sticker with red letters: "National Bank Examiner's Seal". When the time lock released the vault, Byrne stepped inside with three of his assistants, and sealed everything that opens except the customers' safe deposit boxes. He commandeered the bank's board room, toward the back of the building off a public aisle flanked by officers' desks, and deposited the sample cases, which contained the documentation from the last examination of the bank, about eight months before; these documents had been kept in a special safe, controlled by a combination changed at regular intervals, in a corner of the local post office which is permanently assigned to the Comptroller.

At Union Center, following the Comptroller's rules, each teller has control of her (or his) own cash, which is kept in a safe on wheels that is rolled into the central vault every evening and restored every morning to a place below the counter at the teller's window (where it plugs into an automatic alarm system: it is the act of removing all the money from the drawer, not any push on a button, that sets off the silent alarm during a bank robbery). As the tellers arrived for work at about 8.45 (the bank officially opens at 9), an examiner was assigned to accompany each safe to its place and take temporary possession of its contents. The women were nervous and unhappy about having a strange man go through

358

their safe, and bank examiners have learned that any effort to ease the pressure on an individual is likely to backfire. Howard Crosse tells the story of a bank examiner who, on entering the cage, "facetiously enquired, 'And how much are *you* short?' The young lady burst into tears and confessed that she had 'borrowed' ten cents for bus fare the night before." As she opened her safe for the examiner, one of the tellers said nervously to the bank's head teller, Mrs. Elfreide Oliver, "Last night it didn't prove, I had a two-cent difference." Mrs. Oliver said a little touchily, "You had your ticket in there for the two cents, right? Then it's all right."

This tension in the bank is, on the whole, desired. "The examination of a bank," says the Comptroller's *Handbook of Examination Procedures*, "is always begun without prior notice and in a manner that will preserve the element of surprise. Hotel or other accommodations should be arranged so that advance notice of the examination will be avoided. Personal mail should not be directed to banks. The examination staff should assemble near the bank as briefly and inconspicuously as possible. . . . At the beginning of an examination, it is important to obtain immediate control of cash, cash items, clearings, securities on hand, the loan portfolios, collateral to loans and other collateral, customers' safekeeping, deposit ledgers, and all other records and items. . . ." The seals applied by the senior examiner are not to be broken except by an examiner, under any circumstances. If a customer needs the collateral he has left at the bank during the first morning the examiners are there to inspect it, he will have to wait until the afternoon, at best.

In theory, all the branches of a bank are examined simultaneously—and, indeed, several of Byrne's examiners were deployed at the drive-in windows of Union Center elsewhere in this suburb while the counting of cash was proceeding in the main office. In fact, a 1,800-man staff, which is all the Comptroller's office commands nationally, cannot hope to do a complete simultaneous examination of all the tellers' safes at the 1,000+ branches of Bank of America in California. First National City has more branches than the New York regional administrator has examiners; and, of course, no shortage of cash in the safes is going to mean a thing in considering the general solvency and stability of Citibank. So the cash is not counted at the giant banks at all: the Comptroller will accept the print-out figures from the computer. The other side of this coin is that Union Center will have its bank back in a week or ten days, while Bank of America can expect to have examiners from the Comptroller's office in some part of its operation for twelve months out of every twenty-four; and the examination of First National City takes more than two months every time. And examinations are frequent: the law calls for two a year, but relents to permit the Comptroller to authorize only three in two years, if he sees on the surface no reason for concern.

Even after the first tellers' windows had been opened, junior examiners continued to run through the last of the money count in the corridor behind the windows, rifling packages of bills to enumerate with educated fingers, breaking open rolls of coins and passing them through a Brandt Automatic Cashier machine, entering totals on their own sheets to make sure the tellers' proof sheets were correct. One examiner was laboriously proceeding through the ledger of savings accounts, making a monstrously long adding-machine tape; another was beginning the labours of proving the auto loan ledger. "I'll get out of your way", one of the old tellers said nervously to a young Chinese-American examiner who was bending seriously over the piles of bills from her safe. "Uh", he said with some embarrassment, "you've got to stay here". A late-arriving teller came down the aisle behind the counter, wheeling her safe, and began the process of opening it. Mrs. Oliver hurried to her side: "You can't open anything, Esther, until you have a man there."

Byrne was in the windowless board room, methodically pulling from a top-opening file on wheels the quarto-sized cards that represented the bank's largest loans, its loans to its own directors, and the loans that had been questioned by other examiners in earlier examinations. He had his own set of similar large yellow multi-column file cards from the records of those examinations; by comparing the current with the past status of these "classified" loans, and taking a quick look at any big loans made since the last examination, he would be able to make an immediate judgment about whether anything drastic had happened to this bank during the past eight months or so. (This quick judgment can be wrong in small banks: one in south Jersey in 1972 acquired a new president with a friend in the auto business immediately after an examination, and by the time the examiners reappeared eight months later the bank had written $400,000 of bad auto loans, which ate up its entire capital; but the desperate condition of the bank did not appear on the surface until the examiners got down to the small stuff in the instalment loan division.) The fast look through the big loans is probably the least tedious aspect of a bank examination, but on occasion this, too, can get to be a little much. The Comptroller's record card has a place for the examiner to write the name of the borrower, and then the nature of the business. One of the cards in Byrne's file represented a loan to a local hospital, and where the card called for a description of the business, one of Byrne's predecessors had written, "House of ill".

Having taken a quick look at the current status of large loans and previously questioned loans, Byrne began to "pull his lines", that is, to make the list of loans outstanding at this bank for which he or one of his assistants would have to check the documentation. In general, the examiners like to look at loans that total 80 to 85 percent of the total portfolio of the bank, which is done by studying the documents for everything above a certain minimum size. The determination of a minimum size is by rule of thumb, relating to the capitalization of the bank, which is the depositors' first line of defence. An $80 million bank would probably have about $8 million in capital and reserves, and the rule of thumb would demand examination of all loans to one borrower totalling more than $\frac{1}{2}$ of 1 percent of that capital, or $40,000. In smaller banks, the floor level is a little higher as a percentage—in a $20 million bank with $2 million in gross capital, for example, a $\frac{3}{4}$ of 1 percent rule would apply, which means the examiners would look at everything over $15,000. That's a pretty fine-toothed comb.

For instalment loans and loans that are collateralized by marketable securities, there is no floor; *everything* is verified.

While Byrne worked at one end of the table in the board room, two pairs of young examiners looked in every folder in a series of file drawers taken from the vault. One read off the securities the bank was supposed to be holding as the guarantee on each "demand loan", and the other looked at the stock certificates (or mutual fund accounting statements, or E-Bonds, or bankbooks) and announced that yes, indeed, what was in the folder corresponded to the statement on the loan ledger. At computerized banks, the examiners will have a computer run of the most recent price of all the listed securities in the collateral boxes; at a bank like Union Central they are supposed to be alert for any piece of paper no longer worth what it once was. Letter stock (stock authorized by the corporate charter but not registered with the SEC, and thus unsalable) must be heavily discounted as security, and shares of the bank itself are for obvious reasons an absolute no-no.

At Union Center there are no such worries: you never saw so much AT&T stock in your life—"one eighty-four Ma Bell", calls one examiner, and his partner goes through the folder—"fifty-seven and thirty-three and fourteen and twenty-two and fifty-one and seven, it adds up all right." A gum-chewing pretty girl who works for the bank sat at the foot of the table watching all this: the examiners will not lay a finger on a customer's securities unless someone from the bank is present as an observer.

Most of the loans that interest senior examiners like Byrne are perfectly all right. The approved loan application is detailed and legal, a recent CPA's report expresses the borrower's unqualified fiscal good health, all interest payments and amortization (if any) have been made at or near the date due. Some perfectly good loans may need explanation—the most recent certified balance sheet is nine months old, for example, and the lending officer has not put any more recent data into the folder: the examiner would like to talk to him, and may criticize the loan for lack of an adequate credit file even if the lending officer can make a convincing case when queried. There are also loans that look better on paper than they will to the eye of an experienced examiner. "If it's a dress manufacturer," Gerald Lipsky of the New York regional administrator's office explains, "he needs the money for spring inventory. You come around in July and he hasn't paid it back, you question it." And other loans, even on paper, are either in or heading toward default.

The rationale of a bank examination is the need to identify and do something about these loans—or, if there are too many of them, about the bank. There is absolutely nothing in it for a banker to admit that a loan he is carrying as an asset will not be paid back: left to his own devices, he will extend the terms of the loan to avoid writing off an item that appears in black ink on his balance sheet (indeed, he is often, and grievously, tempted to extend still more money to a failing borrower who might otherwise go under with a public smash). The Comptroller requires that every bank with more than $40 million in assets employ a full-time internal auditor responsible only to the directors, who is supposed to force management to write off the bad loans; but directors, too, wish to believe that while there's life, there's hope. And a lending officer who has been spending two days a week at a customer's plant agonizing over the question of whether the bank should put the fellow out of business to salvage something from the sale of the inventory will usually assure an examiner that the borrower's troubles (if any, really) are only short-term, the solution is known and nobody is very concerned. "The banker," first vice-president Eugene Leonard of the Federal Reserve Bank of St. Louis says drily, "feels he knows the character of the borrower, and the examiner doesn't."

The central function of the senior bank examiner, then, is to "classify" the troublesome loans, using his best independent judgment. There are four categories employed by virtually all the examining agencies—"special mention", "substandard", "doubtful", and "loss". A number of factors may trigger concern—failure to meet the repayment schedule specified in the loan agreement, mounting deficits on the profit-and-loss statement or shrinkage of assets on the balance sheet, evidence that the borrower is out borrowing elsewhere, negative newspaper stories or reports of lawsuits. "The fundamental of lending," says New York administrator

Charles Van Horn, "is that when you lend that money you should know how you're going to get it back. When you deviate from that principle you get in trouble." Van Horn, a large, jowly man whose life's work has been the Comptroller's office, paused and added, "All term loans are deviations". In a talk to lending officers in Oklahoma in 1972, Van Horn referred to the cash-flow projections that often support term loans as "dream sheets".

A loan classified by the examiner as a loss must be written off completely, with money taken out of the loan-loss reserve or out of capital on the "liability" side of the ledger to balance the disappearance of the loan from the "asset" side of the ledger. On "substandard" and "doubtful" loans, the examiner may require that the bank add to its loan-loss reserve (from earnings, or from undistributed prior profits) an amount equal to 50 percent of the amount of the questioned loan. "Special mention" does not require any action on the balance sheet, but the bank will be expected to do something sensible about securing this loan before the next examination.

It should be remembered that 80 to 90 percent of classified loans do not produce a loss to the bank; and also that a bank that never makes a bad loan is not serving its community: good ideas for which a bank should be willing to supply money can find bad luck in the marketplace. As Congressman Patman said at the dedication of the Federal Deposit Insurance Corporation Building in 1963, "When we boast of no bank failures, let's remember that several thousand other business firms may have failed because the banks did not take as many reasonable risks as they might have taken." Milton Friedman and Anna Schwartz, not usually on Patman's side, write that "For credit, uniformly high quality can be obtained only by limiting the capital market to an extremely small role in the society. . . [T]he difficulties [of] the early Thirties reflected the unduly high standards of quality then imposed by lenders." But for reasons that lie deep in the history of American banking, the assumption behind bank examinations is that every bad loan endangers the interests of the depositors, and the examiners do not like to see many of them.

The rule of thumb holds that "classified" loans should not total more than 20 percent of the bank's accumulated capital and reserves. "Over twenty percent", says Kenneth Leaf, the overall boss of the Comptroller's examining staff, "it's more than normal wear and tear." If the total gets above 40 percent, the bank is considered a "problem" bank, and the Comptroller will require monthly or even bi-weekly reports on how things are going. (As of early 1974, the FDIC had 156 banks on a "problem" list, including 29 "severe problem" banks; all the "severe problem" banks were small. This argues that the Comptroller's examiners had taken an indulgent view of Franklin National. By early 1976, about 500 banks were on one problem list or another, some as big as Chase Manhattan, Wells Fargo, Republic of Dallas and First of Boston. Some of this was leaked to the newspapers and made big headlines; the banks themselves survived.) If classified loans pass 60 percent of capital, the examiners may be permanently stationed at the bank to supervise its day-to-day activities, and the regional administrator may force the directors to raise additional capital, change management, or even merge the bank into a stronger operation or sell it to a holding company.

Union Center has no troubles. A medium-sized bank with about $80 million in deposits, one of few that size in New Jersey not absorbed by a holding company, Union Center is old-fashioned in its procedures and very careful about the loans it makes. Its white-haired, squared-shouldered, forceful president, Jack McDonnell, works without salary, mostly mornings, to make sure he can take as much time as he needs in his own business. The Epicures Club. He does share in the profits, however, as the largest stockholder in the bank. McDonnell had no worries about examinations: the last time around, his bank had received an "excellent" rating, with classified loans well under 20 percent of capital. Apart from a finding that Union Center would not survive an atomic attack (Congress has mandated upon the examiners a check list of "emergency preparedness measures", up to and including readiness to operate the bank from a prearranged alternate site; nearly all banks flunk this test), the most severe criticism offered in the previous examination had been for failure to replace a deceased director on the board.

As a nationally chartered bank, Union Center is examined by only one agency: the Comptroller of the Currency. About a third of all the banks, with a little more than half of all the assets, are nationally chartered. They are automatically members of their district Federal Reserve Bank and insured by the Federal Deposit Insurance Corporation, but the Fed and the FDIC accept without investigation the reports of the Comptroller's examiners. State-chartered banks, however, usually must undergo two annual inspections, one from the state authorities, and one from either the Fed (for members; state-chartered member banks account for 9 percent of all banks, with 22 percent of all assets), or the FDIC (nearly all state-chartered banks that are not members of the Fed, more than half of all banks, with just under one-quarter of the assets). There are also a handful of banks that are not federally insured, and are inspected only by the states.

The quality of state examinations varies from place to place. New York State, with 260 examiners in the field and 65 in the office, and a salary scale that runs up to $31,000 for a supervising examiner, considers itself in every way the equal of the Comptroller's office (maybe better: chief examiner Bernard Gassman is particularly proud of his roster of real estate appraisers who look at property on which mortgages have been written to make sure the values really secure the loan). Out in the mountains, however, there are state banking commissions with less than a dozen employees. In 1968, the predecessor organization of today's Conference of State Bank Supervisors reported that thirty-five states had inadequate staffs for the examining jobs undertaken. Of course, Nevada *has* only four state-chartered banks.

All told, there are about seventy-five hundred active bank examiners in the country. Most of them are young: the *average* age in the Comptroller's office is twenty-eight. Very few have prior experience at a bank; most enter the corps of examiners right out of college, and learn on the job. Many of them wind up working for banks; Chemical Bank, for example, has a committee of former bank examiners who continuously review the bank's new loans as part of the management information service. When a banking supervisor finds it necessary to put new management into a bank to save it, an examiner often gets a chance to be a bank president, and if he pulls the bank through, he keeps the job. Sometimes—like Alan Mannetter in Walker, Iowa—a bank examiner keeps an eye out for a bank he would like to buy. As salaries improve, however, the examining staffs become more stable: the New York State turn-over has been running only 5 percent a year, and the great majority of that state's examiners have been with the department more than five years. A quiet temperament is required, because any examiner is going to get into arguments with bank managements about the classification of loans; but beneath the quiet temperament a bank examiner is usually a man who rather enjoys giving orders and making judgments. Crosse reports on a study of forty-two examinations of small banks, where the examiners "frequently" characterized the managements as "of mediocre ability but sincere in effort". Wish I could get away with that.

Banks pay the costs of their own examination. New York State specifically charges the bank for the salaries of the examiners plus their out-of-pocket expenses on the job. (This is not nothing: Gassman riffled through file cards, and found a "very, very clean" bank with $25 million in assets, which was examined in only 45 man days—and also a much less clean bank with $50 million in assets, that required 490 man days, at a cost approaching 1 percent of the bank's capital.) The Fed carries examining expenses lightly out of its earnings on the note issue; the Comptroller pays the costs of examination from the general fee assessed nationally chartered banks, which is $200 per charter, plus $50 for each branch office (which would include a "cash machine"), plus $4\frac{1}{2}$¢ for every $1,000 in assets. (That's roughtly $2.3 million for Bank of America, about $4,000 for Union Center.) If the bank has been a bad boy and requires more than the Comptroller's standard three examinations every two years, it will have to pay all the additional costs. FDIC examinations are financed out of the insurance premiums, which run $\frac{1}{12}$ of 1 percent of deposits for all insured banks, with dividends *pro rata* to total two-thirds of the FDIC's "profits" after paying its expenses and setting aside a loss reserve.

FDIC insurance covers individual and corporate deposits up to a maximum of $40,000 per account. Nobody seriously denies that federal deposit insurance, launched in 1933, has been a success. Roosevelt had strongly disapproved of it, considering it a giveaway to a mob of incompetently run rural unit banks to help them compete for deposits against more solid enterprises in the cities. Roosevelt was wrong: deposit insurance was the essential foundation if the credit money system was to become a system of demand deposits and checks on bank accounts.

Except for depositors who are also debtors of the bank (and whose loans from the bank will be offset by the FDIC against their deposits, which can be a bad show), the insurance system works fast and well. A man who is unlucky enough to have his money in a bank that fails will usually be back in business, made whole, within three or four days, and maybe sooner. The faith FDIC has stimulated is quite remarkable in our skeptical world: people today, for the first time in history, simply do not worry about the safety of their money. When the U.S. National Bank of San Diego failed in 1973, the announcement of its collapse was coupled with an announcement that the branches and deposit liabilities had been assumed by Crocker National Bank, and that all parties who used to have accounts with U.S. National now had accounts with Crocker. Traffic in the lobbies of the former U.S. National branches was just about normal the next day, but a reporter did find one man who said he had come to the bank because he'd heard it had failed. Did he want his money? Oh, no—he just wanted to see what a failed bank looked like.

Some banks do feel the premiums are high, even after dividends. Jack McDonnell of Union Central shows a sheaf of correspondence with FDIC about his complaint that the agency was allowing a less carefully run state-chartered competitor to present its condition in an illegitimately favourable light. "I pay them twenty thousand dollars a year," McDonnell fumed, "to subsidize their inefficiency."

As of early 1974, the reserve fund held by FDIC against its risks was $5,600 million. George Benston reports that over the years 1943 through 1969 the total losses to FDIC on its risks ran to $28 million ($168 million disbursed to insured depositors in insolvent banks, of which $140 million was later recovered through liquidation of the portfolio or recoveries from the directors). In the five years since then, however, the losses have risen rapidly. The arrangements made to shut down Sharpstown in Texas and Eatontown in New Jersey, to salvage Commonwealth in Detroit and organize Crocker National's absorption of U.S. National in San Diego, will cost FDIC well over $200 million among them. In summer 1974, without any public fuss, FDIC undertook open-ended laibilities to save medium-sized multi-branch banks in South and North Carolina that were sinking in a declining real estate market; and the insurance fund may have to be tapped to clear up the Franklin National Bank mess in New York. Still, these losses at worst will not approach the $529 million received in premiums in 1973 alone, when the government bond holdings of the funds earned annual interest of $311 million. FDIC is, properly, much sounder than any bank.

How much examination accomplishes is a subject of some dispute. A copy of the examiner's report goes to the board of directors of the bank, but not the whole report: the yellow sheets at the back, containing the supervising examiner's opinions, remain confidential within the agency. In theory, examiners meet with the directors personally to discuss their findings; in fact, such meetings are rare.

Surprisingly little research has been done to verify the accuracy of loan classifications. One report indicates that three-quarters of the amount and almost nine-tenths of the number of loans classified by FDIC examiners fall into that category because they are past due, which means that merely requiring banks to report all such situations to a central office would accomplish most of what is done by examining.

Examiners take the documentation behind a loan at face value; the official line is that "an examination is not an audit". Deliberate cheating, therefore—concealed loans to directors, or loans made by subterfuge to a borrower already over the bank's limit, which are the two most likely trouble spots—would not necessarily be caught in an examination. Of fifty-six banks that failed in the United States between 1959 and 1971, thirty-four had passed their most recent examination in a "no problem" category, and seventeen of the thirty-four had been given an "excellent" rating. (All but five or six of these failures, however, resulted from embezzlement or change of management between examinations.) Kenneth Leaf points out that criticisms based on such figures are necessarily unfair: "If the bank closes, people want to know where the examiners were; but nobody knows how many banks we've pulled back from the brink."

Observers are often surprised at how minimally the banks check out the backgrounds of potential employees; but in fact it isn't the newcomer who makes the trouble. "Most of the defalcations and embezzlements that I have encountered," Henry J. Rohlf of the National Association for Bank Audit and Control told a House committee, "have come from people who have been in [the bank's] employ for a long period of time . . . twenty-five, thirty, thirty-five years." Still, there are undoubtedly unnecessary risks in nearly all banks. An FBI official told the staff of the same House committee that not long ago when G-men went to a local Washington bank to arrest a swindler they found two other people working in the bank whose career paths had taken them through criminal conviction and jail. The foreign exchange trader whose "unauthorized trading" sank Franklin National bank had been fired by Continental Illinois for unauthorized trading. Howard Crosse gave as "examples of laxity . . . the person who was dismissed for cheque kiting by one bank and hired as an auditor by another, or the note teller who was fired for holding his own worthless cheques as cash items and subsequently turned up as a bank examiner." This flow can also work the other way—it was a former assistant bank examiner for the Federal Reserve System who as president of the Eatontown National Bank blew $10 million of its depositors' money on wrong choices in the stock market.

The usual justification for bank examination is that it prevents bank failures, and on that basis George Benston has queried whether it is worth the cost. Years ago the world was full of "call loans", a bank that was going under sought to save itself by calling them, retrenching its activities at the expense of all those in the community who had borrowed from it. Today, however, as Paul Horvitz writes, "The failure of the textile mill in a one-mill New England town is almost certainly a greater community disaster than the failure of the local bank in a one-bank town." The FDIC takes care of the depositors, and some other bank takes over the assets. ("You still have to worry, though," says Thomas Timlen of the New York Fed, "about the guy who runs the local sporting goods shop and has an account there of seventy-five thousand dollars.") In the modern world, it may well be that the major justification of bank examinations is not their prevention of failures but their demonstration that a failure has occurred, forcing a closing that might otherwise be delayed to a time when more harm would be done.

A bank fails, like any other business, when it can no longer pay its creditors—in this case, its depositors. Even the most soundly run bank has days when the call upon it is greater than its immediately available funds. One of the reasons for belonging to a clearing house, historically, was the willingness of the other clearing house members to supply cash to a bank briefly embarrassed by an ebb of deposits. Before the Federal Reserve Act, the Aldrich–Vreeland Act had given extra legal authority to such labours by a clearing house, permitting the issuance of a clearing house scrip that could serve as currency in times of emergency. Still, a bank in need of cash was historically expected to get back on its own feet fairly quickly. This was "asset management", the investment in highly liquid assets that could be cashed in at will.

With the move to "liability management" *all* banks over a certain size rely on their ability to borrow when their depositors demand more money than the bank has just now. This is what the Fed Funds market is all about. Small banks borrow from their correspondents; big banks sell some extra CDs, or buy Fed Funds, or borrow at the discount window of their local Federal Reserve Bank.

During the last half-dozen years, four billion-dollar banks have collapsed, though only one of them—Franklin National—was in fact allowed to "fail". The Bank of Commonwealth situation in Detroit was extremely complicated, a mess of partnerships owning corporations and holding companies, much flim-flam in dealings within the group. The basic difficulty was a misjudgment of the kind of investment a bank should make: management had plunged the bank heavily into discounted, long-term, poor-quality munici- pal bonds, and had lost money trading them. Potential corporate depositors became increasingly unwilling to put money in the bank, and as deposits ran down Commonwealth turned increasingly to the discount window at the Fed to carry its inventory of municipals. There were days in 1970 when Commonwealth's borrowings, steadily over $300 million a day, constituted three-quarters of the total borrowings of Federal Reserve member banks nationally.

The decision to force a new management on Commonwealth was made, essentially, by the Federal Reserve Bank of Chicago, which decided it was being used to keep alive a high-level con game. (What triggered this decision was the pure gall of the Commonwealth group in applying for a charter for an overseas branch.) Then the FDIC moved in, closed down one of the banks in the holding company where there was reason to believe loans had been fraudulently made to the controlling partnership; and encouraged the Chase Manhattan Bank, which held Common- wealth stock as collateral for a personal loan to its president, to foreclose the loan and take over temporary administration of the bank. To make the deal possible, FDIC set up a five-year $60 million line of credit, assuring the liquidity of the bank while the low-grade municipals were being peddled around the country; this money (about $35 million was used) must be repaid. Among the reasons to keep Commonwealth alive, Chairman Arthur Burns of the Fed reports, was the fact that Detroit is a heavily black com- munity. The city's only black bank had been closed as hopelessly insolvent; to close another one, at a time when Detroit was far from prosperous, seemed poor social policy.

The U.S. National Bank of San Diego was controlled by C. Arnholt Smith, an elderly wheeler-dealer whose other investments included an airline, a seafood company, mining enterprises, the San Diego Padres, and the political candidacies of Richard Nixon. (He was among those who watched the 1968 election returns with the next President.) As early as April 1969, a *Wall Street Journal* story claimed that Smith was abusing his position as chairman of the bank to put through loans to other companies he controlled, and to his relatives and friends. But it was not until spring 1973 that the Comptroller's examiners came to a similar conclusion, and by then the "classified" loans at U.S. National of San Diego totalled not 40 percent or 60 percent but *337 percent* of the capitalization of the bank. The FDIC was alerted, and insisted on Smith's removal, but he refused to budge, revealing a weakness in the regulatory structure: the FDIC's only weapon in such situations is the withdrawal of insurance from the bank, which would create a run on it by depositors, forcing liquidation on terms that would be much more costly to the insurance fund. Fortunately, the Comptroller does have "cease-and-desist" powers, and finally— with Smith's conglomerate under attack by the SEC—the Comptroller issued such an order and tossed Smith out.

Nevertheless, the bank remained afloat, despite considerable publicity to Smith's troubles, which presently included the freezing of his personal assets in a "jeopardy assessment" by the Internal Revenue Service. "During the first month to six weeks after our cease-and-desist order," Comptroller James Smith recalls, "about one hundred million dollars in CDs drained off, but that was all. There was the IRS jeopardy assessment, all the newspaper stories that other banks were seeking to purchase, and there was never an adverse effect. Either there was total public confidence or total public apathy. And Fed Funds were sold to that bank till the day it closed, never less than fifteen million and up to forty million, by very substantial Midwest and eastern banks. Had we been unable to achieve a purchase, and gone to an FDIC pay-out, those guys would have been general creditors. . . ." And wiped out.

Teams of examiners worked feverishly every day and every night for two months at U.S. National of San Diego, fearing each night that the next morning the public would panic about its money in this bank and come flocking to withdraw it before the FDIC knew what was there. Finally the Comptroller and the FDIC felt they had a grip on the situation. It was agreed that the bank could not be saved as an independent operation: Smith's Westgate-California conglomerate was never going to be able to pay back its gigantic borrowings. But closing it would involve considerable costs and nuisance—and everybody still thought there was a danger of panic that might affect other West Coast banks. Comptroller James Smith and FDIC chairman Frank Wille decided to treat this failing billion-dollar bank as they might treat a million-dollar bank in some overbanked suburb: by selling it off to a solvent institution that could use a branch.

FDIC substituted its own note for an estimated $160 million in questionable loans, and offered the bank, cleansed of Smith's borrowings, for sale to the highest bidder. Crocker National, which needed San Diego branches, paid $89.5 million for what was left, with the understanding that FDIC was still around to pick up any other loans to Smith interests that might turn bad, and U.S. National depositors suddenly found themselves Crocker National depositors. FDIC is not out of the woods on this one, partly because European and American banks have sued to make the agency honour letters of credit the bank had issued to back Smith's borrowing from them. On the other hand, some of the $160 million paid for the Westgate loans will come back, and FDIC has Crocker's $89.5 million as an offset. As of spring 1974, Wille's "educated guess" on what the U.S. National failure would cost FDIC was $48.3 million. By mid-1975 the guessing figure was over $100 million—every time Crocker turned over a stone the auditor found a Smith loan hiding under it, and the FDIC had to keep buying back bad paper. In early 1976, the guess was near $250 million.

Most observers believe that this loss can be blamed on the failure of the Comptroller's examiners to look more carefully at

374

who really owned all those corporations that were borrowing from U.S. National; others feel that no examination catches outright fraud. On the other hand, if the examiners hadn't finally blown the whistle in spring 1973 there's no telling how great the losses at U.S. National might have been, because neither its depositors nor the banks with money to sell in the Fed Funds market—nor, as we shall see, the giant Euromarket banks in England and France—were in the least troubled about putting their money in this disastrously mismanaged bank.

The San Diego case is disturbing not only because of the size of the bank and the suspicion that political factors delayed action on its unsoundness, but also because the disease may be spreading. "Until recently," says Richard Byrne, shaking his head, "directors' loans *were* 'the best in the bank', as they're supposed to be. Now I have to write up a lot of them." Though the calm reaction to the failure of the San Diego bank argues that times may have changed, the authorities can still make a good case for the secrecy of examiner's reports. Public criticism of a bank does risk a run on it and consequent economic disruption of the community it serves. But the discovery of unsound loans to directors surely ought not to be a matter strictly between the chartering authorities and the board which approved the loans: there is a public interest here. This is the case for bank examinations in England too: the Bank of England cannot really rely on its friends to supply enough information about the true condition of a bank if the friends are lending the bank's money to themselves.

2

"The thing that dawned on me when I came to this job," says Cameron Macrae, the thirty-one-year-old counsel to the New York State Superintendent of Banks, "is that ninety percent of the questions that come here are legal questions. Banks are *totally* regulated."

Most corporations have charters that permit them to do virtually anything that is not specifically prohibited; American banks have charters that prohibit them from doing virtually anything that is not specifically permitted. But the definition of laws and the construction of charters are ever-renewing, and as a practical matter an administrator may have quite a lot of leeway in his interpretations. Which brings us to James Saxon, lawyer, politician, former officer of the First National Bank of Chicago, whom President Kennedy appointed Comptroller of the Currency in 1961. "For years and years," Walter Wriston says, "the Fed was dominated by [Governor James L.] Robertson, who said you couldn't do anything, and the Comptroller went along. The business was stagnating. Then along came Jimmy Saxon, who was some piece of machinery blowing through Washington. He was a change agent—wasn't afraid to make a mistake—wrote a new regulation every morning, all anathema to bureaucrats."

The Federal Reserve Bank of Chicago published in 1970 a summary history of the previous decade, under the title *Midwest Banking in the Sixties*, and included as Appendix A a digest of "Changes in the Legal Environment." Dead-pan, the list includes the following sequences:

1963, September
Comptroller published ruling that federal funds sold are not subject to the lending limit on loans to one customer by a national bank.

1963, September
[Federal Reserve] Board published opinion that sales of federal funds are loans with respect to statutory provisions administered by the Board.

* * *

1963, September 12
Comptroller amended 12 CFR, Investment Securities, to define a general obligation of any state . . . as including "an obligation payable from a special fund . . ."

1963, November 27
Board issued opinion that the only securities that are exempt

from the limitations and restrictions on investment securities are those specified in the statute, the Comptroller is not authorized to expand this category, and it would be unlawful for member state bank to, etc. . . .

* * *

1963, December 24
Comptroller ruled that proceeds of capital notes and debentures may be included in aggregate unimpaired capital funds in determining the limit on loans by a national bank to one borrower.

1964, January
Board published opinion that capital notes and debentures cannot be regarded as capital . . . with respect to statutory provisions of the Federal Reserve Act.

* * *

1964, June
Comptroller published ruling that permitted a national bank to include undivided profits which are earned surplus . . . in computing the lending limit on loans to one borrower.

1964, June
Board published opinion that undivided profits cannot be included in surplus fund with respect to statutory provisions administered by the Board.
* * *

1964, July 2
Comptroller ruled that a national bank may acquire and hold direct stock investment in a foreign bank.

1964, August
Board published opinion that a national or state member bank, under current law, may not acquire and hold direct stock investment in a foreign bank.

Carter Golembe, who now runs a research service for banks, was getting a Ph.D. and a law degree and working for the American

Bankers Association while all this was going on, and had a grand-stand seat. Sometimes he still finds it hard to believe what he saw. "Saxon was an optimist," Golembe says; "he wanted to make things happen. He looked at the '33 Act, and he said, 'There are things you can do'." Golembe shook his head. "Lease personal property! Whoever thought a bank could do that? Multer of New York introduced a bill in Congress to forbid it, and the Fed testified in support."

Saxon made it possible for Citibank to issue negotiable CDs, redefined Fed Funds transactions as purchases and sales rather than loans, okayed the idea of "loan production offices" in states other than the state where the bank was chartered, approved a Citibank proposal to underwrite, manage, and sell a mutual fund, permitted banks to open and operate computer service centres, authorized the operation of messenger services, travel agencies, and insurance agencies by banks, permitted the purchase of finance companies by banks, and authorized "equity kickers" ("a share in the profit, income, or earnings from a business enterprise of a borrower in addition to or in lieu of interest").

Some of this stood up under challenge in court or Congress, some did not. What Saxon thought he was doing is impossible to find out: he is still around, practising law in a small way as a solo practitioner in Washington, but he won't talk to people who are writing books. Congressman Patman feels strongly about Saxon: "He was just no good a-tall, a trickster". General opinion, even in the community of bankers who are most grateful to Saxon for his extraordinary collection of rulings, holds that he was a light-weight; Golembe wrote in the University of Virginia Law Review, "One also suspects that in a few cases he was motivated by an impish desire to shake other regulatory agencies out of their accus-tomed routines."

Saxon was as liberal in chartering banks as he was in freeing them from restrictions: in the ten years 1951–61, only 227 new national banks had been chartered; in Saxon's first three and a half years he chartered 434. Some of them turned out very badly. The Brighton National Bank of Brighton, Colorado, for example, became a conduit for gangsters who siphoned off a million dollars in one year. The case was particularly distasteful because one of the men involved in getting the bank open was former Colorado Governor Stephen L. B. McNichols, who had been Saxon's roommate at college; and for a full month after the FDIC had informed him that the bank was insolvent and corrupt Saxon refused to order it closed. When the FDIC forced the closing of a San Francisco bank he had chartered (to people who presently were in the dock on criminal charges), Saxon was so furious he refused to attend future meetings of the FDIC board, on which the Comptroller is one of only three directors.

Unless a court says No, a national bank can do whatever the Comptroller says it can do: the Fed controls the activities of state-chartered member banks, but not national banks. One of the results of Saxon's initiatives was a draining away of state banks to national charters. The first to go was Mercantile of St. Louis, which had a branch across the river in Illinois that the Fed demanded it abandon—but Saxon, once the national charter was in effect, approved. Wachovia in North Carolina followed, and Wells Fargo, and finally Chase Manhattan. Wriston tells the story: "There was a meeting of the International Monetary Conference in Puerto Rico. They had Kay Randall of the FDIC, and from the Fed Robertson or Mitchell or some other guy who didn't know what was going on. Saxon had said you could do something—sell mutual funds or something—and the Fed had ruled you couldn't. Citibank was going flat out, and Chase was being held back. Robertson said that so long as he was at the Fed it would never be permitted. David [Rockefeller] went down to Washington right after the meeting was over and applied for a national charter—after saying he thought Saxon was crazy. I would have liked to sell tickets to that meeting. . . ."

3

Then, in 1968, Citibank overreached itself, and Congressional reaction to the results of its aggressiveness made what may be permanent changes in the regulatory structure of American banking. The incident that triggered Citibank's inventiveness occurred in 1965, when CIT Financial Corporation bought Meadowbrook National Bank on Long Island (today—CIT does not do things by halves—known as National Bank of North America, with more than $2,000 million in footings). Morris Schapiro, who handled the purchase, remembers that when the officers of First National City heard about it "they pranced about like wild men—if a finance company can buy a bank, why can't a bank buy a finance company?" But not even James Saxon could authorize the purchase of a non-banking business by a bank.

There could be a higher corporate body, however—a holding company—that could own both a bank and a finance company. In 1956, Congress had moved to restrict bank holding companies, like banks, to their own proper banking business, and had turned over the interpretation and enforcement of the restriction to the Federal Reserve Board. In committee discussions on the Bank Holding Company Act, country spokesmen had pointed out that a holding company form of organization was often highly convenient for the small-town banker: it gave him a stock issue less restricted than bank stock for purposes of pledging, and permitted him to put real estate and insurance operations that might be necessary for the financial stability of a really small bank into the same accounting pot. Forbidding a small-town banker to put his bank and his agency operations in the same corporate shell means encouraging him to do these non-banking things on his own, which would weaken the bank and partially conceal what should be an openly expressed conflict of interest. At the end of the debate, Congress exempted the "one-bank holding company" from the provisions of the Act.

Now some genius at First National City found the loophole: a one-bank holding company could own a finance company, and First National City, though the second largest bank in the country, with scores of branches around town, was just one bank. In addition to the long-range conglomerating possibilities of a holding company, there were a few interesting instant advantages: a holding company could sell commercial paper to help the bank get around interest-rate controls and reserve requirements on deposits; and spinning off the bank's traveller's cheque operation to a separate subsidiary of a holding-company structure would free the bank from the need to hold reserves against its traveller's cheque receipts. Union Bank in Los Angeles and Wachovia in Winston-Salem had already reorganized themselves as holding companies, but on the national scene they didn't count. When First National City Bank became First National City Corporation in fall 1968, the announcement was a thunderclap.

Before Citibank's reorganization, there had been 680 one-bank holding companies in the country, with total assets of $18,000 million; less than six months later, there were 783 one-bank holding companies with $108,200 million. By December 1970 there were 1,318 of them, holding a third of the nation's bank deposits.

As the law stood before 1971, there were literally no restrictions on the kinds of business a one-bank holding company could enter, and in fact a survey by the Federal Reserve System showed such holding companies engaged in every one of the 99 two-digit descriptors in the Standard Industrial Classification of the Office of Management and Budget. Thirty-three were into electrical machinery, 29 in machinery other than electrical; 21 in food products, 22 in crude petroleum and natural gas; 478 in real estate. (Some of these, of course, were industrial corporations that also owned a bank, not banks that had acquired other businesses; until summer 1974 Dow Chemical had its own in-house Swiss bank.)

One of the last acts of the Ninety-first Congress was to pass amendments to the Bank Holding Company Act that subjected one-bank holding companies to the same rules that governed the multi-bank companies, and placed all of them under the tutelage of the Federal Reserve Board. "The principal objective of the 1970 amendments," says an unsigned article in the December 1972 *Federal Reserve Bulletin*, "was to maintain the separation between banking and commerce, by defining, in general terms, the kinds of non-banking activities that bank holding companies might enter." But the "general terms" of the amendments gave the Fed in fact considerable freedom to draw its own line between banking and commerce. An activity would be considered appropriate, the law said, if it is "so closely related to banking or managing or controlling banks as to be a proper incident thereto"—and also if it could "reasonably be expected to produce benefits to the public ... that outweigh possible adverse effects."

In 1974, holding companies (one-bank or multi-bank, it now makes no never-mind) controlled banks with nearly 70 percent of all the deposits in the banking system. To acquire an additional bank, a holding company must get approval from the Comptroller if it's a new national bank and the state authorities if it's a state bank, from the Fed—and from the Justice Department, which "advises" the other federal agencies and can bring an antitrust suit to enjoin the acquisition if its advice is not taken. To acquire a business that is not a bank, the holding company must win all the same approvals, plus some sort of *nihil obstat* from the Federal Trade Commission.

But the Federal Reserve Board is the agency charged by the Congress with administering the Act, and as a normal matter it is the Fed's consent that counts. Most of the time at the meetings of the Board of Governors is now taken up with merger applications: "We're like a public utility commission now", says Governor George Mitchell.

The legal authority of the holding company to undertake this new activity is only part of the question the Fed considers; even in fields where other banks have been permitted to move, the Board may deny an application from a holding company for any one of a number of reasons. Bank of America was initially denied the right to buy GAC Finance, a string of small loan offices, on the ground that if it did not acquire existing offices it might open similar offices of its own, promoting competition; this ruling was later rescinded when GAC demonstrated that its own condition was so unsound that in the absence of a bank takeover it would likely have to close the offices. Chemical Bank was definitively denied the right to purchase a company established to supply nuclear fuels to power installations, not because the activity is unrelated to banking (it is, in fact, essentially a financial activity) but because the Fed regarded Chemical's capital position as insufficient for the conduct of its existing businesses, let alone the acquisition of new ones. Chase Manhattan was denied the right to acquire a chain of finance companies on what were announced as antitrust grounds. The cut was particularly unkind because Citicorp less than two years before had been approved on a similar (but smaller) deal. Willard Butcher let himself go enough to say publicly that he was "appalled" by the decision.

That banks should not own other kinds of businesses is among the more obvious organizing principles in an economy. A bank, after all, creates money; people who have to get their money by their own exertions ought not to be put in competition against people who can create it. All businesses borrow from banks for some of their working capital needs, and an independent company in competition with a bank subsidiary is necessarily at a disadvantage. (The rules strongly discourage though they don't forbid a holding-company subsidiary to borrow from its sister bank, but the "halo effect" of the bank's name is such that a major holding company can without question borrow from another bank, at the best rates. Citicorp's sale of $650 million in variable rate notes—which are not obligations of the bank—argues that the halo effect permits easy borrowing from the public too.) Moreover, the money depositors leave at a bank is supposed to be loaned—safely—not ventured.

On the other hand, there are public benefits available from cutting out the middleman in financial transactions: a bank makes personal loans more inexpensively than a finance company that gets its funds by borrowing them from a bank. There is no reason why a credit life insurance policy, guaranteeing the repayment of a personal loan or auto loan or mortgage if the borrower dies, cannot be written by a bank as well as by an insurance company. Both banks and mortgage companies write mortgages; if a banks wants to write some of its mortgages through a wholly owned mortgage company subsidiary, the government has every reason to say, Be my guest. Leasing—though here one's hands begin to sweat a little with contemplation of the tax consequences—is after all just another form of lending. Setting up subsidiaries to compete with management consulting firms, courier services, property managers, travel agencies, and data-processing companies would look more dubious, but all this stuff is small potatoes anyway, as a matter of public concern.

And it should be noted that as "bank groups" the British clearing banks are involved as proprietors or partners in all these activities—plus (through merchant banking subsidiaries) a great deal of work in Stock Exchange matters.

The real fight between the Fed and the American banks in the 1970s has been on the issue of capital adequacy. The idea of the holding company is that the bank can use the same pool of capital to support a large number of different activities, to increase the "leverage" of a given stock issue, and thus the per-share earnings. "It's assumed", says Tom O'Connell, the Fed's lean and witty general counsel—very young-looking for a man who has been with the Fed since 1953 and was an assistant U.S. Attorney before he came—"that we can start off with a kettle and a spoon and eat ourselves silly without anybody ever paying for it."

Since the holding company became commonplace in American banking, experts have been worrying about the degree to which a bank could be endangered by the financial troubles of sister companies in a common ownership. In theory, a Real Estate Investment Trust established and advised by the same holding company that owns a bank is an independent entity, and could go broke without busting anybody except its own stockholders and creditors. Most observers have argued, however, that the bank for its own reputation would have to protect the sister company's creditors as though they were its own. "The fact is," Samuel B. Chase, Jr., then the Fed's Associate Director of Research, told a meeting in 1972, "that bank holding companies would rarely choose to 'walk away' from failing subsidiaries. Rather, at least within the limits of the law, they would use all of the resources of their organizations to meet claims against any part of it."

Chase cited as examples the assumption of responsibility by

American Express in the salad oil swindle that directly involved only a lightly capitalized warehousing subsidiary, and the decision by United California Bank to pay the debts of its Swiss subsidiary after "Adam Smith's" friend Paul Erdman, a novelist trying to run a bank, let his trading desk lose nearly $40 million in cocoa futures. But some people did in fact get hurt in both of those incidents as "Adam Smith" himself has not ceased to point out— and there is another element, which Chase forgot: the bank must take orders from a regulatory agency that couldn't care less about what happens to the holding company.

Late in 1973, Beverly Hills Bancorp, a holding company with a bank and not much else, was struck by the default of a real estate developer on a very large loan made through the holding company rather than the bank because it was way above the legal lending limits of the bank. For once (intelligence levels are high in Beverly Hills), the public got concerned about what was in the newspapers, and deposits began leaking out of the bank. The Comptroller promptly stepped in and arranged the sale of the bank to Wells Fargo, leaving the holding company alone in the woods with the purchasers of its commercial paper, whose money had been loaned to the real estate developer; and presently the holding company was in bankruptcy court while the bank flourished under new management. On the other hand, First Wisconsin Corporation in mid-1974 did agree to assume some $10 million of losses in First Wisconsin Mortgage Trust, virtually wiping out that year's profits for the Milwaukee-based holding company, though the First Wisconsin National Bank (which put up the money) had no legal obligation to bear this load.

Capital adequacy in holding companies is only an extension of a long-standing and growing worry about capital adequacy in banks themselves. Despite James Saxon's remarkable decision permitting banks to include their long-term borrowings (bonds or subordinated notes) as part of their capitalization, the ratio of capital to deposits and especially capital to loans has shrunk dramatically during the last decade. This tourist while in Iowa wandered into a nationally chartered bank that had better remain nameless, where I noted $60 million in deposits and then added up capital, surplus, undistributed profit and loss reserve to a total that did not quite reach $2 million—about 3 percent. "Aren't you", I said to its president, "concerned?"

"Nah", he said. "We've got good loans".

I said, "Isn't the Comptroller concerned?"

He said, "Well, now that you mention it, one of his people was around last week and suggested that we sell some subordinated debentures to beef up the capital ratio. I told him, 'I wouldn't lend money to anybody with a balance sheet like mine, and I don't see how I can borrow money'."

But the regulatory authorities have not had much in the line of tools to force banks to increase their capital. Lucille Mayne reported in 1972 that 30 percent of a sample of Federal Reserve member banks in the Cleveland district had recently been asked by one agency or another to increase their capital; 43·2 percent did as they were told, 27·2 percent did some of what they were told, and 29·6 percent did nothing. "Capital prescriptions . . . have only a limited effect on bank capital positions because of the level of banker resistance to supervisory pressure for more capital."

Now, suddenly, because of its authority under the Bank Holding Company Acts, the Fed has a lever by which it can force banks to increase their capitalization—or, indeed, to do pretty much anything the Fed would like them to do. There are plenty of reasons why the Fed can disapprove a holding-company acquisition, and the real one can be informally communicated without publication. "The Bank Holding Company Amendments of 1970 are not getting the attention they deserve," Governor Andrew Brimmer said in 1973. "Congress told the Federal Reserve Board, 'We've done the best we can—now you make the decisions.' And we are, frequently by split votes, remaking the banking system of this country."

"There's been talk over the years," says Donald Rogers of the Association of Bank Holding Companies, "about the need for a single Federal Banking Commission. Well, under the Holding Company Act we're getting one—by chance."

15/The Federal Reserve: Trying to Police the Economy

The pressures were too great. We were being forced to put large amounts of reserve funds into the market every day in support of the longest-term Government bonds at premium prices, a policy which we considered to be profoundly wrong. Inflationary pressures were again strong. We said, therefore, that unless there was someone at the Treasury who could work out a prompt and definite agreement with us as to a mutually satisfactory course of action, we would have to take unilateral action.

—ALLAN SPROUL (1952)

* * *

A President can hold down interest rates. When Harry Truman heard the Fed was going to let rates rise, he hit the ceiling and called 'em all into the White House. He said, "You're not going to make people pay for the war two and three times over. . . ." During one of the breaks, a newspaperman asked someone from the Fed what was going on, and the man from the Fed said, "He's calling us names". They went out and in thirty minutes they rescinded their order.

—WRIGHT PATMAN (1974)

* * *

"Constitutionally," Congressman Patman wrote in 1964 in the book that celebrated his long-delayed accession to the chairmanship of the House Banking and Currency Committee (he lost the post in a revolt within the Committee in 1975), "the Federal Reserve is a pretty queer duck". It would be a queer duck even without any Constitution, for a more awkward and complicated mixture of private and public, executive and legislative, national and regional, could not possibly be imagined.

The operating entities are the twelve Reserve Banks, each with its own board of directors and roster of executives. Member banks are stockholders in Reserve Banks, each having purchased stock to a value of 3 percent of its capital. There is no market for this stock, which can be sold only to the Reserve Bank itself; it pays a dividend of 6 percent, which was regarded as a terrible give-away to the banks back in the days of low interest but is now considered quite fair by the people who used to attack it. Each Reserve Bank has nine directors, six of them elected by the stockholders; of these six, three may be and three may not be bankers. The remaining three directors, who cannot be bankers and may not own stock in banks, are appointed by the Board of Governors of the Federal Reserve System, and one of these three must be chairman of the Bank board and the "Federal Reserve Agent", in whose name the Bank arranges the details of its note issue. The directors serve staggered three-year terms, and there is one new director in each class each year. They are repaid their expenses in getting to and from meetings, which occur every month, plus a fee per meeting that may not exceed $100 a day.

Andrew Brimmer while one of the Governors published a study of the directors of the Reserve Banks, indicating that the over-whelming majority of them are late-middle age white Protestant males, presidents or chairmen of banks or industrial corporations. In 1970 the first black was appointed to a director's post at a Reserve Bank; there are still no women (though in 1972 one woman, two blacks and two Japanese-Americans were serving as directors of branches of Reserve Banks). There is a scattering of academics in the public category; among those whose terms ended in 1973, for example, were John R. Coleman (Philadelphia), the president of Haverford College, who wrote a book about doing manual labour for a summer; O. Meredith Wilson (San Francisco), head of the Centre for Advanced Study in the Behavioural Sciences at Stanford; and Alan Pifer (New York), the ultrafashionable president of the Carnegie Corporation. More than a fifth of the directors in 1972 did not have college degrees. The officers of the banks are sometimes more surprising. At the New York Fed, Thomas Timlen, vice-president in charge of the discount window, is a lawyer who never had any substantial contact with the nuts and bolts of banking until he undertook this job; and Thomas O. Waage, senior vice-president generally in charge of operations (cheque clearing and the like) was a college English instructor and a newspaperman before signing on at the Bank as public relations director in the early 1950s. And Richard Debs, the new first vice-president, is a lawyer with an additional degree from Cairo University, who speaks fluent Arabic. In St. Louis, the present proprietor of the discount window is Ruth A. Bryant, who started in the Memphis branch as a secretary, went to night school and worked her way up; her predecessor Gerald T. Dunne was a lawyer (he is now a law professor) and historian, author of outstanding biographies of Justices Story and Black.

There is a camaraderie about the Fed, a sense of a secret society working together in the bowels of the economy, keeping confidences with a tenacity quite extraordinary in America, manipulating mysteries the outside world (which includes bankers and monetary economists) does not begin to understand. Among the few Governors who have taken public positions contrary to those of the System was Sherman Maisel, a Johnson appointee politically a little (a very little) to the left of his colleagues. The revenge taken upon him was a (false) rumour, universally believed at all the Banks, that Johnson had *really* intended to appoint him to the Federal Home Loan Bank Board, but being bemused by Vietnam made an understandable mistake. Shortly before he left the St. Louis Fed (because he wanted to teach), Gerald Dunne said, "There are twenty-five or twenty-six thousand people in this outfit, nationwide, but it has resisted the pathology of bigness. I really know most of my colleagues, their weaknesses and strengths, and I think they know mine." Increasingly, the jobs are going to economists trained at the Fed.

The duties of the board of directors of a Reserve Bank are blandly described in law as those "usually appertaining to the office of directors of banking associations." In theory, the directors approve all loans, discounts, and investments. They appoint the president and first vice-president of the Bank, subject to approval of the Board of Governors, and all other officers on their own motion. By law—an extraordinary privilege in American industry or government—they may "dismiss at pleasure" any of their officers or employees. Their budget is subject to approval by the Board of Governors, but as a rule they set the salaries of their employees, except for the two at top. At $100,000, the president of the Federal Reserve Bank of New York is tied with the Vice-President of the United States for second place in the salary sweepstakes among public employees—if indeed he *is* a public employee. The presidents of the Philadelphia and Minneapolis Banks get half as much, the others are scattered in between.

In mid-1974, the twelve Federal Reserve Banks had among them assets of about $95,000 million, exclusive of cash items in process of collection. Most of this represents the result of what are in effect swaps between the Treasury and the Banks, with the Banks issuing to their member banks currency in the form of Federal Reserve Notes and purchasing government bonds with the payments received from the recipients. Ten percent or so is gold, at the official price of $42.22 an ounce, also committed to backing the note issue.

Nearly all the work of the System is done by the individual Banks, which were designed to be its really significant components. A single monetary and banking policy for all the United States is and always was utter nonsense, though most people think we have it and many others think we should. All sectors of the economy and all regions of the country are not equally healthy or unhealthy at the same time. Even in 1972, which taken altogether was the closest thing to total prosperity the United States has ever known, Massachusetts was in serious economic trouble (this is why McGovern carried the state), Seattle was by no means wholly recovered from the blows suffered by Boeing in 1970–71, and in general the metropolitan areas dominated by large older cities were functioning less well than the countryside or the metropolitan areas dominated by smaller or newer cities.

The worst aspect of the previous national banking system, in the view of the authors of the Federal Reserve Act, had been its tendency to draw the ready money of the country off to New York and Chicago, where the short-term markets were. Now each region would have its own Reserve Bank that could supply credit to the local banks to support the needs of trade. There was no need for the discount rate to be the same all over the country; each Reserve Bank would decide for itself what it should charge its members when it supplied them with money by discounting their trade-related paper, and one of the functions of its board of directors would be setting the discount rate and the terms under which the Reserve Bank would lend. Into the 1950s, it was still considered reasonable and proper for different Reserve Banks to charge different rates at the discount window (though not for long). The control over any attempt at regional aggrandizement was not unlike the balance-of-payments discipline historically imposed on nations: no Reserve Bank could accept a note of another, except at a punitive discount of 10 percent; thus a Bank that expanded its note issue too fast would lose reserves to other banks to pay off the escaping notes, and would soon be forced to pull in its horns. This arrangement survived until 1954.

The home offices of the district Reserve Banks were built before the home office of the Board of Governors in Washington; and pompous classical or Renaissance structures they are, from the days when banks were supposed to be solid and look solid, and Reserve Banks necessarily the most solid of all. (However, a new building in Minneapolis, hung like a suspension bridge between two pairs of towers, is among the glories of recent American architecture.) The presidents and in some cases the first vice-presidents of the Reserve Banks are paid more than the Governors of the nationwide System. Each Bank commissions its own economic and statistical studies, maintains its own (often very distinguished) research staff, and publishes its own reports. Some of these are educational, and in great demand: Chicago has distributed a million copies of its *Modern Money Mechanics*. Others are highly technical: those of the Federal Reserve Bank of St. Louis, built on that bank's own computerized model of the functioning of the economy, are the bedrock of Friedmanite monetarism in America.

Federal Reserve examiners work for the individual Banks, not for the Board of Governors, and their power to inquire into the activities of the members is essentially limitless: the Act *requires* each Bank "to keep itself informed of the general character of the loans and investments of its member banks with a view to ascertaining whether undue use is being made of bank credit for the speculative carrying of or trading in securities, real estate, or commodities, or for any other purpose inconsistent with the maintenance of sound credit conditions." It is by no means certain that the Comptroller's examination reports on national banks (which the Comptroller *sells* to Reserve Banks at $100 per report, apparently on the grounds that the Fed has lots of money) meet the demands of the Act, or that the Fed's own examiners go as deeply into questions of bank policy as the law allows.

Both individually and jointly, the Federal Reserve Banks were to perform the functions laid down by Bagehot as those of the central bank, an institution the United States had not known since Andrew Jackson shot down the Second Bank of the United States in the 1830s. By their extension of credit through the discount window, they would both regulate the money supply to match the needs of trade and serve as a lender of last resort when financial panic endangered the functions of the banking system. Further assurance that the Reserve Banks would be able to stop panics was given by a provision in the Act that made their notes legal tender, and thus like the Civil War greenbacks William Jennings Bryan had been extolling up and down the country for a generation; Bryan's support was indispensable for the passage of the Act.

What, then, was to be the role of the Federal Reserve Board, vaguely charged with "general supervision" of the work of the Reserve Banks? This body was to consist of the Secretary of the Treasury, the Comptroller of the Currency, and five others appointed by the President with the advice and consent of the Senate. Each of the five appointed members had to come from a different Reserve Bank district (in the mid-1920s a sixth appointed member was added, specifically to represent the farmers); none of them could have any affiliation with a bank. The Board would pay its own bills by assessment on the Reserve Banks, and would thus be substantially independent of both the Treasury and the Congress. (Other regulatory agencies are also in effect self-supporting through the fees they charge those they regulate, but in every other case the money they collect is paid into the Treasury and they must win a Congressional appropriation to pay their bills.) Until 1936, the books of the Board, like the books of all other government agencies, were audited by the General Accounting Office, which is a branch of the Congress (neither Congress nor the executive has ever had the power to audit the books of the district Banks). Since then, however, the Federal Reserve System has been allowed to hire its own auditors and merely report the results to the Speaker of the House. Congressman Patman has been trying to get the GAO back into the Fed for years, without success.

Once the Reserve Banks were functioning—Treasury Secretary William G. McAdoo got them started less than eleven months after the Act was signed—the Board seemed to have little to do. Wilson's appointees were distinguished; "the men appointed to the Board by President Harding after 1920," Lester Chandler wrote, "were at times capable of obstructing action by others but never of constructive thinking and action". Effective power in the System seemed to reside in the Federal Reserve Bank of New York. When the paralysis of international trade in World War I threatened a financial catastrophe in the United States—because the European lenders who had financed American agricultural production were no longer making such loans and the commercial paper the law demanded as backing for Federal Reserve notes had dried up—Benjamin Strong of the New York Fed single-handedly found and exploited a loophole in the law which permitted his Bank to expand the note issue. (The law authorized the Federal Agent to issue notes to the Bank on receipt of commercial paper, and also authorized the Bank to reduce its liabilities to the Agent by depositing gold. The Bank had lots of gold, but not much prime paper. In one brief period in early 1915, Strong got out $3.4 million of needed currency by pledging the same $100,000 of commercial paper thirty-four times, redeeming it each time immediately with gold, sending it back to the Agent, redeeming it, sending it back, etc.) In his transatlantic correspondence with Montagu Norman during the 1920s, Strong very clearly viewed himself as holding a position functionally equivalent to that of the Governor of the Bank of England, though legally he was merely the chief executive officer of one of twelve Banks supervised by a national board.

Once America entered the First War, the Federal Reserve System was of course committed to helping the government raise the immense sums necessary to carry forward the military effort. At the war's end, the still immature Banks had to make their first major economic decisions. The federal budget moved from a deficit of $13,400 million in fiscal 1919 to a surplus of $300 million in fiscal 1920, with inevitable resulting tightness in the money supply. The Banks followed Bagehot's half-century-old recommendations, making credit available at the discount window to all hardpressed member banks, but charging for it at a punitive rate. The sharpest and shortest depression in American history resulted in 1921, with the wholesale price level dropping 40 percent in nine months and unemployment rising to 12 percent. But within a year the corner was turned, and the road was straight ahead through the 1920s for what was, until the 1960s, the longest sustained prosperity America had ever known.

As the member banks' borrowings ran down in the aftermath of the 1920–21 depression, the Reserve Banks found themselves with a peculiar problem. They were committed to paying their own way, including a 6 percent dividend on the capital stock their member banks had bought, and their earning assets were the loans to member banks that were now disappearing. From 1921 to 1922, as the economy turned back up, the income of the Reserve Banks dropped 41 percent. The Banks went out into the market to buy government bonds to replace the vanishing loans. So many began buying at the same time that conditions in the market became chaotic, and a system-wide "Open Market Investments Committee" was formed to coordinate purchases.

But the buying of government bonds in the market did not in fact increase the income of the Reserve Banks. The banking system took the money they were putting out for bonds and used it to redeem the rest of its high-interest loans at the discount window.

Interest rates in general dropped as the Reserve Banks, in effect, monetized the bonds they had bought. Prior to this discovery, the only known way for the central bank to control the money supply had been through encouraging or discouraging banks to borrow at the discount window. (Presumably, something could have been done by raising or lowering the reserve requirement as a percentage of deposits, but that was fixed by law in the original Federal Reserve Act.) Now, through an accident as startling as those which produced the discovery of X-Rays or penicillin, the central bank learned that "open market operations" could have a significant effect on the behaviour of the banks.

By buying securities, the Reserve Banks would increase the reserves of the banking system, make loans easier to get and reduce interest rates; by selling securities, the Reserve Banks would take money out of the system, diminish reserves, make loans harder to get and raise interest rates. From 1924 on, the Open Market Committee became the basic instrument for the execution of monetary policy in the Federal Reserve System. Among the admirers of the way this device was used in the years right after its discovery are authors not otherwise enchanted with the performance of the Fed: Milton Friedman and Anna Schwartz describe it as "a conscious attempt, for perhaps the first time in monetary history, to use central bank powers to promote internal economic stability as well as to pursue balance in international payments." The introduction of Competition and Credit Control in 1971 was at bottom an effort to copy Federal Reserve procedures in the administration of the British money supply.

What was not realized in America in the 1920s—and indeed is not understood today—was that the use of open-market activities as a major instrument of central-bank policy would subvert the regionalization that was built into the Act. Even today, Congressmen and others fulminate about the extraordinary power open-market operations give the Federal Reserve Bank of New York, because it acts as agent for the System in the purchase and sale of securities. But in fact the dominant role of the New York Bank had been the result of its exclusive and self-energizing access to the most important money market. Once decisions about how to intervene in that market were to be made by a system-wide Committee, New York's independence was gone, and with it the special influence that Benjamin Strong and his successors George Harrison and Allan Sproul in the 1950s could exert from one chair in one district. The first war between the Board and its Banks came over the Board's right to block changes any Bank wished to make in its own discount rate; then over the Board's power to mandate such changes on a reluctant Bank. By the 1950s, when the New York Bank made what was in effect a last stand for independence, the fact that the open-market operations were national gave Washington all the weapons.

Meanwhile, the centralizing tendency of the New Deal had strengthened the institutional role of the Board. Amendments to the Act in 1933 and 1935 eliminated the Secretary of the Treasury and the Comptroller of the Currency from what was now to be called the Board of Governors; restored the size to seven, and established a system of nonrenewable fourteen-year terms, one new Governor to be chosen every two years (which means, as Congressman Patman frequently points out, that even a two-term President cannot hope to appoint a majority of the Board until the end of his second term; but the President does appoint a Chairman and Vice-Chairman from among the Governors, for a four-year term). And the 1935 Amendments gave legal status to the Federal Open Market Committee, which now by law consists of twelve members—the seven Governors, the president of the Federal Reserve Bank of New York (whose bank acts as agent for the Committee), the president of Chicago or Cleveland in alternate years, and the presidents of three of the remaining nine, taking turns once every three years. Thus the seven members of the Board are always a majority of the Committee, though in fact, Sherman Maisel writes from a vantage point as a former Governor, the votes never do break down along those lines.

Among the "reforms" frequently proposed for the Fed has been the removal of the Bank presidents from the Open Market Committee, essentially on the grounds that they are chosen by private boards of directors and the policy set by the Committee is in the highest sense "public policy", which should be established exclusively by the Presidential appointees on the Board. Presumably, the information on regional conditions brought to the meeting by the Bank presidents could be secured just as easily from staff. But "if the presidents of the Reserve Banks were not to participate in the formulation of these policies," Benjamin Haggott Beckhart writes, paraphrasing Allan Sproul, "their responsibilities would be relegated to certain routine functions, and men of stature, vision, and perception could no longer be persuaded to head the Reserve Banks." So important had open-market operations become by the 1970s; and in volume, the transactions of the desk that serves the Committee had risen to $190,000 million a year of trading in and out.

There are two other advertised tools of monetary control in the Fed's kit, but neither is extensively used—or usable. The 1935 amendments gave the Board the power to vary reserve requirements within broad limits, and this power was in fact heavily employed from that date to the mid-1950s. (The authority given to the Bank of England to require "special deposits" under Competition and Credit Control is, of course, similar to the Fed's authority to change reserve requirements.) Requirements first moved up to limit the inflationary effects of a veterans' bonus (the bonus had been Patman's baby, and his hostility to the Fed has been unceasing since this incident), then down a year later as part of the panic reaction to the disheartening return of the Depression, which had seemed to be lifting; then *way* up during and right after the war, when deficit financing had set the banks and the public awash with money.

In recent years the Fed has fiddled with the reserve categories to include new sources of bank funds to which reserve requirements should be applied—commercial paper issued by the holding company, Eurodollars, agreements for the sale and later repurchase of certain assets, etc. But the reserve requirements themselves, except on exotica like CDs and Eurodollars, have been relatively unchanging—partly because the Board regards the use of such a bludgeon as barbaric for civilized scholarly men who have access to a rapier like Open Market operations, but mostly because membership in the Fed is voluntary for state-chartered banks. These banks can leave the System to escape its sterilization of their reserves, which some state law will permit them to keep in interest-bearing investments once they are out of the Fed.

Since 1970, banks have been giving up their Fed membership often enough to decrease the member banks' share of the nation's bank deposits at a rate of about $\frac{1}{2}$ of 1 percent a year, and in early 1974 the Board of Governors formally asked the Congress for legislation to make membership in the Fed compulsory for all American banks. This is not going to happen—the Fed's clout with the Congress approximates zero—and might not make much difference, anyway. The announced purpose is not to free the Fed to change reserve requirements but to improve the quality of its information, which as a daily matter derives from reports by member banks alone. (Thomas O. Waage of the New York Fed has said however, that "the prompt and pervasive impact of a higher reserve requirement" would have significant value.) Opposing compulsory membership in a pamphlet published by the Conference of State Bank Supervisors, Professors Almarin Phillips of the University of Pennsylvania and Ross Robertson of Indiana argue that the power to change reserves is not very significant at best, and propose instead "the restoration of the discount rate to true money market status . . . the best possible Federal Reserve weapon for signalling nuances of change in monetary policy." It should be noted that the danger of losing membership through an increase in reserve requirements is vastly increased by high interest rates. When Fed Funds are at 3 percent, the services provided by the Fed to member banks may seem worth the price of sterilizing reserves that now average out to something less than one-fifteenth of the average bank's time and demand deposits; when Fed Funds sell at 10 percent, the chance to keep state-required reserves in earning assets looks much more attractive.

Changes in the announced discount rate—the interest charged by the Fed on borrowings by its member banks—are still much

publicized and a source of dispute within the System, and sometimes without; it was a Board of Governors decision to allow the
New York Fed to raise its discount rate that provoked the headline-
producing "confrontation" between Lyndon Johnson and William
McChesney Martin in December 1965. But despite what still gets
said in textbooks and in the newspapers, the discount rate today
has virtually no significance in the Fed's struggles to keep a grip
on the nation's money supply. Since the early 1960s—and especially
since 1966—Fed Funds have usually traded at rates higher than
the discount rate; and Fed Funds purchases supply ten to twenty
times as much money for reserves as member bank borrowings at
the discount window. Open-market activities change the rate on
Fed Funds; movements of the discount rate do not.

Abandonment of the discount rate as a measure of monetary
control was signalled almost fifty years ago when the Board of
Governors, for political reasons relating to Congressional relations, first began interfering with the powers of the district Banks
to change their individual rates. The great value of the discount
window was its capacity to serve as the lender of last resort to the
banking system—or to any individual bank. Fire, tornado, hurri-
cane, a bad crop year, a strike in a mining town—any of these
could endanger the continuance of a reasonably well-run bank,
and the Fed had to be ready to go to that bank's aid. But a loan
at a punitive rate, in the Bagehot style, was not the right response
to such situations (which were common in the agricultural depression that accompanied urban prosperity in the 1920s); indeed, for
the Fed to be of real service, its loans would have to be at a rate
below the prevailing rate. At first, the Banks sought to cope with
the problem by establishing a collection of different rates, according to the situation of the bank that wanted the money, but this
was an invitation to pettifoggery. Ultimately, not talking about
what it was doing (maybe not completely understanding all the
implications), the Board abandoned the British model of a controlling bank rate (which Britain itself abandoned in 1971), and
began rationing credit from the discount window by criteria other
than price.

The same month that he decided he had to slam the window on the Bank of Commonwealth in Detroit, Robert Moffat of the Chicago Fed had occasion to make a call to a bank in a town just devastated by a tornado, to inform its officers that if they needed some money the Fed would be glad to help. "Oh, no," came the reply; "the insurance adjusters are already here, and they're writing cheques." After one of the big hurricanes of the 1960s, the Board of Governors leaned on the Atlanta Fed to make sure that rather conservative Bank would be liberal enough in its dealings with the devastated Gulf Coast. "There has to be a showing of need for this money by the institution for reasons that could not have been foreseen," says Chicago Fed economist Karl Scheld. Sometimes there are small local problems—a lawsuit that delays the mailing of school tax bills, forcing the school district to borrow from banks that are already loaned up: that's a good case at the discount window. The rule is that access to the discount window is a privilege, not a right. While movements of the discount rate retained a shock value—an "announcement effect" that would infuriate a President seeking to conceal the domestic economic implications of the Vietnam war—the practical importance of the rate as a governor of the money supply disappeared.

The wisdom of separating the lender-of-last-resort function from the money-supply function was spectacularly demonstrated in June 1970, when Penn Central went under. During the preceding year, the Open Market Committee had been squeezing the banks, and the Board of Governors had set maximum interest rates banks could pay on Certificates of Deposit below the money-market rates, theoretically preventing them from funding new loans. (Actually, the banks had been able to keep expanding their borrowings in the Eurodollar market, but only at heavy cost.) A great deal of business borrowing had moved outside the banking system, into the commercial-paper market; the quantity of these unsecured corporate IOUs had risen from about $9,000 million in 1965 to almost $40,000 million in spring 1970. The Securities and Exchange Commission allows such IOUs to be written without a registration statement for terms shorter than 270 days, and much of the commercial paper was thirty-day and sixty-day notes, or even shorter. The corporations did not pay up on these IOUs when they came due; instead, they "rolled over" their indebtedness, selling new commercial paper to replace the old. Though this market operated outside the banking system—essentially as a substitute for bank loans, which the Fed was restricting—it had a major bank component, for one of the assurances given the purchaser was that the issuer had arranged a "standby line of credit" at a bank which would pay off the IOU if for any reason it could not be rolled over. Penn Central had drawn down its line of credit and spent it for other purposes; and the holders of Penn Central commercial paper were simply out of luck when the railroad filed for bankruptcy.

The business community was already very jittery. American troops were in Cambodia, and the stock market had fallen out of bed. There were rumours all over the country about Chrysler, which was one of the largest borrowers in the commercial-paper market. It seemed clear that billions of dollars of commercial paper coming due in the next few weeks would not be rolled over: in times of perceived trouble, potential lenders prefer cash. And the banks were already bumping their heads against the ceilings the Fed had tried to impose on the money supply. The ground was shifting under everyone's feet; an earthquake of a financial panic had begun.

"I worked on this thing in other ways", Chairman Burns recalls, looking back on what is by common consent the Fed's finest hour, and speaking of the abortive efforts to arrange a government guarantee for new loans to keep Penn Central alive. "Everything fell through. We couldn't lend to them ourselves under the law; it would be wrong." The effort to get a government guarantee for the loan finally collapsed on a Sunday, and Burns was informed that the chiefs of the railroad were going to a federal judge to declare bankruptcy before the start of business on Monday. He called the heads of the Reserve Banks around the country, and told them to get word out immediately that the Fed stood ready to help. William Treiber, first vice-president of the New York Fed, personally called the homes of the chief executive officers of the ten largest banks in the New York area. "Adam Smith" in *Supermoney* has speculated amusingly on what might have happened to the country if the snotty kids of bankers had refused to summon their fathers in from the garden to the telephone when the local Fed called to deliver word that the discount window would be wide open on Monday for any bank that needed money to lend to a corporation that had to pay off commercial paper. Especially Chrysler. On Monday, Burns recalls, "I kept the Board in session practically all day to change Regulation Q so that money could flow into CDs at the banks." Sherman Maisel recalls that the debate was "heated and acrimonious". People at the New York Fed recall that they did all the work, and made the recommendations that Washington finally followed.

Sixty-three years after the money panic of 1907 had started the Congress off on a search for a better way to organize the banking system, the nation got the reward of the creative efforts of the able men who wrote the Federal Reserve Act. The machinery had never been used—the men who ran the Federal Reserve System in 1929–32 apparently did not realize it was there—and when Burns set it in motion it creaked and lumbered as discount officers in all the Banks improvised their telephone calls; but it worked just exactly as Carter Glass in 1913 had hoped it would. Harsh criticisms of the Fed have been spoken in recent years—"I am constantly amazed at their ineptitude" was the opening sentence of the lead story on the financial page of the *New York Times* on September 11, 1973, which reported a poll of 415 business economists in which only 16·6 percent of the respondents had been willing to rate the Fed's policies as Excellent or Good. But not many American institutions have responded that well to emergency in the 1970s.

2

In Washington, life is sweet. The limestone building stands in its own block square of lawn, a wide sweep of stone stairs leading to a massive doorway surmounted with what may be the largest eagle in America. An armed guard at a desk at the door checks the credentials and briefcases of all those who wish to enter, and upstairs on the second floor the corridor that leads to the Governors' offices can be entered only through a small rotunda with another armed guard. The high-ceilinged offices on the Governors' row look out through large windows through the leafy or flowering trees across Constitution Avenue to the Mall. Everything is pleasantly quiet; in American government this group of mostly academic economists is the closest we come to philosopher kings, and it is pleasant to note that (until he left in fall 1974 to become a Harvard professor) one of the most philosophical and kingly was a black, Andrew Brimmer. The fireplaces work; and if a Governor wants a fire in his office he need merely ask. The Fed has arrangements with several of the nation's museums, and for those who care about such things the art work on the walls can be of extraordinary quality. In the waiting room off the rotunda, the visitor can pass the time studying a Vuillard, a Prendergast and a Sargent; and a little plaque thanking Nathan Cummings for his "efforts in advancing the interest of the arts in the Federal Reserve System".

3

When Alan Holmes comes* to his daily work as manager of the System Open Market Account, on the executive tenth floor of the Federal Reserve Bank of New York, he finds a new page in the big black loose-leaf book—"my black bible here"—that he keeps on his Georgian desk. The page is a computer run-down on the money position of the New York City banks as of the night before. He takes a quick look at it, then greets his young assistant, Peter Sternlight, and four traders from the city's big government-bond houses—a different four every morning—who have been invited by to shoot the breeze before the market opens at ten. "They let their hair down", Sternlight says. "They complain to us, we prod them, but mostly these are one-sided conversations; we do most of the listening."

When the traders leave, having conveyed to the bosses of the

* Present tense as of 1974; job assignments have changed.

Fed's traders a sense of the market that could be gathered in no other way, Holmes looks at the rest of the morning's documentation, which is considerable. Reports like those on the New York banks arrive from thirty-eight other large banks around the country, and the eleven other district Reserve Banks wire in statements of condition, detailing the total non-borrowed and borrowed reserves in each district. (It is not yet 7.00 a.m. on the West Coast, but the Fed money-desk people are already at work.) Next comes the computer run on the portfolios of all the government-bond dealers as of the close of business yesterday, reported by the dealers themselves as part of the price of "recognition" by the Fed, which buys from and sells to only the dealers it recognizes.

Congressman Patman is deeply suspicious of this process: "These twenty dealers," he says, "are getting rich on it all the time. One year I had a report from the General Accounting Office that these twenty dealers made ninety percent on their capital." Actually, the twenty dealers are now twenty-four, of which ten are banks; and the GAO report, covering the five years through 1970, analysed only the profits of the then eleven non-bank dealers. In two of the five years (1968 and 1969), the dealers had net losses on their government securities trading, and only in 1970—when interest rates fell, giving the dealers both a mark-up on their inventory and earnings on the bills higher than the cost of the loans needed to carry them—were the profits exorbitant. In 1974, the Treasuries market was a bloodbath for dealers, with declining prices and with interest rates on bank loans so much higher than the rate on Treasury issues that every day was its own disaster. Over the long haul, however, there is no doubt that trading government is a good business for competent dealers, and that the Fed wants them to make money.

Holmes himself decides who will get a chance to buy and sell with the Fed. "It's a free market," he says; "we'll do business with anybody who can prove to us that he's adequately capitalized. The hard thing to find is the talent—there aren't many good bill traders." Does Holmes himself make the judgment on whether or not a man is a sufficiently competent bill trader to justify recognition by the Fed? Pause; then, "Yes".

The next computer run comes from the research department, predicting for today and day by day over the next four weeks the float in the system, the currency in people's hands, the size of the Treasury and foreign dollar accounts, the vault cash at the banks, the reserves of the member banks, and the portfolio holdings of the Federal Reserve itself. A separate forecast on all these items is run every day by the research department at the Board of Governors in Washington, and the two are compared. At ten the Fed's own traders, a dozen men and women who work in an airy little antiseptic amphitheatre of a corner office, make their first calls of the day to the dealers, to determine the size of the positions the dealers expect to be financing that day. Meanwhile, Sternlight is on the telephone with John Carlock of the Treasury Department, who can tell him the dimensions and locations of the calls the Treasury will be making on the Tax and Loan accounts at the banks on this day. The effort is to find out, in Holmes's words, "what factors are going to affect reserves, other than ourselves". Among the significant factors on some days is the activity of foreign central banks, which buy and sell U.S. Treasury bills on the New York market usually but not always through the agency of the Federal Reserve Bank of New York.

By 10.45 the Fed traders know how the stock market opened, how the Fed Funds market opened, and the direction in which prices are moving in the Treasuries market. Sternlight and Holmes talk it over, usually bringing in New York Fed president Alfred Hayes, and decide on what if anything the market needs today. It may need to be left alone. The options are various, because the Fed can purchase or sell short-term or long-term Treasuries—or bankers' acceptances, for that matter, if there are enough of them around. Increasingly in recent years the Fed has operated in the market through repurchase agreements—"buying" from dealers with a prearranged resale tomorrow (in effect, an overnight loan to the market, increasing the supply of reserves for one day); or "reserve repurchase agreements", selling to dealers with an agreement to buy back tomorrow (in effect an overnight borrowing from the market to decrease the supply of money for one day). Both "repos" and "reverse repos" can be made for several days, or even a week, if desired. The reverse repo (always described as a "matched sale-repurchase agreement") is a relatively new tool for the Fed, first authorized in 1966, when an airlines strike delayed the delivery of cheques to clearing houses around the country and increased the float by more than $1,000 million. "We'd always wanted it," Holmes says reflectively, "and we'd never understood why we couldn't have it. Here the Committee agreed we needed it—you couldn't sell off a billion dollars in bills without pushing the interest rate sky high. And we've been allowed to keep it."

At eleven o'clock, Holmes initiates a conference call to the members of the Open Market Committee—as many of the Governors as wish to sit in, plus some of the technical staff in Washington, plus at least one of the Bank presidents around the country. "We describe the market," Sternlight says, "and we lay out our programme for the day, and Alan says, 'How does that sound to you?' The implementation of the decision may be contingent on further developments in the market." If the market opens peculiarly, however, or overnight news seems likely to promote occurrences the Fed would not like to see, Holmes may move early, "touching base" with Hayes and in Washington before issuing his orders. The Fed's traders now call their opposite numbers at the various dealers, who are, to say the least, waiting for the call; and around the Street resounds the cry, "The Fed is in!" If the initial intervention does not produce the results Holmes expected (measured usually these days by the movement of the Fed Funds rate), the bucket can be taken back to the well.

On Wall Street itself, admiration for the technical management of the day-to-day market is virtually universal. "I can't say too much for these guys," says Salomon's Bob Dall, "for their competence and for their independence of judgment." Most of the traders (and Sternlight) are economists, and come to the Fed's trading desk through the research department. "It's considered a particularly interesting place to work," says Sternlight, a rather solemn young man. "We haven't had any trouble getting able people". Holmes is one of those Federal Reserve phenomena. A small man with wispy hair over a broad forehead, and a rather elegant, careful speaking voice, he came to the New York Fed from Columbia University in the 1940s as a Russian expert, of all things, and started as a research assistant on a combined British and Eastern European desk. Somebody decided he had trading talents, and by golly he did. He took over as manager for the Open Market Committee in March 1965, at the end of "a dull period, interest rates not moving. But since 1965," Alan Holmes says, not entirely unhappily (he really is a trader), "it's just been one thing after another." In 1975, he took over the foreign desk, too.

4

The Federal Open Market Committee met the day after the Monday meeting of the Board of Governors following the Penn Central crash in 1970, and issued the following directive to its manager (as printed and released ninety days later, when presumably nobody could make any money by knowing it):

The information reviewed at this meeting suggests that real economic activity is changing little in the current quarter after declining appreciably earlier in the year. Prices and costs generally are continuing to rise at a rapid pace, although some components of major price indexes recently have shown moderating tendencies. Since late May market interest rates have shown mixed changes following earlier sharp advances, and prices of common stocks have recovered part of the large decline of preceding weeks. Attitudes in financial markets continue to be affected by uncertainties and conditions remain sensitive, particularly in light of the insolvency of a major railroad. In May bank credit changed little and the money supply rose moderately on average, following substantial increases in both measures in March and April. Inflows of consumer-type time and savings funds at banks and non-bank thrift institutions have been sizeable in recent months, but the brief spring upturn in large-denomination CDs outstanding at banks has ceased. The over-all balance of payments was in heavy deficit in April and May. In light of the foregoing developments, it is the policy of the Federal Open Market Committee to foster financial conditions conducive to orderly reduction in the rate of inflation, while encouraging the resumption of sustainable economic growth and the attainment of reasonable equilibrium in the country's balance of payments.

To implement this policy, in view of persisting market uncertainties and liquidity strains, open-market operations until the next meeting of the Committee shall continue to be conducted with a view to moderating pressures on financial markets. To the extent compatible therewith, the bank reserves and money market conditions maintained shall be consistent with the Committee's longer-run objective of moderate growth in money and bank credit, taking account of the Board's regulatory action effective June 24 and some possible consequent shifting of credit flows from market to banking channels.

This directive, obviously, did not give Holmes any very clear instructions about what to do tomorrow, or for the remainder of the month before the next meeting of the Open Market Committee. On the other hand, he had sat in on the meeting that produced the document, and knew more than it said—in this case, that what his masters wanted from their manager was that, for God's sake, he should keep the banking system from going down the drain. In less frantic times, however, the directive usually meant no more than a desire that through the open-market account the manager should give the banking system and the business community a feeling that money was easier or tighter. Former Governor Sherman Maisel has written that until the later 1960s this instruction reduced to a pair of specific targets (which were not, however, stated to the public). One was the level of borrowed or excess reserves in the banking system as seen by the Fed; the other was the movement of interest rates in the marketplace. Presumably these two measurements would be closely correlated: if the Fed was creating reserves by purchasing Treasuries, interest rates would drop; if it was taking reserves out of the system by selling Treasuries, interest rates would rise.

The problem with this approach, as economists with political views ranging from Milton Friedman's to Sherman Maisel's kept pointing out, was that it assumed banks and borrowers were passive, sheepishly following the signals given in the market by changing interest rates. If the banks were being made to borrow some of their reserves at the discount window, they could lend less; if rates were higher, businesses would borrow less. But if businesses insisted on borrowing more, and banks kept creating deposits, the Committee's target figure of "net borrowed reserves" would be achieved without for a moment restraining the growth of the money supply: instead of having $25,000 million in reserves, $250 million of which was borrowed, the banks would wind up with $26,000 million in reserves, $250 million of which was borrowed.

Maisel insisted—with growing support on the Committee— that the manager should aim at some figure for the "monetary aggregates". This brought everybody up against the damnable problem that no one definition of "money" suits any two economists. Maisel wanted to use "bank credit proxy"—the total of all deposits in the banking system. (In Bank of England terms, M_3.) The phrase in the June 1970 directive about "moderate growth in money and bank credit" was Maisel's triumph. But it was not really very helpful to Holmes, because activity in the open market did not directly or quickly affect the growth or decline of bank deposits. Ultimately, in February 1972, the Open Market Committee decided that instead of targeting borrowed or excess reserves, Holmes and his traders should target total reserves—or, rather, "Reserves available for the support of Private non-bank Deposits", otherwise known as RPDs.

The *Federal Reserve Bulletin* for June 1973 contains a paraphrase of Holmes's almost anguished report to the Open Market Committee on his first year's experience with detailed quantitative targets—so much expansion of RPDs over a two-month period, so high or low a Fed Funds rate, so much more "M_1" (cash in public hands plus demand deposits), so much more "M_2" ("M_1" plus commercial bank time deposits other than CDs), so much more credit proxy. "The diverse behaviour of M_1, M_2, and the credit proxy in 1972, as in 1971, provided the Committee with different signals at different times concerning the current thrust of monetary policy." Achieving a feeling of ease or constraint in the money markets, and a level of borrowed or excess reserves, had been much easier than staying within the Committee's specified "tolerance ranges" for all the categories monitored. Over and over again in his review of what was in retrospect a particularly bad year for monetary policy, Holmes is reduced to noting that the statistics were misleading and the "Desk" (so-called) was thrown back upon its own judgment of what was going on—which meant, of course, the "feel of the market" that Maisel had tried to push off centre stage.

The problem is too complicated to be solved, and the variables are too independent to be managed together by the single tool of open-market operations. Seasonal factors influence the demand for money and credit: the public wants cash before July 4, Labour Day, and Christmas; corporations need loans to pay tax bills each quarter, and banks need reserves to carry the resulting deposits while the Internal Revenue Service at an unpredictable pace processes the paper; transfers from the Treasury "tax and loan" accounts at the banks to the Treasury's account at the Fed itself (reducing deposits and reserves in the member banks and total reserve needs, but not RPDs) occur in irregular sizes at irregular intervals. With the national debt nearing $500,000 million, the Treasury must sell bonds in great quantities, also at irregular intervals, requiring help from the Open Market Committee. The weather affects the Federal Reserve float. Foreign governments for their own reasons buy and sell Treasury bills, sometimes in quantities that overwhelm the Trading Desk.

In late January and February 1973, when the international monetary system went smash, New York had to face an incredible demand for Treasury bills from foreign governments absorbing dollars to maintain exchange rates. "We had a four-and-a-half billion-dollar day," Holmes recalls; "there was no way our bills market could absorb it, no way for us to buy that many bills. And you didn't want to leave the central banks that were supporting the dollar without assets to put it in. We got the Treasury to issue special certificates. They didn't want to do it, they didn't need the money, they didn't want to tell Congress they were borrowing when they didn't need the money. They have problems all the time. They get criticized by the General Accounting Office and Congress when they run balances too high in the commercial banks, but when they keep the money with us it takes reserves out of the banking system." Money held by the Treasury on account at the Fed is the equivalent of currency in the hands of the public: it drains the banks.

There are nutty technical factors, historical peculiarities, that push the money market in perverse directions. The most remarkable example is the Cook County intangible property tax, which assesses bank deposits and securities holdings in Chicago and environs as of April 1, every year. But Justice John Marshall's decision in *McCulloch* v. *Maryland* a century and a half ago prevents states and municipalities from taxing government bonds or bills. In the old days, when the tax applied to individuals and trusts as well as to corporations, the Twentieth Century Limited took off for New York on March 31 every year with drawing rooms loaded with stocks and bonds, being taken out of the state overnight by armed guards. Since 1972, when the tax was restricted to corporations, the paper is less likely to move, but the banks do a good business transferring company accounts and taxable holdings into governments "over two dates".

"I really have gone after this business," says Tom Herschbach of the First National Bank of Chicago's money desk; "if you're efficient, it's a good way to cover the overhead for April." In 1973, First of Chicago alone swapped for about $450 million of Treasuries to serve its customers and correspondents (down from $1,3500 million in 1970, but still quite a lot for one bank to take out of the market). The rate charged small customers was 10¢ per thousand dollars; big customers got negotiated prices; some no doubt paid for the service through "analysis credit" for deposits maintained at the bank before and after April 1. . . . For the rest of the banking system and for the government-bond dealers, the Cook County tax date makes for strained (though no longer crippled) markets, depleting the collateral on which the market runs. In spring 1973, when the Europeans still had huge holdings left over from the currency crisis, the annual Cook County suction pump virtually closed down parts of the money market. "I never thought I'd live to see the day when there was a shortage of Treasuries," Jim Sheridan of North Carolina National Bank said sourly, "but you can't buy 'em, you can't borrow 'em, the Treasury doesn't have to issue any. . . . It's very detrimental to the country." In late summer 1975, on the other hand, the German government was selling its Treasury bills for dollars to prop a falling mark, the U.S. government was running a heavy deficit, and the banks were asked to absorb almost $10,000 million of Treasury paper in a single month. That was bad for the country, too.

The first charge upon the Fed's money desk every day is not the policy directive of the Open Market Committee but the need to neutralize what the Treasury will be doing in the Tax & Loan accounts, and this activity can easily give the market a false signal. "One April when we were replacing Treasury balances," Holmes recalls, "all the newspapers said we were supplying reserves to ease monetary conditions, which wasn't true at all. But everyone believed it."

Immediately after World War II, the major function of the Open Market Committee was to maintain the price of all U.S. Government obligations at par, holding down the interest the government had to pay on its monumental wartime borrowings. When the Fed managed to break out of this straitjacket, its technicians instituted what was called a "bills only" policy, allowing longer-term government bonds to find their own level (within limits) while manoeuvring the price of short-term Treasuries to meet money-market needs. The Kennedy administration, suitably advised, considered this procedure harmful in two ways: long-term interest rates rose too high, which slowed housing and business investment, while short-term interest rates remained too low, which encouraged a flight of dollars to the better rates of the growing Eurodollar market and worsened the nation's balance of payments. The answer was "Operation Twist", an effort to change the shape of ("to twist") the "yield curve", raising short-term interest rates while lowering long-term interest rates. The Fed went along, and for several years open-market traders would tend to buy long-term governments when the Fed wished to inject money, while the Treasury would tend to sell short-term governments to meet its financing needs. This worked for a while, but not for long, because people and institutions that would once have been in the long-term market shifted their purchases to enjoy the higher short-term rates. (This was not a surprise to the Fed: Robert Roosa, a Fed of New York alumnus at the Treasury who was the inventor of this scheme, had wished to call it "Operation Nudge" to express its limitations.) Meanwhile, open-market activities were hindered by a crazy-quilt pattern of maturities in government debt. Holmes still lives with some of the echoes of Operation Twist a decade after its demise.

But the worst day-to-day problem of the money desk is the inescapably psychological element, the flow of rumour and opinion, in the market. One day toward the end of March 1973 this tourist stood with Ralph Leach in Morgan Guaranty's trading room while he discussed his bank's plans for the day with his chief governments' trader Langdon Cook. Food prices were rising fast, and the air was thick with rumours of price freezes; business had not yet grown disenchanted with price controls, and the stock market was rising, buoyed by the thought that controls were on their way. "Irrational", said Ralph Leach. Collateral was draining to Chicago. "That preposterous horse-trading", said Ralph Leach. The next day would see the publication of Federal Reserve figures for the banking system in the previous week, and as this was the end of a quarter there would be comparisons made against the previous quarter, when the "monetary aggregates" had been distorted by the first big federal payment of revenue sharing funds to the cities and states. The men who would write up the comparisons in the newspapers, however, would not remember the revenue sharing situation, and would comment on how little the money supply had grown in the first quarter. Leach speculated that this would lead people in the market to believe that the Fed must be about to loosen up; the sense that people mistakenly expected a loosening might induce the Fed to tighten. . . . "There are ridiculous things in this market", Ralph Leach growled.

A century ago, Bagehot commented that "money will not manage itself". Milton Friedman and his fellow monetarists say that money can be managed by simply adding to the supply at a steady pace sufficient to make the "aggregates" grow to some predetermined level. Under these circumstances, presumably, the money market would go away—it is quite impossible to see how government-bond dealers could carry their inventory with overnight loans in an atmosphere where every major Treasury financing, every large call on the T&L accounts, every tax date or holiday or storm that grounds airplanes produced a change of five percentage points in the short-term interest rates. Holmes has a hard enough job without being badgered by professors. "The market in the books," he says, just a touch wearily, "is a theoretical perfect market, and not a real market." And, of course, he's right.

The Bank of England operation, for all the superficial differences, is in fact very much like what Holmes and the Open Market Committee run for the Federal Reserve System, except that the Bank give much more information about their intentions than the Fed will. Like Holmes and Sternlight, deputy chief cashier David Somerset and money market manager Rodney Galpin start with information from the government. In Britain, the Treasury estimates its receipts and disbursements for every day over the next seven weeks. These estimates provide a difference figure for today— how much the government will be putting into or taking out of the money supply. The Bank know what gilt-edged settlements occur this day, and how much the discount houses will "take up" from the week's tender of Treasury bills; they keep in touch with the maturities of local authority bills; and because exchange controls are the one thing that is really tight, they have a fair notion of what the overseas settlement picture will be. From history, they can make a good guess about the ebb and flow of note circulation. "We add everything up," says Simon Brearley, "and we come to a net figure, a plus or a minus." The clearing banks (but not the discount houses) are told in the morning roughly what that anticipated figure may be; and in return, they tell the Bank how much they expect to expand or contract their supply of call money.

In America, the Fed's traders get on the telephone with the Fed Fund's brokers and find out how the prices are moving; in London, a bill broker, David Campion of Seccombe & Marshall, walks the market as of old, working for the Bank, finding out at each of the discount houses how the call money is flowing out (it always flows out in the morning), and what the expectations are for the afternoon. ("They know pretty well," says a man at the Bank, "what they'll be able to raise between two thirty and three.") Campion does not tell the bank (or anybody else) which discount houses have which problems; he simply, as Peter Lee puts it, "collates the market", and gives the Bank an estimate of a net figure which may or may not mesh well with the Bank's prediction.

For the predictions are far from guaranteed. In a banking system where loans are made mostly by overdraft, the banks can never be sure how much money they will need for their customers and how much, therefore, they will have for the discount houses (though the fact that money at call with the discount houses qualifies as a reserve asset means that the call money position is not necessarily the first line of defence). When currency exchange rates are volatile, as they certainly were in 1975, money may come into the country or leave it without much notice. Tides of opinion in the gilt-edge market may force the Bank to support government paper —or to damp down too extreme a rise—without reference to the needs of the discount houses. But the fulcrum—by design—is the ebb and flow of money to the discount houses.

The banks in America learn whether the Fed wants interest rates higher or lower by watching its intervention (or its failure to intervene) in the Fed Funds market; the British banks learn what the Bank may want by observing whether Campion buys bills (supplying funds to the discount houses) or sells them (draining funds from the market), or forces the discount houses to scrounge around the market on their own for the money they need, at prices higher than the call money price. Though the textbooks say that the Bank buys only from the discount houses, by the way, practice today does not necessarily follow the model, because the Bank may wish to buy only certain maturities, which the clearing banks have and the discount houses don't. Under these circumstances, the Bank may buy from the clearing houses, with instructions to them to put the money in the call market. "Repurchase agreements" are not—yet—part of the armamentarium of the Bank.

Because everything happens in the square mile of the City, the British mechanism is more delicate than the American; and because it employs men to walk around under top hats, it is a good deal more picturesque. But it's really the same mechanism, very ingenious, very satisfying to contemplate, very effective on a day-to-day basis. Unfortunately, what happens in the world doesn't necessarily happen day-to-day.

5

As everyone knows who gets and spends money these days, the present system is not working well at all, not in America, and not in Britain. The root problem, which we shall take a look at in the last chapter, is our highly abstracted approach to money, which in the name of efficiency facilitates swings back and forth between short-term and long-term money as though they were the same commodity. Operationally, what happens to the policies of the Open Market Committee and the Fed is that users of money, denied additional supplies, make more and faster use of what they have: "velocity" rises. If the squeeze is tight enough, as it was in 1966 and 1969, holders and borrowers of money may find it more convenient to do business with each other outside the banking system: "disintermediation" occurs, as businesses lend to and borrow from each other in the commercial-paper market and individuals withdraw their funds from savings accounts to invest directly in Treasury bills or high-yielding government or corporate bonds. The money touches down briefly in the banking system, and flies off again.

In the U.S., the mechanism is a motion of "money" from current account (for which the Fed requires a high reserve ratio) to term account on CD (for which the ratio is lower). In Britain, the device is the expansion of call money at the discount houses (a reserve asset for a clearing bank) which the discount houses graciously return to the clearing banks through the purchase of bank CDs.

Anyway, in this age of liability management, the central bank or the Bank of England simply cannot squeeze the banks too hard. Once upon a time, at least in theory, a refusal by the Fed to supply new reserves through the open market would force banks to sell their municipals and Treasuries at ever-declining prices to raise the money to make loans. At some point, they would stop making loans, because the cost to them in declining prices for their investments would make the whole business unprofitable. In 1966 the banks and the Fed played chicken in the municipals market, and dumping of tax-exempt bonds drove their price so low that states and localities were virtually unable to raise money for public projects. The Fed chickened first—a letter was sent to the banks to say that any bank that was not outrageously expanding its business loan portfolio could come to the discount window for funds if the alternative was the sale of still more municipal bonds. In 1969–70, there was a gentlemen's agreement between the Fed and the banks that the municipals portfolio would not be touched, and the banks unloaded almost $10,000 million of Treasuries to fund their new loans. Coming into 1974, the banks had less than 10 percent of their assets in Treasuries, and most of that was pledged to the support of T&L or local government accounts. Similarly, in Britain, the ratio of Government stocks to deposits, roughly one third as recently as the 1950s, had dropped to about 10 percent. If the price of investment assets dropped, *tant pis* for the asset-holders; the banks would finance by borrowing.

In an age of liability management, a decision by the central bank to hold the line firm would make the banking system insolvent. Every so often one of the big bankers has this nightmare. Among the best stories of 1969–70—possibly even true—is a tale of Chairman Arthur Burns and Gaylord Freeman of the First National Bank of Chicago meeting in the men's room of the Cosmos Club and standing side by side. Freeman supposedly says out of the blue, "Arthur, would the Fed let what is essentially a well-run bank go under?" And Burns, pipe in mouth, shock of grey hair falling in his eyes, says through clenched teeth, "Maybe". Somehow, the threat must be made believable; but it can't be.

Early in 1973, the U.S. government attempted to make lending a losing game for the banks by demanding that prime rates be held down even though the cost of money was rising rapidly in the Fed Funds and CD markets. The medium through which the demand was made was the Committee on Interest and Dividends of the Cost of Living Council, and Burns was chairman of the Committee. The bankers complained bitterly; Walter Wriston went through the roof, and emitted a memo on the economic idiocy of encouraging corporations to borrow from banks by making loans a bargain at a time of inflation. There was some sarcastic comment about presumed reasons why Arthur Burns had retired as a professor of economics at Columbia University.

The evening his memo appeared in the newspapers Wriston was in Washington for a meeting of the Cost of Living Council, of which he was a member, and he had dinner with Treasury Secretary George Schultz, also a former academic, dean of the business school at the University of Chicago. Schultz, a round-faced man with a manner to match and a pawky wit, began the dinner conversation by saying easily to Wriston, "That was quite a statement your bank published today."

Wriston said furiously, "It would have got me an 'A' five years ago at the University of Chicago."

Schultz laughed and nodded. "At Columbia, too", he said.

Burns is not in the least abashed by this episode. "Many of the bankers," he says, "were insensitive to the political problems they faced. Congress was much too ready to write legislation under which interest rates would be fixed by law. An amendment by Senator McIntyre that would have done that lost in the Senate by only two or three votes. If we hadn't taken quick action the McIntyre amendment would have carried." As chairman of the Committee, not of the Fed, Burns summoned to Washington the heads of five banks that had announced rate increases and told them they had a political problem, not an economic problem, and would have to find a political solution. Perhaps unfortunately, the solution was found: rates would be kept relatively low on consumer loans and on loans to small business, where the political clout was, while loans to prime customers would be allowed to carry a market rate. In 1973–74, the world was treated to the unique spectacle of an economy where the better risks had to pay higher interest rates than the poorer risks when they borrowed money.

Alfred Hayes of the New York Fed drew the heaviest fire from the bankers for a speech to the New York State Bankers Association in which he said blandly, "I think you will agree that self-restraint by bank managements in granting loan commitments is preferable to interest-rate ceilings and other types of regulatory action." Modern businessmen do not walk in the door to borrow: they plan ahead and make arrangements months, even years, in advance. The loans that were straining the banking system in early 1973 had been agreed upon a long time before, in a period when the Fed, in fact, was easing monetary conditions and promoting credit. No banker could walk away from a commitment and stay in business; the Fed, it was said darkly, did not understand the simplest aspects of modern banking.

In theory, the bankers were right; in fact, they were about to behave with a shattering irresponsibility that will cost them dearly over the long run. Twice in 1973, on short notice, funds flowed out of supposedly stretched banks for use in activities that damaged America and the world, and on neither occasion did the banks make the slightest move to control what was happening.

The first of these disasters was beginning as Hayes spoke to the

New York State bankers (and said cheerily that "Faith in the dollar in international markets, while by no means fully restored, has improved markedly over recent months"). Large customers of the banks had already begun borrowing heavily for purposes of buying other currencies, and speculating against the dollar on the world exchanges. Bankers denied that their loans were being used for speculation, and there was much learned talk about the impact of "leads and lags" in a foreign exchange market that had to handle international trade at a rate of $1,000 million a day. (Leads are when people with a claim in marks try to get their marks a little sooner; lags are when people with a debt in dollars try to pay their debt a little later.)

But leads and lags were stretching quite a distance in early 1973. "We would not knowingly make loans to customers purely for speculative purposes," David Rockefeller said. "But what is speculation? A large American company plans to build a plant in Germany, knows they will need a certain amount of D-marks in six months. I don't consider it speculation for him to move now to get the D-marks. There is a legitimate reason for doing it." There was enough of that to drive the value of the dollar down 40 percent in terms of marks in about half a year. These were not commitments the banks had made nine months before; they were customers who walked in the door. Governor Brimmer told a meeting in April 1973 that the banks "contributed on balance some $2.5 billion to the volume of funds which moved abroad in connection with the exchange rate speculation earlier this year." That increase in short-term loans abroad over two months was almost 30 percent of the previous total—and it's only what the Fed knows about. Loans made to domestic branches of multinational corporations, which the corporations then shipped abroad, don't show up in Brimmer's figures, though in many cases the banks knew perfectly well where the money was going.

In midsummer, wheat, corn and soybeans looked as good as marks, and the banks graciously made their facilities available to speculators in the grain market. "How do I know what purpose a customer wants a loan for?" says Robert Abboud of First National

Bank of Chicago. "A big grain dealer comes in and says they need money for a ship charter. I have no way of knowing whether they use it for a ship or in the futures market." The question was on his mind because Gaylord Freeman had recently asked (in response to a question to him from president Robert Mayo of the Chicago Fed) whether Abboud's commodities customers were playing the market with First of Chicago's loans; and all his customers had piously told him that all that money was being used to hedge, not to speculate.

That July, the presidents of the district Banks personally visited the chief executive officers of most of the nation's largest banks and told them to cut it out; and some of them probably did. Donald Platten of Chemical recalls that he went on vacation in July, "came back in August and found our loans had gone from nine billion dollars to nine and a half billion in one month. I lowered the boom; it was very hard to do, very offensive to our young tigers." At least one of his older tigers seems not to have got the message. Speaking a few months later about the difficulties of forecasting loan demand, Richard D. S. Bryan, Chemical's chief loan officer, said that "in July and August, looking toward the end of the year, we substantially overestimated what the commodity loan demand would be." In other words, the commodities market, fortunately, topped out; Chemical had anticipated continuing euphoria in the grain pit, and was quite prepared to bankroll it.

It has always been true that high interest rates make speculators a bank's best customers: the man who is going to play the foreign exchange market or the commodities market or the stock market with the bank's money couldn't care less about paying 12 percent a year, because he hopes to make 20 percent a month. This was a price central bankers were willing to pay for the general restriction on the demand for credit that was supposed to result from higher rates. But in the 1970s that restrictive force has been blunted by the lending policies that write roll-over credits, term loans at a floating rate. A company borrowing for five years as part of its long-range financial plan has no reason to postpone its plans when interest rates go up, or accelerate them when interest rates go down;

over the course of the five years, it must expect to pay high rates in some quarters, and low rates in others. Meanwhile, the banks have no reason not to keep bidding up the price of the money they buy to fund their assets, because they can raise the rates not only on their new loans but also on their outstanding loans. To the extent that Federal Reserve or Bank of England policy has historically rested on the effects of interest rates, it lies wrecked by the side of the road.

Of course, the banks and the Fed did not create inflation. "The deficit in fiscal nineteen seventy-two was fourteen point four billion," says Arthur Burns disgustedly, "and if you count the government agencies it was thirty-three billion. And then you blame the Fed for high interest rates!" Congressman Thomas Ashley of the House Banking and Currency Committee, an Ohio Democrat, agrees: "What we're faced with is the product of our own irresponsibility. There hasn't been an assertion of fiscal responsibility in *any* administration since I've been in the Congress. Maybe Kennedy would have done it if he'd lived." In Britain, the financial analysts (while feeling no affection for the Labour Government) blame the Heath–Barber budgets of 1971 and 1973.

But if monetary policy is to be used as the bulwark against inflation, public policy is going to have to direct, at least in a general way, the streams of scarce money. "Burns says selective controls are really bad news," Ashley comments, "because then it's the Fed that's setting the priorities for the society. But if that's where we are—if Congress and the President have abdicated in spending and taxing, and monetary policy is the last high ground— you have to fight on it. When you go to a credit crunch, the effect is priority-setting—you give preferential treatment to big business. Autos, Revlon, booze, new hotels—those activities aren't slowed down at all. But the ability of localities to dig sewers and of people to build homes is crippled."

The French have developed a system of required reserves related to loans, not deposits, with the percentage to be set aside as a reserve made a function of the purpose of the loan. This may be further than the American or British polity can safely go. The allocation of scarce capital resources will be among the most important tasks of this society during the next decade, and it is vital that the central decisions be made in a market by a variety of men whose life's work and attitudes equip them to envision and evaluate the real plant and equipment that would result from this expenditure of money; to give government the central role in these allocations would gamble the future of the country on the fads and fashions that sweep the academic and intellectual and political elites. What both American and British banks have demonstrated in 1973 and 1974 is that they don't make these decisions very well, either.

6

And there is a further problem. "If we are dealing with a closed system, so that there is only one condition of internal equilibrium to fulfil," John Maynard Keynes wrote almost fifty years ago, "an appropriate banking policy is always capable of preventing any serious disturbance of the status quo from developing at all. . . . But when the condition of external equilibrium must also be fulfilled, then there will be no banking policy capable of avoiding disturbance of the internal system." This is where Britain has been since the end of World War I; America got there around 1960.

PART
V
—
INTERNATIONAL
BANKING

16/Americans Abroad and What Happened to the Dollar

WARSAW, Poland, May 30—The Ministry of Finance of the Polish Peoples Republic and The First National Bank of Chicago today jointly announced the bank will open a representative office in Warsaw—the first to be established in Poland by a bank from the western world. Chauncey E. Schmidt, First Chicago president, said the bank hopes to broaden its existing relationships with Polish industry and government agencies and help expand east-west ties. . . . Schmidt noted that more people of Polish ancestry live in Chicago than in any other city outside Poland. Among the bank's commitments in Poland is an $8·9 million loan to Bank Handlowy Warszawie S.A. to help finance construction by a Chicago company of two sausage factories in Poland, he said.

—press release, First National Bank of Chicago, 1974

* * *

"Suppose I were to set out on a pilgrimage to Jerusalem," Henry Ward Beecher told his Brooklyn Heights congregation in a sermon some time in the 1850s, "and before I started were to go to Brown Brothers and Company and obtain letters of credit for the cities of London, Jericho, etc. Then, with these papers which a child might destroy, which would be but ashes in the teeth of flame, which a thousand chances might take from me, I should go on with confidence and cheer, saying to myself, 'As soon as I come to London I shall be in funds. I have a letter in my pocket from Brown Brothers and Company which will give me five hundred dollars there; and in the other cities to which I am bound I shall find similar supplies, all at my command, through the agency of these magic papers and pen strokes of these enterprising men."

Such enterprising men had been part of the traveller's scene—especially the merchant traveller's—for the better part of five centuries before Beecher made such charming use of commercial custom. (His purpose was to stress that every man bears "the letters of credit of the Eternal God. . . . No fire, no violence, nor any chance, can destroy the cheques of the Lord. . . . No longer dishonour your God by withholding from him the confidence which you freely accord to Brown Brothers and Company.") Hans J. Mast of Credit Suisse in Zurich likes to say that "bankers are risk coverers, not risk takers", but the essence of lending is the assumption of some of the risk of time and place. As international trade developed, these risks were taken not by individual banks with offices in different places but by an international banking system connected through networks of correspondent institutions.

The essence of the correspondent bank relationship across national borders is that the initiating bank keeps an account at the offices of its correspondent. "Obviously, you can't write letters of credit for your customers," says John Roebles, who ran the Banco de Boston at Buenos Aires for about fifteen years, "unless you keep deposits abroad". The letter of credit, one of the two basic documents of international banking, represents a commitment from a bank to its customer to lend him, from the accounts the bank maintains in foreign places, whatever amounts are agreed upon in the letter, at whatever exchange rates may prevail on the day the letter is presented to the foreign bank. (Some letters of credit—probably including the one Beecher carried—are bought for cash by the customer before he leaves, which means in effect that the customer lends the money to the bank and not only receives no interest on his loan but pays the bank for letting it use his money. This is the use of a letter of credit as a traveller's cheque, and not a business transaction.) The value of the letter of credit is not merely the fact that it can be turned into cash in distant parts; it also introduces the customer to a bank abroad, which will adopt him into its local family of customers and do whatever this bank does to help a friend get ahead. The profit to the bank that issues the letter of credit comes from a small commitment fee on the entire amount plus interest to be paid on whatever is advanced to the customer abroad through the use of the letter. The profit to the bank abroad that gives the money to the customer is in the use of the issuing bank's balances and in the small commission for performing a currency exchange. It ought to be risk-free (apart from the loan to the customer), but every so often it isn't: nobody insures the deposits of a correspondent bank if the bank in which they have been placed goes bust. Bankhaus Herstatt of Cologne went down in 1974 with foreign correspondents left to sue for well over $1,000 million of their balances; they got most of the money back, but it was a near thing.

This is the classic letter of credit, involving a balance to the credit of the issuing bank in the accepting bank. But there is no necessary reason why the balance abroad against which the letter of credit is drawn should result from a real prior "deposit" by the bank issuing the letter. If there is a long-standing relationship with the bank accepting the letter, the necessary balance can be borrowed by the issuing bank as needed—deposits, it will be remembered, are created by loans as well as by an actual "deposit". Now the bank issuing the letter receives the commitment fee plus the difference between the interest it charges its customer and the "interbank" rate charged to it by the foreign bank. The bank accepting the letter receives the income from its loan to the issuing bank, plus the exchange commission—and, of course, the opportunity to make similar arrangements in reverse whenever its customers have business to do in the country of the bank that issued this letter of credit.

The letter of credit is the buyer's loan in an international transaction: thanks to his letter of credit, the buyer can pay cash. The "banker's acceptance" is the seller's loan. Here the exporter's bank buys from him a bill representing the importer's promise to pay, guaranteed by the importer's bank abroad. In the acceptance context correspondent relationships are not necessary, as long as the foreign bank guaranteeing the credit is known and trusted in the country where the bill is bought.

429

In modern banking, as distinguished from Renaissance banking, an effort is made to insulate a bank's risk on letters of credit and acceptances from fluctuations in the currency markets. Lending £50,000 for ninety days to an American importer who will pay back in dollars, a bank will immediately buy £50,000 in a "forward market" for delivery in ninety days. The spread between spot (immediate delivery) and forward (future delivery) rates of exchange expresses expectations of the relative future strengths of these two currencies, and where a currency is considered weak people in that country will have to pay higher interest rates to draw foreign money. Usually the spread is very small: a really substantial difference between the exchange rates for immediate and future delivery is an economic pathology, and means that a government is trying to do things the market does not believe it can do.

In spring 1973, for example, speculators were sure the Germans could not prevent a revaluation of the mark; because it was believed that the mark would later be worth more in terms of dollars, there was actually, briefly, a *negative* interest rate on marks in foreign trade: a man willing to borrow "Euromarks" in March for repayment in June could get 500 marks for every 499 he agreed to repay. In spring 1974, on the other hand, the British could keep sterling from leaking out of the United Kingdom only by setting preposterously high interest rates—the annual rate ran as high as 18 percent on a ninety-day instrument. Arab oil money flooded into sterling to take advantage of the rates. and spot sterling became much stronger than forward sterling. A banker borrowing £50,000 for immediate use of an American importer at the end of the first quarter of 1974, and simultaneously purchasing £50,000 in the forward market for delivery at the end of the second quarter, showed a loan to his customer of $119,500 (the spot cost of £50,000) on the asset side of his ledger, and a commitment to pay $117,000 (the forward market cost of £50,000 for delivery in late June) on the liability side, or a guaranteed exchange profit of 8·5 percent on an annual basis. As a result, sterling could be borrowed inexpensively by American importers, splitting the proceeds of the currency exchange with their bank; and the Arabs who were flocking to the London market for the annual rate of 18 percent were really getting only 9·5 percent, like everybody else. But the British home buyer was stuck with a monstrous interest charge on his mortgage.

2

For international banking through letters of credit and acceptances, a bank does not need foreign branches—indeed, branches are likely to get in the way of close correspondent relationships. From the beginning, American banking houses had offices in London, because London was the world money market in the nineteenth century, and America, like any underdeveloped country, had to import capital to grow. *Most* of the money spent to build American railroads was raised in London; even before Junius Morgan there were William and James Brown, Beecher's bankers, predecessors of todays Brown Brothers, Harriman & Co.

Later, American banks tended to tag along wherever American businesses were important to the local economy. They became a major factor in London again at the turn of the century, when Yerkes bought the Underground. The First National Bank of Boston opened substantial branches in Argentina in 1917 and in Cuba in 1923—Argentina, because Boston was the nation's largest wool port and the textile houses wanted a bank on the spot where they bought their wool; Cuba, because several of the largest sugar companies had their headquarters in Boston. In both these cases, the First of Boston branches became very much local banks: Banco de Boston in Argentina even had a tango written about it. When Castro expropriated the American banks in Cuba, First of Boston had only twenty-five Americans altogether in its nine Cuban branches, and there were six hundred Cuban employees. The expropriation did not cost First of Boston much money, either, because the banks' liabilities in Cuba were mostly deposits by Cuban nationals; having seized the banks' assets, the Cuban government could be told to settle up the liabilities by making arrangements with its own citizens.

A. P. Giannini, mostly for personal reasons, acquired a bank in Italy, J. P. Morgan, Sr.—also, one suspects, for personal reasons—started a bank in Paris. When the oil wells began flowing in the Middle East, the Rockefeller banks (Chase and First National City) put banks on the spot to do the business. Bank of America, Chemical, and others followed the mining companies to Chile and elsewhere. But most of this was small potatoes, designed to give service to the local American community and some fraction of exporters to America, not very profitable, much less important than the establishment of the right correspondent liaisons. Bankers Trust, which had been in Paris before Morgan, temporarily gave up its French branch soon after World War II, abandoning in the process one of the choicest locations in the city—the north-west corner of the Place Vendôme, where IBM then built its faintly incongruous European headquarters.

In Britain, "overseas" banks, affiliated with London clearing banks, followed the flag around the globe when so much of it was painted pink. But in the non-colonies of the world, on the European continent and in the United States, the British banks relied almost entirely on correspondent relationships until after American banks had begun dropping offices around the world. Even now, while Barclays and Lloyds (through Bolsa, the Bank of London and South America) have developed extensive Continental and American branches, Midland and NatWest do most of their international banking through "consortium" groups that are essentially formalized correspondent relationships.

3

Letters of credit and bankers' acceptances, and services to Americans abroad, are still the foundations on which American banks build their foreign branches; but the structures raised on these foundations have changed out of all recognition in just the last ten years.

Numbers alone tell the story. In 1947 there were only seven

American banks with foreign branches and only six that operated so-called Edge Act subsidiaries—wholly owned banking corporations dedicated entirely to foreign operations and thus freed from certain restrictions the law applies to domestic banks. (Bank of America has an Edge Act subsidiary on Broad Street in New York with 900 employees and $1,000 million in assets—mostly non-insured deposits—"incidental" to the foreign business of the bank. Its banking floor is one of the half-dozen most grandiose in the city.) Even as late as 1965, there were only 13 American banks with foreign branches and more than half the branches were subsidiaries of one New York bank, First National City. But by 1972, there were 107 American banks abroad, with 588 foreign branches holding something like $80,000 million in assets. (The figures are a little misleading, because 71 of these banks had only one "branch", a letter drop in the Bahamas or the Cayman Islands established to make Eurodollar loans.) In 1974, the best estimate of assets of American banks held abroad was about $140,000 million, more than one-fifth of the total assets American banks held at home. London alone could boast 38 branches of American banks in residence. "There are nineteen more American banks in London," says a Midland officer, "than there are American banks in New York." James Keogh of the Bank of England, whom Danny Davison of Morgan Guaranty irreverently called "the house mother" of American banks in London, said in spring 1973 that to his knowledge (and he knew everything worth knowing) there was only one American bank that could safely risk the expenses of operating in London that had not in fact opened a branch there.

Some of this explosive growth of American banks abroad does reflect the increase in international trade, which now requires more than $1,000 million a day in money flows. But a lot of it represents the creation of local banking business abroad by invading Americans. The Bundesbank in 1972 analyzed the pattern of borrowing from branches of non-German banks operating in Germany. The foreign banks in 1971, the report noted, had been much more likely than domestic banks to lend to German chemical manufacturers and petroleum processors, somewhat more likely to lend to steel construction companies, mechanical engineering and vehicle building companies, electrical engineering firms and makers of precision instruments, optical goods, and metal goods, These industries, the Bundesbank noted, tended to show a higher than usual proportion of foreign ownership and export activity; but they were also, significantly, industries where large firms predominated. In their lending to firms outside the financial industry itself, American banks abroad deal almost exclusively with real big borrowers.

That defines First National City, which talks about its retail business in advertisements but devotes more than two-thirds of its resources and nine-tenths of its talent to the big loans. New York claims to do business with all the top 100 industrial corporations in America; Frankfurt does business with all the top 50 in West Germany. Not quite half of Citibank's total deposit base and more than half its profits derive today from the international business conducted in early 1974 through 311 branches or subsidiaries in 65 countries. Of the bank's 41,800 employees, about 22,000 were working outside the United States at the end of 1973. In its report for that year (published in French, German, Spanish, and Japanese as well as in English), Citicorp announced that it had "business establishments" of some sort in 95 countries. This includes "consumer finance operations" in 20 countries—but in total they involved only $2,500 million of the bank's $42,600 million in footings.

Those who worry about the relationship between government agencies and huge enterprises like Citicorp may be reassured however, by the fact that this bank like all others must get permission of the Federal Reserve Board before it is permitted to open any branches abroad. This means the bank, like its customers, is kept very busy filling out forms. "We applied for a branch in Panama," Wriston says reflectively, "in a hotel. Two pretty girls and a counter. We got a letter: send us a map of the address, how close are you to other banks; what's your rationale? My predecessor wrote back, 'We're opening the bank to make money. I don't know where the nearest bank is. If we don't make money we'll close the branch.'" Wriston left the story unfinished, flashing a toothy smile; no doubt, Citibank got its branch. And should have, too, of course. (The British situation is dramatically different: "If I opened a branch in Tierra del Fuego," says J. Hendley of Midland International, "it wouldn't cross my mind to ask the Bank of England first.")

First National City ties its branches together not only with constant telecommunications but also with short tours of duty on the senior level and a great deal of visiting around. (Citicorp officers on duty always, by bank policy, travel first class. First of Chicago by contrast leaves the choice of class to the officer; but by placing the manager of the profit centre on a bonus-for-performance system Gale Freeman stimulated fresh understanding at the bank of the great truth that the back of the plane arrives at the same time as the front of the plane. Once cost-conscious senior managers began travelling economy class, the bank's lesser officers, sometimes rather wistfully, sacrificed their comfort for a greater good.) A First National City branch abroad has the same flavour as a First National City division in the United States—the same hard-driving, bright, vain people at the helm. And in fact they are the same people, because a tour in top management of one of the overseas branches is now well established as the route to the staff jobs at 399 Park Avenue. "I was the chief lending officer on Penn Central and Lockheed," says Roy Dickerson, now head of Citicorp's British operations, "and I never talked to the press; but I'm told I'm supposed to see you. . . ."

Morgan Guaranty, too, fills the top jobs in its European offices with men who were in high positions in New York a few years ago and will probably return. Fabian K. vom Hofe looks like a professional diplomat, sitting amidst the carved panelling of his grand office overlooking the Place Vendôme (a single decoration on the walls: a magnificent oil of old J. P., bald pate, walrus moustache, W. C. Fields nose and all). But essentially that's because most banking officers at Morgan look like professional diplomats: vom Hofe was the senior v.-p. in charge of lending to the oil companies before he was given the top job in Paris, and the European experience has been strange for him.

435

"There's been a culture shock", vom Hofe says. "I wouldn't want to come to a branch like this in any capacity other than that of boss. The relations between people at work are so much more strained and formal here than they are at home. By their education, the French have become extremely dependent on having everything well defined and laid out. All the important people in French banking come from one club, they're all graduates of one school, and they're all either in the active employ of the government or on leave. They form what is called the technocracy here, and they automatically consult with each other. Of course, once you get to understand this, it makes things more predictable. And they're intelligent, anxious to open up France, open up themselves."

The idea of using the foreign branches as significant stops on the "career path" of a future leader came to the banks very recently. It derives really not from any special thought about the problems of succession in large international enterprises, but simply from the increasing importance of the business done. In the old days, foreign branches were staffed with older men experienced in the bank's routine or well-connected younger men not perceived as likely candidates for major management posts at home: there are still no presidents of really big banks who rose through the overseas branches. But in any big organization a division tends to contribute to top management in ratio to its significance in the operation—the bigger the division, the more likely its executives are to be considered as candidates for corporate staff. As the foreign business grew, the quality and prospects of the men assigned to it improved, and the jobs abroad moved into the chain of succession.

Placing the management of the foreign branches in the hands of people with home-office ambitions serves another important purpose for the big banks: it keeps policy uniform across the world. Because the product is fungible—money is money wherever it comes from and however it is used—banks tend to be run on a more centralized basis than other large organizations, and headquarters would usually like to keep its branches on a fairly short leash. Moreover, there is no way for a bank to insulate its reported annual domestic results from what happens in the foreign branches —the Federal Reserve Act requires that every bank with offices abroad must "at the end of each fiscal period transfer to its general ledger the profit or loss accrued at each branch." But the foreign exchange business moves too fast for any effective control at long range, and building on that necessary freedom the more aggressive managers of the larger branches have been able to achieve a fair degree of independence—especially in situations where they fund their own loans in the local money markets.

"New York knows what I'm doing," says Danny Davison of Morgan in London, "because I send them the figures—a week or so late, much too late for them to do anything about it." (Werner Stange, his colleague in Zurich, who came to international banking from Morgan's trust department, comments that "We always traded the Swiss franc in New York, but now we know what we are doing.") Some obedience to home-office rules can be achieved by installing identical computer procedures and operating manuals (confronted with escalating expenses and diminishing profits in England, Citicorp sent its deputy chief of operations to London to Americanize the paper-handling), but often the American procedures are incompatible with custom in the local market and make more trouble than their economy is worth. Best to rely on the services of managers who are chips off the old block, and expect to slot back into it.

The only obvious alternative to this pattern is the construction of a loose affiliation of essentially separate banks moulded to the patterns of the host countries, which appears to be the sort of organization the nonfinancial multinational corporations will adopt (the automobile companies are there already). But there is, it turns out, a third way to handle the problem, of which the Bank of America is sole proprietor. It makes that Bank, usually (and foolishly) ignored in discussions of international banking, the most interesting and over the long run perhaps the most likely winner among the American banks abroad.

Josef Kramer, a compact, strikingly handsome man who heads the Bank of America operation in Zurich, was born in a country town near Basel, one of seven children whose father died young. He had to go to a commercial high school which offered no access to university, and on completing it he immigrated to the United States, where he found a job at the Bank of America Edge Act subsidiary in New York and remained fifteen years, marrying an American girl and acquiring American citizenship. When Bank of America decided to go to Zurich in 1967, Kramer opened the office. He does not have much in common with his fellow members at the Club Baur au Lac (a very nice club, rather like the City Club in Worcester, Massachusetts); but he knows about them as no non-Swiss possibly could.

Rudolf J. Gebert, Bank of America's number-two area administrator for Germany, based in Frankfurt, worked in a German bank before immigrating to America in 1956 and signing on with Bank of America in San Francisco. He became an American citizen and married an American girl, and in 1966 the bank sent him back to Germany (where it had been operating since 1951, first from Dusseldorf, now from four branches with headquarters in Frankfurt). "Bank of America," Gebert says, "was not traditionally in the business of lending to big corporations; First National City and Chase were. Inevitably, they had the inside track on the German subsidiaries of the American corporations, and we had to develop local business." About two-thirds of Bank of America's loans in Germany are to German companies, and the Bank runs essentially on its own Deutsche-mark deposit base; Gebert estimates that 75 of the 100 largest German companies borrow from Bank of America. The Bank also owns a large German consumer credit bank with twenty-five branches scattered around Germany. (Here First National City is considerably bigger, however, having acquired in 1973 an "indirect majority interest" in a German consumer finance operation with 222 offices in 153 German cities.)

Jeffrey Howles who is in charge of the giant Bank of America operation in the United Kingdom, is an Englishman who immigrated to America, married an American girl, acquired American citizenship, and was sent back to London. Yves LaMarche, born in France, immigrated to California in 1955, a year before Bank of America opened its first office in Paris; to repeat the litany, he married an American girl and became an American citizen. He took a job at Bank of America while studying to be an accountant in San Francisco: "I liked it and was treated well and I stayed". After service in Buenos Aires, he was sent to France in 1969 to oversee the French and other Mediterranean (including Lebanese and Libyan) business of the bank.

LaMarche is at first sight the most remarkable of this remarkable crew. He operates not out of a bank office but from the sixth floor of the Time-Life building near the Champs-Élysées; he is florid in complexion, casual, superbly straightforward. Of the five French branches, he reports, Lille and Strasbourg operate entirely in francs, Lyon is 99 percent in francs, Marseille is 90·4 percent in francs, and even Paris 60 percent in francs. He has much more independent authority than anybody in the Bank of America operation ever had, in California or elsewhere, until quite recently. "Decentralization," he says, "is the best thing the bank ever did to itself." And he uses this authority aggressively, funding his banks long or short according to his views of the money market rather than according to their loan portfolios, demanding lines of credit in francs from the nationalized French banks in return for the backup lines he offers them in dollars, wheeling and dealing with Qaddafy and Boumedienne.

"People will tell you that large banks are full of red tape and cannot make decisions," LaMarche said in spring 1973, "but I got a phone call at eleven at night, another phone call at one a.m., and between the two we committed seventy-five million dollars in Algeria. I went to Algeria to sign the next morning. We syndicated out twenty-five million to Citibank, twenty-five million to Chase, picked up a management fee of two hundred and fifty thousand dollars, quite substantial. That goes on the bottom line of the Paris branch this month. Tom Clausen [Bank of America's president] thinks Paris is doing very well; maybe it is, maybe not. London and San Francisco see what I'm doing. They may say, 'We think you are wrong.' I say, Thank you very much.' I may do what they recommend, I may not."

Ideally, LaMarche would like to move without the need to make the midnight phone calls. "We still have red tape to escape", he said. "We have the G.L.C.—General Loan Committee—in San Francisco. *I* could sell the G.L.C., but I have to go through a guy in San Francisco who doesn't know the deal, and he has to sell it. And if the G.L.C. is in a lousy mood that morning he can get shot down."

The man who put all this together is C. M. VanVlierden, an avuncular Dutchman who (begging your pardon) immigrated to America in 1951 (he had previously married an American girl), became an American citizen—and stayed in California. "I had been with a Dutch bank in Hong Kong," he said one day in early 1973, looking out the tinted windows of the fortieth floor, over the wonderful jumble of San Francisco. "I saw the colonial times drawing to a close, but they were insisting on putting money in Indonesia, so I resigned and came here. When I came, our balance sheet of total resources showed a hundred and fifty million abroad. We had had a branch in London since 1931 but not many people knew about it in the bank. Now we have one hundred and one branches, after losing eight in Chile, twelve and a half billion in resources, eleven thousand people outside the United States, two hundred and seventy of them native Americans. It is what one can do having a broad world view.

"In the State of California we are used to all sorts of nationalities. In the 1960s, we could always find in our domestic system someone who knew the place abroad where we were opening up. We have not even started to exploit the range of different nationalities, educations, cultures, points of view."

The branches of American banks abroad are not as restricted as their domestic offices are in the kinds of business they can do. Though the Fed may not authorize them "to engage in the general business of producing, distributing, buying or selling goods, wares or merchandise"—and they are prohibited from "underwriting, selling, or distributing" corporate securities—the law rather vaguely permits "such further powers as may be usual in connection with the transaction of the business of banking in the places where such foreign branch may transact business." In practice, the restrictions have not prevented American banks abroad from buying or establishing as subsidiaries merchant banks that are virtually indistinguishable from Wall Street investment firms. A number of these houses are consortia of several banks from different countries.

Especially in Switzerland, the American banks have thrived on money management for individuals—not just Americans—who like the idea of combining Wall Street expertise with the guaranteed secrecy of the Swiss banking law. They probably do not get their fair share of Mafia money, however, because the mob feels safer in the hands of the Swiss. (Hugo Frey, a Zurich attorney and bank auditor, takes umbrage at this idea: "If I were an American gangster," he says, "I would put my money under a false name in an American bank." Ever since the Chase Manhattan Bank approved the signature of "H. R. Hughes" on a McGraw–Hill cheque without even attempting to contact Howard Hughes—after the Swiss bank involved had refused to honour the cheque unless Chase specifically okayed it—the Swiss have taken a dim view of the standards of care exercised by American banks in the prevention of large-scale swindle.)

Apart from money management, however, the international bankers take little note of the Swiss: the "gnomes of Zurich" business is strictly British politics and newspaper sloganeering. The Swiss do not permit their banks to have branches abroad: every Swiss office outside the country is separately incorporated under the laws of that country and is treated by the Swiss banking authorities as a foreign bank except when it deals in Swiss francs, which the Swiss authorities keep in their patented hammerlock. (Conversely, American and other banks that wish to have Swiss operations must incorporate those operations separately, and must operate as though the only capital at their disposal were that physically placed in Switzerland to support this subsidiary corporation.) Swiss banks tend to hold more foreign currency than most other banks, because the Swiss government has always kept interest rates on the franc below those available elsewhere, and as a result they took a beating widely believed to have been in the hundreds of millions of dollars on the unexpected dollar devaluation of February 1973. London was full of dry eyes when the news was known: it is entirely proper—even *de rigueur*—to bad-mouth the Swiss in London. "The Swiss have never originated a business in their lives", says Jocelyn Hambro of Hambro's Bank, the largest of the British merchant banks (with $2,500 million in assets). "They charge you a large commission for buying you the wrong stock, and the chap can't complain because he shouldn't have had the money there, anyway."

Swiss banking started on the remittances of mercenary armies (especially the Swiss Guards in the Vatican), and was always based on inflows rather than outflows. Michel Audéod, a Genevois banker of the eighteenth century who bought lifetime bonds of the French crown in the name of young Geneva girls, lousing up the actuarial basis of French finance, was executed in 1789 in Switzerland for exporting money. For a brief period after World War II, when Switzerland alone in the European heartland was solvent, the Swiss banks financed some of the infrastructure of reviving Europe (especially the electrification of the railroads, which made customers for Swiss hydroelectric installations), but since the late 1950s they have preferred to stay out of the hurly-burly and make markets. There is a little culture shock here, too, by the way: in the bookcase behind Hans Mast's desk at Credit Suisse are *Inside USA*, a two-volume history of the Bank of New South Wales, a book called *The Financial Manager*, and Norman Vincent Peale's *Sin, Sex and Self-Control*.

VanVlierden believes the American banks have succeeded abroad because of their dynamism and their freedom from inherited custom and prejudice: "For the first time, European takers [i.e., borrowers] did not have to belong to a club, they were not at the mercy of a few investment bankers who would say, 'I don't like your tie or the colour of your skin so you pay two percent more.'" Citibank's Ronald Geezy, with a different kind of realism, says, "It's regulation at home; you can't see the profitability at home, you've got a five-year plan, so you come where you can fulfil it." But there is a larger cause: a radical change in the world's monetary arrangements and in the structure of the world's industrial enterprise. This story is closely intertwined with the history of the last quarter of a century, and some sense of where we are now in international banking and money, and how we got there, has become literally indispensable for anyone who seeks to understand foreign *and domestic* economic and monetary policy in the years ahead. In as untechnical a manner as possible, let us take a look at this immensely important and widely but ignorantly discussed business of international money flows.

4

What does it mean when we say that an American oil company buys oil from an Arab sheikhdom? It means that somewhere in the world a bank balance is transferred from the account of the oil company to the account of the sheikh. If the sheikh wants dollars, and the balance is in America, presumably there is no problem. But if he wants German marks in Germany, and the oil company has only American dollars in America, clearly some intermediating machinery will have to be set up.

In the hundred years before World War I which were the great age of internationalism this machinery was the gold market. It was not just that paper money was convertible into gold (on demand to a government or to a bank that issued the bank note); most money *was* gold—Yale's Robert Triffin estimates that between 70 percent and 80 percent of all the money in circulation in the period 1885–1913 was precious metals rather than paper. Accounts between countries were settled in theory and to a considerable degree in practice by the exchange of gold, if only by the natural flow of currency. If a country bought more goods abroad than it sold to foreigners, gold flowed out; money became more valuable by comparison with goods, reducing prices; lower prices domestically made exports cheaper on foreign markets and imports more dear; and the "balance of payments" was restored. As an alternative to the loss of gold, the country with the negative balance of payments could provide investment opportunities for countries with positive balances. The expression of these better investment opportunities was usually a higher interest rate. For the better part of a century—into the Great Depression, in fact—the Bank of England regulated the flow of gold into and out of Britain by manipulating the "bank rate" to encourage foreigners to invest in England when the trade balance was negative, encourage British enterprise to look elsewhere when it was positive.

The greatest single weakness of this system (which never worked precisely as described, of course) was that it made no provision for economic growth: if the volume of trade increased substantially but the monetary base of precious metals remained stable, economies would become "illiquid". Moreover, cultural traditions in places like India and France tended to the removal of the precious metals monetary base from the flow of trade. During the nineteenth century, however, the discovery of gold mines in America, Russia, and South Africa—coupled with technological advances in gold mining and extraction—kept the precious-metals base expanding at least as rapidly as the need for it. And the Bank of England's success as overlord for money in the British Empire minimized the problems of a gold shortage. British colonies and commonwealth countries by necessity, and others in the British trade nexus by choice, were willing to use British pounds sterling as the equivalent of gold in the reserves behind the paper portion of their currency, and to settle their accounts by the exchange of pound sterling balances in British banks as well as by the shipment of gold.

The expenditure of treasure in World War I permanently disabled the nineteenth-century system, but for a decade after the end of the war the Bank of England—aided and abetted by the Federal Reserve Bank of New York, which in the regime of Benjamin Strong counted for more than the Federal Reserve Board in Washington—attempted to put all the dominoes back in place. Britain paid a terrible price in deferred economic development and unemployment in the 1920s because Montagu Norman as Governor of the Bank of England could see no substitute for convertibility of currencies into gold and left domestic interest rates high to retain the gold England had. In the light of American actions in the 1970s, however, it should be noted that Norman and his colleagues did keep faith with those who had enabled world trade to expand by accepting the pound as "good as gold". Hans Hock, a partner in the London house of Singer & Friedlander, who can remember money markets in Vienna in the 1920s, says that Churchill in 1926 fixed the pound at the rate it had commanded before the war "because he thought that if you dropped it you were cheating your creditors. Nobody," Hock adds, not criticizing, just commenting, "thinks that way today."

In the tense economies of the 1920s, others besides the Bank of England learned how to manipulate the system, and when the Depression came the United States and Europe sought to deal with it through policies later described as "beggar-thy-neighbour", erecting tariff barriers against imports and raising interest rates to draw gold. The resulting worldwide illiquidity, signalled by the collapse of the Kreditanstalt in Vienna and the failure of its correspondent banks around the world, provoked the worst economic crisis in history. The economy that pulled out of it most successfully before the war, Hitler's Germany, did so in part by abandoning the international monetary system and doing its foreign trade as a series of barter deals, which is about as efficient as requiring a shoemaker to trade shoes for his family's bread but yields an important apparent security in times of chaos—the French reverted to it by instinct at the end of 1973 to assure oil supplies from the Arabs.

The war ended with virtually all the world's gold in the United States, and no reason to believe it would ever leave. The monetary experts of the allied powers met in 1944 at the Mount Washington Hotel in Bretton Woods, New Hampshire, and drafted a new international monetary system based essentially on the interchangeability of gold and two "reserve currencies"—the pound and the dollar. Exchange rates between currencies were fixed within a narrow trading band and could be changed only by agreement. The reference standard—the dollar or pound—was fixed by relation to gold and would never fluctuate. The drastically weakened British economy was never up to the burdens implied by the use of its money as a world reserve currency, and within a few years the pound was dramatically devalued, with great losses to those countries in the British commonwealth and the Persian Gulf that were holding their reserves in pounds. Soon after the collapse of the last British attempt to play imperial master—in the Suez imbroglio of 1956—the world monetary system became a gold-exchange system with the dollar as the exclusive exchange component.

In the hindsight of a generation, it is hard to fathom the faith of the European (and American) monetary experts who believed that the world could safely entrust the creation of its reserve assets to the proprietors of a printing press in Washington. As the Swiss economist Eberhard Reinhardt puts it, "A reserve currency country which can finance a balance of payments deficit cheaply and unobtrusively with the indulgence of others enjoys the economic advantage of being able to extend its people's living standards or its industry's foreign investment far beyond the limits of its own economic potential. That its domestic political parties will not demur to such a situation, as long as it can be maintained, goes without saying." No more touching example could be found for the world's belief in America as the custodian of mankind's dreams than the universal acceptance of the Bretton Woods idea that the United States would stand guard over everyone's money, never taking so much as a tip for itself. The loss of faith in American idealism, too, should be seen not as the result of revisionist history or Asian war but as a natural reaction to the betrayal of the trust America accepted—not knowing very much about what it was doing—in the late 1940s.

If the financing of international trade requires a supply of reserves, then the growth of trade requires increasing reserves. The gold being in America, that growth could come, in the Bretton Woods system, only from an increase in the number of dollars held outside the United States. At first, the dollars were supplied as gifts, in Marshall Plan aid, contributions to the World Bank, etc. Tourism was promoted; defence budgets subsidized; troops were stationed abroad. Capital remaining short in Europe and elsewhere, Americans then supplied capital by expanding their businesses internationally and buying into businesses abroad. By the end of the 1950s, the American balance of payments had fallen clearly into deficit, thanks in large part to American investment overseas. A few of the countries receiving additional dollars became concerned about what General DeGaulle's advisers described as the buying up of European industry with American IOUs; France began to claim gold for some of its dollars. From 1957 to 1962, the value of American private investment abroad rose from $37,000 million to $60,000 million. The American gold stock ran down from $22,800 million to $16,100 million (at $35 an ounce). Gold held at the Federal Reserve Bank of New York "under earmark" for foreign central banks rose from $6,000 million to $12,700 million. But the dollars were needed to provide liquidity for trade under the gold-exchange system; grumbling a little about the Americans' abuse of their privilege of printing a currency accepted all over the world, the other nations continued to accumulate dollars.

By 1962, the American dollar, duly certified as legal tender in the United States, was on the world scene a piece of paper very much like the banknote of the nineteenth-century American bank. In theory, that banknote had been redeemable for specie if presented to the bank; in theory, the dollar was convertible to gold. In fact, the bank had never had enough specie to pay off its entire note issue, and the United States presently did not have enough gold to pay off the dollar holdings of foreigners. The system rested on confidence that the bank was being soundly run. And then, in the late 1960s, the bank began to make loans to its directors and employees—the United States began to run a deficit not only in its balance of payments but also in its balance of trade, using its privilege of printing an international currency to increase the proportion of the world's production that Americans consumed. In 1970, in a desperate effort to sustain the gold-exchange system, the European and Japanese central banks bought no less than $20,000 million of American government securities, fighting to keep the supply of dollars down near the level of the world's need for dollars as a reserve currency. In 1971, the United States threw in the towel: unwilling even to contemplate the management of an orderly and deliberate reduction of the American standard of living by comparison to that of the rest of the world, the Nixon administration devalued the dollar (raised the official price of gold in dollars) and suspended the convertibility of the dollar to gold at any price. The nations that had kept faith with the United States and accumulated dollars when America was still willing to exchange them for gold were stuck with pieces of paper of decreasing value; the nations that had doubted the integrity of the United States and demanded gold for their surplus dollars had won the game. In spring 1974, the gold Charles DeGaulle had bought from America for $2,000 million a decade before was worth $10,000 million.

The bank had failed: its banknotes would no longer be redeemed in specie. For eighteen months, an effort was made to maintain the fiction that a nonredeemable currency could continue to serve as a reference standard, and that exchange rates could be fixed in a world where only drastic intervention by governments in the currency markets could keep them stable. That fiction collapsed in 1973, punctured by the extraordinarily irresponsible second devaluation of the dollar, and the world's economies drifted off onto the stormy seas of "floating rates". The problem now was that the world still desperately needed the dollar as a medium for the settlement of international accounts.

Economists had been saying for a generation that if gold were demonetized its price would drop: Triffin in his book reprinted a futurist piece from a 1961 issue of *The Economist*—allegedly the memoirs of the director of the International Monetary Fund, written in 1971—in which gold, demonetized, dropped in price to the $2.50 an ounce that dentists were willing to pay for it. What would happen if the governments of the world in fact dumped their gold stocks onto the market is an open question—though the economists are probably wrong. What did happen in 1971 was that the governments set a theoretical "price" at which nobody bought or sold, and the stock in nongovernmental hands, theoretically demonetized, was allowed to find its own level, which soared stratospherically above the official price.

Now nobody would use gold for international settlements purposes. By treaty and agreement, a dollar was "worth" ·024 of an ounce of gold; but on the open market, a dollar was worth, in spring 1974, only ·006 of an ounce of gold. So long as the treaties survived, nobody who could pay a debt with a piece of paper would ever use a precious metal to which the market accorded a value of four such pieces of paper. Brave statements about some substitute for both gold and the dollar were heard around the world, and the International Monetary Fund actually created something called a Special Drawing Right (SDR), popularly referred to as "paper gold". There was discussion of the creation of a Common Market currency that could be used for reserve purposes; a number of international transactions were consummated in German marks and Swiss francs. But neither the Germans nor the Swiss were willing to subject their currencies to the pressures that any reserve currency must endure; when the dollar collapsed in 1973—losing 40 percent of its value in terms of marks and francs over a breathtaking six months—both the Germans and the Swiss took stern action to prevent the building up of mark or franc balances by outsiders.

For the benefits derived from the privilege of printing a reserve currency ultimately create costs. Triffin, though also concerned that the Congressmen he was addressing would believe the "absurd theory of a permanent and intractable dollar glut," warned in 1959 against "the totally irrational use of national currencies as international reserves." In this situation, Reinhardt wrote a dozen years later, national authorities "are driven into a policy which pleases no one. To the extent that they succeed in running down their foreign liabilities, they will tend to extinguish reserves instead of creating them, and so cease to fulfil the proper function of a reserve currency, exposing themselves to foreign criticism either of unwarranted interest-rate manipulation or of irresponsible deflation. At home, meanwhile, they are forced into a posture with which the full-employment promises and electoral dictates of democratic governments are increasingly hard to reconcile. Thus step by step, as inevitably as in a Greek tragedy, the moment comes when economically and politically they are doomed to collapse." The Apocalypse is not at hand, and is not inevitable; but we have gone much farther down Reinhardt's road than almost anyone in America (except a few cranks) seems to realize.

17 / The Uses of Eurodollars

In the old days, when monetary control was exercised by central bankers, their primary concern was the stability of the currency in terms of foreign exchange. That objective, in the new era, has been deposed from its old position. It was recognized, even in the initial charter of the I[nternational] M[onetary] F[und] that stability of foreign exchange was not so sacred an object as central bankers had tried to make it in former times. Arrangements were made for agreed adjustment of exchange rates on the occasion of what was called a "fundamental disequilibrium". I would in no way question that this is indeed a real problem. . . . I would nevertheless maintain that it has been quite overshadowed by another, by the inflations (active and creeping inflations) which are traceable, not to "fundamental disequilibrium", but to the implementation of pseudo-Keynesian policies by weak and irresolute governments.

—J. R. HICKS (1967)

* * *

For the big American banks with international interests, the first act of Reinhardt's Greek tragedy was very cheerful: all over the world, everybody wanted to borrow their dollars, at higher interest rates than they could get at home. The money could be loaned, moreover, in dollar denominations: all the risk of currency fluctuation would be borne by the borrower. And a good deal of it went out under government guarantee of repayment. Nearly all this business could be and was conducted from the home office: America, after all, was where the dollars were.

A small pool of dollars, however, remained outside the United States. Like the capitalist countries, the Soviet Union and its satellites needed dollars to participate in world trade. But the

United States had major unsettled claims on the Soviet Union, deriving in part from repudiated Czarist bonds and in part from war matériel shipped to Russia during the war under Lend-Lease. Political relations were awful; the Russians were not prepared to hold dollar balances where an American government could seize them in satisfaction of its own or its citizens' claims. Through agencies abroad, the Russians made loans of dollars, to be repaid in dollars: the Eurodollar was invented at their Narodny Bank in Paris. Technical assistance was available from the Chase Bank, the leading American correspondent for the State Bank of the USSR. Ultimately, in 1966, the Russians opened their very own Swiss bank, Wozchod Handelsbank AG.

In 1956, in a watershed decision so little noticed at the time that historians barely mention it, the Eisenhower administration reacted to the British-French-Israeli attack on Egypt in the spirit of the Neutrality Act of the 1930s, freezing the dollar assets of both the aggressors and the Arab world. Though the Arabs regained control of their assets within weeks, the shock of being expropriated survived for years; presently the Arabs' dollar earnings, like the Russians', fed a pool of dollars retained outside the United States.

Britain's gradual resignation from the reserve currency business provided employment for these external dollar holdings, which flowed naturally into the financing of trade that had once been denominated in sterling. When the Treaty of Rome brought the Common Market into being, the growing pool of dollars held abroad provided a convenient common currency for the rapidly growing internal trade of the European Economic Community. The German machine-tool maker was happy to sell to the French automobile manufacturer for dollars; and the dollars were there in Paris to be borrowed. Beginning in 1959, all the major European currencies were freely convertible to dollars for current account. Thereafter, transactions from guilders to lira, for example, were most easily accomplished in dollars, because the markets trading either against dollars were much broader and deeper than the market trading the two against each other. So a Dutchman needing a loan in lira would borrow dollars, not lira.

It was this separate market for short-term dollar loans that persuaded the Kennedy administration to try Operation Twist. When the dollar outflow persisted, and Operation Twist proved more trouble than it could be worth, the government in 1963 moved to direct intervention, restricting foreign access to the American securities buyer by an Interest Equalization Tax. This created a tax differential between bonds bought from foreigners and bank loans made to foreigners, and thus brought a rash of loan applications from abroad; so Congress passed new legislation that applied the tax to loans, too. Now anyone outside the United States who got his hands on a dollar had a positive incentive to keep it outside the United States: Regulation Q limited the interest American banks would pay for that dollar at home, but nobody limited the interest paid on it if it remained outside the United States. Whatever its value in preventing dollar expatriation, the Interest Equalization Tax greatly diminished dollar repatriation. The quantities held abroad continued to rise, and in 1965, the Johnson administration went a step further, establishing a Voluntary Credit Restraint Programme to diminish lending to Europe; in 1968, with crisis around the corner, the government instituted a Mandatory Foreign Investment Programme.

So long as the balance of payments continued negative, none of this worked very well; in hindsight, it is hard to see why anyone thought it would. As Walter Wriston of First National City told Alfred Hayes of the Federal Reserve Bank of New York in 1964, "There are no exchange regulations that anybody can put into effect that somebody brought up in Brazil or the Argentine cannot find a way to get around." Money *flows*. Charles Kindleberger comments on the inefficiency even of the Nazi "system of controls backed by the death penalty," and tells a story from the 1930s about "a man who had given up smuggling money out of Germany for kicks; it was too easy, he claimed, and he had turned to the more stimulating and equally rewarding game of smuggling out people." Britain, having lived with these problems much longer, has sought to control not the holding of pounds abroad but the holding of foreign currencies by organizations or individuals in London or by British travellers and businesses abroad.

As lendable dollars piled up in Europe, the foreign banks operating in the Eurodollar market became competitors of American banks for short-term business. In the early 1960s the supply of dollars to this market seemed sufficiently secure for lenders to offer longer-term credits, and in 1963 the London firm of S. G. Warburg sold the first "Eurobond", a $15 million issue for the Italian government's toll road corporation Autostrade. Nevertheless, most of even the biggest American banks stayed home, fearing to offend their correspondents: at the end of 1964, there were still only eleven American banks with branches abroad; and in mid-1965, the total assets of American banks abroad added up to only $7·5 billion, of which at least half were deposits denominated in the local currency and used for local purposes. What finally brought the American banks to Europe en masse, in fact, was not the chance to do an expanded business with multinational companies operating there but the chance to get around the Federal Reserve rules that were holding down their domestic deposits.

American banks require the consent of the Fed before they can open branches abroad, but they also—and more importantly—require the consent of the government on whose soil the branch will stand. The branch must then abide by the laws of the host country, and the degree of supervision exercised by American authorities can be no greater than what the host government permits. In London, the British couldn't care less, and the Comptroller of the Currency has opened a permanent resident office to inspect American branches. "It doesn't matter to *me*", said Keogh at the Bank of England, "whether Citibank is evading American regulations in London. I wouldn't particularly want to know. If the Comptroller's people feel they can make their jurisdiction run in London, I say, 'Good luck to them.' "

In Switzerland, on the other hand, bank secrecy laws absolutely prohibit examination of the branches of foreign banks by the authorities of the home country. A pair of Swedish bank examiners who tried to find out what a Swedish bank was up to in Zurich were escorted by the police to the airport a few years ago and forcibly expelled from Switzerland. Morgan Guaranty in Zurich likes to tell the story of a New York State bank examiner who came into the office and identified himself for purposes of cashing a check, begging Morgan not to tell the Swiss that he had so much as stepped in the door: he wanted to go skiing and was afraid that if the Swiss found out he had visited an American bank he would be kicked out. The Swiss are not alone in these attitudes: the New York State banking department in 1973 received a stiff communiqué from the Belgian government instructing it never again to send an examiner to Brussels. "The Fed," says Morgan Guaranty's vom Hofe in Paris, "is interested in understanding foreign exchange, and wants to see our records blow by blow. Under French law, we can't do that".

Even where the local laws permit direct American government regulation, the Fed cannot cripple American branches in their competition with the local banks. If American branches were compelled to keep some of their dollar deposits idle at the Fed, they would have to charge higher interest rates on Eurodollar loans than other banks in the same city. Deposits in foreign branches, then, are free of reserve requirements. Moreover, when Eurodollars are scarce the American branches must be able to bid for them against the local competitors: to hold the branches to Regulation Q would simply eliminate them as a factor in times of high rates. So the branches are allowed to pay whatever interest may be necessary for Eurodollars, even on deposits kept at the branch less than thirty days.

When the Fed turned the screws on the money supply in 1966, banks with foreign branches found that they could replace their disappearing CDs by bringing Eurodollars home from their branches. The squeeze was brief in 1966, and less than $3,000 million was repatriated; but the lesson was learned. By 1969, when the Fed again tried to restrain the growth of the money supply by preventing the banks from selling CDs there were forty-odd American banks with branches abroad, and among them they brought home almost $14,000 million to frustrate the Fed's programme of restraint. First National City alone took $2,000 million out of London.

Finally the Fed introduced reserve requirements on repatriated Eurodollars. At first this was done as delicately as possible, with the reserve requirement to apply only to any excess of Eurodollars imported over and above the levels reached the previous spring. By 1969, the total size of the Eurodollar market was estimated at $35,000 million, and the authorities were concerned about a general collapse if the huge American demand were suddenly removed. This worry turned out to be entirely unnecessary: the American banks ran down their imported Eurodollar balances as quickly as they could, returning the money to Europe, and the Euromarket absorbed the $14,000 million (mostly via central bank purchases of U.S. Treasury securities). By spring 1974 the reported Eurodollar market had risen to an incredible $270,000 million and borrowers were paying more than 13 percent annual interest for pieces of it.

2

What is a Eurodollar? It is not a foolish or easily answered question. "In spite of all the literature," says Raymond Conninx of the London office of the First National Bank of Chicago, "there's very little knowledge about the total situation". In spring 1975, Richard Debs, first vice-president of the New York Fed, told a meeting of banking lawyers that "The Eurodollar market itself is not easily definable, and its legal framework, if any, is even less so." Existentially, a Eurodollar is an entry in dollars on the books of a non-American bank. (In this context, a foreign branch of an American bank is a non-American bank.) Something like half of the Eurodollars are held by foreign governments as part of their currency reserves. One of the reasons to hold dollars rather than gold was always that gold yielded no interest, while dollars could be kept profitably in liquid "money-market instruments". The foreign central banks may lend these dollars to their local banks (sometimes American branches get a piece of this business) or buy U.S. Treasury bills with the money. The other half of the Eurodollar deposits are held by a wide variety of corporations and even individuals.

This money rushes around the world at an unbelievable pace. On the day I was at the New York Clearing House, the computer that is the heart of its CHIPS service (Clearing House Interbank Payments System) batted out page after page of computer paper representing all the transfers of money from account to account by the thousand or so correspondent banks of the Clearing House members. The total balanced (thank God) at about $42,700 million —for one day's transactions. "Slow day", said the Clearing House officer, looking idly at the last sheet. "Back in October we were doing sixty-five billion a day".

How much real money is here, nobody knows. Take a situation where the Dresdner Bank of Germany lends a million dollars to the branch of the Banque de Paris et du Pay Bas in Geneva, which in turn places the money with its Paris home office, which lends it to Renault, which ships it to Detroit to pay for air bags. At the end of this process—which may require an hour or so—there is no surviving Eurodollar: the million dollars have been repatriated. But all three banks will show a $1 million Eurodollar asset—and the corresponding liability (the Dresdner Bank got its $1 million *somewhere*), and a clerk or an economist adding up balance-sheet aggregates in the market will find $3 million of Eurodollars where really there are none. Meanwhile, CHIPS will show a $3 million flow on the computer print-out.

Reports from German and Swiss authorities indicate that about 60 percent of the assets of the foreign banks operating in those countries consist of claims on other banks. Federal Reserve figures indicate that about 70 percent of the assets of foreign branches of American banks consist of claims on other banks. Suddenly the $270,000 million Eurodollar market shrinks to maybe half that figure; but there is so much double counting that nobody really knows.

The fact that the figures "don't add up" has led Milton Friedman, the Princeton economist Fritz Machlup, and the Italian central banker Guido Carli to insist that the Eurodollar market works like a domestic banking system, with a "multiplier" that increases the money supply as the banks create deposits to make loans. The "major source" of Eurodollars, Friedman has written, "is a bookkeeper's pen". But Fred H. Klopstock, an earnest European who is "adviser" on international matters at the New York Fed, points out that credit creation by "a bookkeeper's pen" in American banks works only because the new money stays in the system: the borrower, removing his money from the bank that loaned it to him, takes it one way or another to some other bank— it gets out of the system only to the extent that people decide they would rather hold hard cash. Eurodollars, on the other hand, keep leaking out. A Eurodollar spent or invested in the United States, as most of them are, simply disappears from the Eurodollar market.

When a Eurodollar is converted by a borrower into his home currency, however, his central bank must make a decision either to buy at U.S. Treasury bill or to invest at what are usually the higher rates of the Eurodollar market itself. If the central bank buys the Treasury bill, the Eurodollar is repatriated and there is no "multiplier" in the market. If the central bank gets greedy and puts the money back into the market, the quantity of Eurodollars in the system can indeed be increased without any further payments deficit from the United States. No doubt it happens, and Geoffrey Bell, committed to neither side of the Friedman-Klopstock argument, suggests that "the bets should be placed on the existence of a credit multiplier of more than minimal size". "The Bundesbank deposits the dollar in the market," explains J. H. Atkin, a very sharp young British economist at the London headquarters of First National City, describing the course of events, "and Fritz comes around again with that same dollar".

At this point the finely tuned instrument of the international currency market can turn into a vulgar carousel. Speculators attacking the dollar buy marks hoping for a quick profit when the mark rises in value by comparison with the dollar; the German government returns the dollar to the market, where the speculators borrow it and again buy marks; the German government returns the dollar to the market, etc., ad infinitum. Unfortunately, something not far removed from this coarse comedy can happen even if the German government buys Treasury bills with its newly acquired dollars, for the American banks, their deposit balances increased by the proceeds of the sale of Treasury bills, can lend Fritz the money just as easily as the Eurodollar banks can. (If there is an Interest Equalization Tax, Fritz borrows through an American subsidiary, name of Franz, and quietly cables the cash to Germany.) In the nineteenth century, such tricks were too costly to be worth playing: gold had to be loaded onto a ship, carried to another port, unloaded and so forth. Thanks to the miracles of modern communications, the carousel can now complete a turn and start a new one every fifteen minutes or so. This is why the dollar dropped so fast in early 1973, and why the decline could be halted only by closing the exchange markets for a while. When they reopened, the Germans used their newly acquired dollars for the purchase of special U.S. Treasury issues sold directly to them. Meanwhile, the great quantity of marks created by the Germans to buy dollars inflated the German price level; and American politicians added insult to injury by announcing that the rate of inflation at home, while awful, was after all less severe than the inflation in Germany. . . . This is no way to make friends, or admirers.

By spring 1973, new foreign investment was being prohibited in all the countries of the Common Market except England and Italy, where the currencies were even weaker than the dollar. A foreigner seeking to add to his Swiss franc account was not only denied interest on his money but forced to pay a fee of 2 percent per quarter for the privilege of holding his money in Switzerland. Banks in Germany were permitted to accept new deposits of marks in accounts owned by foreigners only if they deposited the entire sum—a 100 percent reserve—with the central bank. Banks operating in France were required to deposit with the central bank a reserve of 33 percent against any loans made over and above their total loans as of April 5, 1972. The Fed had imposed a 20 percent reserve requirement on any dollars drawn by American banks from their foreign branches. The Eurodollar market was dead: there was nobody who could borrow the money.

INTERNATIONAL BANKING

But if the Europeans didn't want to borrow dollars anymore, there were inhabitants of other countries who did. Blocked from lending to their established customers, the banks went hunting for plausible borrowers in Latin America, Africa, and Asia. Plausibility proved elastic; Geoffrey Bell reports loans to nations like Gabon by bankers "who literally didn't know where those countries were". In 1973 the banks of the Eurodollar market became the greatest single source of foreign aid to the "Third World"— private lending of dollars surpassed the total of grants and loans from Western governments and official international agencies. The Eastern Europeans, too, woke up to this matchless opportunity to borrow their capital needs, few questions asked; and American banks began to open offices in the Soviet Union and the Comecon countries.

To those who think this sort of thing a wee bit risky, David Rockefeller of Chase makes bold reply: "In terms of straight credit risk the presumption is that there is greater continuity of government in certain socialist states than in non-socialist states." Gaylord Freeman of First of Chicago agrees: "It's the less developed countries that have majority governments these days." Peter Ardrin, who runs the international side of Barclay's Bank in London, is less certain: "The idea that the Russians are a good risk," he says, "traces to the after-war years, which exhausts the memories of the young eager beavers from America. I leave these loans to them—I can't take a ten-year view on Romania." There is also a third position: "I have never lost a penny on Russia or Poland or the Congo," says a Swiss banker, "but we had made loans to Penn Central and Equity Funding. . . ."

In 1974, the Eurodollar market revived in Europe itself, as the Common Market countries, their balance of payments plunged into deficit by the jump in oil prices, borrowed from the banks the dollars the oil exporting countries were depositing in those banks. The sums were enormous: $1,500 million in one piece to France; $2,500 million in one piece to Britain; $4,000 million in several pieces to floundering Italy. By September 1974, the Comptroller was instructing American bank examiners to question all loans to

460

Italian government agencies, and rumours about Britain's ability to pay its debts were flooding the money centres. The oil exporting nations had put the world's monetary system on a carousel, charging more than the importing nations could afford but freely lending back the proceeds to maintain the appearance that the bills were being paid. As the risks multiplied, the Arabs tried to lay them off on America, using American banks and even the Treasury as intermediaries for their European loans. As the carousel speeded up—with American banks decreasing the proportion of their Eurodollar loans made for terms longer than a few months (in England, a few *days*)—it became increasingly hard to see any way for anyone to get off before the machinery broke down. In summer 1975, the fact that it had not broken down yet was considered hugely encouraging—but nobody had managed to get off. For the time being, though, the wheels continue to spin—especially in London.

3

"The name 'London Banker'," Bagehot wrote a century ago, "had especially a charged value. He was supposed to represent, and often did represent, a certain union of pecuniary sagacity and educated refinement which was scarcely to be found in any other part of society. In a time when the trading classes were very much ruder than they now are, many private bankers possessed variety of knowledge and a delicacy of attainment which would even now be very rare. Such a position is indeed singularly favourable. The calling is hereditary; the credit of the bank descends from father to son; this inherited wealth soon begins inherited refinement. Banking is a watchful, but not a laborious trade. A banker, even in large business, can feel pretty sure that all his transactions are sound, and yet have much spare mind. A certain part of his time, and a considerable part of his thoughts, he can readily devote to other pursuits. And a London banker can also have the most intellectual society in the world if he chooses it. There has probably very rarely ever been so happy a position as that of a London private banker; and never perhaps a happier."

The first contribution of the Eurodollar market to the lot of man was the creation of Swinging London, a place unlike the London of Bagehot's private banker because its refinement was questionable (a generation of young men and women were barbarously deafened in its nightclubs), but still an unusually sweet and cheerful ambiance. And few places in the world could have accepted prosperity so grandly as the City of London, the famous mile-square between St. Paul's and The Tower—the streets with the splendid names (Lombard Street, Cornhill, Threadneedle Street, Old Jewry); the cultivated history (Soanes's neo-classic Bank with the ushers in the mauve coats, behind it the Renaissance Royal Exchange; a sign just above eye-level of a cat playing a gamba with a pre-Tourte bow, announcing the Royal Bank of Scotland); the words on the plaques on the walls ("Here lived a man 8 times Lord Mayor of London, 1274–1281, and 1285"). New buildings and old, the rentals were the highest in the world: $35 per square foot per year. Tom Storrs of North Carolina National Bank, visiting his London branch, told its young manager that he could build a sizeable bank building at home for less than the annual rental in London.

Though London became the postwar lord of finance only when the Interest Equalization Tax signaled an American abdication, its supremacy soon seemed inevitable enough. "You've got the personnel, the communications, the time zones," says Dan Davison, who runs the Morgan Guaranty branch. "We're open when Hong Kong, Singapore and Tokyo are open, but also when New York is open." But there is more to it than that. "London has everything," says First National City's Atkin. "If you want to import wheat from Australia to Africa, you do it in London. London has a big equity market, and bonds; and the exchange market is here, because here is where the central banks intervene. In New York the exchange markets get out of whack, because they don't know what the central banks are doing. And though England was the first to industrialize, we are not an industrial nation—but the City can take any other financial market to the cleaners. Salaries in the

City are double those in British industry, and it's hard to find grey hairs. The City is full of young men who are expert. But I'm convinced that the major factor was something so mundane as the common language: it's much easier to transfer operational people from a small U.S. bank to London than to a place where the clerical staff speaks another language."

London was where the loans were funded; the strength of the Americans in the market was their complete understanding of liability management, of the idea that the man with the money counts for more than the man with the customers. "We spend all our time looking for deposits," says Morgan's Davison; "the British banks are out looking for loans". One of the reasons for the great volume of interbank lending was the extent of restrictions placed by governments on the operations of banks on the Continent, which often meant that the easiest place to "book" the loan was London, where there were almost no restrictions at all, provided the borrower was not British. It would not be unusual for Geneva to find the borrower, Frankfurt to take the credit risk, and London to supply the cash.

Loans in the Eurodollar market were written as a percentage over the interbank lending rate. If the loan was a term loan, the interest to be paid by the borrower was usually recalculated every six months, and the bank sought to match maturities—i.e., to fund the loan through a six-month interbank borrowing of its own. Nearly all the borrowers were prime names or governments. Rates on the best names were for a long time 1 percent per annum over the interbank rate; then they dropped to $\frac{3}{4}$ of 1 percent; in 1972, to $\frac{1}{2}$ of 1 percent, and in 1973, in a very controversial breakthrough billion-dollar loan to the nationalized British Electricity Board (guaranteed by Her Majesty's Treasury) to $\frac{3}{8}$ of 1 percent on the shorter maturities of a sinking fund situation (i.e., on the earlier repayments of a loan to be paid back in instalments rather than in a lump at the end.) For underdeveloped countries and not quite prime companies, the rates were 2 percent or even 3 percent over the interbank lending rate.

Where several different branches are involved in a single loan, the allocation of this return to the separate profit centres may be a source of political jockeying within the bank. A. Robert Abboud, deputy chairman of the First National Bank of Chicago—young, small, dark, with a prize-fighter's face and attitudes, up from Lebanese immigrant stock through the Harvard Business School —says that the pattern of government controls "makes it tougher for the branch manager, he has a less comfortable life. Fine, it's good for him." First of Chicago's formula for allocating proceeds, which seems typical, gives $\frac{1}{8}$ of 1 percent to the branch that books the loan, $\frac{1}{3}$ of 1 percent to the branch that takes the credit risk on a standard loan at $\frac{1}{2}$ of 1 percent over prime. That leaves $\frac{1}{24}$ of 1 percent as a finder's fee for the branch that developed the business. Yves LaMarche of Bank of America in Paris rather resents the $\frac{1}{8}$ of 1 percent his headquarters allocates to London for booking the loan: "I would say, Give them nothing: if they manage their funding right, they should make money out of booking the loan"— that is, they should be able to play with their maturity schedules in a way that reduces their cost of funds below the matched maturity rates on which the borrower's interest payments and the branch's earnings are calculated. LaMarche has high standards for his colleagues, and likes to live a little dangerously. If the loan is something less than prime, and the rate is more than $\frac{1}{2}$ of 1 percent over the interbank rate, the extra margin goes at all the banks, as it obviously should, to the branch that takes the risk.

These figures illustrate the problems of the branches that must live off the Eurodollar market—$\frac{1}{24}$ of 1 percent on $1 million is $416.66, or the rental of a dozen square feet in London for a year. The banks that have been around for twenty years or more are much better off: First National City, Morgan, Bank of America have long-standing local business to pay the costs of running a bank in Britain. "A lot of our profitability," says Ronald Geezy, a young American vice-president in the First National City London branch, "comes from a base of business for which we are the bank of account". "And when you have *that* business," adds David Reid, an older English colleague (since moved on to become head of Williams and Glyn's), "you have to be *awfully* bad to lose it".

In spring 1973, First National City London had 108 employees with twenty-five years or more of service in the bank. It also had a new chain of "money shops"—small loan offices—it had scattered around England, and a 40 percent interest in National & Grindlay's, a long-established nationwide British commercial bank. Morgan, which shares a British small-loan operation with Household Finance, has a large base of sterling business with the British sub-sidiaries of companies like Michelin and Siemens, because when they invaded the British market Morgan was almost the only bank active in their home country that also had a large London operation (Morgan has 575 employees scattered around London).

The two dozen American banks that opened their London offices in the later 1960s and early 1970s must pay all their bills, however, out of the small spread between the interbank rate and the bor-rowers' rate in the Eurodollar market—and competition has steadily driven the spread down. Keogh of the Bank of England estimates that the minimum cost of a London branch for an American bank runs between half a million and a million dollars; at $\frac{1}{2}$ of 1 percent, the break-even point is then between $100 million and $200 million in loans. Borrowers in Europe are not willing to supply as much information and security as borrowers in America—"I was used to amortizations and covenants," says Citibank's Dickerson; "no, we don't have any of those". And even if the information were more extensive, the smaller branch offices would not have the resources to make a realistic credit investiga-tion. "It's a constant battle", says George Campbell of North Carolina National Bank, "between placing earning assets on the books and keeping safe."

Most of the London branches of American banks are doing what Governor Andrew Brimmer of the Fed has called "essentially a money brokerage rather than a banking business". The difference is that a broker arranges for one party to get money from another, and is long gone before any problems about repayment may arise; the banker runs a risk. "Lots of people in this market," Sam Armacost, Bank of America's number-two in London, said in 1973, "are not considering risk at all; it's pure money rental." By

1974 risk factors were in everyone's mind—but the cost of money was so high that spreads remained comparatively small.

Most Eurodollar borrowings are short-term credits associated with the flow of world trade. But in 1973 something not far from $20,000 million (nobody could know for sure) was written in term loans in Eurodollars. There are also Eurobonds, written to be sold supposedly from places like Luxembourg and the Bahamas, which do not collect taxes on bond interest at the source (as most European governments do).

To the extent that this development merely revealed multinational companies using the full extent of their multinational standing to borrow in the cheapest market (and much of the term borrowing in Eurodollars was just that), a case can be made for it. Nor can anybody criticize the Euromarkets for lending to operations in underdeveloped countries where the local financial markets could not conceivably raise the necessary funds. But there were also borrowers from cosmopolitan countries who were in the Euromarkets because they could no longer convince people to lend them money at home: in the gentle words of R. H. Lutz of Crédit Suisse, "Underwriters occasionally try to represent borrowers as first class who, in fact, hardly deserve that classification and who would not be acceptable to the authorities of their own countries." And even in a time of worldwide and accelerating inflation (which makes all fixed debts easier to repay), the borrowing entities in some underdeveloped countries have unquestionably put themselves so deep in the hole that the lending banks are really relying on subsequent intervention by the governments of rich countries to bail out the loans they have made. "The only question is whether they can roll over this debt—cover it with new borrowings—as it comes due," Gerassimos Arsenis of the UN Conference on Trade and Development has said. "They can't pay it."

Most of these loans are what the French call "dry" and the Americans call "clean" credit—that is, all the money goes out of the bank; and quite a number of them are what the English call "one-off jobs"—that is, this bank and this borrower have never done business together before and may never meet again. In a portfolio of loans at $\frac{1}{2}$ of 1 percent over the interbank rate, the default of a $1 million credit eats up the net receipts (not just the profits) on $200 million loans, which is a pretty stiff penalty to pay for a misjudgment. As the loans lengthened—five years was a lot in the late 1960s, ten years was nothing remarkable in 1973— the dangers increased. Moreover, it is simply not true that the banks are matching maturities: that $42,700 million skipping along through the Clearing House computer in New York demonstrated the immense sums of overnight money were changing hands to fund loans that were much longer than overnight.

Of course, as Dan Davison puts it, "A short-term mismatch might embarrass me with my head office, but it won't endanger the Morgan Guaranty Trust Company." David Rockefeller says, "International banking is not a business for kids and country bumpkins," and despite some skepticism among British banks about what Ardrin of Barclay's calls "the First of Boot Hill" there are no kids or country bumpkins from America in this business in London. Though there is in theory no regulation, in fact nobody hangs out a shingle without talking to the Bank of England who know very much more than they say they want to know. Banks as big as Atlanta's Citizens & Southern have got a pursed lip and a shake of the head—the functional equivalent of "I don't think you'd be happy here"—from the Bank.

The failure of the U.S. National Bank of San Diego in autumn 1973 gave impressive evidence of the durability of what looks like a gossamer structure. As part of its effort to keep afloat the other enterprises of its chairman C. Arnholt Smith, U.S. National had arranged with syndicates of foreign (and a few domestic) banks to lend sister companies in Smith's Westgate-California conglomerate some $90 million, secured through standby letters of credit issued by the bank. When the Smith enterprises went into bankruptcy, the FDIC, shepherding the reorganization of the bank, refused to pay off these loans. The foreign syndicate, headed by Britain's National Westminster and Société Générale in France, claimed the loans as an interbank transaction for which FDIC or Crocker National (which had absorbed U.S. National) must stand responsible. FDIC insisted that the losers had known exactly what they were doing (apparently the interest rate on these loans, which has not been made public, was considerably above the normal inter-bank rate), and that normal prudence should have led even foreign banks to suspect that the purpose of this roundabout standby letter of credit was to enable U.S. National to make loans to West-gate corporations beyond its legal lending limit without showing them on its books. "Of course," says Comptroller James Smith, "they read much into the future of that bank by what they considered Mr. Smith's relations to the President of the United States. Europeans are rather naïve about Americans."

Regardless of the merits of the situation, from the European point of view a group of British and French banks were left holding the bag for $74 million in the interbank market. Frank Wille of FDIC quietly consulted with the Federal Reserve Bank of New York, the Fed's agent for international matters, about what the dangers were, and the Bank said with considerable courage that the Londoners needed the market so badly they would do no more than howl and sue, which turned out to be true—the CHIPS computer never skipped a blink. But for a few hours in 1973, until the Nat West group reacted, the world stood on the brink of a new Kreditanstalt and a worldwide economic collapse. In July, 1974, FDIC okayed $47.7 million of the disputed loans as valid obligations of the bank, but definitively denied any obligation to repay the other $42.4 million. National Westminster got its full $15 million back, but Société Générale was out $7.5 million, Coutts in London lost $5 million, Hypobank of Luxembourg lost $5.3 million, and the semiofficial Westdeutsche Landesbank Girozentrale lost $3 million. In the aftermath, even those who believe the American government agencies acted outrageously, which includes most European bankers, admitted that there was a certain value in the lesson that even in the interbank market a lender should pay attention to the purposes and solidity of a borrower.

Because the funds for individual loans derive from a collection of interbank transactions, a single failure could knock down a lot of dominoes very fast. The market survived a freeze of several hours' duration in the early 1960s when Intrabank of Lebanon went under—but only because Chase in an act of faith permitted its correspondents to go very nearly 1,000 million dollars in the hole for a few hours (*not* overnight) to start the engine again. That was a long time ago, and the balloon has been blown much bigger since. In summer 1974 it very nearly blew up in response to a pinprick: the collapse of Bankhaus Herstatt in Cologne.

The Herstatt story argues that the real danger to the international monetary system, even beyond the Arab threat, may be the stupidity of a government agency. Most of the losses suffered by American and British banks when Herstatt went under came not from misjudgment in the extension of credit but from necessary international courtesy in the execution of cash transactions. As part of its routine currency trading activity, Herstatt had purchased —for dollars to be paid out in New York from its account at Chase —marks that were in fact delivered in Germany by Morgan, First National of Seattle and Hill, Samuel of London. At 2.30 in the afternoon, at the close of the local banking day, the German regional authorities moved in on the bank, which was indeed insolvent.

But 2.30 in Cologne was 9.30 in the morning in New York: the banks hadn't opened yet. Chase was confronted with a situation where the management that had authorized payment to Morgan and the others from the Herstatt account was no longer in control of the bank, which had passed into the hands of official liquidators. Though $156 million of Herstatt's money was on hand and ready to be paid out, Chase on advice of counsel held it all pending receipt of instructions from the liquidator. (All, that is, except for $5 million that offset Chase's own deposits at Herstatt: that money Chase, perhaps unwisely, took for its own account.) To the liquidator in Cologne, Morgan, Seattle First, and Hill, Samuel were just unsecured creditors of Herstatt, and they would have to wait on line with everybody else for the distribution of the surviving assets.

People who like to blame Americans for everything that goes wrong can make a fairly good case here. After World War II,

Allied Military Government at American insistence reorganized German banking on the Federal Reserve pattern, with a central Bundesbank no more powerful than the Board of Governors had been in the early days of the Federal Reserve Act, and most authority reserved for supervisory regional official Banks. With the passage of time, the Bundesbank in Germany (like the Board of Governors in America) took over most governmental decision-making about banks; but the regional authorities continued to be the examining bodies and the morticians of the system. Normally, to reduce complications, insolvent banks are closed down at the end of a business day, and to the Cologne authorities that meant 2.30. But a German bank doing an international business really ends its day about nine at night, when the New York money market begins to pack up. So far as can be learned in New York, the provincial types in Cologne simply forgot that the world is full of different time zones.

The upshot was that the CHIPS computer choked to a halt: its members—which include all the fifty largest banks in the world —were no longer willing to enter their payments to correspondent banks until other correspondent banks had entered the balancing payments to them. But the essence of a clearing house is that it handles multilateral transactions, which cannot happen instantaneously unless each one involves a rehearsed "closing". The New York Clearing House rose to the occasion. Because erasers are needed on computer terminals as well as on lead pencils, the CHIPS rules had always permitted a bank to withdraw a credit previously entered, up to a cut-off hour long after the close of the banking day. Now the Clearing House offered everyone a chance to get out of an aborted deal overnight, at a meeting of all CHIPS members every morning at ten o'clock, while the domestic clearings were being accomplished downstairs.

The only room available for this meeting was the second-floor boardroom with its nineteenth-century furniture and artwork, and it was not big enough to seat representatives of all the 50-odd banks that subscribe to the CHIPS service. Psychologically, the fact that some bankers had to stand was unfortunate, because in the clearing nexus a bank failure is like a game of musical chairs, where on each round one of the participants must expect not to have a seat. And in the July 4th week there was one withdrawal of a $50 million transaction, which provoked no fewer than fifteen other hasty cancellations around the room. Between them, however, the Clearing House Association and the Federal Reserve Bank of New York (which was represented at the daily meetings by a very senior officer) managed to stem the panic. On the understanding that the modern Clearing House would stand behind its members (as its uncomputerized predecessors had for more than a century)—and on a less precise understanding that the Fed and the European central banks would somehow stand behind the Clearing House—the bankers got the international payments mechanism moving once more, with no more damage than one of the many unexplained nose-dives in the world's stock markets that punctuated 1974. By autumn 1974, the volume on the CHIPS computer was nearing $40,000 million a day once again. But it was a near thing, and it left a worrisome residue in the growth of a premium; smaller banks were compelled to pay if they wished to borrow in the interbank market.

"There are still risks in banking", says David Rockefeller. "We recognize that." Uh-huh.

4

The increasing number and importance of bank failures is part of the cost of the move from the fixed-currency exchange rates of the Bretton Woods system established right after World War II to the floating currency exchange rates of the catch-as-catch-can system forced by American balance of payments deficits in the early 1970s. So long as the dollar was the reserve currency and reference standard, and the American and other governments were committed to the maintenance of set ratios between other currencies and dollars (within a narrow band of permissible fluctuations), banks with international business could hold their assets and do business for their customers in any currency, making expenses by their commissions on the exchanges. Because volume was so large, and transaction speed so swift, experts could milk interesting profits from movements of as little as $\frac{1}{8}$ of 1 percent in currency exchanges; and some banks (especially the Swiss banks) allocated considerable capital to this sort of low-key speculation in the currency markets.

As the dollar weakened, the Euromarket expanded into other currencies, and since the late 1960s, some of the loans that would once have been made in Eurodollars have been made instead in Euromarks, Euroyen, Eurosterling, and Euro(Swiss) francs. The nations that are the proprietors of these currencies did not like this at all (the Swiss have threatened expulsion to the Swiss branch of any foreign bank that participates in a publicly announced Swiss franc loan outside Switzerland), but there is no way a government can control the trading or use of its currency outside its own borders. As the available pools of Eurocurrencies grew, loans denominated in different countries' money began to carry different rates of interest, and banks began to deal seriously in "forward markets". To make a loan in marks, an American bank would buy marks today with dollars, and contract to sell marks for dollars at the forward market price for the date its loan was to be repaid. This insulated the profits on the loan from any possible movement in exchange rates, and enabled the bank to adjust its interest rates on loans in foreign currencies to the financial community's expectations of the relative future values of those currencies.

When exchange rates began to move around freely, currency traders—in and out of banks—could play roulette with the monetary system, holding inventories of currencies they thought would appreciate and selling short in the forward market currencies they thought were going down. A bank that put its chips on the right number could add hugely to its profitability; but a bank that bet wrong could take a bad shellacking—and the risks were compounded by the fact that governments which did not like what was happening in the market could (expecially with the co-operation of the central banks of other countries) intervene effectively in the "free" market to change prices. (This was called "dirty floating".)

Banks that make money in this casino rarely talk about it: they lump these profits with the profits from more conventional international operations, and happy stockholders are incurious stockholders. But when a bank takes a major loss in currency trading management will often seek to reassure stockholders by announcing the one-shot "extraordinary loss" and firing the trading desk executives who can be held responsible for it. In 1974, several large European banks—including the Union Bank of Switzerland, Lloyds Bank in England, and one of the semipublic German regional banks—admitted to losses in the tens of millions of dollars from misjudgments in currency dealings.

Though they are forbidden to play the stock market, American banks can legally gamble in foreign exchange; but this business is foreign to the American banking temperament, and they usually don't. Currency traders for American banks are restricted to small positions, long or short, at the end of each day's work—$5 or $10 million "exposure" would be a considerable overnight risk in one currency at a $10,000 million American bank. If it is for some reason inconvenient to sell off an inventory or buy in an indebtedness today, the trader is expected to "cover" the bank's risks in the forward market; and nearly all the currency speculation done by American banks involves only the limited risks and profits in the margin between the "spot" rate and the "forward" rate. This is sissy stuff to a real gambler, and when Michele Sindona took over control of New York's Franklin National he told Arthur Roth, who was still the second-largest stockholder, that his path to increasing the profitability of the bank would lie through the employment of greater resources in currency trading—a field where Sindona had European experience and expertise that should give Roth and the other stockholders great confidence. When Franklin blew in spring 1974, the official explanation (conceivably true) was that unauthorized exposure in the currency markets by a relatively junior trader had cost the bank something like $40 million. A knowledgeable but shy observer commented in pity and terror that "Sindona thought he could outguess the Bank of England". In August 1975, the junior trader and several of his colleagues and supervisers were indicted on criminal charges in a federal court.

In an era of liability management when international banks find a third or more of their deposits and "usable funds" abroad, an aggressive banker may be tempted to fund his loans through what are in effect foreign exchange dealings. Illustrating the range of options available to First National City on April 6, 1973, executive committee chairman Edward L. Palmer said, "Euro D-marks are now available for six months on a one and a half percent basis. Domestic CDs are seven and a half percent. Are we willing to make a six-month bet that the D-mark won't be revalued more than three percent? For one hundred million dollars? Well, we were and we did. I made that decision this morning; that's why I was late for this interview."

When I was in Germany six weeks later, and the mark was beginning its flight to the stratosphere, I inquired of First National City's people in Frankfurt about Palmer's $100 million Euromark borrowing. "What hundred million dollars?" said my interlocutor. "Well," quoth I, "he told me himself that he'd just taken a hundred million dollar D-mark interbank loan for six months. Didn't he consult you?" There was a moment's pause, then: "Oh, shit, if Ed told you I don't see why I can't tell you. He didn't consult me. I found out about it a couple of days later, and I called him, and I said, 'Look, Ed, if you want to give us a hundred million dollars to play in the foreign exchange market, give it to us, and we'll make you some money. But don't you try to do that sort of thing from New York; you don't know what you're doing.' We ran it down in a couple of weeks." If Palmer had held his $100 million six-month Euromark loan to maturity, the loss on the exchange to First National City would have been $20 million. It should also be noted that this did not happen, and that Citibank's man on the spot was able to overrule his boss.

5

Many bankers abroad felt that the United States had created the Euromarket by restricting the outflow of dollars, and that the business would return to New York as soon as the Americans regained their sanity. But by the time the Nixon administration got around to eliminating the last controls on international currency flows, in January 1974, everybody was thinking about Arabs. Arabs have always liked London, and they don't like New York at all: too many Jews. Not that they would have to do business with Jews at the New York banks, of course; but they couldn't easily avoid Jewish cabbies and shoe salesmen and real estate agents. Moreover, if Treasury regulations on dollar flows had been eliminated, the Federal Reserve was making suggestions and other noises about the desirability of keeping reserves against dollar deposits actually on the books of American branches and agencies. Though the Arabs soon began sending their money to England through roundabout American routes, the market remained, at least for the time being, in London.

Even before the controls had been lifted, the European and Japanese banks came to America, in a flood. Branch banking across national boundaries can be done only on a basis of reciprocal rights: if the Dutch allow an American branch in Holland, they will expect the United States to allow a Dutch branch in America. This turned out to be a little more complicated than the Europeans could have believed before they started. Federal law prohibits the ownership of nationally chartered banks of deposit by foreign corporations, and prohibits also federal insurance of deposits in foreign banks. If European banks wished to open American branches, they would have to get their charters from the states.

Some states will charter foreign-owned banks; some won't. In California, a foreign bank can open a branch but can't take domestic deposits, because California law requires deposit insurance. On the other hand, California will charter a separate American subsidiary corporation, wholly owned by a foreign bank, to do a banking business in the state. Deposits can then be insured

—but the lending power of the bank is limited by its domestic capital. Sometimes this capital can be built up rapidly and profitably, because foreign-owned banks in California, like any other California banks, are permitted to branch virtually without limit. The Japanese banks thrive on a base of ethnic trade; and Barclay's Bank, rather to its own surprise, spreads rapidly across the state on the basis of a snob trade. (Barclay's, in fairness, are also good merchandisers: they invented the free traveller's cheque as a promotion device. Since the profits on issuing traveller's cheques are in the float rather than in the fee, this gives Barclay's a profitable promotion gimmick, which is any businessman's dream.) On a reciprocal basis, Bank of America is allowed to open branches all over all the countries in which it sets up shop.

Because nations must establish their reciprocal arrangements with American states, the foreign banks can take advantage of the federal rule which permits a holding company to operate banks in more than one state on the invitation of the state authorities. Normally, this rule is just paper in a law book: if First National City Corporation applies to the Massachusetts State Banking Commission for permission to buy a Massachusetts bank, all the Massachusetts bankers form serried ranks of opposition. But when Barclay's wanted to open a Boston subsidiary, the First National Bank of Boston had meekly to urge approval, because otherwise the British authorities might disapprove a London operation for the Boston bank.

Congress is not likely to contemplate quietly forever the spectacle of foreign banks doing in America what domestic banks cannot, but the solution to the problem has not yet presented itself. Governor George Mitchell, speaking for a Fed committee seized of this problem, has proposed federal chartering of foreign banks, which would then stand on all fours with domestic bank holding companies, but Congress is likely to see this as the camel's nose in the tent.

What bothers the American banks more than this relatively small poaching on the retail preserves is the continuing advantage of the Euromarket wholesale banks, domiciled abroad, in competing for American lending business. Nobody quarrels (seriously) with their edge in developing loans to American subsidiaries of European manufacturers or to American importers of European goods, or with their aggressiveness in seeking business from American firms that operate also in their home country; that's reciprocity for what American banks do abroad. But because they can hold Eurodollars in their home offices without reserve requirements, their funds come to them in effect cheaper than the bought funds of American banks (which must sterilize some of their CD receipts in non-interest-bearing reserve accounts at the Fed), and they can profitably undercut the American banks' interest rate.

Still, the foreign agencies cannot take deposits, and cannot perform any banking services other than lending: the American banks with their compensating balances and range of auxiliary services can probably compete acceptably against the agencies, for all their grumbling. (And the American banks with overseas branches can make Eurodollar loans themselves.) What hurts is the competition of New York State-chartered foreign *branches*, which can take deposits (though they are not insured), and can enjoy the full benefits of not being members of the Federal Reserve Bank. New York State requires its nonmember banks to maintain $108 of assets for every $100 of deposit liabilities, which means in effect an 8 percent reserve—but these reserve assets may be kept on account at other banks, which means they can earn interest. And the state rules require nonmember banks to show these reserve assets on their books only at the start of the business day, which means that the whole kit and caboodle can be sold in the Fed Funds market every afternoon on the system by which the big banks buy funds by extinguishing their correspondents' accounts overnight, restoring the deposit the next morning with the interest added. We are talking about immense sums of money: New York State Superintendent of Banking Harry W. Albright boasted in a speech to the New York State Bankers Association in June 1973 that "The foreign banking community in New York has become a twenty-billion-dollar industry—larger than the entire banking systems of most states." At the end of 1973, Governor Mitchell told a bankers' convention in spring 1974, foreign banks operating in the United States held total assets of $38,000 million in their American branches and subsidiaries and this figure was up $10,000 million from that reported ten months earlier.

Even before the foreign credit restraint programme was dropped by the Nixon administration, the foreign branches and agencies could play what they called "the Thursday-Friday market". Eurodollars borrowed Thursday in the interbank market moved through CHIPS that day to become "good funds" in New York on Friday. Fed Funds sold on Friday, it will be recalled, count triple, because the Fed calculates average reserves on a seven-day basis. But the European clearing systems do not work on the weekend, so the agencies and branches could sell Fed Funds Friday for three days' interest while making their repayments to their Eurodollar sources at the same time, secure in the knowledge that these legally kited cheques would not clear until Monday. At its most complete development, this scenario has the foreign branches borrow from the Eurodollar market overnight on Thursday a sum large enough to fulfil the total reserve requirement in New York for the week. These "reserves" are then placed in the Fed Funds market for the weekend, and in 1974 a branch with luck could earn a higher return on its "reserves" than it earned on its loans. . . . As a result, overnight borrowing on the Eurodollar market now costs substantially more on Thursday than on other days of the week.

But the problem presented by the distortion of the London market is trivial next to the problem presented to the Fed by the ease with which the foreign banks and foreign branches of American banks can arbitrage the Eurodollar market against the Fed Funds market, moving money in and out of New York on the computer—often via their own leased channels in the communications satellite—by pushing a few keys on a terminal. In effect, by accident, the Open Market Committee has become the central banker for the entire world. The Eurodollar and the Fed Funds market have been united. Under Governor Mitchell's proposals for federal chartering, branches of foreign banks would have to be members of the Fed, but that merely lifts the Eurodollar and Fed

Funds rate a notch; it does not brake the slide to chaos. The Herstatt collapse and the German government's clumsiness in handling it—coupled with the Labour Government's decision to exorcise the slouching approach of England's doomsday with a graceful ballet of old-fashioned socialist gestures—drove Euro-dollar rates a point or two higher than Fed Funds rates, but the principles remained the same.

If the Fed tries to ease credit conditions in the United States by purchasing Treasury bills and lowering the Fed Funds rate, dollars flow out to the higher rates of the Eurodollar market and the dollar sinks on foreign exchanges. If the Fed tries to restrict credit conditions in the United States by selling Treasury bills and raising the Fed Funds rate, dollars flow in to take advantage of the greater return in New York and the dollar rises on foreign exchanges. And in the all-paper money system an outflow of funds is as inflationary as an inflow of funds. Prices in terms of gold or any other external standard may be reduced—but prices in terms of dollars rise because foreigners can without cost to themselves raise their bids for domestic commodities. (A bid of 120 marks for 10 bushels of wheat translates to $4 a bushel when the dollar is worth 3 marks; if the dollar drops to 2·4 marks the same 120 marks for 10 bushels translates to $5 a bushel; and this is a significant part of the explanation of what happened to us in 1973.) The United States may or may not have become what President Nixon in a Disneyish phrase called a "pitiful, helpless giant"; but the dollar certainly has. "There will be some control over Eurodollars," says Hans Hock in London from an old man's perspective, "because otherwise Washington has no control over its own economy. After all, it's a man-made situation." But like a physician's brilliant diagnosis, the control could come post mortem.

Lord Keynes in 1943 dreamed of an International Clearing Union that would give to the growth of international trade and the development of all the world's economies the advantages that unified banking systems had given to national economies. With the linkage of the Fed Funds and Eurodollar markets, this dream has been accomplished—the mechanism looks American but in reality it is as impersonal and universal as the gold standard. In 1975, this linkage achieved institutional recognition, when Alan Holmes replaced Charles Coombs as head of the foreign exchange desk at the New York Fed, without relinquishing his Open Market Committee responsibilities.

How this system will settle down is still unclear, despite numerous high-level international "agreements". There can be no doubt it has worked better than I thought it would when these pages were first written. All that has actually been proved, however, is that international inflation can be controlled when a positive American balance of payments drains reserves from the Eurodollar market. The cost has been heavy in terms of economic distemper around the world, but it has been borne mostly by the previously "emerging" nations that now seem likely to stop emerging.

If in fact the new system imposes discipline on America, and on those who profit from American international deficits, it may be more workable than I would have expected. Hans Hock was right: the situation is very dicey, but not doomed.

PART
VI

—

CONCLUSION

18/Living on the Edge of an Abyss

The apparently private and technical theme of corporate financing leads us step by step to the heart of major problems of national policy. . . . We are dealing here with serious and far-reaching matters which deserve our undivided attention. For, as a great French poet once said, "Criminals do not always find their penalty in this world, but mistakes are always punished—mercilessly and without exception".

—HANS J. MAST, Crédit Suisse

* * *

"We live in an age of concern", said Walter Wriston of First National City. "People are concerned about everything—about parking tickets, about potholes, about banks." Among the things that concern them are the two great interrelated pathologies: our desperate inflation and the ruinously high interest rates that accompany it. The adjectives are not carelessly chosen: at this writing, inflation truly is a source of despair for the future of democratic institutions; and interest rates are still at a level that will indeed ruin American enterprise as it has already perhaps irretrievably damaged British enterprise, and a lot of banks with it.

How much Congressman Wright Patman really understands about the operations of the banking system is a question close associates are by no means prepared to answer simply. At the age of eighty-one, dean of the House, a gentle, charming, round-faced cherub of a man with a weak memory and no acquaintance with current literature in the field, Patman was not an impressive spokesman for his side of the nation's monetary debates. But if Patman is not a fox that knows the many smaller things, he is certainly a hedgehog that knows the one great thing—the harm done by high interest rates.

We have already noted that high rates draw money from long-term investments (housing, public improvements, utilities) to short-run speculations (tax dodges, commodities, foreign exchange) and consumer credit. High rates make it immensely more difficult for new businesses to get started, by reducing the margin between even optimistically projected earnings and the overhead costs that must be carried. Increasing inventory valuation protects established business from the full penalties of high rates, but at a time when nearly half the capitalization of industry is in debt rather than equity—and increasing chunks of that debt are in the form of bank loans with floating interest rates rather than in bonds with fixed interest rates—the prices for money customary in 1974 threatened large-scale insolvency, a worry the banks seemed to treat with blithe unconcern. ("It is a terrific burden", Serge Semenenko said in spring 1974. "The banks now should be more realistic. They should be willing to accept lower interest rates, accept the cash flow as reduction of principal, get their money back and help these companies. If you're dealing with the right people, you will get it back in the future. Any banker would think that way; but we don't have bankers now, just computers. So they will charge the higher interest rates, and in the end they will not get their money back, because the borrower will go broke.") And high rates necessarily increase the share of the nation's production that goes to the rentier class—the people who have money on which they can earn this fantastic return—at the expense of the rest of society. In mid-1974, Senator Russell Long publicly and maybe seriously advocated a confiscatory 100 percent tax on all interest receipts over 10 percent per annum, reviving a tradition long dormant but strongly expressed in our history by (among others) his father, Huey.

Increases in interest rates are themselves inflationary. Maisel writes, "Interest plays a major role in the consumer price index, especially through the housing and consumer credit component. It is a large factor in utility costs. . . . Tightening monetary policy has an effect on productivity and efficiency. Investment for the next several years will be less and its costs more because of past interest-rate gyrations." And at today's rates the interest on the national debt—more than $30,000 million a year—contributes significantly to inflationary deficits in the federal budget. This is a minority view. Bankers unanimously deny that interest-rate increases have any significant inflationary impact: "We've done studies," George Scott said while vice-chairman of First National City, "and they show that the money-cost component in industrial prices is less than one percent." And the whole thing sounds a little silly to most economists, for whom increases in interest rate are results, not causes of inflation—it is because people believe their money will be worth less in a year than it is today that they insist on high interest rates before they will lend.

But social as well as economic forces move an economy. The fact that high interest rates benefit the rentier class provokes a political mind-set that half-consciously accepts the need for inflation to avoid redistributions of wealth that would worsen existing disparities. Popular horror of inflation persists, but its expression is dulled by the debtors' felt need to repay these expensive debts in a depreciated currency. At the end of 1973, American consumers were $180,000 million in debt for consumer credit, up from $138,000 million at the end of 1971. Accepting Harry Johnson's insistence that consumption in the American economy is largely "using the services of capital goods" (i.e., the car or the TV set should be seen as "consumer capital" which the consumer correctly pays off "concurrently, as he enjoys the services"), $180,000 million remains an immense amount of debt, and gives most households a debtors' stake in continuing inflation.

Nevertheless, inflation really is a horror, because it demeans work. In a developed economy, people necessarily work for money.

CONCLUSION

Obviously, they want money to buy something, but at the time of work, and of thinking about work, they do not normally have in their heads the idea of what they are going to buy with the proceeds. If the money they receive in return for their labours is continually diminishing in value, they feel an insult to themselves and to their function in society, even if as instalment debtors they benefit by it. Ultimately, they seek an authoritarian government that will protect them against this degradation in their lives.

Benjamin Franklin pointed out two hundred years ago, in his comments on the Continental currency, that inflation is really a tax. (Keynes says this was understood by the Romans before the birth of Christ). Each person through whose hands the money passes finds that it is worth a little less when he spends it than it was when he acquired it; thus the burden of a depreciating currency is shared, like other burdens of government, by the entire community. It was, Franklin noted, an unscientific tax; it hits the middle class, who have liquid assets that depreciate, far harder than it hits the poor, who lack the assets, or the rich, who find ways to invest their money at suitably high rates of return. Worse, it is a tax nobody has voted: it is something government has done against the wishes of the people. With rare exceptions (and most of those in or near wartime), electorates in democracies throw out governments they hold responsible for inflation. The stability of Gaullist France—after the rat-race politics of the Fourth Republic—was the result of DeGaulle's success in stabilizing the franc; and the American economists who made fun of the hard-money types around the General lacked his sense of the real sources of his strength.

No doubt there are times when the "cause" of inflation is the exercise of monopoly power by big labour and big business, but such "cost-push" elements tend to burn themselves out in the marketplace. Sustained, socially damaging inflation is, simply, a result of too much money in the system; and that happens for one of two reasons. Either the government is spending beyond its receipts in taxes, or business is spending for capital expansion (or replacement) beyond the savings (or depreciation provisions)

486

available to match such investments. In the first case, the "tax" of inflation is imposed, like other taxes, by government, out of cowardly reluctance to make voters face the costs of the programmes they demand.* In the second case, the inflationary "tax" is imposed by private industry, forcing people to consume less than they wish to consume by reducing the purchasing power of the money in their pockets.

Sometimes the two forces work in harness: by pushing the federal housing programmes out into the marketplace through the establishment of FNMA and GNMA, the American government transferred the inflationary pressure of aid to housing from its failure to tax to the public's failure to save; by mandating heavy investment in pollution control without providing subsidies the government compelled both price increases in the industries involved and greater imbalance between the demand for capital and the supply of savings. And domestic price controls, unless accompanied by export restrictions, ultimately promote inflation by causing the export of scarce goods and commodities that can be sold more profitably abroad. Argentina is a perfect case in point. A negative balance of trade damps inflation, because it supplies streams of foreign goods to sop up local money; but, the delay, in the end, exacerbates. When the American balance turned in 1973 the United States for the first time had to face up to the consequences of almost fifteen years of irresponsible management of the American economy.

But in the search for "causes" of our current distress, it is too easy to forget that at this time, in this place, there is essentially only one mechanism for creating too much money: the banks. When the

* This is, obviously, a little too simple. A first amendment necessary in Britain is that inflation may also be caused by declining production for domestic consumption. The Labour government measures of spring 1975 were doomed to failure (as the currency exchange markets realized) because they continued to subsidize from public funds the employment of workers truly redundant to their employers, and continued the pernicious practice of permitting public authorities to borrow abroad. The payment of interest on such borrowings must be in terms of real British goods exported without offsetting imports, which will be a continuing major source of inflationary pressure. The measure taken in autumn 1975 are more convincing.

government runs a deficit, the Fed or the Bank of England permits expansion of bank credit to enable people or institutions to buy the bonds. When industry decides to spend for capital formation more than is being saved by individuals and corporations, the banks make up the difference by lending. Meanwhile, the bank loans that support speculation in foreign exchange, commodity futures, common stocks, and real estate add to inflationary pressures in the economy without producing any increase whatever in the Gross National Product.

The increasing interest rates associated with inflationary pressures—or, more likely, private fears that family financial security is being jeopardized by rising prices—do tend to increase the flow of private savings, thus providing some minor degree of corrective for the imbalance in the national income accounts. But the rate of inflation of the 1970s provoked, in Britain especially, the beginnings of a flight from money, a desire to buy now because prices will be higher later or to hoard the precious metals or land that would seem certain to appreciate in terms of a steadily inflating currency. There was more talk than action: "It's all very well to say I should put my money in grand pianos," said R. S. Sayers. "Where am I going to keep them?" But it was the sort of talk that could, at short notice, trigger action.

"Too much money" in the system refers not simply to quantity, but to the velocity of that quantity. Twenty years ago, a man paying his bill from the electric company sent off a cheque which went to the offices of the electric company, was appropriately processed by clerks and deposited in the bank which did not give usable credit for it until the third or fourth business day after its deposit. Now the cheque comes to a lock box maintained by the bank, and is credited to the company's account before the company registers the payment on its ledger. The company's need for cash balances to pay its bills is much reduced; money once idle or floating is put to work much faster by the company itself. The proliferation of short-term money-market instruments gives every corporate treasurer an ever-increasing stake in "cash management" that boosts the velocity of money. And the banks trade what Thomas

Waage calls "high-powered money" in the Fed Funds or interbank market.

Attention has been paid in these pages to the banker's bugaboo of borrowing short and lending long—using demand deposits that may be withdrawn tomorrow or short-term CDs that run out in thirty days as the source of funds for loans that now run for years. But "maturity transformation", as the modern bankers insist, is what banks do: lending is a way to bridge time for the lender as well as for the borrower. What happens in the euphoria of an inflationary economy is that maturity transformation begins to work in reverse—money that is in effect borrowed long, through savings accounts, time deposits, the sale of debentures, comes into the overnight market to be loaned short. The constant arbitraging back and forth of long-term and short-term money acts as an over-drive for velocity.

The banking system loses what Keynes identified as its central social function: its power to mobilize the idle balances of the economy. Under the eye of eternity, what justified the banker's profits was the fact that through a banking system—and in no other way—tributary streams of transaction balances held by households and corporations to pay forthcoming bills could be joined into great rivers of working capital for productive enterprise. Now the transaction balances are rapidly diminishing as a source of funds: in 1974, despite the requirement of compensating balances, demand deposits accounted for only 30 percent of the funds used by the eight big New York banks. Current accounts made up almost 60 percent of the deposit liabilities of London clearing banks as late as 1960, but little more than a third of total deposits by 1975. These figures are not published. In conversation, Midland Bank estimated "one-third free accounts, one-third cheap accounts, one-third expensive deposits". The banks buy what they lend and live off the "interest differential" between the price they pay and the price they charge.

These conditions produce an increasingly unequal division of rewards between the people who have money and the people who have productive uses for it. Attention focuses too much on the pieces of paper themselves, too little on correctly employing the money. Greed drives balances out of demand deposits and into interest-bearing instruments, multiplies velocity, fuels inflation, raises interest rates. The profitability of enterprise is determined less by the quality of management and the need for the product than by the impact of inflation. In those businesses that benefit from inflation, mistakes are hidden rather than illuminated by the abstractions of the balance sheet; misallocation of resources persists, extends, ultimately undermines the foundations of the economy. It is all terribly risky: in an age of interest differential banking, the interest rate, however high it goes, does not begin to cover the risk factors. There are billions of dollars of potential loan losses in the system, and the clock ticks toward the moment of their detonation. The clock began to strike in Britain in 1974, in America in 1975; we have by no means heard the last bell.

Apparently tiny changes in the technical procedures of banking have stimulated today's overexpansion. The Fed Funds market can move $25,000 million a day—70 percent of the entire reserve requirement of the banking system—because savings banks and savings and loan associations were permitted to treat their deposits at the commercial banks as Fed Funds for sale and the foreign agencies were freed of restrictions in arbitraging the Eurodollar and Fed Funds markets. With Fed Funds at 11 percent and even more —and mortgages at 8 percent—the incentive was irresistible for the savings institutions to employ their long-term deposits in the short-term market. In Britain, the fact that discount houses could buy CDs and banks could put the money back into the discount houses "at call" meant that the "call money" component of reserve assets required under Competition and Credit Control was expandable virtually at will.

Economists in general believe that the kiss of competition makes everything feel all right; but competition works only in the real world, where ultimate purchasers consume what they buy and first sellers live on the proceeds of what they sell. Then the market pretty well must be cleared by a price; the better the information, the more accurate the price as an expression of the values received and the costs of production. But the financial market is an unreal world, where prices are made by opinions, by perceptions grossly influenced by the fashion of the time. In depressions, we have Keynes's "liquidity trap", in which both lenders and borrowers are so concerned by the need for safety that investment fails to absorb savings. In a boom we have the "economics of euphoria", brilliantly described by Hyman Minsky in 1966:

"The confident expectation of a steady stream of prosperity gross profits [produces a] willingness . . . to take what would have been considered in earlier times undesirable chances in order to finance the acquisition of additional capital goods. . . . Those that supply financial resources live in the same expectational climate as those that demand them. . . . Demanders with liability structures that previously would . . . have made them ineligible for accommodations become quite acceptable. . . . The shift to euphoria increases the willingness of financial institutions to acquire assets by engaging in liquidity-decreasing portfolio transformations."

Because "it is possible to finance investment by portfolio transformations . . . the amount of investment financed can be independent of monetary policy. The desire to expand and the willingness to finance expansion by portfolio changes can be so great that . . . an inflationary explosion becomes likely. . . .

"The tight money of the euphoric period is due more to runaway demand than to constraint upon supply. Thus, those who weigh money supply heavily in estimating money market conditions will be misled.

"The run-up of short- and long-term interest rates places pressure on deposit savings intermediaries and disrupts industries whose financial channels run through these intermediaries. There is a feed-back from euphoria to constrained real demand in some sectors.

"An essential aspect of a euphoric economy is the construction of liability structures which imply payments that are closely articulated . . . to cash flows due to income production. . . . Under pressure, various financial and nonfinancial units may withdraw, either by necessity or because of a defensive financial policy, from

CONCLUSION

some financial markets. . . . Withdrawals on the supply side of financial markets may force demanding units that were under no special strain and were not directly affected by financial stringencies to look for new financing connections. An initial disturbance can cumulate through such third-party or innocent-bystander impacts. . . . Financial instability occurs whenever a large number of units resort to extraordinary sources for cash."

Minsky in 1966 underestimated the sturdiness of a banking system with deposit insurance ("a powerful offset to events with the potential for setting off a financial crisis," he wrote in 1970) and also the degree to which, as he wrote in 1972, "the Federal Reserve and the government were both willing and able to turn pauses around and to ameliorate the consequences of financial stringency." Unfortunately, as Minsky insists, the resourcefulness of the banks cannot legislate an end to the business cycle any more than Congress or Parliament can. In the end, by following the universal prescription that they must not allow shocks to become disruptions, the Fed and the Bank of England create a situation where only a disruption can administer the corrections that should come from shocks. As noted earlier, the weakness of the banks in an era of liability management makes government the prisoner of their follies.

2

In brief, what has happened to us is that our technology has outrun our management capacities. Greed, curiosity, and pride join to push the best people in the system toward maximum exploitation of the emerging technology, with the Devil to take the hindmost: we have seen the phenomenon elsewhere. But this is a big Devil, and very dangerous. Getting him back in the bottle will take major investments of good will and intelligence from men some of whom are not very nice and some of whom are not very bright.

Perhaps the most frightening aspect of the technology is the ease of transfer between money and credit, or money and "near money". It was said earlier that only the banks can create the "too much

492

money" that makes inflation, but this is not quite true. At a time of rising prices and high interest rates, for example, people begin to pay their bills more slowly, especially in situations where no penalty is involved. In effect, willingly or otherwise, creditors create "money", and by their tolerance of a situation which moves goods without cash they speed up the measured velocity of ordinary money.

Then, in a euphoric economy, as Minsky points out, all sorts of people begin to emit near moneys, especially securities like commercial paper. "Banks are competing with business corporations", Gaylord Freeman of First of Chicago said in 1973. "If we were smart, we would recognize that our competitor is not Continental Bank but Allstate Insurance, with two thousand offices around the country. GMAC is in our business. We shouldn't look across the street and say, 'That's my competitor'. We should say, 'That's my brother'." At the end of 1972, Sears Roebuck alone carried consumer receivables totalling 80 percent of the entire outstandings of all the bank credit cards issued by 8,000 American banks. Among them, General Motors, Ford, and General Electric held consumer credit of $12,500 million, three times as much as that held by Bank of America, Citicorp and Chase-Manhattan combined. They are gigantic customers of the banks, the finance subsidiaries of the great industrial corporations, but most of their money is raised elsewhere.

Early in 1971, Lawrence L. Crum and Dennis W. Richardson submitted to the American Bankers Association a study called *Competition for the Commercial Banking Industry in the Establishment and Operation of an Electronic Payment System*. It was, for the bankers, a cheerful document. Competition could be expected, the authors thought, from third-party payments systems devised for savings and loan associations, and possibly from American Express, but those were known antagonists. The Post Office was not likely to get a giro scheme in operation (it was having too much trouble delivering the mail); the insurance companies were not interested in doing banking business; the retail establishments were losing money on their credit operations and were fragmented anyway, being unable even to form a single sizeable trade association (but Sears might be a danger all by itself); IBM had too much anti-trust trouble already; the communications companies were absorbed by internal competition and technological change; the oil companies had never done anything with their existing credit cards; the airline companies were in no position to fight the banks.

But proprietorship of the payments mechanism looks less and less like the way money is going to be made in the financial market in the years ahead. Improvements in technology mean that both businesses and households will require much smaller transaction balances to get their business done: current accounts will certainly represent a steadily decreasing proportion of bank funds. At the same time, that portion of bank lending that serves purely trans-actional needs—that bridges time lags in payments—must also diminish. Freeman is (as usual) correct in his perception that the battles of the future will be fought between banks and non-banks that can in one way or another perform banking functions, emitting liabilities to garner funds and then lending them to borrowers who might otherwise be borrowing from banks. The aggressiveness that came with Citicorp's revolution can reasonably be seen as really defensive in intent—without the CDs and the holding-company activities (in Britain, "banking group"), the banks were going to get clobbered in what were going to be their best markets by institu-tions nobody thinks of, or regulates, as banks.

The case for the banks is strong. Surely we are better off with banking functions in the hands of institutions charged with a public interest and accountable in a detailed way to public bodies. More-over, the banks do most things more cheaply and more efficiently than their rivals could hope to accomplish them. And banks are of course much more democratic—that is, businesses and individuals that could not hope to borrow in an open market (except from sharks and shylocks) are more than welcome to borrow at banks. It is probably no exaggeration to say that most of the new businesses started in the United States and Britain every year would never get started at all without help from banks. We can no more keep an economy from activities we dislike by prohibiting banks from engaging in them than we could stop drinking by shutting down the saloons. Actions which encourage the shifting of financial business from banks to non-banks are chancy, probably expensive, conceivably destructive. Restraining bank lending, as Lord O'Brien put it while Governor of the Bank of England, does not mean "we have necessarily been operating a restrictive credit policy. We may by our very actions stimulate the provision of credit through non-bank channels . . . and we may indeed be distorting in harmful ways the deployment of the real resources of the country." But allowing matters to take the course they are now on will be certainly destructive.

The problem is that bankers really do navigate on time horizons that are low even by the standards of our impatient and short-sighted age, and emphasis on bought money—which is very rarely bought for periods as long as six months—may have lowered their horizons still further. In theory, the old system of reliance on transaction balances meant insecurity, because the deposits could drain off "on demand": this is why reserve or liquidity requirements were instituted in the first place. In fact, the system was very stable in the absence of a crisis that provoked a run on the banks; in the words of the Radcliffe Report, only fifteen years ago, "Individual balances go up and down, depositors come and depositors go, but the total on current account goes on forever." Now the banks live on hot money that has no reason to be where it is except the rate that is paid for it. Many of the big American money-centre banks must deliberately roll over 10 percent of their liabilities *overnight*, 50 percent every two or three months. It concentrates the attention of their leaders on the very short term.

Research departments of large banks issue forecasts from time to time, but they rarely attempt to extrapolate their trend lines as far out as a full year. It does not matter much to the banking system whether the money that circulates from its windows through the life of the society returns to the windows after nourishing the construction of a power plant, the purchase of a television set or a speculation in silver futures. The money is loaned, removed, spent, and redeposited in the same way. Bankers really live the economists' fallacy, the proposition that short-term and long-term money are the same animal in different clothes.

But the truth of the matter is that short-term and long-term money are very different animals. Transaction balances are not savings, and the financing of trade expresses societal needs very different from those expressed by the financing of investment or of government. One of the great causes of economic instability is the inevitable blurring of these distinctions in any money market. The proximate cause of the 1929 crash in America was the draining off of savings into brokers' loans—*not*, by the way, by banks, which did not increase their lending to Wall Street, but by business corporations that could make more in the high-interest call-money market than they could by investment in their own businesses. (In October 1929, there was $8,500 million of brokers' loans in the market, $1,900 million from banks and $6,600 million from "others".) To the extent that banks become the controlling operator in both short-term and long-term money—and this is what the term-loan phenomenon means—a necessary distinction becomes *institutionally* blurred, and stability decreases. The fact of decreasing stability has been hidden for the last ten years by the greater capacity of government to shore up the structure whenever any part of it shakes; but this capacity is not infinite, and we are nearing its limits.

The generation since World War II has been profligate in many ways, and any number of decisions have contributed to what can now be seen as unwise policies. It is no longer so clear as it once was, for example, that earnings used to pay dividends are "income" to be taxed at 50 percent or so, while earnings used to pay interest on bonds or loans are not "income" and should not be taxed at all. Partly because of this official encouragement, business has increasingly financed its modernization and expansion by borrowing rather than by selling stock. Meanwhile, inventory appreciation in an inflationary time gets reported as profits, which are taxed though there is no cash coming in to pay the taxes. Industry's capacity to finance itself is eroded, and loan demand soars.

In 1974, nearly 40¢ of every dollar of gross earnings by American business—compared to about 15¢ as recently as the early 1960s—was committed to interest payments, which were running at a rate of almost $50,000 million a year. The British ratios cannot be greatly different. In 1964, in America, according to Henry Kaufman of Salomon Brothers, "total credit market debt exceeded the market value of equities . . . by two hundred and ninety-six billion dollars." A decade later, this "spread" had passed the $1 *trillion* mark.

A debt-based society, where managers must look first of all to the coverage of their interest and amortization, is clearly less flexible and innovative than an equity-based society, where the stock of capital is permanent and consciously at risk, and entrepreneurs and stockholders expect profits to fall in some years as they rise in others. However much change is talked at the universities or on the television networks or in the House of Commons, a society in which productive enterprise is financed mostly by debt cannot be changed very much.

In America deposit insurance has put an end to runs on the bank, and the Keynesian "liquidity preference" that makes people avoid investments now leads to purchases of mutual funds that hold money-market instruments, to bonds rather than stocks, to short-term rather than long-term assets. In the end, inflation creates a false "liquidity" of things—silver bars, gold stocks and (perhaps the most rapidly inflating commodity) farm land. At some point in this process, crisis materializes again: the economy becomes vulnerable to a decline in a handful of key prices—a decline that may not be reversible through action by the government.

Historically, American industry has been fortunately situated by comparison with European industry: a much higher proportion of its capital was financed by equity rather than by debt, and a much higher proportion of its expansion was financed by internally generated funds rather than by bank loans. Now American industry's capacity to generate its own financing is steadily eroded by the pressure of interest payments; reliance on banks rather than the mobilization of savings in the marketplace is increased by foolish tax laws and by the shift in liquidity preferences. Europe has lived for generations, not always happily, with financial markets dominated by banks and a few other large pools of available capital. During the decades of the Americanization of Europe, we have seen in our financial markets a persistent and accelerating Europeanization of America. Neither our banks nor our political institutions are geared to handle it; and it is the wrong way to go, anyway. Britain occupied, naturally, an intermediate position between American and Continental custom. By opting for American banking procedures with Competition and Credit Control in 1971, while simultaneously accepting a role in the Common Market, the Tory government accepted the presence of economic contradictions that soon proved unmanageable.

3

Like most revolutions, the banking revolution of the 1960s happened because it was needed; now we need a reaction. Punishing the banks is not going to do anybody any good; but on the evidence of 1973–74 they need more rather than less public control of their activities. America and Britain both need discreet means to insure the separation of long-term money and short-term money and the maintenance of reasonable balance between real savings and investment (plus government deficits) on the swings of the business cycle. (The "book-keeping identities" beloved of economists do not express the true situation adequately.)

Within the commercial banking system, there should be a requirement—enforced loosely and with discretion, in terms of averages rather than minimums—that term loans and mortgages match up with the total of savings accounts and term deposits. Roll-over credits should be discouraged: to the greatest extent possible, the risks of interest rate fluctuations should be borne by the banks, which are professionals in this business, and not by their customers. To the extent that their earnings on their assets change slowly, the banks would be seriously discouraged from collaboration in rapid movements of money-market rates.

Unless private investment will be too small to absorb private and corporate savings, government really must—ya gotta believe —balance its budget through open-and-aboveboard publicly imposed taxes rather than through the hidden tax of inflation or the flim-flam game of foreign borrowings. Government must face up manfully to the fact that the goods and services we purchase collectively must be paid for, just like the goods and services we purchase as individuals. This is not a new idea, and it is not controversial, but neither the British nor the American government (of any party) seems to have been able to keep a grip on it.

Whether involuntarily or voluntarily—through higher taxes to pay for capital projects, through inflation, or through deliberate saving and purchasing of stocks and bonds—both countries are going to have to save a higher proportion of their Gross National Product in the years ahead. Once the wilderness paradises are gone, and most men never considered them much in the line of paradises, the "quality of life" becomes a function of the energy resources at the disposal of the individual and the capital investment that multiplies his benefits from his efforts. The ecologists are basically right, but when they talk about reduced consumption what they means is not what they seem to think they mean—a general slowing down of the machinery of existence, a kind of reduction in the pulse rate by government fiat—but an increase in recycling through savings. There are many reasons why the Europeans and the Japanese have done better economically in the postwar world than Americans have, not least of them our export of capital and technology, but among the large facts that glares out from the statistics is the very much greater savings rate in Japan and all the European countries except England—which is, not by coincidence, in really bad trouble. Swinging London can stand as a symbol of the short-term, its brief contents and its morning after.

Maintaining a free market but gearing investment more closely to savings will keep housing production on the roller coaster that seems to unsettling to many critics of today's financial system. But on time horizons of a decent height it is hard to understand why housing should *not* be a residual user of funds. We are not so far from the 1930s that we should have lost all sense of the value of an investment demand that persists through good times and bad; organizing ourselves to meet that demand more adequately in bad times is no more than commonsense. There are amongst us many who believe that we can all at once control pollution, expand energy production, perfect the delivery of medical services to all, guarantee the good life to the aged and infirm, put everybody in college, renew our transportation infrastructure, feed India, put 5 percent of our Gross National Product into housing and 7 percent into education every year, extend the leading edge of weapons technology and continue to increase everybody's "net real disposable income". Britain also provides a home for Peronists in the left wing of the governing party—people who believe some wonderfully nourishing national soup can be concocted from frozen prices, rising wages, prohibition on lay-offs and government heat to force a boiling boom in capital investment. If the English-speaking peoples insist on electing to public office people who make such promises, we shall of course get the dishonest government, tearing inflation, and ultimate depression we invite.

Any honest estimate of our chances over the next decade is not going to be very cheerful. Most of the world's savings for the next few years will be by Arabs, who have notoriously low time horizons when it comes to the employment of money; they may finance some major capital improvement projects near home, but they are all but certain to employ their mounting Eurodollar resources in loans to banks as intermediaries, and no banker in his right mind will use—or should use—an oil sheikh's CD as the source of funds for a mortgage loan. And the great demand for money in the Eurodollar market will be for the purpose of paying the Arabs for their oil, establishing a merry-go-round most inappropriate to the seriousness of the world's problems. From the American point of view, the Eurodollar market will expand still further, leaving the control of the domestic economy an almost impossible task for the Fed or the Congress in the absence of massive debt repudiation. The partial debt repudiation represented by inflation is clearly the path of least resistance—indeed, Britain has already shown the way.

Ultimately, some way will have to be found to sterilize these immense dollar balances held outside the United States, but that will require a level of intelligent international co-operation we are very far from reaching in the political life of the middle of the eighth decade of the twentieth century. (Left to their own devices, the central banks might come up with something, but they will not be left to their own devices.) Most of the sacrifices that will be involved will have to be American: these are, after all, *our* debts. Observers who see a spirit of self-sacrifice rising in American political life are a rare and endangered species; we must cherish them, irrelevant and ignorant nuisances though most of them are, in hopes that one of these days they will produce a useful idea.

"I know a bank with a long-range plan to earn twenty-three percent on equity in 1980," says bank-stock dealer Harry Keefe. "IBM and Xerox do less well". That won't do. Bankers did not create these problems and cannot resolve them. But they do have some obligation to pay attention. The institutional structure of banking, the forms (sometimes the technicalities) of operation, the goals that bankers set for themselves and that they are told to set —all these will significantly influence how hard a bump we get. One of the bad things about revolutionaries is that they never care what happens to other people. That will not be an acceptable attitude from bankers in the years ahead. There is a counter-revolution in their future.

EPILOGUE

In the year that has passed since the first publication of this book, the American counter-revolution has indeed begun. First the collapse of Franklin, Herstatt and Beverly Hills showed the money market that bank liabilities not insured by a government—large-denomination Certificates of Deposit and correspondent balances, Federal Funds, commercial paper sold by bank holding companies —were not necessarily as safe as they seemed. Then the multiform disasters of the Real Estate Investment Trusts—and the frightening run-off of liquidity in corporate borrowers squeezed by the recession—demonstrated to the banks that fluctuating interest rates did not in the least improve (and might even diminish) the chances that the debtors would pay back what they owe. And the journey toward bankruptcy by quasi-governmental bodies as removed from each other as New York City and the Indonesian state oil company cast doubt (to say the least) on the once unquestioned safety of loans to official bodies.

With loan losses mounting rapidly, it became obvious that the Internal Revenue Service formula for contributions to loan loss reserves—a five-year moving average of actual loss experience— would leave bank stockholders subject to some exceedingly unpleasant shocks in years ahead. Starting in the last quarter of 1974, the larger banks rapidly increased the proportion of their earnings that they squirrelled away as a loan loss reserve. They are entitled to some credit for this use of what could have been claimed as profits. It did them no good in their dealings with either their stockholders or the regulators who were pressing them to enlarge their capital base, which would at least have seemed to grow if these earnings had been slotted on an undistributed profits line rather than into the loss reserve.

Still, the fact is that these additions to loan loss reserves came out of apparent profits that rose spectacularly fast and far in the first half of 1975. In the old days, when banks lived mostly on their demand deposits, a decline in money market interest rates meant a decrease in their profits—the cost of servicing the cheque accounts remained roughly the same, but the income from lending out the money declined. Under conditions of liability management, however, declining interest rates produce windfall gains for the banks, because the cost of the very short-run money they buy drops more rapidly than the interest they charge on their loans. The rule of thumb in modern banking has set the interest rate on prime loans at a number somewhere under 2 percent above the bank's cost of funds.* In early 1975, the big banks were charging their best borrowers as much as four percentage points more than the Federal Funds rate. This left an unprecedentedly large margin for profit— and for the channelling of money to the loan loss reserve.

The counter-revolution starts here. Through the 1960s, a steadily increasing proportion of American borrowing—by large corporations with direct access to the money market as well as by small businesses and consumers—had been done through the banks. The banks funded these loans through the issuance of large-denomination CDs which purchasers believed to be insured by the government on the argument that "the Fed would never let a really big bank fail." The CDs drew money out of the bond market, and indeed out of the stock market. And because the banks were lending at variable interest rates, they could offer roll-over credits at prices that did not include a risk premium to cover the contingency that during the term of the loan the market rates for money would rise.

---

* This is, as the reader of the preceding chapters realizes, a very tricky calculation, because some of the bought funds are sterilized in reserves at the Fed, and some of the funds loaned to customers are kept in the bank as compensating balances; moreover, there are questions of average or "melded" cost of funds versus marginal cost of funds, and of the allocation of expenses to "cost of funds" rather than to some other cost centre.

EPILOGUE

In 1975, the American banks—stretched, a little scared by the prospect of mounting loan losses—were no longer bidding so aggressively for funds on the CD chassis; CD rates dropped rapidly, and money ran out to the bond market and the stock market, which rose steadily in the United States (and also in Britain, where IBELs controls began to bite) through month after month of bad news in the newspapers. Large corporate borrowers with names good enough to give them access to the securities markets found that the cost of borrowing in public had fallen some distance below the immediate cost of borrowing from the banks; they sold bonds and paid back their bank loans. Meanwhile, both producers and retailers began to use up the extremely heavy inventories they had laid aside during the shortage scares of 1974, and banks loans to support inventories—still by some margin the largest single category of business lending—ran down. If the surface sign of what I called the American revolution in banking was the steady increase in the proportion of the nation's credit needs supplied by banks rather than by other intermediaries, the surface sign of the counter-revolution was the reversal of this trend. Indeed, it became a matter of real concern that a kind of White Terror would be imposed by conservative loan officers frightened by the increasingly visible excesses of the revolutionary era, and that a necessary recession could be deepened to a long-lasting depression by the maintenance of tight credit conditions at the banks at a time when money should have become easy.

The concern was real enough; its expression in the United States, unfortunately, was rather stupid. From press and pulpit, economics department and Congressmen came demands that the Fed "increase the money supply" to help the country out of the recession. As most of the money supply is created by banks in the process of making loans, there was a King Canute quality about this demand: if the banks weren't making loans or investments, there was no way the money supply would go up. But the American federal budget was rapidly (and properly) sliding into massive deficit, and the diminishing loan demand from corporations and individuals would soon be more than made up by increased issuance

504

of government debt instruments. In terms of the "monetary aggregates", it does not matter whether the money the banks create is used for loans to private borrowers or for purchases of newly minted Treasury bills. As 1975 proceeded, the American money supply did begin to grow, reflecting the activity of the banks in monetizing the federal deficit. The British money supply, of course, never stopped growing, as the mess created by Tory fecklessness was compounded by Socialist doctrine.

In terms of the future operation of the banks, the replacement of loan agreements by Treasury paper (and in Britain by Treasury-backed local authority paper) has profound systemic implications. It drops the other shoe of counter-revolution, a return from liability management to asset management in the day-to-day operations of the banks.

A Treasury bill in the asset portfolio of a bank is quite different from a loan. A loan may or may not be callable, may or may not be saleable, if the bank needs cash to pay off a depositor or to live up to a commitment to make another loan. A Treasury bill must always be saleable to the central bank, because the interest rate on Treasuries is the floor below which no other public interest rates will fall, and quite apart from the government's cost in carrying the debt, the central bank cannot permit the effective rate on Treasuries to rise above a certain (admittedly moveable) point.

Having created money once, to monetize the government deficit, the banks can now in effect rely on the aftermath of that same transaction to create money again by monetizing a private sector borrower's newly emitted liability. And the Fed or the Bank, because they cannot permit Treasury prices to sink too low, will be *compelled* to create the reserves that make this subsequent monetization possible. This is the story of 1951–52, an inflation in America every bit as bad as 1973–74, fuelled by bank loans funded through the liquidation of the banks' very large portfolios of government paper. Every first-year student in economics learns that the use of monetary stimuli to promote economic recovery is, in Keynes's famous analogy, like pushing on a piece of string; Keynes forgot to note the corollary that string thereupon accumulates, and when loan demand revives the authorities have no means of controlling it.

The inflationary pressures on the economy in 1977–78 will be much harder to restrain than those that arose in 1951–52, for two technical reaons. In 1951–52, a higher proportion of the Treasury paper held by banks was long-term paper, which moves considerably in price on the stimulus of a relatively small change in the interest rate—a ten-year bond that yields 5 percent a year will sell for 100 when the interest rate is 5 percent, but for only $93\frac{1}{2}$ when the interest rate rises to 6 percent. (Arithmetic: $\$5 \times 10$ years $=$ $\$50 + \$6.50$ appreciation to maturity$= \$56.50$; 6 percent on $\$93.50$ $= \$5.61$). A six month bill that sells for $97\frac{5}{8}$ when the interest rate is 5 percent will sell for $97\frac{1}{8}$ if the interest rate rises to 6 percent. A bank that owns a ten-year Treasury will think twice before it takes a shellacking of $65 per thousand for the purpose of funding a loan that will not yield enough additional profit to repay this loss for at least a couple of years, but it will scarcely think twice about sacrificing $5 per thousand by selling a six-month bill to make a loan that will more than repay this loss in ninety days. This, of course, is why the Treasury and the Fed worked to finance as much as possible of the 1976 and 1977 deficits by selling longer-term securities; but with both the market and the Congress demanding short maturities, we saw very heavy sales of bills and short-term notes.

The second technical reason why the Fed will find it harder to control inflation from aggressive asset management in 1977–78 is that we will be starting from an interest rate base not far from 6 percent, rather than the 2 percent base of 1950. And one lesson that I think—I hope—was learned in 1974 was the social harm done by very high interest rates. George Brown, former chief of the U.S. Census Bureau and now an economist with the National Industrial Conference Board, has urged the need to find "some non-price means for the allocation of credit". That's a troubling thought, but these are troubled times.

Recovery from the recession will be less cheerful at the banks, especially at the big banks, than elsewhere in the economy. The additions to loan loss reserves mentioned earlier do not, I fear, begin to cover the actual losses that will have to be taken by 1978, as the excuse that business is bad all over ceases to cover the particular badness of many loans and investments made during the euphoric boom. A number of R E I Ts and even more fringe banks will have to be put to sleep (the property market not only won't recover, it shouldn't—not if "recovery" means restoration of the hectic boom of 1972–73). The bankruptcy of New York City will have ripple effects that will take a long time to work through the system, because the financial condition of the casualty insurance companies and other large holders of New York paper will be significantly impaired.

Internationally, a number of the consortia loans to the Third World are very shaky—the Philippines, Chad, Zambia, Sri Lanka, Uruguay, Argentina and Chile are already over their heads. Still, the money keeps rolling out—$5,500 million of new Eurodollar bank loans to developing countries in the first half of 1975, most of it, one suspects, to maintain the fiction that these borrowers are paying their interest. Not all the loans to the industrialized countries are so hotsy-totsy, either. As a guest in the house, I do not wish to be unnecessarily nasty about Britain, and I imagine some way will be found to maintain British appearances. But I should not wish to have to feed my children on the cash flow from the loans that were made to England earlier in this decade. The increased "profits" from an improved spread between cost of funds and interest rate in the Eurodollar market should be seen as a risk premium—which is almost certainly too small to cover the real risks. And there are, as widely advertised in spring 1975, some billions of dollars of financing of laid-up oil tankers which are now worth on the open market perhaps half of what the banks loaned to their owners.

Now that the panic of early 1975 has passed, I think Americans can look with some equanimity on the writing-off of the mistakes of the boom; the real danger to our society is not that we will make mistakes, but that we will fail to acknowledge them and pigheadedly persist. Banks, because they can always cover over even the worst loan by advancing the borrower still more money to keep his interest payments current, are the very font of this kind of dangerous pigheadedness, and their behaviour in the second half of the 1970s will need careful scrutiny by both friends and enemies.

The British prospect is, in all honesty, very sombre. R. S. Sayers said in spring 1975 that he thought the age of credit money was over, at least in England; the Germans and the Swiss would be able to keep the system working, probably the Americans, and perhaps the French, though there Professor Sayers thought "wait and see" was the best attitude. The English, rather to Sayers's surprise, had turned out to lack the necessary self-control. The lesson of 1968, when the U.K. had to make real sacrifices of sovereignty to qualify for vitally needed International Monetary Fund credits, had been quickly forgotten once friendly Arabs and aggressive Americans offered to finance a profligacy that expressed itself not so much in overconsumption (for the British more or less cheerfully accepted a gradual decline of their standard of living relative to that of their Continental neighbours) as in a general and spreading unwillingness to pay attention to business. The fashion is to blame the worker and his unions, but in my observation, for what it may be worth, the real villains are the educated classes.

It is not surprising, on second thought, that the new aristocrats of educational merit would adopt the attitudes toward trade common among the old aristocrats of blood; what has been remarkable is their apparently unlimited ability to bureaucratize, to constrain, to make political, to assure that the new works manager will be one of ours, not (like his predecessor) one of theirs. I understand that I have been critical of a revolution in banking that was in fact one of the shining spots of energy in the dull background of post-1950 British enterprise. But the very fact that all this talent went into the generation of abstractions rather than consumables may have been a symptom of the underlying malaise.

Well, we have seen its like before: Disraeli's two nations (the north and the south, *not* the rich and the poor) managed to coalesce against even greater odds, when the management of credit money was so new that its significance completely escaped so attentive an observer as Karl Marx (who was never, as Engels observed in a

pathetic footnote in Volume II of *Kapital*, very good at arithmetic).
At worst, as Sayers insists, there are other ways to organize the
medium of exchange. Though depressed about what the hyperinflation he foresees will do to people and institutions he loves,
Sayers does not for a moment think that the world has come to an
end, or that there will be no more cakes and ale—and he relishes
the prosperity of the village people who live near his country retire-
ment, a prosperity made possible in part by the monetary mani-
pulations he deplores. But he does feel that the history he has
written, carrying the Bank to World War II, is of no possible
present utility because that system is dead.

It may well be that the revolutionized system I have written
about in these pages is itself dying, drowning in the ocean of inflation, as Sayers believes. My own hunch is that there is life in the
Old Lady yet, if people (especially politicians) will heed her soft,
dignified cries for help. Soon.

ACKNOWLEDGMENTS

A book like this one can be written only with the cooperation of literally hundreds of people, who consent to be interviewed and think about the answers to questions; and I owe a considerable debt to those whose names are in the pages that have passed, and in the index that follows.

The indispensable person in the writing of this book was Tom Waage of the Federal Reserve Bank of New York, who in 1947 sat at a desk near the desk where I sat at the *New York Journal of Commerce*. He was a wise counsellor then and has supplied guidance as well as information more often than he remembers in the years since. When the idea for a book about bankers was proposed to me, the first thing I did was call Tom and ask whether it could be done; and he said sure it could, so long as I didn't write the book he was going to write after he retired. I know I haven't done that, because I can't. On a number of occasions in the course of the work for this book, I found paths smoothed before me because Tom Waage had made a phone call, less from a status as senior vice-president of the New York Fed than from a personal position that can be earned only by being right and being fair, all the time. This book would be much less complete and much less accurate (not that he will think it complete or accurate enough) without his help.

I am grateful for personal kindnesses from William Stott, formerly of Morgan; Gerald T. Dunne, formerly of the Federal Reserve Bank of St. Louis; Arthur Roth, formerly of Franklin National; Warren Marcus of Salomon Brothers; Geoffrey Bell of Schroder, Wagg; Edward Herman of the Wharton School; Robin Bell of *The Banker*; Murray Rossant of Twentieth Century Fund;

Martin Griffin and Ralph Leach of Morgan; and the late Bryce Fisher, Esq. of Cedar Rapids. And to a number of friends who supplied information, insights or introductions that would have been difficult to come by any other way—Robert Hodes, Fred Wilson, Wilbur Cowett, Mary Moers Wenig, J.-F. Bernheim and Maurice Feldman, among others. And to Truman M. Talley, my publisher, who had the idea for the book, badgered me into writing it, and now must sell it.

There are also unsung heroes, who cannot be quoted, but whose assistance is heaven-sent: the p.r. staffs who assemble the material, make the appointments for interviews, arrange introductions at the foreign branches, and find (or have) the answers to all sorts of niggling little questions. A number of these, it seemed to me, gave services well beyond the call of duty, and the least I can do is thank them: Jim Brugger, Don Colen, John DeBoice, Mel Adams, Edward O'Toole, Ray Toman and Michael Eden.

The great pleasure associated with the work on this book was acquaintance with Bray Hammond's *Banks and Politics in the United States Between the Revolution and the Civil War*. For scholarship, organization and personal grace, this book alone establishes Hammond in the pantheon of American historians, with Parkman and Prescott and Motley, Mason, Woodward and Merk: it does honour to its Pulitzer Prize. People often ask a writer what he hopes to accomplish with a book, to which the cant answer is a question about what people hope to accomplish when they have a baby. In this instance, however, I do have a purpose: I should like to convince lots of people to read Bray Hammond.

Milton Friedman's and Anna P. Schwartz's *Monetary History* was of course invaluable, and so were several books by R. S. Sayers. Re-acquaintance with the work of Walter Bagehot, Karl Marx, John Maynard Keynes, and J. R. Hicks was important and useful, and R. W. Clower's Penguin anthology *Monetary Theory* brought me (almost) up to date on significant subjects. The many book-length reports on meetings forwarded by the Federal Reserve Bank of Boston are models of what such documents should be: informative and argumentative at the same time.

ACKNOWLEDGMENTS

I have already expressed in my dedication my gratitude to my professors of years ago. I should probably note that what they gave me was an abiding interest in this subject, and the habits of mind that facilitate understanding it. I do not burden them with the responsibility for the information that appears in these pages. In fact, knowing something about banking as it was thirty years ago was at first a hindrance rather than a help in making sense of what I saw when I began work on this book: there really *was* a revolution. Intellectually, the absorbing exercise of this job was casting out of my head all the stuff that might block me from perceiving what today's bankers think they are doing. But I would have been lost without my lifeline back to those accumulations of human experience that are not only our past but also the seeds of our future.

A last note on the technique of work toward this book. Early on, a choice had to be made between trying to cover lots of banks and looking hard at a more limited list. I decided I would know more about banking when I was done if I restricted my numbers. On three visits to Boston, for example, I went only to the First National Bank of Boston; on three to San Francisco, only to Bank of America; and on four to Chicago, I spent the great bulk of my time at one bank. By returning to the same scene as my angles of vision sharpened and deepened, I believe I have acquired a better understanding of how the business works; and because a number of my most important sources of information are not affiliated with any bank I think I have been able to get a reasonable grip on what is typical and what may be idiosyncratic at the institutions I examined. Seeing two or three people at each of a hundred banks might have produced a book quite different from what you have just read; but I do not think the differences would have made it better, and they might have made it worse.

NOTES

ix. Motto: John Maynard Keynes, *Essays in Persuasion*, Norton Library, N.Y., 1963, p. 178.

Chapter 1
The Revolution
3. Epigraph: Henry Harfield, "Legal Considerations in Industrial Banking", *Banking Law Journal*, Aug. 1974, p. 629.

6. "Kremlin Decree Mobilizes Soviet to Get 1974 Harvest In on Time", *New York Times*, May 12, 1974, Sec. I, p. 3.

13. Gaylord Freeman, *The Goal of the First National Bank of Chicago and the Means of Attaining That Goal*, Mimeo, 1950, p. 72.

14. Walter Bagehot, *Lombard Street*, Richard D. Irwin, Inc., Homewood, Ill., 1962, p. 119.

15. Randall quote, in *Post Assembly Summary*, The Assemblies for Bank Directors 1973, The Foundation of the Southwest Graduate School of Banking, Southern Methodist University, Dallas, Texas, p. 108.

16. Freeman, *op. cit.*, p. 1.

17. Howard D. Crosse, *Management Policies for Commercial Banks*, Prentice-Hall, Inc., Englewood Cliffs, N.J., 1962, p. 11.

19. Nadler quote, in Bill Hieronymous, "More Local Banks Are Making International Deals, Partly Defensively", *Wall Street Journal*, April 22, 1974, p. 30.

19. Peter Drucker, *Management*, Harper & Row, New York, 1974, pp. 406–407.

21. Storrs quote, in *Post Assembly Summary*, p. 129.

21. Bagehot, *op. cit.*, p. 113.

Chapter 2
Introducing Money
24. Ward quote, in Bray Hammond, *Banks and Politics in America from the Revolution to the Civil War*. Princeton University Press, Princeton, N.J., 1967 (paperback), p. 19.

24. Karl Marx, *Capital*, Charles H. Kerry & Co., Inc., Chicago, Ill., 1906, vol. I, p. 144.

24. Wright Patman, *A Primer on Money*, Subcommittee on Domestic Finance, Committee on Banking and Currency, House of Representatives, 88th Congress 2nd Session, 1964, p. 1.

24. Robin Pringle, *Banking in Britain*, Charles Knight & Co. Ltd., London, 1973, p. 9.

25. R. H. Clower, in Clower, ed., *Monetary Theory*, Penguin Books, Harmondsworth, Middlesex, England, 1969, pp. 14–15.

25. Marx, *op. cit.*, p. 101.

25. R. S. Sayers, *Central Banking After Bagehot*, Oxford University Press, London, 1967, p. 9.

NOTES

26. John Maynard Keynes, *General Theory of Employment, Interest and Money*, Harcourt, Brace & Co., New York, 1936, pp. 215–216.
26. Theodore Geiger and Winifred Armstrong, *The Development of African Private Enterprise*, National Planning Association, Washington, 1964, p. 46.
28. Keynes, *loc. cit.*
29. Hume quote, in J. R. Hicks, *Monetary Theory and Keynesian Economics*, in Clower, ed., *op. cit.*, pp. 258–59.
29. Hicks, *ibid.*, p. 260.
30. Lincoln, in Patman, *op. cit.*, p. 16.
30. Paine, in Hammond, *op. cit.*, p. 61.
30. Bagehot, *Memoir of the Right Honourable James Wilson*, in Norman St. John-Stevas, ed., *The Collected Works of Walter Bagehot*. Harvard University Press, Cambridge, Mass., 1968, vol. III, p. 339.
31. Hammond, *op. cit.*, p. 30.
31. Michigan commission, in *ibid.*, p. 601.
32. Biddle, in *ibid.*, vol. I, p. 51.
34. Radcliffe Report: *Report of the Committee on the Working of the Monetary System*, HMSO, London, 1969, para. 345.
34. Edison quote, in Patman, *op. cit.*, p. 47.
37. Maisel, in *Controlling Monetary Aggregates*, Proceedings of a Conference Held in June 1969. Federal Reserve Bank of Boston, 1969, p. 152.
38. Holmes, in *ibid.*, p. 73.

Chapter 3
Introducing Banking
39. Paine, in Hammond, *op. cit.*, p. 60.
39. Marx, in *Capital*, vol. III, p. 713.
40. Iris Origo, *The Merchant of Prato*, Knopf, New York, 1957, p. 149fn.
41. Raymond de Roover, *The Rise and Decline of the Medici Bank, 1397–1494*. W. W. Norton & Co. (paper edition), New York, 1966. pp. 138–139.
44. Hamilton, in Hammond, *op. cit.*, p. 37.
44. Morris, in Redlich, *op. cit.*, vol. I, p. 24.
45. Hamilton, in Hammond, *op. cit.*, p. 131.
46. George J. Vojta, *Bank Capital Adequacy*. First National City Bank of New York, 1973.
47. Steuart, in Redlich, *op. cit.*, vol. I, p. 6.
48. Bagehot, *Lombard Street*, p. 45.
49. Hammond, *op. cit.*, p. 550.
49. Suffolk Bank, in *ibid.*, pp. 551–552.
53. *United States Investor* X, May 27, 1899, p. 705, in Vincent P. Carosso, *Investment Banking in America*. Harvard University Press, Cambridge, Mass., 1970, p. 47.
53. "solemnize marriages", in W. Nelson Peach, *The Security Affiliates of National Banks*, in Carosso, *op. cit.*, p. 272.
53. U.S. Treasury Annual Report 1920, pp. 1223–1224, in *ibid.*, p. 273.
54. Joseph A. Schumpeter, *The Theory of Economic Development*. Harvard University Press, 1936, p. 111.
55. Hammond, *op. cit.*, pp. 677, 679.

Chapter 4
How to Start an American Bank
67. Hammond, *op. cit.*, pp. 696–697.
68. Bernard Shull and Paul M. Horvitz, Branch Banking and the Structure of Competition, *Studies in Banking Competition and the Banking Structure*, articles reprinted from the National Banking Review, Office of the Comptroller of the Currency, Washington, 1966, pp. 107–108.

68. *Post Assembly Summary.* The Assemblies for Bank Directors 1973, pp. 19, 20, 42.
69. Kentucky case, in Herbert Bratter, *A Bank Director's Job: Banking*, The Journal of the American Bankers Association, New York City, 1970, p. 8.
69. Comptroller quote, in *Duties and Liabilities of Directors of National Banks*, Comptroller of the Currency, Washington, June 1972, p. 2.
70. New York State Banking Code, Sec. 10.
70. Charles F. Haywood, *The Potential Competition Doctrine.* Association of Registered Bank Holding Companies, Washington, 1972, p. 59.
71. 1812 Bank of America story, in Hammond, *op. cit.*, pp. 162–163.
71. deposit solicitation letter, in Redlich, *op. cit.*, vol. I, p. 22.
71. Jefferson quote, in Richard Hofstadter, *The Idea of a Party System*, Univ. of California Press, 1972, p. 160.
71. Bray Hammond, *Sovereignty and an Empty Purse*, Princeton University Press, Princeton, N.J., 1968, p. 15.
74. Morrill quote, in *ibid.*, p. 304.
75. David P. Motter, "Bank Mergers and Public Policy", in *Studies in Banking Competition*, p. 14.
82. Bagehot, *Lombard Street*, pp. 43–44.
82. Golembe: in Herbert V. Prochnow and Herbert V. Prochnow, Jr., *The Changing World of Banking*. Harper & Row, New York 1974, p. 19.
82. Patman, *op. cit.*, p. 2.
85. Corns quote: in Crosse, *op. cit.*, p. 100.
85. Ernest Kohn, Carmen J. Carlo and Bernard Kaye, *Meeting Local Credit Needs.* New York State Banking Department, 1973, p. 18. See also, Ernest Kohn, *Branch Banking, Bank Mergers and the Public Interest.* New York State Banking Department, 1964.

Chapter 5
A Bank of One's Own
94. Emmanuel Celler, "The Philadelphia National Bank Case: A Rejoinder", in *Studies in Banking Competition and the Banking Structure*, p. 49.
107. Bowen, in *Post Assembly Summaries*, p. 15.
108. McNew, in *Bankers Handbook*, p. 219.
108. Conn, in *Post Assembly Summaries*, p. 28.

Chapter 6
The Cheque System
115. Thomas O. Waage, "Giro Credit-Transfer Plan Could Be EFTS Alternative", in *The American Banker*, Oct. 29, 1973, p. 7.
129. priest story: "Paine Webber Sued by Priest Over Sales Tied to Margin Rule", in *Wall Street Journal*, 6/27/74, p. 22.
129. Thibaut de Saint-Phalle and John Heptonstall, "International Banking Services in Europe: A User's View", in *Euromoney*, February 1973, p. 1.
132. float figures: from Carter H. Golembe Associates, Bank Float in a New Payments System. American Bankers Association, Washington, D.C. 1971, p. 51.
139. *Constitution of the New York Clearing House, With Rules and Regulations*, p. 18.

Chapter 7
Operations
147. G. W. A. Dummer, F. P. Thomson and J. Mackenzie Robertson, *Banking Automation*, Pergamon Press, London, 1971, p. vi.
159. "Fed diffidence", Functional Cost Analysis, Federal Reserve System, Washington, D. C. 1973, p. 1.

160. Crosse quote, in Howard D. Crosse, *Management Policies for Commercial Banks*, p. 75.
163. Case M. Sprenkle, *Effects of Large Firm and Bank Behavior on the Demand for Money of Large Firms*. American Bankers Association, Washington, D.C. 1971, pp. 5–6.
163. Sprenkle figures, in *ibid.*, p. 4. FCA figures, *op. cit.*, table 7.2; some calculations by author.
167. Gerald T. Dunne, *Variations on a Theme by Parkinson on Some Proposals for the Uniform Commercial Code and the Checkless Society, Yale Law Journal*, vol. 75, p. 792.
168. Francis P. Thomson, *Giro Credit Transfer Systems*, Pergamon Press, London, 1964, p. 22.
169. *Banking Automation*, p. vii.

Chapter 8
Bought Money
177. George Garvy and Martin R. Blyn, *The Velocity of Money*, Federal Reserve Bank of New York, 1969, pp. 86, 88.
187. Stephen H. Axilrod, *Liquidity and Public Policy*, in *Federal Reserve Bulletin*, October 1961, pp. 1170, 1176.
193. Anderson and Eisenmenger quote, in *Policies for a More Competitive Financial System*, Federal Reserve Bank of Boston, 1972, p. 168.
193. Dentzer quote, in *ibid.*, p. 214.

Chapter 9
Fancy Bought Money
198. Bagehot, *Lombard Street*, p. 1.
201. Strong letter: Lester V. Chandler, Benjamin Strong, *Central Banker*, Brookings Institution, Washington, D.C. 1958, p. 172.
205. "practically all": Parker B. Willis, "A Study of the Market for Federal Funds", in *Reappraisal of the Federal Reserve Discount Mechanism*, vol. III, Federal Reserve Board, Washington D.C., 1972, p. 77.
207. Benjamin H. Beckhart, "Federal Reserve System", American Institute of Banking, American Bankers Association, Washington, D.C. 1972, p. 74.
209. Alan Holmes, "Open Market Operations in 1973", *Monthly Review*, Federal Reserve Bank of New York, May 1974, p. 113.
220. Lyon quote, in *Bankers Handbook*, p. 562.
222. Morris and Little quote, in Herbert V. Prochnow and Herbert V. Prochnow, Jr., *The Changing World of Banking*, Harper & Row, New York, 1974, p. 115.
223. Federal Reserve Board, Regulation Q as amended effective 1/1/71, p. 4.
224. *ibid.*, Sec. 217.1(f)(3)(i).
226. Milton Friedman and Anna Jacobson Schwartz, *A Monetary History of the United States*, 1867–1960, Princeton University Press, Princeton, N.J., 1963, p. 227.

Chapter 10
Lending to Producers
229. Bagehot, *op. cit.*, p. 3.
229. Eugene Manlove Rhodes, *Copper Streak Trail*, Hillman Periodicals ed., New York, 1950, pp. 25–27.
232. Benjamin Graham, *The Intelligent Investor*, fourth revised edition, Harper & Row, New York, 1973, pp. 238–239.
234. R. H. Tawney, *Religion and the Rise of Capitalism*, Penguin Books, New York, 1947, p. 130.
236. "bigger loans to bigger farmers": *Farm Borrowing in the Midwest*, Federal Reserve Bank of Chicago, 1966, pp. 26–31.
244. Bank of America, *Term Loans to Business*, San Francisco, 1970, p. 25.

246. *ibid.,* p. 53.
249. Frederick C. Klein, "The Acquisitor", in *Wall Street Journal* 1/4/74, pp. 1, 16.

Chapter 11
Interest Rates and Other Problems
264. Tawney, *op. cit.,* p. 150.
265. "Risky?" Sanford H. Rose, "Is This Any Way to Run 10 Banks?" *Fortune,* December 1968, p. 145 @ 197.
266. Maisel, *op. cit.,* p. 278.
269. Radcliffe Committee Report, p. 134, para. 393.
269. Okun, quoted in Maisel, *op. cit.,* p. 79.
271. Burns quote, in Storrs' talk, Post Assembly Summary, p. 128.
272. Craft quote, in *Bankers Handbook,* p. 311.
273. Morgan Guaranty, *The Financing of Business in the United States,* New York, 1974. p. 20.
277. Henry Kaufman and James McKeon, *Supply and Demand for Credit in 1974,* Salomon Brothers, New York, 1974. p. 4.
288. Sprenkle, *op. cit.,* p. 16.
289. Crosse, *op. cit.,* p. 208.
291. Wille testimony, in Bank Reform Act Hearings, p. 32.

Chapter 12
Bad Loans, Municipal Bonds, and Still More Problems
293. Frederic Solomon, in Bankers Handbook, p. 1053.
301. John Brooks, *The Go-Go Years,* Weybright & Talley, New York, 1973, p. 122.
301. on Mill Factors: from Abraham Briloff, *Unaccountable Accounting,* Harper & Row, New York, 1972, p. 130.
302. Staggers, in *The Financial Collapse of the Penn Central Company,* a Staff Report of the Securities and Exchange Commission to the Special Subcommittee on Investigations. U. S. Govt. Printing Office, August 1972. p. iii.
303. Joseph R. Daughen and Peter Binzen, *The Wreck of the Penn Central,* Mentor Edition, New American Library, New York, 1972, p. 203.
303. SEC Report, p. 97.
306. Renchard memo: *ibid.,* p. 307.
308. Paul Delaney, "Mafia Links to US Bureau Found," *New York Times,* 2/28/74, p. 24.
311. Crosse, *op. cit.,* p. 15.
314. George J. Vojta, *Bank Capital Adequacy,* First National City Bank of New York, 1973, fn p. 22.
315. Schapiro quote: *Bank Stock Quarterly,* April 1972, pp. 6, 7, 8.
315. Richard J. Whalen, "The Big Skid at Yale Express," *Fortune,* 11/65, p. 145 @ 148.
320. *Principles and Presentation,* Peat, Marwick, Mitchell & Co. New York, 1973. p. 233.
321. David C. Cates and Frank L. Harwell, Jr., "Bank Accounting Versus Security Analysis," in *Bankers Monthly,* March 15, 1972, p. 1.

Chapter 13
Lending to Consumers
323. Otto Friedrich, *The Loner,* Crown Publications, New York 1964, pp. 18–19.
326. Regulations U, 12CFR 221.3(b).
331. *Handbook of Instalment Lending,* Bank of America, San Francisco 1970, pp. D–3, D–4, D–5.
333. Turner, in *Bankers Handbook,* p. 505.
335. Jackie Robinson, as told to Alfred Duckett, *I Never Had It Made,* G. P. Putnam's Sons, New York, 1972, p. 204.

339. Alan Abelson, "Up and Down Wall Street," in *Barron's*, 2/18/74, p. 23.
339. Francis Pollock, "Toward Protecting Consumers," in *Columbia Journalism Review*, Mar./Apr. 1974, pp. 22 @ 24.
340. Bank of America, *Advanced Sales Training Workshop on Auto, Mobile Home and Recreational Vehicle Dealers*, San Francisco, 1972, p. 59.
340. Juster quote, in *Consumer and Monetary Policy*, Federal Reserve Bank of Boston, 1971, p. 185.
341. Falstaff: *Henry IV, Part II*, Act 1, Scene 2.
344. *Bank Credit-Card and Check-Credit Plans*, A Federal Reserve System Report, Washington, 1968, p. 75.
344. *ibid.*, p. 32.
350. Robert Johnston, *Nation-Spanning Credit Cards*, Fed of San Francisco Monthly Review Reprint, March 1972, p. 4.

Chapter 14
Regulators and Supervisors: Policing the Banks

357. Hammond, *Banks and Sovereignty*, pp. 349, 351.
359. Crosse, *op. cit.*, p. 95.
359. *Handbook of Examination Procedures*, Comptroller of the Currency, Washington, 1972, pp. 1, 2.
364. Patman quote, in George J. Benston, "Bank Examination," *The Bulletin*, New York University Graduate School of Business Administration Institute of Finance, Nos. 89–90, May 1973, p. 63 fn.
364. Friedman and Schwartz, *op. cit.*, p. 247.
367. Crosse, *op. cit.*, p. 41.
370. Rohlf quote, *Crimes Against Banking Institutions*, p. 90.
370. Crosse, *op. cit.*, p. 97.
371. Horvitz quote, in Benston, *op. cit.*, p. 16–17.
374. U. S. National Bank figures, from Shirley Scheibla, "Big Bank Failure," in *Barron's*, April 1, 1974, p. 3.
376. *Midwest Banking in the Sixties*, Federal Reserve Bank of Chicago, 1970, pp. 162, 165, 169.
378. *ibid.*, p. 170.
378. Carter H. Golembe, "Our Remarkable Banking System," *Virginia Law Review*, vol. 53, no. 5, June 1967, p. 1091 @ 1106.
380. "holding company legislation"—12 USC 1841, Sec. 4(c) (8).
381. outside activity figures: "One-Bank Holding Companies Before the 1970 Amendments," in *Federal Reserve Bulletin*, December 1972, table A99; quote, p. 1001.
381. law: *The Bank Holding Company, Its History and Significance in Modern America*, Association of Registered Bank Holding Companies, Washington, 1973, p. 9.
384. Samuel B. Chase, Jr., "The Bank Holding Company—A Superior Device for Expanding Activities?" in *Policies for a More Competitive Banking System*, Federal Reserve Bank of Boston 1972, p. 77 @ 83.
386. Mayne quote, in Benston, p. 45.

Chapter 15
The Federal Reserve: Trying to Police the Economy

387. Sproul quote, in Beckhart, *op. cit.*, p. 200.
387. Patman, *op. cit.*, p. 121.
391. Federal Reserve Act, Section 3 (8).
392. on Bryan and Federal Reserve Act passage generally, *see* G. T. Dunne, *A Christmas Present for the President*, Federal Reserve Bank of St. Louis, 1964.
393. Chandler, *op. cit.*, p. 43.
397. Beckhart, *op. cit.*, p. 43.

398. Thomas O. Waage, The Need for Uniform Reserve Requirements, address to The Executive Seminar, November 8, 1973. Federal Reserve Bank of New York, mimeo, p. 11.

398. Ross Robertson and Almarin Phillips, *Optimal Affiliation With the Federal Reserve System for Reserve Purposes is Consistent with Effective Monetary Policies*, Conference of State Bank Supervisors, Washington, 1974, p. 24.

402. Maisel, *op. cit.*, p. 44.

402. "ineptitude," Edwin L. Dale, Jr., "Economists Lose Respect For Fed," in *New York Times*, Sept. 17, 1973, p. 49.

404. profits figures: Improvements Needed in the Federal Reserve Reporting System For Recognized Dealers in Government Securities: Report to the Vice-Chairman of the Joint Economic Committee by the Comptroller-General, Oct. 6, 1971.

407. Monetary Aggregates and Money Market Conditions in Open Market Policy, *Federal Reserve Bulletin*, February 1971, pp. 99–100.

409. Open Market Operations in 1972, *Federal Reserve Bulletin*, June 1973, p. 416.

419. Remarks of Alfred Hayes . . . Before the 45th Annual Midwinter Meeting of the New York State Bankers Association, Federal Reserve Bank of New York, mimeo, 1973, p. 5.

420. "Brimmer Says U. S. Banks' Dollar Outflow Had Key Role in This Year's Currency Crisis," in *Wall Street Journal*, April 3, 1973, p. 11.

423. John Maynard Keynes, *Treatise on Money*, Harcourt Brace & Co., New York, 1930, vol. I, p. 149.

Chapter 16
Americans Abroad and What Happened to the Dollar

427. Beecher quote, in John A. Kouwenhoven, *Partners in Banking*, Brown Brothers, Harriman & Co., New York, 1968, p. 113, 114.

437. Federal Reserve Act, Section 25 No. 9.

440. *ibid.*, Section 25, No. 10.

443. Robert Triffin, *Gold and the Dollar Crisis*, Yale University Press, paper edition, New Haven, 1968. p. 21.

446. Eberard Reinhardt, "The Role of Key Currencies," in Wolfgang Schmitz (ed), *Convertibility, Multilateralism and Freedom*, Springer-Verlag, Vienna & New York, 1972. p. 278.

449. Triffin, *op. cit.*, p. 3, p. 90.

449. Reinhardt, *op. cit.*, p. 279.

Chapter 17
The Uses of Eurodollars

451. Hicks, in Clower, *op. cit.*, pp. 267–268.

453. Charles P. Kindleberger, *Power and Money*, Macmillan & Co., New York, 1970, p. 172.

456. Debs, in Federal Reserve Bank of New York *Monthly Review*, June 1975, p. 123. Geoffrey H. Bell, *The Eurodollar Market and the International Financial System*, Macmillan, London, 1973, p. 53.

457. Milton Friedman, "The Euro $ Market: Some First Principles," in *The Morgan Guaranty Survey*, October 1969, p. 4.

461. Bagehot, *op. cit.*, p. 130.

465. Andrew Brimmer, "American International Banking: Trends and Prospects," in *Revue de la Banque*, No. 6 1973, p. 491.

466. R. H. Lutz, "The Banks and the International Money and Capital Markets", Crédit Suisse, Zurich, mimeo, 1973, p. 13.

466. Arsenis quote in Charles N. Stabler, "Outpouring of Credit to Developing Nations Seen Spelling Trouble," in *Wall Street Journal*, May 21, 1973, p. 1.

NOTES

Chapter 18
Living on the Edge of an Abyss

483. Hans J. Mast, "Corporate Financing in Europe," in *Euromoney*, London, Sept. 1970, p. 7.
485. Maisel, *op. cit.*, pp. 18–19.
485. Harry G. Johnson, *Money, Trade and Economic Growth*, Harvard University Press, Cambridge, Mass., 1967, p. 172.
486. Franklin, from *The Writings of Benjamin Franklin* (Albert H. Smyth, ed.), vol. IX, pp. 231–234; cited in Bray Hammond, *Sovereignty and an Empty Purse*, Princeton University Press, 1968, p. 254.
491. Hyman P. Minsky, "Financial Instability Revisited," in *Reappraisal of the Federal Reserve Discount Mechanism*, Federal Reserve System, Washington, 1972, pp. 100–105.
492. *ibid.*, p. 118.
493. 1972 quote: Minsky, "An Evaluation of Recent U. S. Monetary Policy," in *The Bankers' Magazine*, London, December 1972, p. 6.
493. Lawrence L. Crum and Dennis W. Richardson, *Competition for the Commercial Banking Industry in the Establishment and Operation of an Electronic Payments System*, American Bankers Association, Washington, D.C., 1971.
495. O'Brien quote, in Pringle, *Banking in Britain*, p. 12.
495. Radcliffe Report, p. 43.
496. 1929 figures, from Chandler, *op. cit.*, p. 426.
497. Henry Kaufman, *Forces of Change in the American Credit Markets*, Salomon Brothers, N. Y., 1974, p. 14.

INDEX

INDEX

Lipp, Bob, 156–7
Lipsky, Gerald, 362–3
liquidity trap, 491
Lisbon Bank & Trust Company, 104–106
Little, Jane, 222
Lloyds Bank, 263, 352, 432, 473
loan losses, 24, 101, 295; adjustment of, 295; bank policy on, 77–81; and bank profitability, 230–4; to big business, 252–8, 300–306; defaults on, 293–7, 310–17; of Eurodollars, 463–4, 466–71; examiner's classification, 363–5, 369–70; history of, 39–43; non-bank, 257–8; sale of, 223–4; self-amortizing, 200, 244; specialization in, 79–80; speculative, 256–7, 326, 419–23; syndicated, 255–6. *See also* specific types, i.e. auto loans, farm loans
Lockett, Walker, 240, 242–3, 263
Lockheed, 252, 315
Lombard loan, 42
Lombard rate, 42
Lombard Street (Bagehot), 14
Long, Huey, 485
Long, Robert, 14, 236
Long, Russell, 484–5
Lutz, R. H., 466
Lyon, Roger, 166, 220

M1 definition of money supply, 35, 36, 37, 410
M2 definition of money supply, 410
Mabon, Nugent & Company, 209, 210, 219
McAdoo, William, 393
McCulloch, Hugh, 74
McDonnell, Jack, 365, 368
McFadden Act, 83
Machlup, Fritz, 457
McIntyre, Thomas, 174, 419
McKeon, James, 277
McNew, Ben, 108
McNichols, Stephen, 379
Macrae, Cameron, 375
Madison, James, 45, 72, 266, 389, 396, 402, 408–9, 485
Mandatory Foreign Investment Program, 453
Mannetter, Alan, 106–7, 205, 367
Manny Hanny. *See* Manufacturers Hanover Trust Company
Manufacturers Bank, 79, 83, 102, 186
Manufacturers Hanover Trust Company, 62, 65, 86, 112, 117, 125, 159, 186, 257, 304; cheque processing, 131, 135, 138, 141, 142, 147–54
Manufacturers Trust Company, 52, 90–1, 186
Marcus, Warren, 233, 289
Marine Midland Bank, 344, 346
Marine National Bank, 76, 79, 84
Mark Twain Bankshares, 13, 79, 84, 102, 224

Mark Twain Northlands Bank, 77
Mark Twain State Bank, 77
Martin, William McChesney, 99, 184–5, 399
Marx, Karl, 25, 508–509
Mast, Hans, 428, 442
Master Charge, 330–1, 345, 347–8, 349, 350, 352
Mastercharge, 346
maturity transformation, 489
Mayne, Lucille, 386
Mayo, Robert, 179, 421
Maytum, William, 173
Meadowbrook National Bank, 312, 380
Medici, Cosimo de, 59
Medici Bank, 40, 41
Memorex, 316
Mercantile Bank of St. Louis, 379
Merchants National Bank, 164, 175
Metzler, Karl, 133
MICR code, 117–19, 122, 135
Midwest Banking in the Sixties, 376–7
Mill Factors, 301, 315
Minnesota and Ontario Paper Company, 101
Minsky, Hyman, 249, 269, 491–2, 493
Mitchell, Charles, 109
Mitchell, George, 174, 176, 379, 382, 476, 477–8
Moeller, A. P., 299
Modern Money Mechanics, 391
Moffat, Richard, 202, 207, 400
monetary policy, 395, 397, 398–400, 416–23
money, 24–8; creation of, 33, 35, 43–4. (*See also* demand deposits); development of, 26–8; velocity of, 488–9
money brokers, 465
money shops, 465
money supply, 5, 28–9, 35–8, 395; definitions of, 35, 36, 409; interest rates and, 408–409
Mooney, George, 16, 55–6, 180
Morgan, J. P., 4, 14, 257
Morgan, J. P., Sr, 432
Morgan (J.P.) & Company, 187, 204–205
Morgan, Junius, 431
Morgan Guaranty Trust Company, 12–13, 18, 60, 65, 74, 86, 140–1, 203–205, 213–14, 252, 257, 269, 273, 289; foreign branches, 435, 464, 465, 469–70; "tenth floor group", 215–19
Morrice, State Bank, 291
Morrill, Justin, 73–4
Morris, Arthur, 323
Morris, Frank, 222
Morris, Robert, 44–5
Morris Plan, 323–7, 329
mortgage warehousing, 261
mortgages, 56, 58, 61, 90–1, 95–7, 178, 192, 199, 235, 248, 383
Mott Brothers, 90–1
Motter, David, 74